Language Arts

Charles Temple

HOBART AND WILLIAM SMITH COLLEGES

Jean Wallace Gillet

UNIVERSITY OF VIRGINIA

Language Arts

LEARNING PROCESSES AND TEACHING PRACTICES

LITTLE, BROWN AND COMPANY

BOSTON   TORONTO

Library of Congress Cataloging in Publication Data

Temple, Charles A., 1947–
    Language arts.

    Bibliography: p. 463
    1. Language arts (Elementary) 2. Activity programs
in education. 3. Child development. I. Gillet,
Jean Wallace. II. Title.
LB1576.T445 1984   372.6'044   83–19606
ISBN 0–316–83676–1

Library of Congress Catalog Card No. 83-19606

ISBN 0-316-83676-1

9   8   7   6   5   4

HAL

Published simultaneously in Canada by Little, Brown & Company (Canada) Limited
Printed in the United States of America

Acknowledgments
Photographs:
    Photographs on pages 16 and 33 are by Jan E.
Regan.
Text:
    Chapter 3   *Page 48*: From James Moffett and
Betty Jane Wagner, *Student-Centered Language Arts
and Reading, K–14: A Handbook for Teachers*, 3rd
edition. Copyright © 1983 by Houghton Mifflin
Company. Used by permission. *Page 53*: From Ruth
Craft, *Play School Play Ideas* (London: BBC Publi-
cations/Knight, 1971). Reprinted by permission of
the author.
    Chapter 4   *Pages 111–115*: From Jean Wallace
Gillet and Charles Temple, *Understanding Reading
Problems: Assessment and Instruction*. Copyright ©
1982 by Jean Wallace Gillet and Charles Temple.

Reprinted by permission of Little, Brown and Company. *Page 116*: From Stephanie McConaughy, "Using Story Structure in the Classroom," *Language Arts*,
Vol. 57, no. 7 (February 1980). Reprinted by permission of the National Council of Teachers of English.
    Chapter 5   *Page 163*: Reprinted by permission
of the publisher from Glenna Davis Sloan, *The Child
as Critic: Teaching Literature in the Elementary School*
(New York: Teachers College Press, © 1975 by
Teachers College, Columbia University. All rights
reserved.). p. 78. *Page 164*: From Bill Martin, Jr.,
and Peggy Brogan, *Sounds I Remember*, p. 10. Copyright © 1974 by Holt, Rinehart and Winston, Inc.
Reprinted by permission. *Page 164*: From Bill Mar-
(continued on page 473)

For Anna Brooke, Jessica, Mary Tyler, Frances
and for Jennifer and Tim

Preface

Language Arts: Learning Processes and Teaching Practices is intended as a primary text for undergraduate and graduate courses in the methods of teaching the language arts. In this text we have integrated principles of child development and current theory and research in language and cognition with detailed descriptions for teaching speech, listening, reading, writing, spelling, and grammar.

The contents and organization of this text reflect our belief that informed, effective teachers must know both the *how* and *why* of language arts teaching. Knowledge of what to do in the classroom must be based on an understanding of how children's self-directed learning shapes their language use, what roles invention and discovery play in language learning, and why particular approaches, methods, and materials may be more successful at fostering learning than others. We believe it is essential that teachers understand how children learn, and be able to shape their teaching practices to work in concert with these learning processes.

What sets this text apart from others is that both learning processes and teaching practices are treated in rich detail that integrates and relates them to each other. It is not enough for a text to focus on teaching methods and deal with developmental learning processes only in passing. If this developmental material is to be useful, it must be presented elaborately and clearly. Without an understanding of the processes that make learning possible and teaching successful, teachers cannot evaluate programs or materials, modify lessons, or critically judge their own effectiveness. Nor is it sufficient for a textbook to deal with principles of language and learning and leave the actual "nuts and bolts" of teaching — planning and implementing instruction and evaluating children's progress — to the imagination. Every teacher, particularly the preservice teacher, needs practical, concrete direction in methods of instruction. No matter how imaginative a teacher you may be, it is always possible to benefit from the ideas of other resourceful, successful teachers.

Our primary goal, then, is to help students understand both theory and practice. To do so we have used a *paired chapter* organizational scheme for the major portion of the text. Developmental principles, learning theories, and relevant research are discussed in the first chapter of each pair. The following chapter integrates research and theory with ongoing teaching methods. The chapters and within-chapter sections entitled "Understanding" not only feature numerous examples, but also build on prior information. Chapters and within-chapter sections entitled "Teaching" are richly detailed and provide specific direction that allows even novice teachers to implement teaching activities successfully in each area of language arts.

Learning in language arts is too often conceived of as a passive process of receiving language skills, which themselves are often fragmented from each other and from the rest of the curriculum. Examples of this fragmentation are the artificial separation of skills in speaking and listening, and the teaching of handwriting, grammar, and spelling as separate from each other and from the process of composition. In this text, therefore, we strive to reintegrate the language arts with themselves and with other subject areas, so that children's growing language abilities can support and foster each other across the full range of school activities and subjects.

Although we advocate an integrated language arts approach, we could not compose a book with only one long chapter. We had to break our material into discrete chapters devoted, for convenience, to the various language arts. The paired-chapter organization is used in our treatment of oral language, Chapters Two and Three; reading, Chapters Four and Five; and writing, Chapters Six and Seven. Spelling, handwriting, and grammar, however, are each treated in a single chapter that combines theory and practice. Finally, we focus on overall aspects of teaching the language arts in Chapter Ten.

Many people helped and encouraged us during the development of this book, and we owe them a great debt. We particularly wish to thank these individuals for their special contributions: Mylan Jaixen, Cynthia Mayer, Cynthia Chapin, and the staff of the Little, Brown and Company College Division; our reviewers who encouraged, challenged, questioned, corrected, suggested, and helped shape our work: Bonnie Lass, Boston College; Michael L. Michlin, Duke University; Nancy C. Millett, Wichita State University; Wanda Powers, The University of North Carolina at Greensboro; Sam Sebesta, University of Washington; Linda D. Stefl, Illinois State University; Eileen Tway, Miami University of Ohio; our students at the University of Houston at Victoria, Hobart and William Smith Colleges, and the University of Virginia; our colleagues who shared ideas with us, especially Ruth Nathan (co-author with Charles Temple of a previous book), Oakland University, and Pat Crook, Herb Richards, Chris Cherrington, Ellen Garfinkel, Ann Fordham, Kathy Oliver, and Susan Drigant Robinson, University of Virginia. For the ideas on invented spelling that are mentioned throughout this book, but especially in Chapter Nine, we are heavily indebted to Edmund Henderson and his students at the University of Virginia; especially Jim Beers, Shane Templeton, Richard Gentry, and Jerry Zutell. We also thank the teachers who welcomed us into their classrooms and shared their children's work with us: Juanita Hazelgrove, fourth grade, Cumberland, Va.; Marsha Jones, first grade, Cumberland, Va.; Midge Burns, second and third grades, Geneva, N.Y.; Marilyn Pope, Title I, Victoria,

Texas; Gail Brown, first grade, Lynchburg, Va.; Linda Williams, kindergarten, Lynchburg, Va.; Pam Williams, sixth grade, Lynchburg, Va.; Bobbie Lee, fourth grade, Lynchburg, Va.; Jenny Wajciechowski, third-fourth grade, Lynchburg, Va.; Holly Perrow, parent, Lynchburg, Va.; the children whose art and written work appear here and the parents who kindly gave us permission to reproduce their children's work; the teachers and librarian who made the arrangements for us to take the photographs that appear in this book: Juanita Hazelgrove, Midge Burns, Ann Ryan, Michela DiDuro and, of course, their children; special thanks to Jan Regan of the Hobart and William Smith Colleges Communications Office for generously sharing her photographs; to those who helped us with permissions and related matters, and whose flying fingers created ordered typescript out of our chaotic drafts: Shirley D'Augustine, Hobart and William Smith Colleges; Helen Collier, University of Virginia; and Brenda Kelley, University of Virginia.

Brief Contents

Contents

CHAPTER THREE

Teaching Oral Language 41

CHAPTER FOUR
Understanding Reading and Literature 97

CHAPTER FIVE

Teaching Reading and Literature   133

CHAPTER SIX

Understanding Written Expression   203

CHAPTER SEVEN
Teaching Written Expression 237

CHAPTER EIGHT

Understanding and Teaching Grammar   303

The Language Arts Program 431

Language Arts

CHAPTER ONE

Children and Language Arts

CHAPTER OUTLINE

The most powerful of all human attributes is language. Through language we come to know, to organize, and ultimately to control our world; we give form to our experiences, thoughts, and emotions; we share ourselves with others and form the relationships that shape our lives.

Language arts is sometimes thought of as a fairly unified school subject, but in reality it is a topic that sprawls across the school curriculum, resisting attempts to define it neatly. Teaching language arts is defined most simply as teaching reading, writing, speaking, and listening; some might add teaching handwriting, spelling, and grammar too. Yet there is no school subject, or indeed any process or activity that goes on in school, that does not require most or all of these skills. Schools are set up especially to promote learning, and for human beings beyond infancy learning is inextricably bound up with language. It is the foundation of all teaching and learning, and language arts is the curriculum area where a child's language is nurtured in all its forms. Since language arts instruction includes talking, listening, reading, and writing, it may be considered to be the most important of all school subjects and indeed the heart of the elementary school program.

As director and orchestrator of the language arts program, the elementary classroom teacher stands at the center of the entire curriculum — a position that implies an awesome responsibility because instruction does not end when the basal readers are put away, nor does it wane in importance as children progress to upper grades and beyond. Like language itself, it fills the entire school day, pervading every other subject and activity. Learning to teach language arts means learning to teach everything else too.

As a teacher in this area you will have a dual responsibility: first, to teach those skills that are traditionally considered a part of the language arts; and second, to build and reinforce children's language skills in the context of the other subjects and activities they undertake throughout the school day.

What are the skills that are taught directly in language arts? They are:

— *Speaking*: including fluent self-expression, the ability to use language for different purposes and in different settings, and the ability to articulate clearly and effectively

— *Listening*: including the ability to pay attention to a speaker, to follow the speaker's message, and to identify the significant parts of what is said
— *Reading*: including the prereading experiences and concepts that make successful beginning reading possible; forming effective, meaning-oriented reading strategies; experiencing and appreciating literature, both prose and poetry; and reading and learning from other nonfiction forms of text
— *Writing*: including handwriting, the ability to form letters quickly and legibly; composition, the ability to express ideas effectively on different topics, to different audiences, for different purposes; and the ability to edit one's own writing and revise it to make it better
— *Spelling*: including both the learning of correct spellings and the development of a sense of how English spelling is structured
— *Grammar and usage*: including the ability to speak and write in ways that express one's ideas colorfully, precisely, efficiently, and appropriately for the situations in which the language is used

Each of these skills can and should be extended and practiced in the subjects that make up the elementary curriculum. Children's speaking ability advances when they are encouraged to discuss such things as the weather or the feeding of gerbils, or current events or number concepts, and when they use their language to inquire, investigate, reason, and report. Their listening skill is called into play every time they listen to a discussion or an explanation, watch a film or hear a speaker, or when they are told the steps and rules for solving a problem or playing a game. Their writing ability is improved and extended when they record observations of weather, plant growth, or traffic patterns in their neighborhoods; transcribe interviews with older relatives; write out instructions for playing a game or solving a mystery; or write invitations to a guest speaker or letters to a public official. Their spelling ability grows when they explore the etymological bases of science words like *thermometer* or *photograph* or math words like *dividend, pentagon,* or *equation.* Both by careful planning and by taking advantage of the opportunities that arise from moment to moment, effective language arts teaching means constantly keeping language development on the teaching agenda, whatever the subject at hand.

Let's take a look at some language arts teachers in action, and observe how each puts language at the heart of daily activities.

A Window on Language Arts Classrooms

Reading in the First Grade

Mary Carter likes to treat her first graders to an experience of successful reading on the opening day of school. On that first morning she produces a large, colorfully illustrated storybook, and she tells the class that they are going to learn to read this book this morning. Justin looks doubtful; he has heard enough about school from his older brother to believe that learning to read is difficult and tedious, and he wonders how he can learn to read a whole book in one day. Ms. Carter begins to read the book aloud, inviting the children to "join in whenever you like." As she reads, they realize that each page has almost the same words on it: "Brown bear, brown bear, what do you see? I see a redbird looking at me. Redbird, redbird, what do you see? I see a yellow duck looking at me. Yellow duck, yellow duck, what do you see? . . . " (Martin, 1970). The words that are different, they realize, are the ones illustrated on each page: a gray mouse, a green frog, a redbird. Hesitantly at first, then with growing confidence, they begin to join in the reading, supported by the highly repetitious text and well-placed illustrations. The book is short, and when they reach the end Justin looks astonished; he'd been *reading*! Ms. Carter leads the children through the book again; they now know the message on each page, so the reading is buoyantly confident. When they finish, Ms. Carter praises their success and says, "When you go home I want each of you to tell your family that you read a whole book today." Justin grins; they might not believe it, but he *knows* it's true.

"Now that you've read a book, the next thing we're going to do is write one of our own," Ms. Carter announces. She produces a large tablet on which she has printed the basic pattern from *Brown Bear, Brown Bear, What Do You See?* on successive sheets, leaving blanks where each color word and animal name occurred in the original. She invites volunteers to read the printed words and name a new color and animal, which she writes in the blanks. The children eagerly volunteer new combinations: a brown dog, a gray rat, an orange cat; Justin, thinking of his pet at home, volunteers "a white mouse." After she has written up eight pages, Ms. Carter passes out the individual sheets and asks pairs or groups of three to illustrate a page, repeating for each group what their page says. Crayons fly as the children draw the animal. Then Ms. Carter collects the illustrated pages and staples them together with a paper cover. After the children have made up a title, she writes it on the cover: "We See Animals." Ms. Carter places their book on the library corner table with the original storybook, so they can look at both in their spare time. "When you go home today," she tells them, "I want each of you to tell your family that you read a whole book *and* that you helped write a book!" Justin reaches out to touch the class book as he goes by; he never thought the first day of school would be like this!

Using Computers in the Third Grade

Third-grade teacher Ellie Harris was not a computer whiz. Anyway, when the principal announced that three desk-top computers had been bought for her school by the district, she assumed that they would be snapped up by the upper grades. A month later, however, when there were still a pair of them sitting unused in the media center, she began to have ideas. She had read articles in *Instructor* and *Language Arts* about using computers in the classroom, but the thought of using them herself had seemed out of the question until her own fourth-grade daughter began describing the fun she was having using the microcomputer in *her* classroom. That did it. Ms. Harris moved both of the computers into her room the next day.

They gave the classroom a space-age look, those two metal machines with their cluttered keyboards and blank screens, and they reminded Ms. Harris of the control panel of the starship *Enterprise*. The strangeness wore off very quickly, however, when a pair of students — both video game veterans — came in early the first morning and turned them on. Then the screens lit up in cheerful colors as words and graphics flitted across the screen to the commands punched in by these two knowledgeable students. Actually both machines were programmed with software packages that made it very clear what the students were to do.

By the end of the week everybody in the class had used one of the machines. Already, procedures were beginning to evolve: Ms. Harris instituted a sign-up sheet to give each student fair access to a computer. When the demand for time on the machines began to result in long waits, she instituted a "buddy system," after which the students worked in pairs at the computers. For a month or so things went smoothly. Ms. Harris was borrowing software packages, preprogrammed instructional activities, from the school media center. But although the students still approached the computer with enthusiasm, she began to want something more of her students. It seemed to her when she looked at them closely that most of the programmed instructional activities, while motivating to the children, were only slightly useful instructionally. Most, in fact, were on the order of electronic workbook pages. There must be more to computers than this, she thought.

A talk with a friend who taught at another school put her on a better track. One clear advantage for computers in the language arts period, her friend told her, was in getting children to write. Software is available to turn small computers into *word processors*. What is needed is the program itself (which comes in the form of a small piece of celluloid called a "floppy disk") and a special electronic typewriter called a "printer." Luckily, Ms. Harris found that her school's media center had both.

The word processing program enabled the students to use the typewriter keyboard to type their writing onto the computer's television screen or CRT ("cathode ray tube," as Ms. Harris, to her own amazement, found herself able to explain). Ultimately the writing on the screen could be printed out on paper by a printing machine located in the media center. The real advantage of the word processing program, however, was that the students were given the opportunity to write and change around their ideas many times and in many ways before they printed out the work. The computer allowed them to remove, reorder, or substitute a word, a line, or even a whole paragraph on the screen simply by punching in instructions on the keyboard. What is more, the students could store work indefinitely on their own floppy disks, printing it out only when it was developed as far as it could go.

During the language arts time period, from 8:45 to 10:45 A.M. daily, Ms. Harris kept the word processing package in the computers and assigned students to work for periods of twenty minutes each throughout the period. With two machines, twelve children were able to use the computers for a generous period of time each day, thus allowing each one access nearly every other day. Those students who were particularly involved in a writing project at any one time were scheduled into the computer for extra time at odd moments throughout the day.

Ms. Harris had been teaching her students to write the way professional authors do: to choose and narrow down their own topics, to write their first drafts experimentally, leaving themselves open to new ideas that may occur to them as they write, and writing second and third drafts after hearing reactions to their papers from her or even from their classmates. Her approach to teaching writing was successful. Most of her class enjoyed writing and wrote meaningful things. If there was one sticking point in her method of teaching writing, however, it was this: For some children the basic act of putting words on paper did not come easily, and her suggestion that these particular children reconsider what they had written and write it another way met stiff resistance.

It was with these students that the word processor was the greatest success. Even using the "hunt-and-peck" approach, typing on the keyboard was easier and faster than writing by hand (she found that when the school librarian gave them some basic instruction in touch typing, they became even faster). What is more, they *enjoyed* revising what they wrote when they could do it so magically on the computer! They wrote more, they read over what they wrote, and they rewrote more than they ever had previously. By year's end, Ms. Harris was sure she could see signs of improvement in all the writing done by her students, even in the things they did not write on the computer.

Writing in the Fourth Grade

Whether a beginning reader or more advanced, every youngster in Randy Kellerman's fourth grade does a great deal of composition. Mr. Kellerman is convinced that only through extensive exposure to writing practice do children become fluent, expressive writers, but he feels that in general they don't do enough writing. So he has made composition a routine component of the daily work schedule.

Each child has a large folder in which to keep writing-in-progress. Every morning during the language arts period time is planned for composition, and the folders come out. Mr. Kellerman has taught his students to focus initially on content, to write first drafts, and then to revise their work by reading it aloud to others, adding new ideas and moving sentences and words around. Only after the students are satisfied that their writing is complete and conveys what they intended is attention turned to spelling, punctuation, and other mechanical aspects of composition. In Mr. Kellerman's class no one complains, "I don't know what to write!" or "I don't know how to spell _____."

Here children use a variety of strategies to help them over the spelling hurdle so that they can get their thoughts and words down on paper first and then work on correctness. They use their word banks as sources of words, as well as referring to the bulletin board displays they've created, collections of pictures, and related words by the dozens. They also ask one another, and their teacher, for help, but prior to the final-draft stage they usually put down their best guesses for spellings and go on from there.

These "invented spellings" may take many forms, depending on the child's degree of reading ability and knowledge of sounds, letters, and words. Some invented spellings don't look much like their correct forms, but all the young writers know that, at first, getting down what they mean is more important than correctness.

If we were able to watch Mr. Kellerman's students at work, we would see a number of writing processes going on simultaneously. Several groups of two or three children retire to corners to listen to one another read their current drafts aloud. After Audrey reads, her partners offer criticism and comments: "You used a lot of *he's* and *she's*; I got mixed up about who's talking." "How come you didn't say what happened when you got home?" At a low table Mr. Kellerman meets with individual students who bring their current drafts with them; he asks each one questions like "Where are you in this draft? What are you going to do next with this? What part do you like best? What else might your readers need to know about this?" Such questions help the children solve problems, gain objectivity about their work, and discover new information they didn't know they had. All the youngsters leave the short conference with a clear idea of what they would like to do next with their compositions.

Some students are working at revising earlier drafts. Some cut their drafts apart and rearrange parts on larger pieces of paper, taping down the cut-apart strips. Others use stars, arrows, or balloons to mark where changes and insertions will be made. Bill, who has revised his composition on dolphins twice, is now combing his paper for possible spelling errors. During his most recent conference Mr. Kellerman asked him to underline five words he was sure he had spelled correctly and circle five of which he wasn't sure. In their next conference Mr. Kellerman will help him check a dictionary for correct spellings.

Katie and John are at the final-draft stage; they have edited their revisions, checked punctuation and spelling, and read their work over and over. They have both chosen to have their final drafts "published"; that is, they will create their own illustrated books with sewn bindings for their work, which will go into a special class library collection. Because John and Katie have worked hard on these particular compositions, they feel they are worth making permanent.

If you asked Randy Kellerman why his students are willing to work so long and so hard at revising, editing, and publishing their compositions, he would tell you that it is the pride of authorship that motivates them. His students have learned that good writing isn't something that just happens, or that some people can produce while others can't. They know that good writing is the result of careful, thoughtful crafting, requiring the objectivity to cross out, move parts around, and add or change information. They realize that writers have to consider not only what they themselves know but also what their readers may or may not know. And they are aware that most writing is for sharing with others, not just with the teacher. Because much of their writing is intended for others to read, and because what they write is consistently treated as worthy of sustained effort, they are willing to work at making it effective. They themselves act as judges of which compositions will be revised and polished, so they maintain responsibility for their own writing. Mr. Kellerman's fourth graders are already confident, effective writers in large part due to the way their teacher has structured the writing program.

Language Arts in a Social Studies Class: Fifth Grade

Jack Sloan, a fifth-grade teacher, loves history. He wants to make history come alive for his students and help them gain a sense of their own community's roots, but he is not sure how to do this. When a colleague mentions an elderly neighbor who retired after teaching school in the local community for almost fifty years, Mr. Sloan invites her to visit his class and talk about what school was like when she began teaching. He carefully prepares his students for the visit by helping them draw up questions they'd like to ask her and by planning reading and creative writing assignments to follow up the visit. The children are fascinated by what their community used to be like and what was taught in "the olden days." When one student comments that he was reminded of his grandfather's reminiscences about growing up, Mr. Sloan's unit on local history is born.

Working in groups, the students begin to come up with ideas for other visits and interviews. Starting at home with parents and other relatives, the children plan and conduct interviews with older adults to learn more about their experiences in growing up, going to school, working, and leisure activities. After planning and conducting interviews and writing up their results, the youngsters discover that there are many more topics uncovered than they can really handle. Special interest groups form to use their contacts and the library to learn more about topics like early farming methods, arts and crafts, hunting and trapping, wartime experiences, and folk remedies. The students invite other speakers to their class, report on topics and compile what they've learned in class books and in newspapers. One group begins compiling oral histories of older people in the community into an illustrated book for the school library, and another researches and creates a display of books and borrowed memorabilia, also housed in the library.

Mr. Sloan soon realizes that without a wider audience than just themselves, the students' interest will wane and the project will lose impetus. First he tries to think of ways they can share what they've learned with others, but then he decides to let the students themselves tackle this problem too. In brainstorming groups they generate ideas, then evaluate each, and finally vote on the best alternatives. Their eventual decision is to host a Local History Day at their school. Gaining permission for such an event, planning and inviting speakers, choosing materials and books for displays all start them on yet further rounds of discussions, letter writing, library research, interviews, and the like. There are days when Mr. Sloan wonders what he and his class have gotten into, but when he looks at the work his students have generated and compares it with the textbook/lecture/worksheet cycle he might have used, he is certain that the path they chose was the better one.

Mr. Sloan's unit on local history has its own roots in a program called *cultural journalism*, first developed by Eliot Wigginton, a Georgia high school journalism teacher, as a way of involving his students in their local cultural heritage and preserving some of the rapidly disappearing skills of their older relatives and neighbors. Many people who have never heard of Rabun Gap, Georgia, or cultural journalism have read some of the *Foxfire* magazines or books, which are products of these students' efforts. Without really planning it out, Mr. Sloan has effectively tied together instruction in social studies, reading, composition, oral communication, and a variety of other topics and skills.

An Understanding of Language and Language Processes

In the several sketches of language arts teaching in the previous section there was a common theme: Each teacher had a clear understanding of what particular language abilities are like, knew how they develop, and knew how to carry out teaching procedures to help the children develop these abilities. We have the feeling that these teachers might rely a little or a lot on commercially published language arts texts and materials but that they would not hesitate to pick and choose from lessons in these materials, or substitute their own lessons altogether. They know when the textbook is working and when, in the case of a few or even most students, other approaches would be more productive.

Where do they get this knowledge? Experience is one answer. Certainly with experience we get to know the books, skits, poems, exercises, games, and routines that are part of teaching the language arts. We also get to know a particular age group of children — first grade, fourth grade, middle school, and so on — and while no two groups of young people are ever really the same, experience with children can enable us to get to know within broad limits their concerns, powers, and particular ranges of interests.

Experience alone, however, will not make us really good teachers. We sometimes hear it said of two experienced teachers that one has five years of experience, while the other has had one year of experience repeated five times. The extra ingredient that helps a teacher turn each year's experience into learning and growth starts out as a fundamental set of ideas about what there is to be learned in language arts and the processes through which children come to learn it. The developing teacher must, in short, acquire a sense of the issues and possibilities in language development.

What do we mean by issues and possibilities? Take, for example, the issue of teaching grammar. Most of the language arts texts children use in the United States today emphasize the teaching of grammar, but decades of research have turned up no evidence that teaching children to analyze sentences and identify parts of speech does any good at all. In fact, some researchers have concluded that it is harmful in the respect that it takes class time away from more productive activities (see Chapter Nine). On the other hand, a group of teachers working with middle-grade children and older has developed a "hands-on" approach to teaching grammar that has been repeatedly shown to improve the sentences that children write. The method, called *sentence combining*, can be adapted for use in the elementary grades. Surely a language arts teacher should be aware of the issue of grammar instruction: aware of the success record of the methods that have traditionally been tried, aware of the new goals that many teachers and professional organizations have adopted for learning grammar, and aware of the newer methods that are now being promoted. Without considering these things, the teacher and the students both may experience

many hours of frustration, trying to teach and learn textbook units on grammar, which are of little or no value.

Another factor to consider is that children are sometimes capable of achievements in language arts that their teachers do not suspect. Until recently, very few of even the most experienced teachers would have believed that primary-grade students could learn to write elaborate pieces of prose for many different purposes, could learn to edit and revise their writing to make it more and more effective — and could even help classmates become better writers by critiquing their peers' compositions. Yet a group of teachers and researchers in New Hampshire found that with the proper encouragement, their students could do these things; and when their story circulated to other attentive teachers, it was found that *their* primary students could become dedicated and skillful writers too. Today, there is a revolution in writing instruction in many primary and elementary classrooms throughout America and the rest of the English-speaking world — but only in those classrooms where the teachers have pushed beyond the level at which tradition and most textbooks had indicated that a child's writing could go.

There have been similar breakthroughs in other areas of language arts instruction: in the ways children learn and thus should be taught spelling and handwriting and talking and listening and reading. We have included in the following chapters all of the most important ones that were known to us up to the time this book went to press as well as the best of the traditional wisdom and the "tried-and-true" methods of teaching language arts — many of our best techniques have been known for centuries. More breakthroughs in instruction will undoubtedly come to light after you read this book, but we have sought in the chapters that follow to go beyond trends and styles of teaching and to explain the *why* of it all: the underlying intellectual and linguistic processes that make language learning possible, and upon which any effective methods of teaching should be based. With a grasp of these background concepts, you should be aptly prepared to put into practice the best ideas for language arts teaching that we know of at present. You should also be able to evaluate new ideas that come your way and select the truly valuable ones from the fads.

The Plan of the Book

The language arts are sometimes listed separately as speaking, listening, reading, and writing, and the curriculum usually includes handwriting, spelling, and grammar. Most experts in the field argue, however, that it is both ineffective and dreadfully dull to teach the language arts one at a time, as separate subjects. We agree, and at several places in this book we suggest ways that the separate language arts can be combined with one another and also with other school subjects. For the sake of simplicity, however, we have elected to break up the language arts for presentation in this book. It is the first instance where we as authors must do things with you our readers that we would not have you do with your students.

The second instance comes in the amount of background discussion we give to each of the topics of speaking, listening, reading, writing, handwriting, spelling, and grammar. Most authorities contend that the best way to learn language is to use it, while the worst way is to analyze it. Here again we agree. We ask you, however, to bear in mind that your goal as a reader of this book is not to learn language yourself but to find out how to help children develop theirs. As a teacher, you must develop considerable analytical skills so that you can see where your students' language development is going and plan activities — be they tightly or loosely structured — to help them make progress. Occasionally, a child's language will not develop as it should, and here again your ability to analyze language will be called upon, as well as your judgment and knowledge of corrective procedures.

An understanding of language and the ability to analyze it by themselves are a sufficient background for a linguist or a psychologist of language, but teachers need to know "what to do on Monday." A good teacher has a repertoire of techniques for introducing, practicing, and applying language skills. These come from various sources: Many are in the teacher's manual to the textbooks they use. Others they remember from their own elementary school days. Still others they learn at workshops, from other teachers, and from reading. In the chapters that follow, we have described in detail procedures for teaching every aspect of the language arts. Our intention has been to provide you with a basic professional repertoire of techniques, techniques that you will undoubtedly modify and supplement over the years but which we nonetheless hope will form the core of your "tools of the trade." Together with the basic concepts on children's development in spoken and written language as well as procedures for analyzing this development, the proper blend of conceptual and practical approaches is the best preparation for teaching language arts.

For the most part, the format of this book consists of paired conceptual and practical chapters. Chapters Two and Three are devoted to oral language and listening. Chapter Two introduces the concept of developmental learning, and then provides the background you will need to understand what it is exactly that children learn when they use oral language, as well as the processes by which this learning takes place. Chapter Three discusses techniques for helping children develop oral language, as well as procedures for evaluating and helping those whose language requires special attention. Chapters Four and Five provide, respectively, a conceptual and practical look at reading instruction. In Chapter Four we look at the reading process and how it develops. We also look at children's literature and its contributions to elementary education. In Chapter Five we present techniques for teaching reading from beginners to fluent readers, with special attention to reading problems and their correction. We also include approaches for dealing with literature in the elementary school. Chapters Six and Seven are devoted to writing, or composition instruction. Chapter Six describes the evolution of writing ability. Chapter Seven presents major topics in teaching writing.

With Chapter Eight, we depart from the paired chapter format. This chapter is devoted to spelling and handwriting. The conceptual background to spelling instruction is presented first, followed immediately by a section that explains methods of teaching children to spell. The second half of Chapter Eight is devoted to handwriting, first a discussion of the perceptual-motor learning that handwriting involves and then a discussion of ways to teach handwriting. Chapter Nine is devoted entirely to the subject of grammar. In the first half, we review the background of grammar instruction and then explain the nature of the grammar that children should learn in school. In the second half of that chapter we describe techniques for teaching grammar that have been supported by recent research. Finally in Chapter Ten we address the general issues of teaching the language arts that are not fully addressed in the preceding separate discussions of talking, listening, reading, writing, handwriting, spelling, and grammar. These include the issues of grouping for instruction, evaluating the program, combining the language arts with one another and with other subjects, and the question of how you continue to become a better teacher year after year.

CHAPTER TWO

Understanding Oral Language

CHAPTER OUTLINE

"Start where the children are." That may be the most valuable piece of advice about teaching that can be passed from one person to another. Learning theorists tell us that children learn best those ideas that can be related to what they already know and that are pitched on a level of difficulty close to the one on which they can comfortably work. Behavior experts tell us that children are easier to get to know and to teach when they are not frustrated by material that is too difficult or abstract for them. With these thoughts in mind, we can see that "starting where the children are" is an easy piece of advice to accept. It is only the application of it that is difficult.

Roughly put, the business of teaching language arts is to draw out, elaborate, and refine children's language. With this as our area of concern, how do we go about deciding where our students are in language ability? Clearly we must begin by deciding what language ability is. Then we must seek to understand the ways in which it develops, for, as we shall soon see, the development of language, or *language acquisition*, follows an orderly and predictable course which is dictated by the nature of language itself, and by a set of basic learning strategies that seem to form a part of human nature. In this chapter we will explore the nature of language and children's language learning process.

Language Development

What is a language, exactly? We can define it as *an arbitrary system of arbitrary vocal symbols used by a human society to conduct its affairs.* We say "vocal" symbols because language is primarily spoken. Writing and sign language are both derived from, and therefore secondary to, spoken language. The emphasis on "arbitrary" simply means there is no necessary connection between words and the entities they stand for. An item that you wear on your head can be called a *hat*, a *sombrero*, or a *chapeau*. The only thing that matters is what a group of people choose to call it. Similarly, the system that organizes the symbols can be arranged in any way a group of people agrees that it should

17

be. In English we usually put a "sss" or "zzz" sound on the end of words when we want to indicate that we are speaking of more than one thing, as in *house* → *houses*. Nearly a billion Chinese, however, get along quite well without making any distinction between singular and plural nouns. If you want to indicate plurality in Chinese, you simply say how many things you are thinking of, or say "a group of house," or whatever you mean. This works in Chinese, but it would be met with raised eyebrows in English. Why? Because the English language has an ordinarily unspoken rule that plural nouns should be marked with "sss" and "zzz" (the rule is actually more complicated, as we shall see).

Such a rule would exist even if it were never put into words and expressed out loud. It exists as a pattern of regularity that governs the relations between words and other words, and between groups of words and meanings. Children who learn to talk apparently do so by discovering or *acquiring* these rules of language from listening and observing as those around them use language in meaningful ways, and by imitating and inventing and trying out language on their own.

This act of discovery is perhaps the greatest intellectual achievement any of us ever makes. It begins in the first year of life but gets going in earnest after age two. There are many distinct tasks involved in the acquisition of language. They include the acquisition of words, developing a sense of grammar or syntax, learning the functions of language, developing metalinguistic awareness, overcoming egocentrism, and learning to use language in different settings. Let us now look at each of these in turn.

Names for Things

The naming of objects and simple actions occurs very early in the sequence of language acquisition; between twelve and eighteen months the average child begins to produce single words, most of which are names for objects in the environment like *ball, doggie, mama* or for familiar actions like *give, go, bye-bye,* (Nelson, 1973). Single words are used to represent entire utterances for about the next six months: One-word utterances are obviously ambiguous, and the listener must depend heavily on the context in which they are used to fully understand them. These early one-word utterances comprise a stage called *holophrastic speech;* holophrases are "words that are sentences" (Brown, 1973).

Children acquire their very first labels for things in their environments by hearing those things named by others; most often the first labels are the ones a child interacts with frequently, such as *mama* or *daddy, doggie, bottle, milk,* or the like, much more commonly than other objects like *chair, trees,* or *stove* (Hetherington and Parke, 1979). Once a few words have been acquired, vocabulary growth moves at an astonishing rate. When children begin to try to apply labels to new things or figure out what something might be called, we can see self-directed learning in action.

A typical example is seventeen-month-old Katie's experience with *doggie*. Katie learned *doggie* early, at about twelve months, to refer to the neighbor's friendly setter. Soon she was using *doggie* to refer to other dogs, even when they differed greatly in size and color from the first dog. Her first real-life experience with a cat happened to be a very large cat in the neighborhood; she confidently called it *doggie*, apparently on the basis of its similar features: four legs, fur, general body configuration. Katie had examined the new object, cat, compared it with the features of the items in her mental category or scheme for dogs, and found the cat sufficiently like the dogs she'd seen to classify it as a dog.

Soon after, Katie was riding in the car when she saw a large brown cow standing near the road. Looking at it carefully, she said "doggie?" with a clear interrogative inflection. Apparently the animal was sufficiently unlike a dog or cat that she doubted its identity. "No, that's not a doggie, that's a cow. A cow says moo and it eats grass," her mother responded. By pointing out its unique features and giving it a name, Katie's mother is helping the child establish a new category of reality that can be named, as well as providing the name itself. On seeing other cowlike animals Katie might be expected to call them *cows* too, lumping them into that category, but as she experiences more and more new things, she will also spontaneously begin to establish new categories by asking "What dat?"

Katie's experience with "doggie" shows a concept formation process that is not unlike the one adults use in discovering terms for unfamiliar things. On a drive through the mountains, for example, we might say, "Oh, look at the lovely bushes!" but have our naturalist friend correct us: "That is a rhododendron." Later we might say, "Oh, look at the lovely rhododendron!" only to be corrected again: "Actually, *that* is a mountain laurel." Eventually, if we didn't lose interest in plants altogether, we would have learned more specific names for different kinds of "bushes."

Sometimes, however, a child's early concept formation follows an entirely different direction. The Russian psychologist Lev Vygotsky (1962) noted that children's early concepts may lump things together with an object for which they have a name but on the basis of *different* features (see Figure 2.1). A boy might say "doggie" to refer (a) to the family beagle, (b) to a shiny black olive (because it looks like the doggie's nose), (c) to a wooly rug (because it resembles the doggie's fur), or (d) to the sensation of having his hair brushed (because it reminds him of the doggie's scratchy claws) (DeVilliers and DeVilliers, 1978). Vygotsky called these oddly matched groupings *spontaneous concepts* and pointed out that they give way to *scientific concepts*, the hierarchically arranged categories that adults use, but only gradually and by means of interaction with adults.

A child may also make up a name for a new object, which often happens when children begin combining two or more words. At age three Annabrook coined the term *chainsaw bike* for the first motorcycle she'd ever seen; already familiar with bicycles and with her father's chainsaw, she combined features of both to accommodate the new, unfamiliar object. This creation of unique names for things is common in young children and has even been observed by scientists

Figure 2.1   Some spontaneous concepts for "dog"

studying the ability of primates to generate language using signs and other nonverbal means (Gardner and Gardner, 1971; Premack, 1971).

The Rise of Grammar

Holophrastic speech gives way to the combining of words, first in two-word utterances and then longer strings, at about the age of two. This is an important development because the appearance of word strings signals the beginning of the child's use of *syntax*, or *grammar*. Grammar is the element of language that shows the meaning of words in combinations. It has two ways of showing such meaning: One is by *word order*, and the other is by *inflections*. In English, for example, the order of the two strings

The man bit the dog

and   The dog bit the man

shows us who did the biting and who was bitten. In Latin, inflectional endings were used instead of word order to signal such differences. In Latin, for example, with *canus* meaning "dog," *mordet* meaning "he, she, or it bites," and *virum* meaning "the man," one can say

	Canus mordet virum
or	Canus virum mordet
or	Mordet canus virum
or	Virum mordet canus

and all of them mean "The dog bites the man." How? Because it is not the word order but the inflectional endings *-us* and *-um* that tell us which noun is the subject and which noun is the object.

Although ordering rules are never taught to children directly, they are acquired by speakers of every language very early. In their two-word utterances children sometimes use ambiguous orderings, but they very quickly modify them so that they make sense, probably because when they produce ambiguous utterances others question them or show they don't understand.

Here is an example of such an interaction: (Jamie, twenty-two months old, is in his highchair drinking milk from his cup; nearby is his mother's coffee mug.)

JAMIE: Cup.
MOTHER: Where's your cup?
JAMIE: Cup. Jamie cup.
MOTHER: That's right. That's Jamie's cup.
JAMIE: Cup mama. (pointing to mug)
MOTHER: What, honey? What's that?
JAMIE: Mama cup.
MOTHER: Yes, that's mama's cup.

By listening to the speech of others, as well as by interactions such as the one above, which help the youngster clarify the meaning of utterances, ordering rules are discovered and internalized. As utterances grow longer, ordering becomes more complex, but most youngsters have little difficulty figuring this system out for themselves.

Compared with Latin, English grammar uses relatively few inflections. There are plural and possessive inflections for nouns, number and tense markers for verbs, and comparison inflections for adjectives. Few as they are, they are nonetheless important, and they comprise one problem of language development with which all children must grapple. Two very interesting phenomena show up in a child's mastery of grammatical inflections. First, as Table 2.1 shows, all English-speaking children everywhere begin to use these inflections in roughly the same order. Since it is clear that they must be exposed to all of the inflections all of the time in the speech of those around them, this finding suggests that the course of language development is controlled by language

Table 2.1 Order of acquisition of some grammatical features

1. Present progressive	*-ing*	Him sing*ing*
2. Plural	*-s*	Two shoes; two knees
3. Irregular past		I *went*; you *saw*
4. Possessive	*'s*	Kitty*'s* tail; John*'s* book
5. Articles	*the, a*	I want *the* ball; that's *a* dog
6. Regular past	*-ed*	She shout*ed*; they play*ed*
7. Third-person singular	*-s*	He run*s* fast; she throw*s* hard

NOTE: Language researchers have found that most English-speaking children begin using the above-listed grammatical features in exactly the order in which they appear here.

learning processes inherent in children, as well as possibly, by structural difficulties in the grammar of the language itself.

The second interesting feature of learning grammatical inflections has to do with the mistakes children make. Inflectional endings are used according to both regular and irregular patterns. In the case of plurals, for example, we affix the sound /s/, /z/, or /Iz/ on the ends of nouns to indicate that they are plural: thus *goat, goats; hog, hogs; ash, ashes.* Some irregular nouns either show no marking of plurals at all or show their changes internally, such as one sheep, two sheep; one foot, two feet. When young children use these irregular nouns, however, they go through a stage in which they pluralize them as if these nouns followed the regular pattern. Hence we hear: *I got tiny foots,* and *I seed two sheeps.* These *overgeneralizations,* as they are called, are amusing, but they are more than that; they are extremely informative behaviors, because they dramatically show two important principles of language learning. One is that children learn language by invention, not solely by imitating what they hear. All children predictably produce utterances like those above, which they have never heard before. (This is also true of the invention of unique labels, such as the "chainsaw bike" example.)

The second principle is that very young children have the ability to abstract regularities out of an environment where examples are not presented in any orderly sequence, rules are not explained or even directly stated, and little or no attempt is made to emphasize patterns (Chomsky, 1975). Yet out of this maelstrom of language, children intuit what the regularities are, test their hunches by trying out unique utterances to see if they are responded to, and then modify them so that they are most clearly understood. That they master these systems in all languages, in all cultures, between the ages of about two and five is a monument to the astonishing intellectual capability of the very young child.

From simple two-word utterances preschoolers quickly move to longer ones, grouping words in predictable ways until by age four or five their language is just about as complex and fully developed as that of older children. "Fine-tuning" of sentences goes on at a rapid pace in these years, including mastery of the formation of questions, the use of negatives, pronouns, active and passive sentences, relative clauses, modifiers, and so on. At the early stages of sentence formation, often beginning before or around the age of three, a child's sentences are *telegraphic*; that is, some words and word endings are omitted, and only the words most critical to meaning are included. Here are some examples of telegraphic sentences.

Mary Tyler at twenty months:
> Where you go?
> Want down, Mama.
> Not bad girl.
> Up'tairs, Nanny.
> Go you bed.
> Want "Mama side you" [at bedtime].

Mary Tyler at thirty months:
> Thunder going kill you, Daddy.
> Her not puppy; her Cleo.
> Jessie say spider at Stacy house.
> I hear that coming—
> That my daddy in him bus.
> Bye, Mama. I'm going Cathy's house.
> I'm not going to watch it Mushow [Muppet Show].
> Tell Nanny go stairs take bubbles Ty Ty.
> My tooth hurt back in mouth.
> Them my favorite sisters.
> I need it boiled peanuts.

School-age children also articulate more clearly than preschoolers, use longer utterances, and may double their speaking vocabularies between the first and sixth grade (Smart and Smart, 1973b).

By the age of school entry most children have mastered most aspects of their oral language. Phillip Dale's (1972) data on children at different ages show that average six-year-olds have over 2500 words in their vocabulary (see Table 2.2).

Table 2.2 Average sizes of children's vocabularies at ages one through six

AGE (IN YEARS)	NUMBER OF WORDS	GAIN FROM ONE YEAR PREVIOUS
1	3	3
2	272	269
3	896	624
4	1540	644
5	2072	532
6	2562	490

By six or seven almost all children can understand and use active and passive sentences, questions, imperative commands, negative statements and negative affixes, present, past, and future verb tenses, noun plurals, inflections to make subjects and verbs agree in tense and number, pronouns, possessives, and verbs that include auxiliaries. As a rule, however, not all these forms appear spontaneously — younger children rarely use passives, for example — but then such forms are heard relatively less often in adult speech too. Also, not all adult syntactic forms are mastered by six or seven. Mastery of imbedded sentences like "the dog that chased the cat sat up" and of complex sentences like "Mary asked Jane what she should wear" is generally not achieved until the middle grades, when children are nine or ten (Chomsky, 1969).

Also slow to develop are complex sentences, sentences that combine two or more short sentences into single, more elaborate strings. A second-grade child is likely to say (or to write):

> We went to the store.
> It was the hardware store.
> We bought nails there.
> They were expensive.
> They took all the money we had.

A sixth grader, however, might say or write:

> We went to the hardware store to buy some nails.
> They were so expensive, though, that they took all the money we had.

In addition to the kinds of sentences described by Carol Chomsky, the problem of combining short, "stubby" sentences into longer, smoother ones has been identified as perhaps the most important item on the grammar-teaching agenda in the elementary grades (see the detailed discussion of this issue and related teaching strategies in Chapter Eight).

Functions of Language

As children's language becomes more and more complete and elaborate, so too does their ability to use it socially and to interact on a personal level with others. In fact, when we view language as communication between people, it is clear that children are able to use at least a primitive form of language before grammar, or possibly even words, have begun to emerge. Infants are able to communicate the message that they are upset, or happy, or hungry, or frightened. Eight-month-old babies can indicate through speech certain things they want, like, or observe. A one-year-old can use sounds to query, express anger, build bonds of affection, give commands, and express personal states, all before learning a single English word.

One linguist, Michael Halliday (1975), has observed that learning to talk is basically "learning how to mean." Much of this learning is accomplished before children acquire English vocabulary or grammar, and even after that

stage their ability to use language to meet their needs in a social setting seems to depend as much on patterns of behavior they have learned as on words or grammatical structures. In other words, a child must learn *to do things with language* as well as to learn the language.

From a careful observation of one preschool child, Halliday found that there were seven main uses or functions of language that children may learn (see Box 2.1).

There are two other points that are of interest with regard to Halliday's findings. First, even though he acknowledges that adults probably have many more identifiable functions, these seven serve to describe the uses to which young children put their language. Second, it is obvious when we think about it that adults can serve several functions with a single utterance: The sentence "It's certainly stuffy in here" can be as much a request for someone to raise a window, open a door, or extinguish a cigarette as it is a comment on the quality of the air. In children's language, however, each utterance serves only one function at a time.

Educators in England have been aware of Halliday's research for some time and have examined its implications for language in school. Joan Tough (1973) found in the study of kindergarten children that they could develop unevenly

BOX 2.1
Halliday's Models of Language Functions

1. "Gimme!" (*the instrumental model*). Language is used as a tool to get something for the speaker.
2. "Stop that!" (*the regulatory model*). Language is used to control another's behavior but not for the direct benefit of the speaker.
3. "What's that?" (*the heuristic model*). Language is used to find things out: to ask questions, assess answers, and form new questions.

4. "How are you feeling?" (*the interactional model*). Language is used to build a "we-ness" between speaker and listener.
5. "I'm scared." (*the personal model*). Language is used to explore and communicate the speaker's feeling and his or her point of view.
6. "Knock, knock, who's there?" (*the imaginative model*). Language is used purely for the fun of it, for the "feel" of sounds and for the fun of combining words and ideas, or repeating old ones to amuse or entertain.
7. "It's snowing!" (*the representative model*). Language is used to represent reality and convey information to others.

After Halliday, 1975.

in the seven functions Halliday listed, depending on the opportunities for language use their home environment provided. She illustrates this point very clearly in the case of one little boy. When Joey brings a frog home to his mother and begins to tell her about it, she cuts him off and tells him to get rid of it. When he asks her a question about a flower growing in the yard she declines to answer and tells him to go do something else. The result of such language interaction day after day is that the child fails to develop very far in the heuristic function, in the ability to ask questions and understand answers. Furthermore, his growth in the instrumental and regulatory functions encompasses only the most direct forms, which is clearly evident at the preschool level. When his teacher uses a polite, indirect form of command with the class, Joey fails to understand properly. "Those boys and girls who have cleaned up their places can have some cookies and juice," she says, and Joey, desk still littered, sprints for the snack. The teacher comes to realize that his problem is not so much one of manners as simply not understanding certain forms of command. When it comes to joining with a small group inquiry about a growing bean sprout, Joey has little to say. Again, speculates the teacher, this is because he has not developed very far in the language of inquiry.

Teachers can think of similar illustrations from their own experience: children who understood the language of regulation but were limited in their ability to express personal feelings, or children who had difficulty using language to build good relations with others, or children who seemed to take little delight in the fanciful and playful uses of language. If Halliday is correct, then helping children learn to talk is not helping them with a single ability but rather with at least seven somewhat different abilities: one for each of the functions of language.

Thought and Language: Internalizing Speech and Overcoming Egocentrism

We've been talking in this chapter about children's language, but the issue of their thinking has always lurked just outside of the limelight. When we spoke of their finding names for things, for example, we saw that having names depended as much on having mental categories or concepts of reality as on knowing words. In this section, we meet two more linguistic developments that are related very closely to developments in a child's thinking: *internalizing speech* and *overcoming egocentrism*.

Internalizing speech relates to what many of us think of when we reflect on what it is we do when we think — namely, we talk to ourselves. Of course, this talk is silent and not all of it is verbal. There are dimensions of the way we feel about events as well as images and sounds that make our thoughts richer than words alone. Neither are our thoughts bound to a linear presentation as our speech is. They can jump around, race ahead, change instantly. Still, there are words in our thoughts. Our thoughts are close to language and for children they are even closer.

The Russian psychologist Lev Vygotsky (Flavell, 1977) believed that children are first dependent on others for the language of their thoughts. Though they may have concepts for things, they are unable to generate elaborate ideas about things or plan and execute complex tasks by themselves. What they can do is understand the communicated ideas and elaborated plans of the mature speakers around them. Vygotsky refers to this early period as a stage of *other-external speech*, which lasts roughly from the age of one and a half to three. During this period, children are dependent on others for language that elaborates ideas and commands that lead to complex activity.

At the same time they hear the language of others, however, they are learning to speak themselves. Gradually they begin to encode elaborated ideas and plans for behavior into their own speech, and eventually they can express their own complex thoughts and formulate and execute more complex plans. Yet these thoughts and plans are still tied to overt or external speech. To have a thought, in other words, a child must say it out loud. Vygotsky calls this stage the period of *self-external speech*, and it lasts roughly from the ages of three to four and a half years.

After the age of four and a half, children begin to *internalize speech*. Now, while their thoughts and plans are still tied to language, the language can be run through their minds covertly. They have reached the stage of *self-internal speech*. With age and experience, their thinking will rely less and less on being elaborated in inner speech and will become less strictly verbal and more adultlike. At the same time, there will be many occasions when their thoughts will need to be expressed aloud. It is not at all unusual for a nine-year-old to mutter to himself or herself when thinking through a dilemma or putting together a puzzle. This is not so unusual for adults either!

There are two clear implications of these stages of inner speech for language arts teaching. First, they underscore the importance of having good language models around when children are engaged in activities. According to Vygotsky, inner speech and thence thought are imitated by children from the speech they hear used around them. The richer the language they hear, the richer their thinking can become. Also, they need opportunities to talk to themselves and others as they go about their work. Young children cannot "work quietly" the way adults can. If Vygotsky is correct, then to silence children's language in the early grades is to silence their thoughts.

The other area of language development closely related to thought is *overcoming egocentrism. Egocentrism* is a characteristic that was first highlighted by the Swiss psychologist Jean Piaget (1954). The concept refers not merely to selfishness but to an assumption children apparently make that others see what they see and know what they know. Put another way, egocentrism is a failure to recognize that others may have a point of view different from one's own: A five-year-old girl who is looking through a magazine may come across something especially interesting and say, "Look at this!" — yet hold the magazine so that only she, not we, can see it.

Piaget noted that egocentrism can make a child's language very difficult to understand. To demonstrate this point, he conducted a series of experiments in which child A was told a story while child B was out of the room. When child B returned, child A retold the story to child B. The retold version was almost always inadequate in several respects. The characters and things in the story were referred to with the pronouns "he," "she," or "it" without its being made clear to whom or to what the pronouns referred. Important parts of the story were sometimes left out, and events were arranged in a different order from the original. These findings were repeated when instead of being told a story child A was given a demonstration of, say, the way a faucet works. On being questioned, it was shown that child A usually *comprehended* the story or the demonstration. The problem lay not in understanding but rather in the inability to consider what child B needed to know, and the account was thus distorted by egocentrism.

Egocentrism may persist until children are as old as nine or ten. According to Piaget, overcoming it is not a sudden or once-and-for-all accomplishment but a gradual one that takes place throughout the primary school years. The reason children can overcome egocentrism and begin to take others' viewpoints into account is because other people demand it of them. When the five-year-old says, "Look at this!" but doesn't show us the magazine, an older brother or sister is likely to say, "Turn it around, silly, so I can see it!" Similarly, youngsters who fail to tell others what they need to know in order for the others to understand them will be pressed for more information and will gradually learn to anticipate the questions others may have.

Overcoming egocentric language is a task many children need to master during the early elementary years. Probably because in speech the audience is present and able to press for immediate clarification when messages are incomplete, most youngsters use egocentric language in writing long after they have overcome it in speech. In both speech and in writing, however, they need regular and frequent opportunities to communicate with real audiences in order to avoid or eliminate this problem.

Metalinguistic Awareness: Saying What You Know About Language

One of the latest-developing abilities involves being able to think about and talk about language; that is, to use words to analyze and discuss language. This ability is called *metalinguistic awareness*, and it requires a high degree of verbal fluency as well as the ability to think objectively. Metalinguistic awareness emerges after about the age of five. Before that, children may have acquired a great deal of knowledge about language, but that knowledge is at the *tacit*, or unconscious, level; they use that knowledge every day in their speech, but they find it virtually impossible to describe what they know about or how they use language. Metalinguistic awareness brings that tacit knowledge to a conscious level, where it can be described as well as used.

With many youngsters, metalinguistic awareness doesn't emerge until well into the primary grades, which has important instructional implications because right from the beginning of school we use terms like *word, sentence, letter, sound, noun, verb*, and the like every day. Since these terms are meaningful and specific to us as adults, we expect the children to use them correctly and precisely. We also expect, as early as first grade, that youngsters be able to perform quite complicated analyses of sentences, such as choosing the correct verb form to complete a sentence or make nouns and verbs agree in number. Although these are fairly typical exercises in language arts, they may be extremely difficult for those whose metalinguistic awareness has not yet fully emerged. The ability to state and understand (and not just parrot) rules governing various aspects of language use emerges in middle childhood, well after the ability to use such rules in speaking. Metalinguistic awareness is one of the crowning achievements of language development.

Using Language in Different Settings

The last aspect of children's spoken language that we will discuss in this chapter deals with their ability to use language appropriately in different speech situations. Linguists have often observed that the same individual may use language quite differently in different settings.

Marvin Klein (1977) has differentiated four different kinds of circumstances that he finds lead to important differences in language use.

Ceremonial Settings. These settings would include courtrooms, civil or religious ceremonies like weddings and funerals, formal debates, graduation exercises, and drama. This language is formal and somewhat artificial. The events of the language use convey more meaning than the words themselves: Students who participate in a graduation exercise are not really informed of anything new when they are granted a diploma with all the rights and responsibilities pertaining thereto. They genuinely would be surprised if instead of diplomas, the school had decided to bestow books of coupons redeemable at a local fast food restaurant, but they wouldn't believe it because the graduation proceeding in itself would communicate more than the words. Ceremonial circumstances require the speakers to use particular types of language structures and words, speak with clear enunciation and dramatic pauses, and, in general, to key in properly to the tone of the proceedings.

Formal Settings. Formal language is usually reserved for speeches or lectures delivered before an audience. Although there may be personal friends in the audience, the speaker is still expected to speak in such a way that even strangers could follow the presentation. The tone is usually serious, the informational content of the message is high, and the logical structure of the ideas presented is expected to be clear and strong. Formal language is usually prepared beforehand.

Occasions when we use ceremonial and formal speech are rarer than occasions for the kinds that follow. Nevertheless, when those occasions arise, we want to perform well because we are displaying ourselves in front of large groups of other people. Since using formal language improves with practice, it is important to remember it in planning a language arts program.

Unlike conversations, the language of formal settings consists of monologue. The speaker presents an entire spoken text from beginning to end without prompts, interruptions, or other contributions from the listeners. Though we are getting ahead of ourselves a bit, we can say here that monologues are the form of speech that are most like writing, since writing too requires us to convey a whole message without the intervening support of an audience. Helping children draw out their speech more and more in the fashion of monologues is therefore a helpful practice for writing.

Informal Settings. The language of informal settings, unlike that of formal settings, is not usually prepared beforehand, and the speaker does not have to construct the whole text of the talk, as is the case with monologues. Thus informal talk may seem easy and relaxed. In truth, however, informal talk puts some of the greatest demands on speakers. For one thing, informal talk engages all the purposes of language, from relating, to persuading, to explaining, to storytelling, and language play. Informal talk also requires that speakers be able to shift rapidly from one topic and purpose to another, which places a great burden on listening ability. Not only must they be able to follow language that shifts abruptly among topics, purposes, and other speakers, but they must also be able to monitor the speech of others at the same time they are planning their own contributions. They must further be able to follow a complex set of rules that comprise the "etiquette" of conversation: rules that govern when they should contribute, how they should tie their contributions to what has already been said, when they may interrupt another speaker, and what sorts of expressions and body gestures they should use while doing so. The impression we make on others as well as our general popularity is startlingly dependent on our ability to use language in informal settings.

Intimate Settings. When two people who know each other well are talking off by themselves, they use another form of language, which tends to be more abbreviated than the other forms, with one speaker often finishing a comment begun by another. Body language, and sighs, groans, and laughter may communicate as much in intimate situations as fully expressed sentences. As Klein points out,

> . . . it is important to remember that this setting is more private than the others but not necessarily less important, or, for that matter, less commonly employed. It is simply that the occasion is often nonpublic. Hence, its role in a school setting is often relegated to very specific and limited situations, as in teacher-student talks on personal matters, or in role-playing or dramatic activities.
>
> — Klein, 1977, p. 14

Informal language in classrooms is found in the form of small group discussions and in out-of-classroom chatter of groups of students.

The effect of settings is an important one to remember in language arts teaching. If we accept the idea that children learn to talk by (a) having language used meaningfully in their presence and (b) by having opportunities to use language for real communicative purposes, then it follows that they need both exposure and opportunities to use the language appropriate to different settings. For most students, the classroom is perhaps the only group setting in which they spend significant amounts of time. In school, teachers have the opportunity to vary both the size and the degree of formality of the groups in which children use language.

One researcher, Jill Richards (1978), has urged that elementary school teachers take seriously these opportunities to vary the language settings and hence expand the language of their students. Without some attention to this variable, she finds, elementary classrooms tend to use informal small group language (with a well-known and supportive audience) almost exclusively. High schools, however, with their rotating classes and objective, subject-discipline–oriented discussions, call for a dramatic increase of formal and much more explicit discussion. Children who cannot make this transition often fail to succeed in high school — not from a lack of preparation in the subject matter but from an inability to participate in the discourse of high school subjects. Steps that elementary school teachers can take to vary a child's language experience with regard to the settings of speech will be discussed in Chapter Three.

Listening

Of the four verbal communicative acts — talking, listening, writing, and reading — listening is the one we begin with in early life, and the one we spend the most time doing from then on. As Sara Lundsteen has put it, "We listen a book a day; speak a book a week; read a book a month; and write a book a year" (Lundsteen, 1978, p. 75). Yet when it comes to the amount of time school instruction devotes to cultivating skills in talking, listening, reading, and writing, listening comes in dead last.

In past years, we used to say that talking *and* listening were neglected in schools. Today, talking is coming in for more emphasis, but we do not see a similar amount of stress on listening, partly because many educators assume that listening ability can be handled along with the greater emphasis on talking. When, for example, we set up small group discussions, each of the students will necessarily spend more time listening than talking. This line of thought is at least partially correct, and it agrees with our preference stated throughout this book that those instructional activities are preferable that involve children in real language use for important communicative purposes. Nevertheless, there are times when we must pay attention to the skill of listening itself, in order to ensure that children properly develop this skill in the language arts program. Let us look, therefore, more closely in this section at what it is that listening ability entails. In the next chapter we will discuss techniques for helping to develop it.

Listening as a Language Act. As it concerns language arts, listening is a *language act*. We cannot help children develop much listening skill without helping them understand sentences and paragraphs and stories and essays and conversations. Conversely, experiences that help them gain control over a variety of forms and uses of language will pay off in listening ability. By practical listening skill we mean listening and following directions accurately, listening to stories with understanding and appreciation, participating fully in conversations, learning from spoken deliveries, and evaluating truths and distortions in advertisements, political speeches, and the like.

You would be correct in assuming that this sort of listening skill overlaps considerably with skill in reading, talking, and even writing, but it would be more accurate to say that listening skill precedes and makes possible the development of skill in reading, talking, and writing. If children are not able to follow an argument that is spoken to them, they will not be able to say it, read it, or write it either. What we need to do in this section is to clarify in what ways listening *is* different from other language acts, and how it is similar. Then we will sketch some principles that can enhance the teaching and nurturing of listening skill in the classroom, principles that will be extended into practical methods in Chapter Three.

When we listen, we do so on three levels. On the first level is *hearing*. Technically speaking, we hear sound when the sound waves strike the eardrums with sufficient strength to set up an excitation that is converted to nerve impulses and transmitted to the brain. If a sound is too faint, or if the ears are impaired, we will not hear a particular sound. On a higher level, we *perceive* sounds. Perception might be defined as educated hearing; that is, we hear a sound and identify it with a class of sounds that we had previously stored in our memory. When we perceive a sound, we intuitively compare it with sounds we had heard before. If it is sufficiently similar, we judge the sound as being "a so and so."

Human beings are uniquely adapted to perceiving speech sounds, which seems to be a capability that we are born with. According to Eimas (1974), within the first week of life infants are more aroused by the sounds of human voices than by other sounds. Moreover, through a series of experiments he found that newborns are able to distinguish between individual speech sounds, the differences between which are extremely slight. /b/ and /p/, for example, are separated only by a delay of about forty-thousandths of a second in the onset of the vibration of the vocal cords (in the case of /p/) — yet newborns reliably responded to such difference in Eimas's research.

On an even higher level, we understand that sounds constitute a message. We understand that combinations of sounds are words, sentences, and larger units of language. In one sense we could say that all three of these levels of listening are built on each other; first we hear sound, then we perceive speech sounds, then we recognize combinations of sounds to be words and combinations of words to be sentences, paragraphs, and larger messages. But this is too simple. The fact is that we do not hear every speech sound of every word, or even every word of every sentence. The messages that strike our ears are rarely that clear. People slur sounds in words and even whole words, but that rarely hinders our understanding because when we listen at the highest level, when we listen for whole messages, then the parts we do hear distinctly enable us to mentally fill in the parts we don't hear. This works best, of course, when we are listening to language about familiar topics, in familiar situations, as when we are talking informally with friends. If we listen to a lecture on nuclear physics, most of us need to hear more of the message, because we have less knowledge of the subject — and the language in which people customarily talk about the subject — to serve as the basis for filling in gaps in the message.

Listening depends on the listener's thinking in terms of and expecting sensible messages, and not just accumulating speech sounds. As a demonstration of this point, a friend recounted an event that took place while he was visiting the Dominican Republic, a small Caribbean nation where Spanish is spoken. A relatively fluent speaker of Spanish, he had been hearing and speaking only Spanish during his visit. One afternoon while he sat talking in a restaurant, he became aware of a conversation at the next table. The sounds seemed hauntingly familiar, but he could not understand what was being said, nor could he place the language. At first he wondered if it were Spanish, but he had heard no identifiable Spanish phrases. Then he thought it might be French, but he recognized no French vocabulary either. Then it struck him that it was English, spoken in a very pronounced Brooklyn accent. As soon as he made this realization, he understood every word the people were saying! The speech sounds, which he both heard and perceived, did not constitute any messages for him until he decided in what language they were to be understood.

All of the foregoing would suggest that when we undertake to teach children listening skills, we should provide them with experiences with real language. Discriminating doorbells from bird chirps is irrelevant to understanding speech. Discriminating "bat" from "pat" and similar exercises that deal with phonemes are not worthwhile either: first, because school-aged children can already make these discriminations, as we saw earlier in this section, and second, because distinguishing phonemes or isolated words is not sufficient to an understanding of spoken messages.

What does contribute is experience using and listening to real language. Moreover, children need practice with *different kinds of language*. Halliday, you will remember, suggested that there are seven different functions of language, each of which constitutes a demonstrably different style of use and each of which must be learned adequately by children if they are to become fluent speakers. Jill Richards found that in school there are modes of talking associated with school subjects. There is a "language," or *register*, of language arts, another of mathematics, another of science. These consist not only of vocabulary items but also of sentence structures, of things like stories and poems in one subject, definitions and structural explanations in another, hierarchical relationships and cause and effect in another. Richards found that failure in school subjects could often be traced to a child's failure to learn these subject area registers, or variations of language. She argued that teachers must take deliberate steps to see that students become adept at learning the language of the school subjects at the same time they are being taught the subjects. She was talking about listening and reading, speaking and writing, but primarily about listening.

Reading specialists have long been aware that listening and reading are both related in an important way to one's ability to understand language structures. Many upper elementary grade students who are poor in comprehending on-grade level material when they read it do not adequately comprehend the same material when they listen to it read aloud to them either. The difficulty seems to lie in a lack of familiarity with the language structures in which the material is couched. Normal readers learn these language structures through the experience of reading. Poor readers, lacking this reading experience, do not learn the structures, but repeated opportunities at being read to improve their listening comprehension, and it usually improves their reading comprehension at the same time. It is not necessary to call the familiarity with complex language structures "listening skill" or "reading skill." Basically it is a *language skill*, which facilitates first listening, then reading.

In summary, the first and most important kind of listening skill turns out to be nothing less than the knowledge of language itself. This knowledge comes to us first and foremost through listening, and in this sense our listening experience provides the foundation for growth in the ability to talk, to read, and to write. Nevertheless, we should not forget that it is mostly *language ability* that is learned through listening. What does this language ability consist of? Essentially it is the familiarity with the grammatical structures of sentences, in addition to the structures of larger message units. The latter include story structures, as well as the forms of language used in explanation, description, argumentation, and the like (these structures are treated in detail in Chapter Four). They also include the different functions that Halliday describes: language used to get things, to regulate behavior, to find things out, to build interpersonal relationships, to explore one's own thoughts, to play with sounds and images, and to report observations about reality to others.

Listening skill has another important dimension that language skill does not fully take into account. That is the question of *attention*, which we turn to next.

Listening and Attention. Our teachers sometimes used to shake their fingers at us and say, "Give me your undivided attention." We suspected even then that it was impossible to do so fully. Psychologists have since told us why.

It is a psychological fact that the mind cannot maintain a steady focus on one thing for more than twenty seconds (Moray, 1969). Thus, as young students, even when we resolved to give our teacher our undivided attention, the deal was off in less than half a minute! This does not mean that listening is impossible, of course, but it does mean that *passive* listening is doomed to be a tug-of-war that pits the speaker's message against the listener's distractions.

Another psychological fact is that listeners can understand speech at twice the rate that speakers can produce it (Friedman, 1978). This fact is important in explaining what people do when they listen, for if we can understand speech so rapidly, it means that half of our mental capacity for comprehending is not engaged when we are listening to someone speak. This capacity is always going to be used for something; if it is not we soon find ourselves nodding off to sleep.

What, then, is active listening? Active listening is what listeners do when they acknowledge that their minds are going to be occupied with something in addition to the literal comprehension of the speaker's words. Rather than let their thoughts drift aimlessly, however, they deliberately exert their attention to do something with the speaker's message. There are several things they can do. They can run a mental commentary on it: They can doubt it, talk back to it, or extend it. They can rehearse it in order to remember it; that is, they can repeat interesting points back to themselves. They can formulate questions to ask the speaker, if permitted. They can take notes, jot down key words, or key phrases, if they are listening to a lecture. They can nod assent and interject words of agreement, if they are listening to a conversation. They can move to the words, if they are participating in a listening game. They can tap their feet if they are listening to music, or try to identify the instruments that are playing the different parts. They can plan a response to what the speaker is saying, if they are in a conversation. They can wonder if what they are listening to is true, or what motives the speaker has in saying it, or whether the speaker is revealing personal feelings rather than objective assessments. The kind of mental activity an active listener engages in depends on what is being listened to.

Guidelines for Developing Listening Habits. We can teach children to develop active listening habits. Games such as Simon Says and exercises in following directions are helpful in this regard, but there is much more that can be done. A sound program of instruction in this area can be developed along two lines:

1. *The teacher should make sure that the children can understand the language structures—sentence forms, functions of language, and school subject registers—that are necessary for productive learning at their grade level.* This is a tall order, and one that may not be entirely possible to achieve at the present time, because we do not have an exact idea of the language structures that are useful at each grade level. Nor do we have any foolproof means of evaluating children's language ability in so many different areas of use. This guideline is an ideal, then, a goal that teachers should keep in mind as they go about talking and listening to their students every day and planning instruction for them. We will, however, present some specific approaches to this goal in the next chapter.

2. *The teacher should show the children ways to listen actively, ways to respond both overtly and covertly to what they are listening to.* The various means of responding will vary with the grade level. The goal of this teaching is to demonstrate and practice ways of responding to listening so that the students will work them into their listening habits. Some techniques for helping to develop these habits will be presented in the next chapter.

Summary

A child's language development has implications for teaching language arts. Learning language, we have seen, is an active process. Children must hear language used and have opportunities to use it themselves in order to grow linguistically. Classrooms must be places where they talk, listen, read, and write; places where language is richly modeled for them, and where they are given many opportunities to initiate language use for their own purposes.

An early function of language is in naming things. Names can be categories for things, but, as we noted, these categories can at first be over- or underextended. Another possible problem, as Vygotsky has demonstrated, is that children may use names for *spontaneous concepts*, classifications based on a horizontal grouping of features. In teaching, it is thus important for us to use well-chosen words when students are exploring objects on their own.

With the development of grammar, or *syntax*, children first proceed through a stage in which they use single words, or *holophrases*, to express whole sentences. Next come two-word sentences and then three- and four-word sentences, sometimes called *telegraphic* speech because the less meaningful words are left out. In the development of grammar children make many systematic errors, errors indicating both the fact that they are exploring language and *need* to make errors before they master adult forms of speech and also that they are learning grammar as *rule-governed behavior*. These errors are sometimes called *overgeneralizations*, and their study can teach us much about children's concepts about language.

Michael Halliday tells us that learning language is not a unitary achievement, but entails developing in the seven *functions of language*: the *instrumental*, *regulatory*, *interactional*, *personal*, *heuristic*, *imaginative*, and *representational* functions. These might be viewed as prescriptive of language experiences the curriculum should provide.

Thought and language are interwoven. Specifically, we saw in this chapter that thought may begin in children as language borrowed from adults. For a time, their thinking will be verbalized aloud until it is internalized as inner speech.

Egocentrism affects language. Egocentric children assume that others know what they know and thus leave gaps or use pronouns with unclear referents.

Egocentrism usually persists in writing even after it has been eliminated from speech.

Youngsters may use language for years before they can talk about it. The awareness of language as an object for study, *metalinguistic awareness*, is surprisingly slow in developing, thus making it difficult for many children to talk about "nouns," "verbs," "sentences," and so on, even though their usage suggests that at least they can use the forms correctly.

The *settings* in which language is used calls upon different skills on the child's part. Settings may be *ceremonial*, *formal*, *informal*, or *intimate*, and classrooms should give children regular opportunities to use language in all types of settings.

Listening is a language skill, and humans are uniquely suited for making and listening to speech sounds. Listening is the channel of language we use first, and most. Nonetheless, what is often considered listening skill is really language skill: understanding words, sentences, stories, and other structures of discourse. The aspect of listening probably most in need of separate treatment is the matter of *attention*, sometimes treated as *active listening*.

In Chapter Three, methods for helping children develop ability in talking and listening are explained.

CHAPTER THREE

Teaching
Oral Language

CHAPTER OUTLINE

Oral language forms the basis of children's literacy. It is the primary way they communicate both before and after they have learned to read and write, and whatever will be learned and mastered in print is based on this foundation.

Almost all children are fluent oral language users when they come to school and have usually had three or four years of extended experience speaking and listening. The preschool years encourage particular aspects of oral language development, however, while the school years usually require children to master different kinds of oral language. Also, the kinds of oral experiences preschoolers have vary widely. Some home and preschool experiences prepare youngsters for school communication better than others. A language arts program must systematically help them to master new skills and prepare them for the unique academic and social demands that school places on their language ability.

Although oral communication requires both speaking and listening — sending and receiving messages — speaking and listening are not separate processes. Rather, they are slightly different facets of the same process: communication. If someone speaks and no one listens, communication has not taken place. Some of the activities in this chapter focus primarily on one aspect or the other, but all oral activities require both speaking and listening.

Oral Language Goals

For a language arts program to help children develop the oral language skills they need for school and for life, we must develop both general and specific goals. The methods and materials we propose spring from these general curricular goals:

— Children should receive instruction in and have many opportunities to use all of the functions of language with equal facility.
— They should be given opportunities to communicate effectively in a variety of language settings.
— They should be shown how the language registers of the content areas differ from other types of language and should become familiar with their predictable language structures.
— Speaking and listening should be integrated, not separated from each other. Listening should be active and responsive rather than a passive receptive process.

Children grow and change radically during the elementary years as their cognitive, emotional, and social abilities and needs modify and develop in unique ways. The goals of language arts in the primary grades must be differentiated from the goals of the middle and upper grades.

Preschool and Primary Grades

Goals for the preschool and early primary grades should focus on:

— *Spontaneous expression*: a multitude of concrete experiences to talk about; an environment rich in adult language modeling
— *Vocabulary development*: labeling of things; practice in simple categorization; the introduction of written labels to accompany learned oral labels of things in the environment
— *Syntactic development*: exposure and practice toward fluent use of the basic grammatical forms; experience giving and following simple directions; elaboration of everyday language forms
— *Social use of language*: development of clarity of articulation; much practice in social aspects of informal discussions such as turn taking and disagreeing; rich use of different language functions through activities like describing, dictating stories, telling stories, and dramatics
— *Development of listening and sense of stories*: listening to many types of stories told and read aloud; critical listening through use of prediction during story reading and storytelling; exposure to a variety of literary forms

Middle and Upper Elementary Grades

Goals for these grades should include and focus on:

— *Forms of expression*: practice using all of the language functions, with particular emphasis on facility with the "school functions," the heuristic and representational; practice using all of the language settings, with particular emphasis on the "school settings," formal and informal; facility in communicating with different types of audiences
— *Vocabulary development*: emphasis on the development of more precise vocabulary and the special terms and usages of the various content areas
— *Syntactic development*: rich exposure to and practice in using more elaborated and complex grammatical forms, especially those most often used in print; giving and following more complicated directions and sequences; exposure to and practice using the various registers of the content areas; growing facility with the syntactic forms of standard English for all speakers
— *Social use of language*: attention to the "rules" of group discussions; more sensitive and responsive listening to others; greater awareness and use of appropriate turn taking, disagreeing, arguing, and convincing; appropriate use of standard English in the various settings requiring it
— *Listening development*: greater awareness and use of story and text structures in listening to fiction and nonfiction; use of logic and prediction in comprehension activities; responsive and evaluative listening through note taking, outlining in various ways, sequencing, and illustrating; using story and text structures to remember and retell stories and nonfiction accounts

The following sections describe many types of oral communication activities that will help you implement these goals.

Discussions and Dialogues

Oral communication is social, and discussing things with others is a fundamental communicative act. Since discussion also forms the basis of communication through reading and writing, a natural place to begin instruction is by having students talk with one another.

Children engage in much social talk in school, but much of it is unstructured, informal, and unplanned. Therefore, if we are preparing them to use oral language flexibly and for many purposes, not just *any* talk will do. Through a variety of conversation, discussion, and dialogue techniques we can expand their repertoire of social language.

Discussions and dialogues help children learn to:

— use the language functions most called for in school, those we use to find things out, convey information, and express feelings and opinions (the heuristic, representative, and personal functions)

— use language in a variety of settings, particularly those that are structured and more formal than informal conversations
— communicate with different audiences and respond to their different information needs and reactions
— expand their repertoire of sentence structures, usage forms, and vocabularies
— develop poise and confidence

Conversation Activities

A *disconnected telephone* is useful for role playing and conversing. A pair of toy telephones for primary classrooms can be used to teach children "telephone manners" and survival skills like calling the operator in an emergency. For older children, a pair of real telephones can be obtained from the telephone company and used to relay messages, make appointments, seek consumer or employment information, or describe an event or a book one has read. They are good props for classroom dramatics too.

Show and Tell is a classic activity of the lower grades, because it allows children to talk about something familiar and interesting.

Your role is to help the speaker with leading questions when necessary, to model good questioning and listening, and to encourage interaction. Some children may hesitate to participate or think they have nothing to share; creative suggestions will help. Since youngsters love to talk about their families, a snapshot or a child's drawing of the family will elicit much sharing. You can ask the children to bring something small enough to fit into a lunch bag and describe, but not name, the object. They will get valuable practice in describing various aspects of size, color, function, and composition as others try to guess what is in the bag. You can also encourage them to bring in something seasonal, something they made or drew, an interesting object they found outdoors, or a picture of something they would very much like to have.

Show and Tell should not be limited to lower grades. Older children can also benefit from planning and presenting a brief monologue from time to time, although they will probably prefer calling the activity by another name. We know a teacher who refers to the activity as "News 'N Goods," and children share "something new or something good" in their lives, so the topics often revolve around their small triumphs and novel experiences. At the upper levels students should be encouraged to use more complete descriptions, precise vocabulary, and elaborated sentences in their presentations.

Small Group Discussions

The more children can talk and be heard in the classroom, the better. Simple arithmetic will show that they have six times the opportunity to talk and be heard in a group of five than they have in a group of thirty. In groups of three the increase would be tenfold, but here is where mathematics fails us. Experience shows that in a group of five there is a diversity of viewpoints that keeps discussion interesting, as well as a "critical mass" of participants to keep up the momentum of the discussion. Below five, however, these qualities are lost. Five to seven students are ideal for small group discussions.

Kindergarten and primary school teachers know that it is preferable to conduct discussions with small groups of students. From third or fourth grade on up, many teachers find that students can very profitably conduct their own small group discussions without the teacher's direct participation. Small discussion groups can carry out such tasks as:

— raising questions about a unit that will be studied
— finding solutions to a practical problem, such as excessive noise in the cafeteria
— planning a project that can be undertaken together, such as an after-school interview with a neighborhood expert on rocketry
— researching a topic together and planning a report for the class
— discussing schoolwork-related questions that have been set by the teacher

Making groups work in the classroom takes deliberate planning and patient orientation of the students to this mode of learning. Here are some steps to keep in mind:

1. *Teach the procedure.* You should conduct your first few weeks of exercises primarily for the purpose of teaching children to function in groups. Make your first assignments short, very explicit, and immediately inviting. If small group work is completely new to the class, you might begin by setting up only one group at a time, making sure it is dominated by your most responsible students. It can meet a few times while all the other students do seatwork or work under your supervision. Without making "saints" out of the children in the first group, you can call attention to what they are doing and explain that everyone will shortly be working in small groups from time to time. The first group may thus establish a positive model for other students to follow when their turn comes to participate in the group.

2. *Construct the first groups carefully.* Gerbrandt (1974) suggests that children's first experiences in small groups be in groups assigned by the teacher, especially if they have not had prior experience working in groups. He recommends that the teacher give some thought to the different types of behavior each student manifests, and then distribute equally among the groups students with the following characteristics: "the vocal leader, the quiet leader, the follower, the attention getter, and the child with severe attitude problems" (p. 10).

He further suggests that the teacher take charge of many of the decisions of this first group experience, determining, for example, the best place for each group to meet, and the quietest and least disruptive route that the children can take to get from their desks to the group meeting area. He suggests that this movement be practiced with the whole class several times so that everyone knows how to get from desk to group quickly and quietly.

3. *Make first assignments concrete and interesting.* Some topics for these first experiences in group work might be several brainstorming exercises, followed by some consensus-building exercises.

Brainstorming means getting out all the ideas you can in answer to a question within a specified time limit. In brainstorming, all answers are acceptable, the goal being quantity of ideas, uninhibited participation, and uncritical acceptance by the group members. Logistically, brainstorming requires that one group member be appointed to be the recorder, to write down the ideas of all the other members. This job should rotate, in order to avoid burdening one student. Questions for brainstorming are at first quite literal. "What if . . ." problems are good for brainstorming, which requires a problem that can be solved many ways. For example, what if . . .

— you had to find as many uses as possible for a thousand pounds of peanut shells?
— you were to designate a new national holiday or National _____ Week?
— you had to invent an entirely unique candy bar or breakfast cereal?
— you were to come up with as many ways as possible to use a brick (or an inner tube, an empty thread spool, a bag of styrofoam-packing "wiggles," a broken umbrella, a junked car)?
— your group were put in charge of reducing litter in and around the school?

Brainstorming is a good prelude to more structured problem-solving group processes.

Consensus building is a task that follows on brainstorming. After the students have gotten the idea of loosening up, of having everyone participate, and of accepting all ideas from all sources, the next logical step is to find ways to decide on the best ideas of those available. The cardinal rule of consensus building is that the solution arrived at must be satisfactory to every member of the group. If it is not, then the discussion must proceed until a solution is found that does satisfy everyone. Exercises for consensus building usually require group members to agree on a short list of alternatives derived from a longer list. An example of a consensus building task is as follows:

An airplane crashes in the snowy mountain wilderness during winter time. The pilot and one passenger survive but both are badly bruised and limited in what they can carry the fifty miles to civilization. They are limited to five items between them, from the following supplies on board the plane: a knife, a compass, a mirror, a rope, five pounds of fresh meat, a gallon of water, a gun, a blanket, matches, firewood, an ax, and a frying pan. Which five items should they take?

Later consensus building activities can draw first on suggestions made by group members and then arrive at a consensus as to the best ones. Examples of topics for such discussions are the following:

1. Your group will be able to choose new playground equipment (or library books, band uniforms, science books, gym equipment, etc.) for the school. You have a budget of $1000 (or some other amount) and you *cannot* exceed this figure. You must choose what will be useful or agreeable to the most people. (The teacher provides catalogues and the like for selections.)

2. Your group must decide on activites for an All-School Day (or parents' open house, field trip, etc.) that will involve, entertain, and be useful to all students in the school. Problems like costs, transportation, facilities, and parents' approval must be considered.

3. Other "dilemmas" might include devising a new grading scheme, report card, or daily schedule; responding on behalf of the entire school to a community problem or controversy; or planning a "dream" classroom or school building. Younger children might work on developing a set of classroom rules, selecting toys for the classroom with a simple budget, or choosing a pet for the class.

It is a good idea when introducing a consensus building task to encourage students to brainstorm first and think of as many items as possible. After they have done so, you can tell them to choose the best three or four or five alternatives, or to rank-order the ideas. Later, after they have become skillful at the tasks of brainstorming and consensus building, you can encourage them to use both procedures in approaching other group topics.

Panel discussions are good for older students, since they require the division of labor within a group, preparation of individual presentations, and the co-ordination of individual efforts for a group outcome. Like consensus building, a panel discussion can be an outcome of a problem-solving group process. Students can present their solution to a problem if they were able to arrive at a consensus, or the two best alternatives if they didn't agree. (Such an outcome may lead to a debate too.) They should present their research, facts and figures, results of polls they may have taken or need to take, and their solutions to various potential problems. If opinion is strongly divided, groups can split or recombine to plan a spirited pro-and-con debate on the issue.

To take a problem to these lengths, you should try to select a basic issue that offers the children some *real* input. If you want to have them respond to a community controversy, culminate the activity by having them write and mail real letters to a newspaper editor or politician, invite a speaker to hear and respond to their panel or debate, or make arrangements for them to speak at a principals' or school board meeting. Student involvement in real issues with real outcomes will be high, but they will not carry through on issues where what they decide really doesn't matter anyway.

Grouptalk is a discussion activity described by Moffett and Wagner (1976) and Carlson (1976). In groups of four to six, students practice keeping to the point and accurately summarizing what others have said. A group leader is selected to help keep the discussion moving; a question is posed, to which the other members respond by calling on their own experiences and what they have read. In Grouptalk, the discussion proceeds under a specific and demanding set of rules. The rules come in three sets: *starting rules*, *discussion rules*, and *ending rules*. Starting rules guide the group's activity as they become oriented to the topic to be discussed.

Starting rules:
— *Read (or listen to) today's question.*
— *Understand it:* tell yourself what it means.
— *Discuss its meaning:* tell others what you think the question means.
— *Decide on one meaning:* agree on the meaning before you start answering the questions.

Once these rules have been followed the students are ready to begin discussing the question, at which point each student now begins to observe the *discussion rules:*

— *Contribute:* give your answer to the question.
— *Be relevant:* stick to the subject.
— *Listen:* try to understand what someone else is saying.
— *Respond:* comment on what others have said.
At the close of the discussion, the students follow the *ending rules:*
— *Sum up:* help in the summary by trying to remember the main ideas discussed.
— *Evaluate:* listen to the playback (if the discussion was recorded on tape) and comment on how well the Grouptalk rules were followed.

               — (Moffett and Wagner, 1976, pp. 76–77)

This activity should be kept fairly short, say fifteen or twenty minutes. Move from group to group, aiding students without interrupting or taking over the dialogue. Example discussions could involve describing alternative ways a story character might have acted, or situations that might make one feel lonely, afraid, angry, or proud.

A danger to be avoided in Grouptalk as well as in brainstorming and consensus building exercises is that they become so stylized that discussion becomes isolated from other activities in the school day. As Moffett and Wagner point out, some of the best discussion children take part in is directed toward getting things done in the classroom.

Tasks for Small Groups

Small groups work effectively only when there is a clearly stated task for the members to perform, and when all the members know how to perform it. The task is not simply to talk, but to *talk to some purpose.* Small groups are most interesting and more productive when you have students apply themselves to a variety of tasks. Moffett and Wagner (1976) describe two sorts of talk that take place in small groups: *task talk* and *topic talk*. Task talk is discussion that arises in the course of doing something else, such as planning and painting a mural, designing the layout for the classroom reading corner, or deciding which papers should go into a book produced by the group. Topic talk, on the other hand, is usually removed from some present concrete project and tends to be addressed toward more disembodied subjects. The participants must exert effort to structure their discussion in topic talk; they do not have a concrete task that structures their talk for them.

Moffett and Wagner identify four kinds of topics for topic talk, arranged according to level of sophistication. They are *enumeration, comparison, chronology*, and *analysis or illustration*.

1. *Enumeration.* Enumeration is the simplest level, the one where groups should begin. It is relatively simple because it relies on a more basic thinking process than the other kinds of topics. The thinking is essentially a kind of classification. If the topic is "ways to earn a living," the students must think of ways that fit that category and exclude those that do not, such as cutting the grass (unless cutting the grass can be made into a living). This level of topic is also simpler because for the most part it requires little interaction among the participants. Everyone's ideas are welcome, so long as they fit the category demanded by the topic. There is no need here to debate or arrive jointly at a complex solution.

2. *Comparison.* Comparisons require thinking that is more limited and more abstract. Instead of thinking of whole objects or actions that fit a category, students must now think of qualities of particular objects: "How is a horse like a cow?" "How is an airplane like a fish?" "How is football different from soccer?" Moffett and Wagner note that it is easier to find either likenesses or differences first and become adept at making comparisons of this sort before both comparing and contrasting in one activity.

3. *Chronology.* Chronology involves thinking up steps and arranging them in a sequence. Writing a group story is one such topic. Reconstructing the process by which something was made is another. Planning a strategy for publishing and distributing classroom-produced magazines is yet another. In all three examples it may be necessary to brainstorm events or steps that are relevant to the task at hand, to separate the essential ones from the nonessential ones, and to find the relations among them that would dictate the order in which they should fall. Such discussion calls for more sophisticated thinking on the part of the membership, and more skillful interaction as well.

4. *Analysis or illustration.* "These topics call for analyzing, explaining causes, or furnishing some sort of evidence such as anecdotes, logical reasons, or facts and figures" (Moffett and Wagner, 1976, p. 81). Topics for such discussions are open-ended and as close to the experience of the participants as possible. Moffett and Wagner suggest that questions with a *yes* or *no* answer

are often less successful than ones where the students must choose and defend a more elaborate position. "Which is the best position to occupy in the family: youngest, middle, or oldest?" and other questions of this sort are recommended both because they are close to everyone's experience and because students must go beyond *yes* or *no* in choosing and defending a position. Moffett and Wagner also recommend selecting a proverb and deciding whether or not it is always true: "Does he who laughs last always laugh best?" "Does the early bird always get the worm?" Arranging choices in order of priority, as in the consensus building exercise described above, is another topic that fits this category.

Classroom Dramatics

Dramatics should be a cornerstone of the language arts program. Drama activities range from the simplest fingerplays and imaginative play with dolls and toys through somewhat more elaborate choral speaking and improvisations to making up and putting on puppet shows, radio plays, and readers theater productions. Drama activities can take five minutes or sustained effort over several weeks; they can involve one child, several, or a whole class; they can develop spontaneously from a discussion, a story or film, a fragment of music, or a box of empty containers. Dramatics in the classroom provides one of the very best settings for growth in oral communication.

Children use dramatics to explore their own feelings, to "try on" different roles and ways of acting, to act out alternatives without risk and to put events and emotions in the context of their own lives. They use their senses, emotions and reactions, wishes and fears, and impressions of adult life in their dramatic play.

The teacher's role in dramatics is that of a facilitator, a guide, and a means of extending horizons. The teacher models active involvement, appreciative listening, and sensitive response. The guidelines in Box 3.1 will help you use classroom dramatics positively and productively.

Dramatic Play

A child's first spontaneous drama experiences spring from play. In primary classrooms dramatic play should predominate over other, more structured forms of drama, to help children build a base of spontaneity, imagination, and unfettered creativity. The classroom should provide the physical means for endless combinations of making things, playing with them, making up dialogues and actions, and inventing new alternatives. The simplest, cheapest raw materials are the best, since they offer so many possibilities for trying out and inventing.

Dressing up is a sure-fire drama stimulus. Keep a box or garment bag in your room, stocked with items like scarves, gloves, shawls, hats, belts, large shirts with sleeves cut off for tunics and capes, curtain panels, briefcases and purses, umbrellas, plain aprons, old boots, and discarded wigs. (Parents can donate these items.) Yard and rummage sales and thrift shops can yield special

BOX 3.1
Guidelines for
Classroom Dramatics

Seize the moment! Let drama evolve naturally from daily activities.

Emphasize movement and action rather than dialogue.

Get involved yourself!

Give everyone something to do; they should be doing, not watching.

Deemphasize "production"; drama should be for the children themselves, not for an audience.

Respond positively; don't judge or criticize.

Don't keep intervening with suggestions or directions, since this diverts attention from the activity itself.

Make sure every child has a chance to take every role at some time.

Never take away drama activities as a punishment.

Be prepared for some noise and disorder; too much restraint stifles dramatics.

items like old military, postal or other uniforms, top or cowboy hats, helmets, net or lace curtains, or bits of fake fur. Avoid commercial Halloween costumes and masks; their possibilities are limited and they are rarely durable.

A few simple homemade props or costume items lend themselves to many skits and improvisations: cardboard-and-foil crowns with glued-on button "jewels"; cardboard swords and wands (blunt ends); decorative belts with bits of foil, buttons, and so on attached; beards made of cut-up wigs tied on with shoelaces or elastic; macaroni or "dough" beads painted and strung or shaped into brooches, medals, and the like; a pair of "wings" made of wire or cardboard and gauze, net, or lace; a shoulder bag and used envelopes for mail delivery; play money; old glasses with lenses removed; empty grocery containers; plastic dishes and simple housewares.

Masks can add a great deal to spontaneous dramatics, and are easily made (see Figure 3.1). A basic mask that leaves the nose and mouth free can be made from a sheet of 8-1/2" x 11" duplicator paper and a pair of shoelaces or a bit of string: 1) Fold paper in half horizontally; 2) cut on dotted lines, remove triangle and eye holes; 3) attach string at sides to tie behind head. Decorate by coloring or gluing on extra features such as horns, feathers, fur, beards, or whatever.

Choral Speaking

Choral recitation and speaking are excellent oral activities for children throughout the grades. At first, children should focus on *doing*, not just saying; they are more interested in physical response than the words, and activities should focus on rhythm and tempo. Fingerplays and responding with movement are good starting places. Later children can choral-read poetry and other literature forms.

Figure 3.1 Making a basic mask

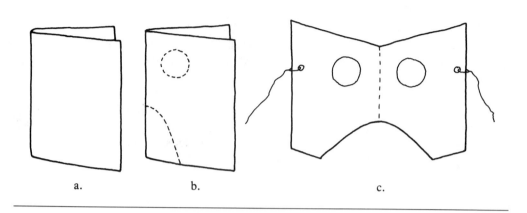

a.   b.   c.

Fingerplays are simple verses that are accompanied by hand gestures. Children should first practice the gestures, and then recite the verses as they do the gestures.

Here is the sea,	(SEA: one hand held horizontally makes wavy motion;
The wavy sea.	
Here is the boat	BOAT: other hand cupped on sea;
And this is me.	ME: Thumb wiggling from "boat.")

— (Craft, 1971, unnumbered)

This is the church.	(CHURCH: Fingers laced together inside palms;
This is the steeple.	STEEPLE: Forefingers raised and touch at tips;
Open the doors.	DOORS: Thumbs held together vertically, opening;
And see all the people.	PEOPLE: Turn hands palms up to show fingers sticking up.)

The following books are good sources of fingerplays and related activities.

Brown, Marc. *Finger Rhymes.* New York: Dutton, 1980.

Glazer, Tom. *Eye Winker, Tom Tinker, Chin Chopper: A Collection of Musical Fingerplays.* New York: Doubleday, 1973.

Grayson, Marion. *Let's Do Fingerplays.* Bethesda, Md.: Robert Luce, 1962.

Poulsson, Emilie. *Finger Plays for Nursery and Kindergarten.* Santa Fe, N.M.: Gannon, 1971.

Self, Margaret, ed. *Two Hundred Two Things To Do.* Atlanta: Regal, 1968.

Choral verses can be effectively acted out during recitation, with children stamping, clapping, whispering, hunching over, or using similar means to act out words and sound effects. Here are a few example verses:

> Jack-in-a-box
> Is a funny old man
> He hides in his box
> As small as he can
> He hides in his box
> As small as he can
> Then SUDDENLY OUT
> he jumps!
> UP! DOWN UP! DOWN
> Funny Jack-in-a-box.

OLD MRS. STUCK-IN-THE-MUD

> Both boots stuck in the mud,
> Both feet stuck in the boots,
> Both feet stuck to my legs,
> Both legs stuck to me,
> HELP!
> I'm old Mrs. Stuck-in-the-Mud!

MISS GLORIA GRAND

> Miss Gloria Grand got ready for the dance,
> She did her eyelashes,
> Painted her mouth,
> (Very carefully, no splodges)
> Powdered her nose,
> Combed her long, long hair
> Put on her earrings,
> Fastened her necklace,
> Stepped into her grand, gold-buckled shoes,
> Picked up her long swishy skirts,
> Opened her door
> AND
> Tripped over the milk-bottles!
> CRASH! BANG! SPLASH.
> (She wasn't hurt — but she had to start all over again!)
> — Craft, 1971, unnumbered

Refrains are verses in which one person recites the main verse and others respond with a refrain or chorus.

In *antiphonal arrangements*, two groups alternately recite verses with dialogue formats.

A refrain
LEADER: Old MacDonald had a farm,
CHORUS: Ee-yi-ee-yi-oh.
LEADER: And on this farm he had a pig (cow, goat, dog, hen, etc.)
CHORUS: Ee-yi-ee-yi-oh.
ALL: With an oink oink (moo, baa, bow-wow, cluck, etc.) here and an oink oink there,
CHORUS: Ee-yi-ee-yi-oh.

An antiphonal arrangement

COME OUT TO PLAY

GROUP 1: Boys and girls, come out to play,
        The moon doth shine as bright as day;
GROUP 2: Leave your supper and leave your sleep,
        And come with your playfellows into the street.
GROUP 1: Come with a whoop, come with a call,
GROUP 2: Come with a good will or not at all.
GROUP 1: Up the ladder and down the wall,
GROUP 2: A half penny roll will serve us all.
GROUP 1: You find milk and we'll find flour,
GROUP 2: And we'll have a pudding in half an hour.

— Mother Goose

Mime and Improvisation

Mime, acting out without words, and *improvisation,* spontaneously acting out a scene with impromptu dialogue, are both excellent devices. Both can cause self-consciousness, so it is wise to use a "warm-up" activity to get children up, moving around, and involved in the activity. Mimes and improvisations are excellent stimuli for writing assignments done by older students. Several of the following activities were suggested by two of our students, Susan Robinson and A. Kathleen Oliver.

1. Warm-ups: Pair students for a "mirror game"; facing each other, one moves slowly and the other mirrors his or her motions as precisely as possible. Group students for a "ball game": standing in a circle, they throw an imaginary ball back and forth, watching its progress and occasionally changing its size and weight (Ping-Pong ball, football, bowling ball). In a circle, students pass around a "glob"; each one reacts to it in some way and passes it on. They might explore how they would handle it if it were very hot, very cold, slimy, sticky, very tiny, or slippery.

2. Pantomimes, acted out without words:
   a. Act out an occupation or sport; others guess the activity, as in a game of charades.
   b. Spill spaghetti on a borrowed shirt or blouse.
   c. Break a vase and try to clean it up before you get caught.
   d. Discover you've lost your house key, lunch box, or homework.
   e. Offered a snack or drink at someone's house, you try it and find it tastes horrible.
   f. On a hike you wander off and suddenly realize you're lost and all alone.
   g. Wrap an odd-sized, cumbersome gift.
   h. Try to thread a needle with a very small eye.
3. Improvisation, brief scenarios acted out with minimal planning and spontaneous dialogue:
   a. At a meeting at school between principal or teacher, parent and child, the child was caught cheating but denies it.
   b. A shoe store clerk has to wait on a parent buying shoes for a "bratty" five-year-old. After a minute or so, add another customer or two demanding to be served.
   c. While using a borrowed bike, a rider hits another bike, which turns out to be very expensive, or scratches a parked car. After the initial confrontation has proceeded for a minute, add a police officer or other adult.
   d. An older child is setting the table, dusting, or doing some household chore; a younger sibling comes in and breaks or spoils something. Add a tired, harassed parent after a minute.
   e. A child buying a gift in a department store is patronized by a clerk who doesn't want to wait on children.

Klein (1977) suggested ways of structuring improvisations that require various language settings. Many of these can draw on events children have read about in social studies, science, and other content areas. *Ceremonial* language settings, for example, could include acting out a wedding or funeral, a coronation or inauguration, the surrender of an army or a declaration of war, the birth of a new king or queen, or the signing of an important peace treaty. *Formal* settings might include delivering a speech to Congress, a graduation, addressing a ruler or president, winning the Nobel Prize, or a court trial. *Informal* settings could include talking to a friend's parents, inviting people to a party, planning a big play during a game, or getting information on a product or service. *Intimate* settings might include sharing good or bad news with a friend, asking someone to dance, working with a tutor or with a classmate on a project, asking a parent for money, or describing a good book or movie to a friend.

Role Playing and Puppetry

Role playing usually refers to moderately structured, preplanned dramatics where children develop a story, create characters, plan dialogue ahead of time (rather than spontaneously, as in improvisation), write or dictate a script, rehearse parts, and then stage a final production. These activities can, of course, range from simple one-scene dialogues to complex plays and presentations. Children often use puppets instead of acting themselves or in conjunction with human players. Ideas for making puppets are given later in this section.

"Scripts" can be written out, either in full form or in the form of more cryptic notations; they can be dictated by younger children or poor readers onto a tape and transcribed later from the tape. Preparing scripts is a powerful creative writing activity which requires much thinking, writing, and rewriting, but however the scripts are constructed, it is important to remember that role playing is not "putting on a play." Memorizing lines is not a productive practice, unless dialogue is very brief and simple. Memorizing lines almost completely prevents creative, spontaneous activity. It puts thoughts and words in a strait-jacket. It makes students self-conscious, wooden, and fearful of forgetting, and contributes to their perception of dramatics as something to be avoided by all but the "best actors." If they are used at all, scripts should be used as a tool to help children feel comfortable and spontaneous, but they should be put away before the final runthrough. Divergence from the script should be encouraged. Leave memorization of lines to professional adult actors.

Situations for role playing arise naturally from books and stories read in language arts and from all the content areas. Situations should involve some sort of conflict, plenty of physical action as well as words, and natural, everyday dialogue and characters, whether human or animal, that seem real and understandable. Let children suggest role playing situations as well as coming up with them yourself. A few suggestions are listed here to spur your imagination. (These are equally appropriate for puppetry.)

1. Act out or use puppets to re-create part or all of a basal story instead of using the usual comprehension activities.
2. Act out part of a good book as a book-sharing activity, or role-play a character in the book telling about his or her adventures, or the author of the book telling about writing it.
3. For social studies/history, create a skit, pantomime, or short play based on a historical event you've been reading about.
4. Take a trip in a "time machine," stopping at various points in the past for a brief visit with famous or ordinary people of the time.
5. Plan and present a travelogue of a place you're studying in geography or history. Use travel brochures and books and other references to plan and illustrate your travel talk; optionally, role-play events during your trip.
6. Take a book or story you liked and create a new ending or outcome for it; role-play the new version.

7. Experiment with photography and film making when you do role playing. Accustom children to working before a camera by using a camera without film for a while; soon they will forget the camera is there at all. "Freeze" action and photograph consecutive scenes that can be made into slides and shown to accompany taped or live dialogue. Use a movie camera and 8-mm film to produce a silent movie; tape dialogue or let children use signs and gestures as old-time silent movie actors did. Or use videotaping equipment if your school has it; the "instant playback" feature of videotaping gives immediate feedback and allows the participants to be their own audience. Since videotape can be reused over and over it is a more economical means if your school already has the equipment, and it requires no waiting for film to be developed and returned. And seeing themselves on TV is an almost magical experience for children!

Puppetry is a wonderful vehicle for encouraging oral communication growth. Young children especially enjoy puppets and often engage in puppetry with enormous enthusiasm and creativity because they come to believe the puppets are real. Older children will be able to make more elaborate puppets, create more involved situations and plots, and can stay with a puppetry project

longer. The focus should always be on the process, not on the puppet construction or on producing a polished show.

In puppetry the puppet, not the child, takes the part of actor, so shy or self-conscious youngsters frequently feel freer and less constrained by their nervousness. Often the children are hidden, at least partially, behind a puppet theater and they can focus on the puppet's movement and dialogue rather than on the audience's reactions, which is why puppetry is such a good alternative for self-conscious students.

Puppetry can be highly motivating, but too often the effort and creativity are put into *making* the puppets, not into *using* them. In fact, some teachers have children make puppets but then simply take them home or hang them in displays, with no role playing done at all! Puppets are a means to an end; the end is oral communication and experimentation, not puppet construction. It is better to spend time making a few durable puppets that can be used over and over in many ways than to try to make every type and have no time or energy left to play with them. Puppetry is not a craft but a performing art.

Puppets can be made in many different ways; some are quickly created from simple materials and are good for spontaneous dialogues and acting out short, simple scenes. Others are somewhat more elaborate and more durable and can be kept for numerous activities in their present form or with changes of detail. The following are descriptions of construction and suggestions for using a number of puppet and puppet theater types (Jenkins, 1980).

Puppet Types. Puppets fit into general categories from simplest to most complex: stick puppets, shadow puppets, finger puppets, hand puppets, people puppets (humanettes), rod puppets, and string puppets (marionettes) (Figure 3.2).

1. *Stick puppets:* Easiest and fastest to make, a good instant puppet. Movement limited to bobbing about. Made by gluing, impaling, or otherwise attaching an object to a stick or an object with a handle.

Possibilities

— Paper shapes on tongue depressors.
— Envelopes on rulers.
— Small toys, clay figures on pencils.
— Apples, potatoes, or whatever on sticks.
— Shapes cut from kitchen sponges.
— Faces taped to long-handled spoons.
— Ping-Pong paddles.
— Plastic bottles inverted onto sticks.

2. *Shadow puppets:* Stick puppets used behind a lighted screen, throwing a shadow or silhouette on screen. Flat, undetailed shapes work best. Bent coat-

hanger wire often substituted for stick so support is less noticeable. Moving position of light can change puppet's shape and size.

Possibilities for staging

— White sheet strung across door or corner
— Suit box or carton lined with white cloth, wax paper, tissue, or white trash can liner.

3. *Finger puppets:* Small, easily carried, but hard for a group to see; best for puppet play alone or with a partner.

Possibilities

— Draw faces right on the fingers with felt pens.
— Gather scraps of cloth around finger below face.
— Decorate cut-off glove fingers and wear.
— Push decorated peanut-shell halves, small bottles, boxes, or small paper tubes over fingers.
— Cut out a head-and-trunk from paper and decorate; attach paper ring or rubber band to back; slip over two fingers with fingertips as "feet."

4. *Hand puppets:* Most common and varied puppets; two basic types are all head with movable mouth and head-and-body with movable arms.

Possibilities for "mouth" puppets

— Lunch bags with hand in folded bottom.
— Halved paper plates, eyes on top, hinged at back of mouth.
— Individual cereal or pudding boxes cut and folded, fingers in top half and thumb in bottom.
— Socks pulled over hand with "mouth" in toe.

Possibilities for "arm" puppets

— Use large cloth square draped over hand with holes cut in sides for thumb and little finger to protrude; push head down over cloth-covered fingers.
— For head use a paper cup, styrofoam ball, hollow rubber ball, or Ping-Pong ball, broken-off doll or stuffed toy head, fruit or vegetable, papier mâché head formed over cup, ball, or balloon.
— Stuff toe of sock or end of mitten; tie off loosely below stuffing; insert finger into stuffing and cut holes in sides for arms.
— Cut a simple shape from two pieces of heavy cloth, felt, wallpaper, or thin foam rubber; sew or glue edges and wear like mitten.
— Stuff a ball of stuffing into back of a glove; tie off below stuffing; attach eyes to ball and wear glove with fingers as legs for an octopus, insect, or spider puppet.

Figure 3.2   Types of puppets

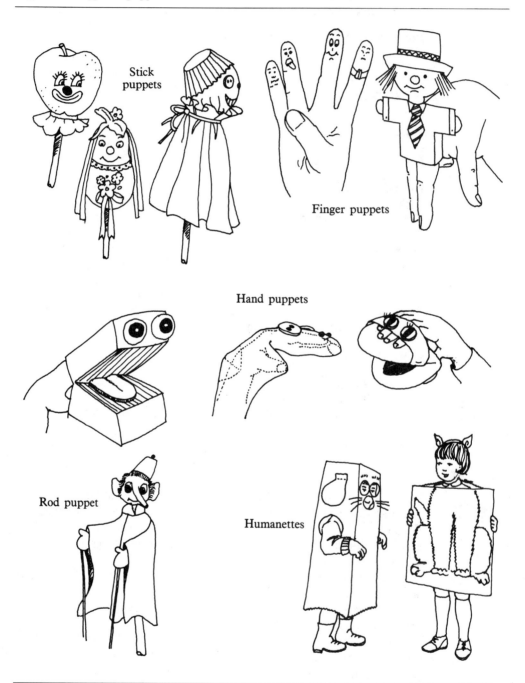

Stick puppets

Finger puppets

Hand puppets

Rod puppet

Humanettes

Figure 3.2   continued

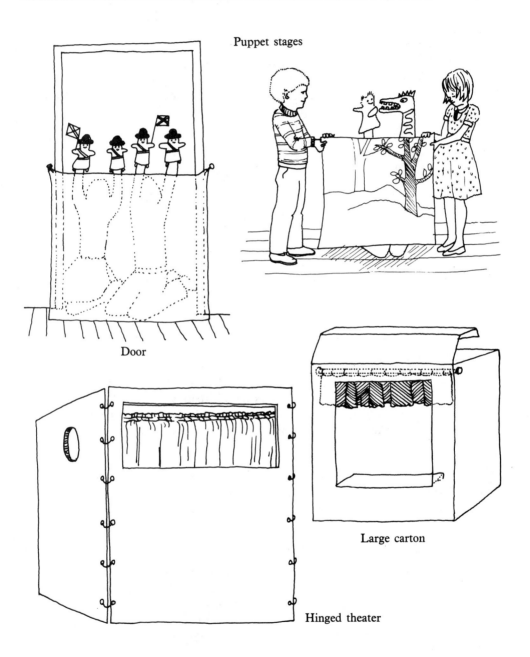

Puppet stages

Door

Large carton

Hinged theater

5. *Rod puppets:* Like arm puppets but not worn; instead, supported on sticks, requiring two-handed operation. Best for pairs of older children where one works puppet and partner read its lines or does the dialogue.

Possibilities

— Use old arm puppet by inserting long stick under costume and into head; attach thin sticks to hands so they can move.
— Use upper half of discarded dolls, action figures, and stuffed toys in same manner; drape bottom of figure to hide stick.

6. *Marionettes or string puppets:* Most complex puppet requiring one or more operators and another to provide dialogue; too complex for most classroom construction.

Possibilities

— Use a commercially available toy marionette and change its costume, hair, and other features.
— Two-string puppets are made by suspending a shape on strings to a horizontal stick; move by bobbing.
— Make two-string animals by cutting an "H" shape, folding horizontally along crossbar; attach head and tail.

7. *Humanettes:* Costume fitting over puppeteer's body that transforms human into a "live puppet."

Possibilities

— Put large box or bag over child's upper body (often decorated as an enormous head). Cut *large* holes for adequate vision and breathing!
— Cut bib-style flat shape to tie over upper body with child's face exposed; child's arms and legs are free; head is puppet's head; shape ties behind neck and perhaps at waist.

Puppet Staging. The simplest staging devices are the best, for they allow spontaneous play and are easy to set up and dismantle. The puppeteer need not be hidden, since the audience quickly focuses on the puppet rather than the puppeteer.

Puppet stage possibilities include:

— A towel draped over puppeteer's arm, puppet held behind.
— An old purse, bag, or box; cut hole in back for arm; let puppet protrude from top; hold on table or in puppeteer's lap.
— A sheet, held at upper corners by two students with others behind sheet.
— A card table lying on its side, with puppeteers behind table and puppets held above.
— A sheet-draped table; use as above.

— A large umbrella opened on floor, puppeteers crouching behind.

— Low or medium-height freestanding bookcase, carton, or couch; use as above.

— A sheet tacked across lower half of doorway, or held in place with tension rod.

— Large appliance carton cut to make a booth; hole in front for stage, door in back.

— Discarded TV cabinet with tube and insides removed; set on a draped table.

— Three- or four-sided hinged plywood screen, with windows and simple curtains. Windows must be high for most puppets but low for marionettes; for the latter, turn screen upside down.

— Low bookcases placed diagonally in corner with clothesline above to hold curtain; shelves hold puppets and supplies.

— Light puppet stage from the front to highlight puppets; use gooseneck desk lamp, clamp-on reading lamp, projector light, or large flashlight.

You might consult the following books for more information on role playing and puppetry.

FURTHER READINGS ON ROLE PLAYING

Chesler, Mark and Robert Fox. *Role-Playing Methods in the Classroom.* Chicago: Science Research Associates, 1966.

Furness, Pauline. *Role-Play in the Elementary School.* New York: A & W Publishing, 1976.

Gartner, Alan. *Children Teach Children: Learning by Teaching.* New York: Harper & Row, 1971.

Hawley, Robert C. *Value Exploration Through Role Playing.* New York: A & W Publishing, 1975.

Pinkerton, Todd. *Breaking Communication Barriers with Roleplay.* Atlanta: John Knox Press, 1976.

Sarason, Irwin G. and Barbara R. Sarason. *Constructive Classroom Behavior: A Teacher's Guide to Modeling & Role Playing Techniques.* New York: Behavioral Publishers, 1974.

Shaftel, Fannie R. and George Shaftel. *Role-Playing for Social Values: Decision-Making in the Social Studies.* Englewood Cliffs, N.J.: Prentice-Hall, 1967.

Shaftel, George and Fannie R. Shaftel. *Role-Playing in the Curriculum.* 2d ed. Englewood Cliffs, N.J.: Prentice-Hall, 1982.

Thompson, John F. *Using Role Playing in the Classroom.* Bloomington, Ind.: Phi Delta Kappa, 1978.

Wohlking, Wallace and Patricia Gill. *Role Playing.* Englewood Cliffs, N.J.: Educational Technology Publications, 1980.

FURTHER READINGS ON PUPPETRY

Ackley, Edith F. *Marionettes: Easy to Make and Fun to Use.* New York: Harper & Row, 1939.

Alkema, Chester. *Puppet-Making.* New York: Sterling, 1971.

Baird, Bil. *Art of the Puppet.* Boston: Plays, Inc., 1966.

Boekholt, Albert. *Puppets and Masks.* New York: Sterling, 1981.

Gates, Frieda. *Glove, Mitten and Sock Puppets.* Englewood Cliffs, N.J.: Scholastic Magazines, Inc., 1979.

Green, M. C. and B. R. Targett. *Space Age Puppets and Masks.* Boston: Plays, Inc., 1969.

Jagendorf, Moritz. *Puppets for Beginners.* Boston: Plays, Inc., 1952.

Jenkins, Peggy Davidson. *The Magic of Puppetry: A Guide for Those Working with Young Children.* Englewood Cliffs, N.J.: Prentice-Hall, 1980.

Muppet Show People. *The Muppet Show Book.* New York: Bantam Books, 1979.

Reiniger, Lotte. *Shadow Puppets, Shadow Theatres and Shadow Films.* Boston: Plays, Inc., 1975.

Rutter, Vicki. *ABC Puppetry.* Boston: Plays, Inc., 1969.

Supraner, Robyn and Lauren Supraner. *Plenty of Puppets to Make.* Mahwah, N.J.: Troll Associates, 1981.

Readers Theater

Readers theater is a dramatic form in which participants read aloud from scripts or other material, use minimal props and physical action, and convey ideas and emotions principally through facial and vocal expression. According to Coger and White (1973), the goal of readers theater is ". . . to present a literary script with oral interpreters using their voices and bodies to suggest the intellectual, emotional, and sensory experiences inherent in the literature" (p. 3).

Readers theater focuses on oral reading and oral interpretation. It is an excellent way of combining practice in fluent, expressive oral reading with creative dramatics. It also frees students from always having to act things out physically and encourages them to focus on the material and on how gesture and vocal expression communicate with an audience.

In readers theater lines are never memorized but always read aloud; participants carry their scripts or books about with them and sometimes use the scripts as simple props such as books, fans, or masks. Much of readers theater can be acted out sitting or standing in one place; a few chairs carefully placed sometimes serve as the only "stage set." Often all characters are on stage continually; characters that are not involved in a scene sit with their backs to the audience and turn forward or stand to mark their entrances. Costuming and staging are simple — the point of readers theater is to *suggest*, not to *represent*.

Readers theater requires more imagination on the part of the audience than other dramatic forms. It is subtle and suggestive and thus an effective way of dramatically dealing with literature that you want children to discuss and evaluate.

Because of the emphasis on fluent oral reading, readers theater is a good way to get children to practice oral reading and reread the same text numerous times. Repeated oral reading of the same text is a little-used but very effective method of helping children develop larger sight-word vocabularies, increase their reading rate and fluency, and develop confidence in their oral reading (see the discussion of the method of repeated reading in Chapter Five).

Readers theater can be an effective procedure to use with remedial readers. It (a) allows focused study and interpretation of a story or play, (b) requires extensive practice in oral reading, (c) focuses on interpreting rather than acting out, (d) requires reading practice during every stage of rehearsal and production, and (e) provides poor readers with a supportive setting for reading and role playing.

The following activities show how readers theater can be made the basis of many ongoing activities simultaneously:

1. Read the entire text to the participants or let them read it through silently.
2. Let students summarize the story orally or in writing.
3. Scramble the story events and let students put them in chronological order.
4. Let students role-play parts of the story, pantomime action scenes, or use puppets to dramatize the story.
5. Let students draw or use other artistic means to illustrate story scenes.
6. Encourage students to write alternative story endings, dialogues, or descriptive prose for the story, or have them do nonfiction writing such as newspaper articles about story events.
7. Let students do their oral reading practice in pairs in class, alone at home, and as repeated reading material.
8. Use words from the text for spelling lessons, word study, and handwriting practice.
9. Use phrases, sentences, and paragraphs from the story for exercises in grammar and related activities for which you would use workbook exercises or make up sentences.
10. Use words from the text for crossword puzzles, word searches, and similar puzzles and games.

You can consult these or other books for more information on readers theater:

Coger, Leslie Irene and Melvin R. White. *Readers Theatre Handbook: A Dramatic Approach to Literature*, rev. ed. Glenview, Ill.: Scott, Foresman, 1973.

Henry, Mabel W. *Creative Experiences in Oral Language*. Urbana, Ill.: NCTE, 1967.

Maclay, Joanna Hawkins. *Readers Theatre: Toward a Grammar of Practise.* Philadelphia: Philadelphia Book Co., 1970.

Trotter, Judy. *Beyond Borrowed Bathrobes: Guide to Readers Theater.* Cincinnati: Standard Publishers, 1976.

Storytelling

People all over the world have always been fascinated by stories. In earlier centuries storytelling was a valuable social skill and the storyteller enjoyed considerable prestige. Today we learn stories from books, TV, and movies, and the latter two are omnipresent in children's lives. TV and movies, however, put the listener in a passive role whereas storytelling involves children in stories actively and positively.

When you use storytelling in your class you involve your students directly and intimately with the story. Storytelling allows you to move around, use gestures and eye contact, clown a bit, and even involve your own students as characters in the story. These things can make stories come alive for listeners.

Storytelling also helps children become familiar with story language and story structures. Familiarity with these aspects helps them read stories themselves more easily and enjoy them more. It also helps in introducing them to the plots and themes that run through all literature.

Storytelling and reading aloud to children are both important classroom experiences. Sometimes storytelling is a good substitute for hearing a story read, as when a particular story is too long for comfortable reading aloud or is written in a difficult style. You should use the same guidelines for choosing stories to tell that you would use for choosing stories to read; that is, stories that are appropriate in length, topic, and language for the ages and interests of your students.

In general, good choices for preschool and kindergarten are stories about familiar things: children, animals, home, toys, machines. Humorous and nonsense stories and poems, Mother Goose rhymes, and simple, relatively nonviolent nursery tales like *The Three Little Pigs, The Three Bears, Little Red Riding Hood*, and *The Teeny Tiny Woman* also are good.

For grades one through three animal stories, stories of children's lives in other ages and cultures, classic fairy tales, holiday stories, folk tales, and simple myths are appealing. Both old and new stories should be used. Classic tales like *The Elves and the Shoemaker, Hansel and Gretel, The Bremen-Town Musicians, Sleeping Beauty*, and *Rumpelstiltskin* should be included.

For grades four through six good bets are true accounts of adventure and invention, mysteries, hero tales, and stories about both children and adults. Preadolescents usually enjoy more complex myths and legends, epic tales of ancient heroes and heroines, historically accurate fiction or nonfiction, and sports stories. Some good choices would include the legends of Arthur and Guinevere, Robin Hood, stories of gods and goddesses from many religions, tall tales like Pecos Bill and Paul Bunyan, and so on.

Guidelines for preparing and telling stories are shown in Box 3.2.

In primary grades a *flannelboard* is a good storytelling device. Follow these pointers in using flannelboards:

1. Create only the most essential characters and scenery to illustrate your story, such as the people, animals, trees, and houses that figure most prominently in it.
2. Carefully check each piece to make sure it sticks to the flannel. Nothing breaks up a good story more than drooping or falling flannel pieces.
3. Number each piece on the back in the order in which you will put it on the board. Then before you tell the story, lay the pieces face down beside you with the numbers showing.
4. Take each piece off the flannelboard as soon as it is no longer needed, so as not to have distracting clutter on the flannelboard.

Children love to tell stories, and storytelling provides them with excellent opportunities to organize their thoughts, communicate effectively with others, and get actively involved with literature.

Storytelling places very different demands on the speaker than informal conversation, however. It requires the teller to explain the setting, the characters' appearance, motives and actions, the sequence of events, and other aspects clearly and colorfully. It also requires that the teller sustain a monologue.

Practice in these language skills helps children become more articulate, confident speakers and lays a necessary foundation for composing stories in

---

BOX 3.2
Guidelines for Storytelling

Choose stories *you* like; your enthusiasm for the story is critical.

Tie storytelling to various holidays and to topics studied at the time: stories about Columbus, St. Valentine, Christmas or Chanukah, stories from other lands, Betsy Ross and the flag, etc.

Invite others as guest storytellers.

Avoid stories you can't paraphrase, because forgetting can shake your confidence.

Don't try to memorize a story verbatim.

Visualize characters and settings in your mind so you can describe them as though you'd seen them.

If you need to, jot down details or an outline on cards you can hold in your lap. But don't read from them!

Plan in advance ways you can lengthen or shorten a story depending on time and your audience.

Practice your story before you deliver it, either in front of a mirror or to other people.

Find a device you can use to set an expectant mood whenever you tell a story; light a candle, wear a shawl or hat, or whatever you choose, and use this device every time.

Practice varying your voice to convey mystery, excitement, anger, etc.

Look directly at the faces of your audience.

If you use props or puppets, keep them simple; check them over before you begin.

writing. Students should be invited to participate as storytellers regularly and often. At first they will have the most success with familiar stories they have heard others tell or stories from books.

As soon as they express a desire to do so, they should be encouraged to make up and tell original stories, even though these stories will probably not be as well structured as others, particularly the creations of a young child. You may recall from Chapter Two that children follow a developmental sequence in learning to create stories. At first, their efforts consist of simple chaining of ideas, even if the ideas are not closely related. With sustained practice in developing stories as well as continuing exposure to well-formed stories, youngsters begin to include more consistent structures and sequences in their stories, and although their first attempts may not be very well organized, they need this practice if they are to develop a good "sense of story."

Wordless picture books are an excellent storytelling vehicle. These books contain only pictures and no written text, or in some cases a very limited text. Following the pictures allows children to tell a structured story in their own words. Not all wordless books tell a story in the true sense; some are like Tana Hoban's *Shapes and Things*, pictures of related shapes or objects for identification, or like *Look Again!*, also by Tana Hoban, a collection of unusual photographs that sharpen observation and stimulate conversation and questions. Wordless books are especially good for very young students, and some of them give information, such as Iela and Enzo Mari's *The Apple and the Moth*, which shows the life cycle of a moth.

You should introduce a wordless book to the children yourself, and encourage them to discuss the pictures and construct the story line, if the book has one, by asking them "what's happening on this page." This method works best in small groups of less than five or six, since in larger groups there is less interaction and involvement with the book. After your introduction, members of the group can pair up with other classmates and use the book to tell the story. This procedure provides each storyteller with a structured approach to the book as well as plentiful opportunity to share with others. Be sure to keep some wordless books in your classroom library so that children who enjoy them can return to them over and over.

Here is a brief list of titles of wordless (or nearly wordless) books. Check with your school librarian and with library reference sources and annotated bibliographies of children's literature for other titles.

WORDLESS (OR NEARLY WORDLESS) BOOKS

Aliki. *Go Tell Aunt Rhody*. New York: Macmillan, 1974.

Alexander, Martha. *Bobo's Dream*. New York: Dial Press, 1970.

Anno, Mitsumasa. *Topsy-Turvies: Pictures to Stretch the Imagination*. Salem, Mass.: Weatherhill, 1970.

Ardizzone, Edward. *The Wrong Side of the Bed*. New York: Doubleday, 1970.

Carle, Eric. *Do You Want to Be My Friend?* New York: Crowell, 1971.

Carroll, Ruth. *Rolling Downhill.* New York: Walck, 1973.

Cristini, Ermanno and Luigi Puricelli. *In My Garden.* Boston: Neugebauer/ Alphabet Quincy Press, 1981.

Goodall, John. *The Ballooning Adventures of Paddy Pork.* New York: Harcourt, 1969.

Hoban, Tana. *Shapes and Things.* New York: Macmillan, 1970.

————. *Look Again!* New York: Macmillan, 1971.

Hutchins, Pat. *Changes, Changes.* New York: Macmillan, 1971.

Keats, Ezra Jack. *Kitten for a Day.* New York: Watts, 1974.

————. *Pssst! Doggie—.* New York: Watts, 1973.

Kent, Jack. *The Egg Book.* New York: Macmillan, 1975.

Koren, Edward. *Behind the Wheel.* New York: Holt, 1972.

Krahn, Fernando. *April Fools.* New York: Dutton, 1974.

Mari, Iela and Enzo Mari. *The Apple and the Moth.* New York: Pantheon Books, 1970.

Mayer, Mercer. *Ah-Choo.* New York: Dial Press, 1976.

————. *Bubble Bubble.* New York: Parents Magazine, 1973.

————. *Frog Goes to Dinner.* New York: Dial Press, 1974.

————. *The Great Cat Chase.* New York: Four Winds, 1974.

Ormerod, Jan. *Sunshine.* New York: Lothrop, Lee & Shepard, 1981.

Simmons, Ellie. *Family.* New York: McKay, 1970.

Ward, Lynd. *The Silver Pony.* Boston: Houghton Mifflin, 1973.

When children take part in storytelling, there is much you can do to make them comfortable. Let them tell their stories to a "buddy" or a small group instead of the whole class. Let them sit, if they wish, rather than having to stand. Encourage them to use an illustrated book, a puppet, a flannelboard, or some other prop if they'd like to. Make sure they have practiced their story. Model good listening yourself.

Both the stories you tell in class and those by your students should lead to other, related activities. Students may wish to mime a story as a storyteller narrates or use role playing to act it out. They may enjoy composing written forms of their stories, illustrating and collecting them in a class collection. They may want to experiment with lighting and music to complement the storytelling and then share their creations with other classes. You can also consult some of the following sources for more information.

American Library Association, Children's Services Division. *For Storytellers and Storytelling: Bibliographies, Materials, Resource Aids.* Chicago: ALA, 1968.

Bryant, Sara Cone. *How to Tell Stories to Children.* Detroit: Gale, 1924/1973.

Cathon, Laura, ed. *Stories to Tell Children*, 8th ed. Pittsburgh: University of Pittsburgh Press, 1974.

Chalmers, Aidan. "Storytelling and Reading Aloud," *Introducing Books to Children*, ed. Aidan Chalmers. Exeter, N.Y.: Heinemann Educational Books, 1973.

Hardendorff, Jeanne B. *Stories to Tell: A List of Stories with Annotations*, 5th ed. Baltimore, Md.: Enoch Pratt Free Library, 1965.

Iarusso, Marilyn. *Stories: A List of Stories to Tell and to Read Aloud*, 7th ed. New York: New York Public Library, 1977.

Pellowski, Anne. *The World of Storytelling*. New York: R. R. Bowker, 1977.

Sawyer, Ruth. *The Way of the Storyteller*. New York: Viking Press, 1962.

Tashjian, Virginia A. *Juba This and Juba That: Story Hour Stretches for Large or Small Groups*. Boston: Little, Brown, 1969.

———. *With a Deep Sea Smile: Story Hour Stretches for Large or Small Groups*. Boston: Little, Brown, 1974.

Ziskind, Sylvia. *Telling Stories to Children*. New York: Wilson, 1976.

Listening

Listening cannot be separated from the expressive aspects of oral communication. It is impossible to "teach listening" separately from speaking, or to set aside a portion of the instructional time for listening instruction and ignore it the rest of the time. Listening is as much a part of group discussions, dramatic play, or puppetry, for example, as the dialogues and actions created. When children develop their communicative powers they also develop their ability to listen appreciatively and receptively. Some activities, however, focus more on listening than on oral language, and these activities are helpful in improving listening skills.

Listening and reading are the two primary *receptive* processes through which children receive information in school. In the lower grades, when reading is just beginning, listening is the more important and more relied-upon process. As youngsters become better readers, much of the emphasis shifts to learning through reading, especially in the upper elementary grades and beyond, but the importance of listening remains throughout school. In the upper grades children must learn how to listen effectively to lectures, demonstrations, and films; in high school and beyond much of their reading is done outside of class or work, and the majority of classes, meetings, and presentations require active sustained listening.

Good listening is much more than a matter of will. Although teachers and parents frequently deliver comments like "You weren't listening!" as though all one had to do was pay attention, there is more to listening than trying. There are limits to the length of time one can "pay attention" without doing something; about every twenty seconds attention shifts and the mind may wander. Also the listening situation itself can be conducive or unconducive to attentive listening.

Pilon (1978) described such conditions.

Listeners are more apt to listen attentively when:

— The speaker can be heard and understood comfortably, without distracting outside noise, too-low volume, or interruptions.
— They are interested and involved in the presentation, preferably *actively* involved.
— They have positive feelings toward the speaker.
— They are motivated to interact and respond.
— They know they will be expected to respond.
— They do not have to listen for too long without doing something active.
— The presentation is forceful and clearly organized.

Listeners are apt to be inattentive when:

— They cannot comfortably hear the speaker.
— The speaker's manner of speaking is monotonous, poorly organized, rambling, or flawed by annoying or distracting mannerisms or an unpleasant voice.
— The speaker's language is convoluted or too advanced in syntax or vocabulary.
— They disagree with the speaker and stop listening in order to think about their own objections or feelings.
— The speaker insults their intelligence, talks down to them, or makes unpleasant or derogatory remarks; or any other conditions that cause them to have negative feelings toward the speaker.
— They know there will be no "payoff" for listening; no response will be required, or only the same few people will be called on, selected, or asked to respond in some other way.
— They have been "conditioned" not to listen, as by a parent or teacher who habitually repeats the main point or directions numerous times.

Box 3.3 lists ways you can critique yourself and help maximize good listening in your classroom.

Listening Games

Many listening activities can be conducted as games. They provide modeling and practice in attentive listening and appropriate responding in a fun setting. Some of the following games will be old favorites familiar to you and your students.

Everybody Talks can trigger discussion of why we should take turns talking (Cottrell, 1975). Seated in a circle, children prepare to tell something about a favorite pet, game, food, or whatever. At a signal, all talk at once (but no

---

BOX 3.3
Guidelines for Fostering Good Listening in Your Classroom

Don't expect youngsters to "sit still and listen" for long. Vary activities.

Be a model listener yourself. Never daydream, mark papers, etc. while students are speaking.

Tape record or videotape yourself teaching. Review it critically for negative behaviors that may "turn off" listeners. Ask a friend to help.

Practice reading aloud on tape and analyze your delivery critically. Ask a friend to do the same for you.

Do you call on the same children repeatedly? Think about ways to involve more children in discussions with eye contact, physical proximity, and conversation.

Practice getting the children's attention without raising your voice: Blink the lights, ring a bell, blow into a pitchpipe or harmonica.

Avoid negative comments like "If you'd been listening you'd have known that" or "You should know this; I talked about it already."

Work at getting rid of annoying speaking mannerisms such as pacing, abrupt pauses, and "fillers" like "Umm . . .," "you know," "well. . . ."

---

shouting). Then they try to recall what others said; only near neighbors will be able to do so. They can then take turns talking and repeating what others said. This game demonstrates the practical need to take turns and listen to others.

Add-a-Sentence consists of building a group story by having each child around a circle add successive sentences. Alternatives are developing a summary or descriptions of special events, trips, experiments, and so on.

Simon Says can be easily modified as a vehicle for auditory discrimination and phonics activities; children can pantomime actions of words with a specified sound, like "*pick* an apple" or "*pat* the dog"; or respond to rhyming directions like "Says Gail, wag your tail" while ignoring nonrhyming directions like "Says Ralph, sweep the floor."

Elephants Fly (Cottrell, 1975) is another adaptation of Simon Says, in which children mime actions in true statements but not in untrue ones; for example, they would flap their arms after hearing "Sparrows fly" but not after hearing "Elephants fly."

Yes I Can helps develop listening to directions. A leader asks a question such as "Marcella, can you brush your teeth?" Marcella responds "Yes, I can brush my teeth" and mimes the action, then addresses a new question to another pupil. This game should be kept fast-paced.

Place Names focuses on sounds in words and is played by chaining place names (or other related words). Each addition begins with the same sound as the ending of the previous word, as in Texas–Seattle–Lexington–Newark, and so forth. Older children enjoy this game, which can be used in any content area to review categories of words.

I Packed My Bag is an old party game; each player "packs a bag" by naming an item beginning with successive alphabet letters. Older children can also try to repeat in order each item "packed" previously, as in "I packed my bag and in it I put an apple, a bulldog, a car, a dish, an eggplant, and . . . a firetruck." Younger children may have to limit their efforts to letter order.

I Like is a game of deduction and categorization. The object is to infer relationships and add items that share them. A leader begins with an example statement: "I like *dresses* and *sneakers*, but I hate *skirts* and *shoes*." Players try to guess how the first two are alike but different from the second pair. One volunteers, "I like *raisins* but I hate *bread*," which is correct; another offers "I like *dogs* but I hate *cats*," which is incorrect, so the leader responds by modeling: "No, I like *horses* but I hate *dogs*." (Here the "liked" words have two syllables.) The game continues until each player can supply a correct original pair by inferring, but not stating, the relationship.

The Directed Listening-Thinking Activity

Listening to literature and nonfiction text material is an extremely important classroom activity.

A Directed Listening-Thinking Activity (DLTA) is one that helps children listen to stories (and other written text) actively and critically, engaging all their thinking abilities and prior experiences as they listen (Stauffer, 1975, 1980). The procedure is uncomplicated: Children examine illustrations and listen to part of a story read aloud, then predict what might happen in forthcoming portions based on what they have already heard, clues in title and illustrations, and their own experiences and knowledge. They particularly listen to subsequent parts so as to confirm or disprove their predictions, and they are encouraged to modify their predictions as the story unfolds. Since the children are predicting what *might* happen rather than answering questions about what *did* happen, they engage in divergent thinking and the creation of alternatives. There are no right or wrong answers, but there are more likely and less likely alternatives, which they must weigh and evaluate. A DLTA encourages creative divergent thinking, the use of logic, and heightened curiosity and interest in stories.

Here are the steps in preparing and conducting a directed listening-thinking activity:

1. Select a story with an obvious plot structure and attractive illustrations. Look for one that has some conflict or problem to be achieved, some clear attempts at the goal, and a clear resolution. (Most stories fit this format; fairy tales and folk tales are excellent.)

2. Plan to stop reading several times just *before* some important event or revelation so that the students can predict what might happen next. Don't stop too often; two to four stops is about right. Too many stops fragment the story line and frustrate the listeners' attempts to understand.

3. Allow children to look at the title and illustrations for their first predictions. Since they have little information about the story at the beginning, their predictions will probably be hazy and unspecific.

4. At each stopping point, ask for summaries of what has happened so far, and then for predictions of what might happen next. This procedure encourages pupils to use what they have already heard to structure and refine their predictions and also helps clear up misunderstandings.

5. Accept all predictions *noncommittally*; the creation of alternatives, not "guessing right," is the point of a DLTA. Ask students to use prior story events and logic to back up their predictions if they can. Avoid using terms like "right" and "wrong"; instead, use terms like "likely" or "unlikely." Ask what "*might* happen" rather than what "*will* happen," and say "Why do you *think* so?" rather than "How do you *know*?"

6. When confirming predictions, focus on the idea rather than on who volunteered it. "*Which idea* turned out to be true" or "... was the most likely?" are better than "*Who* gave the best guess?" The latter response turns the children's attention away from the story itself.

7. Perhaps most important, keep the discussions short and spirited; keep up the pace! Long-drawn-out discussions dull the children's interest in the story and decrease their desire to participate.

A DLTA is an alternative to just reading a story to your students from start to finish. It should not be used *every* time you read to them. Some text should be listened to just for enjoyment, with little or no requirement to discuss the material. Likewise, occasionally listening to a story straight through before discussing is fine, but because a DLTA is a powerful tool for involving children actively and arousing their curiosity, it should be used frequently. If you read to your students daily, which we strongly recommend at every elementary grade, you might plan to use a DLTA format twice a week.

Guidelines for DLTA's are summarized in Box 3.4.

Listening to Develop Study Skills

As children progress through the elementary grades, their listening needs change and expand. In the upper grades it becomes increasingly important for them to apply listening skills to the content areas. Listening, reading, and writing skills converge when they begin to practice taking notes during lectures and demonstrations, keeping observational records, and creating summaries and outlines. These strategies are most often applied by writing things down, but before information can be encoded it must be heard, understood, and mentally organized. Listening is the basis for these study skills. There are a

BOX 3.4
Directed
Listening–Thinking
Activity Guidelines

Choose a story with clear episodes and action.
Plan your stops just before important
events. Two to four stops is plenty.

At each stop, elicit summaries of what happened so far, and predictions of "what
might happen next."

Accept all predictions as equally probable.

Ask the children to explain why they made

particular predictions and to use previous
story information for justification.

Avoid "right" or "wrong"; use terms like
"might happen," "possible," or "likely."

After reading a section, review previous predictions and let the students change their
ideas.

Focus on predictions, not on who offered
them.

Involve everyone by letting the children show
hands or take sides with others on predictions.

Keep up the pace! Don't let discussions drag;
get back to the story quickly.

number of speaking and writing activities that can be used to help students
develop the listening skills they will have to apply in content areas.

Transcribing. Writing down live or recorded speech is an excellent activity
that helps students sharpen their listening, handwriting, spelling, and punctuation all at once. When transcribing, or taking dictation, is used primarily
as a listening activity, you should put emphasis on the accuracy of their listening
and deemphasize the encoding aspects of handwriting, spelling, and punctuation. If we demand a high degree of accuracy in *all* these aspects, we can make
transcribing a very difficult and frustrating task. Focus on the main point —
good listening — and work on neatness and accurate spelling at another time.

Transcribing the teacher's speech is a common activity in European schools
but has never been widely used in the United States. If it is not overused or
overemphasized, it can be a very useful exercise. Here are several ways you
can structure transcribing as a listening activity.

1. Use different types of material for transcription, particularly material
you want your students to remember and to use when they practice writing.
Classroom rules, material to be memorized such as the Pledge of Allegiance,
or steps in a procedure you want them to follow are good examples. When the
daily schedule changes, you can describe and discuss what the schedule will be
and culminate the discussion with a transcribing exercise: "Tomorrow we will
have our class trip. Don't forget to bring your lunch. We will ride a school bus
downtown. . . ."

2. Include material that is fun to listen to and easy to remember, such as
short poems and jump-rope rhymes, limericks, tongue-twisters, nursery
rhymes, riddles, and even recipes.

3. Let children dictate stories to each other, and then have them work together to proofread and correct spelling and punctuation errors if they can.

4. Arrange with a teacher of younger children to let your students take dictated stories from the young pupils. Work with your pupils to correct spelling errors and make a neat copy of each story, and return them to the other teacher. His or her students can use them as individual language experience stories for rereading, voice pointing, and sight word practice, or they can illustrate and display their stories. (See Chapter Five for a discussion of these methods.)

5. Older remedial readers can try taking their own dictated stories, by recording an individual or small group experience story on a tape recorder, then playing the tape back and trying to write down what they said. Working with taped material is excellent for those who write poorly or have much trouble keeping up with group transcription, because they can stop and reverse the tape as often as necessary.

6. Use transcribing when you or the students give a brief summary of a story, news item, or event.

7. Have pairs or threes play a story-building game, where each adds a sentence to create a story. As one composes and says his or her sentence, another transcribes it; then the first transcriber composes a sentence and the next youngster writes it down. The process continues back and forth or among the three until the stories are concluded. Then they can be read to the class, acted out, or pantomimed. This activity combines storytelling and transcribing and limits the dictation to one sentence at a time.

Summarizing. Students at all grade levels should have a great deal of practice in giving a summary both orally and in writing. Summarizing is a very important study skill, since it requires synthesizing information, putting important items in proper sequence, discriminating between important and unimportant detail, and condensing information into concise forms. Students should have sufficient oral practice so that they can easily and confidently summarize aloud before they have to compose written summaries. You can help the process along as follows:

1. Remember that it is critically important for children to see and hear the teacher model summarizing so they will know what to do. Every day you will have opportunities to summarize: stories read aloud, news events, things accomplished during a lesson, things described in Show and Tell or other discussions, steps in a procedure to follow, sequences of events in science experiments or math problems, decisions reached in a class meeting. Take advantage of these opportunities and model what you want your students to be able to do in summarizing.

2. Make use of summarizing as a way to help children remember information in science, math, and social studies. These subjects particularly lend themselves to summaries. Your students should have frequent practice in composing summaries of both discussions and the text material they have read. They could summarize the steps in solving a multiplication problem, the important events and outcomes of a war, or the stages of development from egg to adult frog. Whenever new information is presented in sequences, stages, or causes and effects — structures that are common in social studies, math, science, and health — children should practice summarizing as they proceed.

3. Have students include brief oral or written summaries of books they read when they do book-sharing projects. For books read but not shared, they can complete a short summary on a file card to keep track of what they have read independently. (Keep these summaries short, so they don't begin to discourage the class from reading in the first place.)

4. Make summarizing a routine culminating part of Show and Tell, current events discussions, class meetings, and related oral activities. A very brief synopsis of what went on is sufficient.

5. For those who are not fluent writers, use tape recorders to break down the composing and writing of the summary into two manageable acts. Taping allows students to focus first on what to say and how to say it, then to concentrate on writing mechanics separately as they transcribe their words.

Outlining. Outlining is not an important skill in itself, but it can help to organize information and perceive order in text structures. Most often we immediately think of the traditional outline form with Roman numerals, Arabic numerals, upper- and lower-case letters arranged in hierarchies, each subordinate portion carefully indented. You have probably constructed hundreds of such outlines in your years in school, yet chances are you still aren't sure what comes *after* the Roman numerals: Upper case letters? Arabic numerals? And what about those rules like "Don't use an A unless there is also a B"?

Although there are many other forms of outlines besides the "Roman numeral one" type, we often neglect to demonstrate any other types. Also, outlining simply means perceiving and arranging things in superordinate and subordinate categories. Allen (1976) suggested several innovative ways this process can be introduced and practiced.

1. Take your students for an "observation walk" around the school building, the library or kitchen, the neighborhood, or to a park or nature trail. Beforehand, assign groups of students to watch (or listen) for and remember examples of specific categories of things. On a nature walk, for example, some could be asked to remember what animals they see, while others watch for types of plants, different shapes of leaves, and varieties of wildflowers, and still another group could listen for various sounds in the environment. On a walk through the library some could note different types of furniture, major categories of books, examples of art and other decorations, and all the different activities people were engaged in at the time.

Back in the classroom, write the headings you selected on the board and below each heading list the examples that the students "collected." This activity sharpens their powers of observation and memory, gives them something specific to do during the walk, and models classifying and outlining very effectively. It can be modified in numerous ways.

2. A "skeleton outline" can be put on the board (or on a ditto) to be filled in as students read and discuss a selection, especially nonfiction text. Before reading, they practice skimming to get major ideas and then read sections carefully to fill in subordinate details. If they do this activity individually or in small groups of two or three, the skeleton outlines serve as a type of study guide to the reading selection.

3. Recipes are an excellent vehicle for practice in outlining and sequencing. (There are many, many recipes for cooking in the classroom that require no actual cooking at all, or only simple equipment like a hot plate, electric frying pan, or slow cooker.) After they have read a recipe through completely, they sequence the steps in outline form:

MAKING APPLESAUCE

I. Gather materials we need
  A. Equipment
    1. slow cooker
    2. vegetable peeler
    3. sharp knife
    4. measuring cups
    5. measuring spoons
  B. Supplies
    1. apples
    2. sugar
    3. cinnamon
    4. water
II. Cooking steps
  A. Prepare apples
    1. Peel apples
    2. Cut cores out of apples
    3. Cut apples in pieces
  B. Measure ingredients in recipe
    1. Measure sugar
    2. Measure cinnamon
    3. Measure water
  C. Combine all ingredients in slow cooker
  D. Cook for specified time
  E. Cool applesauce before eating

4. Other types of directions are also useful in the same ways: Steps to complete a science experiment, an art project, a model, a puppet show, or a photography or film-making project have the same kind of superordinate and subordinate sequences that recipes have. Outlining can be modeled and practiced painlessly when incorporated into these activities.

5. Show children how to construct and use a variety of different kinds of outline forms, such as timelines, flow charts, ladders, concentric circles, even "paths" like those commonly seen on game boards. Make up a variety of outline forms, run them off on a duplicator, and have the students fill them in as they discuss activities, complete sequences, and make observations.

6. Vacca (1981) suggested several outline forms appropriate for upper graders: free-form outlines with terms or concepts freely arrayed on paper with arrows connecting the related items; pyramids, which resemble business flow charts; radial outlines, with interlocking and line-connected circles containing concepts.

Helping Children Who Have Language Problems

Our understanding of children's language problems has grown tremendously over the past decade, in part as a result of our increased knowledge about their language in general. You will have considerable responsibility for identifying, referring for assessment, and carrying out corrective instruction for those with special language problems.

What sorts of language problems are there? Language is a multifaceted skill, and the problems may be diverse. Some of the most important ones have to do with general spoken fluency: that is, the quantity, grammatical complexity, and expressiveness of what children have to say and what they can understand. Problems of fluency may stem from *delayed language development*, which usually manifests itself in the quantity and complexity of a child's language. Another area of fluency where problems can arise is in the *functions of language* a child can use. This area is related more to home environment than maturity, and has to do with whether a child can use and understand language when it is used for different communicative purposes. Another problem area stems from the *variations of language*; that is, a child who may not be fluent in the standard English spoken in the classroom may be quite fluent in some other dialect spoken in the home, such as Black English. Or the child may be fluent in some other language altogether, such as Spanish, French, Vietnamese, or Arabic.

A different kind of language problem involves *articulation*, how clearly and accurately children can pronounce the phonemes or speech sounds of English. A related area of potential concern is the *quality of voice*: whether a child's speech is shrill, rough, too loud, or too soft for the classroom.

Assessing Children's Speech for Language Problems

Speech pathologists usually use commercially published tests for screening children for language problems, which are most useful in assessing articulation. In practically all other areas, however, these tests are controversial, and varying amounts of confidence are placed in them by experts. In the case of general language fluency, a person who is in daily contact over a long period of time with the children to be screened can usually tell as much or more about their language as a specialist who gives the youngsters a "single-shot" examination.

Children who have delayed language development are often shy and withdrawn. Rather than being aware that their language is limited, our impressions may be more that we don't hear much from them, that they always seem to stay on the periphery of what is going in class.

When we suspect that a child may have delayed language, there are several procedures we can use to check out our suspicions. Two are presented here: *sentence modeling* and *mean length of utterance*.

Sentence Modeling. Sentence modeling, proposed by Ursula Bellugi (1971), provides an indication of the kinds of sentences a child is able to understand. The procedure uses a collection of small props, such as dolls, puppets, blocks, or other items. Children are directed to manipulate the props in ways that demonstrate how well they understand sentences that contain different grammatical constructions. These constructions are basic ones, such as modification by adjectives, negation of sentences, passive constructions, constructions with "greater than/less than," and others.

The sentences are very carefully worded so that children can follow the instructions correctly only if they understand the grammar of the sentence. In everyday situations, when we give children verbal instructions there are many cues other than grammar alone to help them apprehend the meaning of a request. The gestures we use, the objects themselves that can be manipulated only in certain ways, and the meanings of individual words can be interpreted together to arrive at the meaning of most commands. In the sentence-modeling task all of these other cues are controlled so that we can observe a child's understanding of grammatical constructions in isolation from other cues.

The procedure is carried out with one child at a time, and it is important to administer it in a reasonably quiet and distraction-free area.

The following version of the sentence-modeling test was adapted from Bellugi (1971). The entire series requires the following props: dolls and/or puppets both male and female, one larger than others; three or more blocks, one larger than others; a shoe that ties; a small toy animal; a piece of cloth to be used as a washcloth.

SENTENCE-MODELING TASK

Directions: Put the needed props before you and put the others away for each task. If a task names a doll, name the dolls for the child and make sure that he or she knows the names of the dolls. Show the child how the action may be demonstrated; for example, if a task requires dolls to speak to each other, model how one doll speaks to the other. If the task is not modeled correctly, record what the subject did or said.

1. Sentence order: agent-action-object
   Props: Two dolls, puppets, etc. Give each a name.
   Say: Show me, *John pats Bill.*
      Show me, *Bill pats John.*
      (Optional: use other simple active verbs: washes, hugs, etc.)
2. Noun plurals
   Props: Two or more dolls or puppets, two or more blocks.
   Say: Show me *a doll.*
      Show me *dolls* (or *the dolls*).
      Show me *blocks.*
      Show me *a block.*

3. Possessives

Props: Two dolls or puppets, one larger than other; larger is "mother/father," smaller is "child."

Say: Show me *the child's mother (father).*

Show me *the mother's (father's) child.*

4. Negative statements

Props: A doll or puppet that can be made to sit down.

Say: Show me, *the doll is sitting.*

Show me, *the doll is not sitting.*

Show me, *the doll is not standing.*

Show me, *the doll is standing.*

5. Singular and plural subject-verb agreement

Props: Two dolls or puppets.

Say: Show me, *the dolls walk.*

Show me, *the doll walks.*

Show me, *the doll sits (falls, etc.).*

Show me, *the dolls sit.*

6. Modifiers and comparatives

Props: Larger and smaller dolls, larger and smaller blocks.

Say: Show me, *the little doll has a big block.*

Show me, *the little doll has a little block.*

Show me, *the big doll has a little block.*

Props: Two dolls, five blocks.

Say: Show me, *Mary has more blocks than Jane.*

Show me, *Mary has fewer blocks than Jane.*

7. Negative affixes

Props: Three or four blocks, shoe.

Say: Show me, *the blocks are stacked.*

Show me, *the blocks are unstacked.*

Show me, *the shoe is untied.*

Show me, *the shoe is not untied.*

8. Reflexive pronouns

Props: Two dolls, washcloth.

Say: Show me, *John washed him.*

Show me, *John washed himself.*

Show me, *Bill talked to him.*

Show me, *Bill talked to himself.*

9. Passives

Props: Two dolls, toy animal, blocks.

Say: Show me, *John was kissed by Mary.*

Show me, *the blocks were stacked by the children.*

Show me, *the child is chased by the dog (cat).*

10. Self-imbedded sentences

Props: Two dolls, boy and girl, or two puppets, different animals.

Say: Show me, *the boy (dog, etc.) chased the girl.*
  Show me, *the boy that chased the girl fell down.*
  Show me, *the girl (cat, etc.) waved to the boy.*
  Show me, *the girl that waved to the boy ran away.*

11. Complex verbs
  Props: Dolls made to "speak" to each other.
  Say: Show me, *Mary asked Jane what to wear.*
    Show me, *Jane asked Mary why she was late.*
    Show me, *Mary promised Jane she'd bake some cookies.*

The syntactic structures numbered 1 through 9 have developed in most children by the time they enter first grade. The last two do not usually develop before the age of nine or ten (Chomsky, 1969). Occasionally children are either well ahead or well behind their peers in syntactic development. Those who are behind are likely to experience difficulty in listening and following directions, both in class discussions and in reading.

Mean Length of Utterance. Another simple means of language assessment is to measure the child's *mean length of utterance,* or MLU. This procedure was originated by Roger Brown and his associates to aid in research on young children's language development (Brown, 1973). The measurement of the MLU is based on the assumption that the longer utterances are, the more grammatically complex they necessarily must be. While this assumption is valid in the case of beginning speakers, it does not hold true beyond a certain level of development, the point at which children begin to use sentences with more than one clause in them. Nevertheless, the MLU can be a valuable means of keeping track of progress in language development in school-aged children who are significantly language delayed.

To evaluate language by means of the MLU, it is necessary to get a sample of ten or more sentences spoken by each child. The sentences should be typical of their self-initiated expressions: They should not be one-word answers to your questions. For the body of utterances in the sample, count all of the words *and the inflectional morphemes* (discussed in Chapter Two). If a child says "Dog barking," "dog" counts as one, "bark-" counts as another, and "-ing" counts as another, since "-ing" is another meaningful element of language that the child is controlling in the utterance. In the same vein, count verb inflections such as *-s, -ed;* negative particles such as *-n't;* comparative adjective inflections like *-er* and *-est;* and noun plural markers, *-s.* Once a total count of words and morphemes has been reached for the whole sample, divide the total by the number of utterances in the sample. This yields the mean or "average" length of each utterance.

Box 3.5 shows an MLU count of a young child that was made by Laura Fricke, one of our former students. Christopher, age two years, eight months, was playing outside under the supervision of his sister, Mischelle. Christopher made a total of fifteen utterances in this sample, with a total of fifty-six words

---

BOX 3.5
MLU Count of a Language Sample

WORDS +
MORPHEMES

3	C.: (coming out of house): My here, Missy.
	M.: I see you.
5	C.: (sees shrimp boat) Some one shrimp right there.
	M.: Yes, they are shrimping.
3	C.: (sees car drive up next door) See it car.
	M.: Yes, who is it?
2	C.: Somebody. Lady. (goes to other side of patio to see what other sister is doing)
6	C.: You can't hurt me that. (sister teasing with palm branch)
	M.: Tauscha, don't do that. You might hurt him or make him fall down.
7	C.: Now, you make me fall down that.
	Tauscha: Come here.
3	C.: No, my not.
4	C.: Can't reach me.
5	C.: Ow, don't do that.
2	C.: You not.
4	C.: You not spank me.
2	C.: Tauscha not. (He leaves and goes to tricycle.)
	M.: What are you doing?
3 + 3	C.: My bicycle here. My bicycle here. (pulling on tricycle)
	M.: Do you want me to help you?
4	C.: My bicycle up here.

C = Christopher, M = Mischelle.

---

and inflections. Dividing 56 by 15 we get 3.5, which is Christopher's MLU for this sample.

Compared over a period of time, calculations of a language-delayed child's MLU can give an indication of whether or not he or she is gaining fluency.

Assessing Children's Use of Different Functions of Language. It was pointed out in Chapter Two that language development consists of more than growth in control over grammatical structures. As Halliday (1975) has shown, developing well-rounded language fluency includes the ability to use language for a variety of different purposes. Joan Tough (1973) has found that children sometimes develop unevenly in their ability to use language for different purposes. Thus it is important when assessing language to observe systematically which language functions a child can use. A checklist such as Table 3.1 can serve as

Table 3.1   Checklist for language functions

NAME: _____ Period of observation: _____ to _____
                                                    (date)   (date)

Did the child use language to: How often? How well?	
Get something for self? *Instrumental* (permission, a favor, etc.)	
Direct others' actions? *Regulatory* (give directions, commands, etc.)	
Find something out or learn about something? *Heuristic*	
Express a personal feeling? *Personal*	
Interact socially with others? *Interactional*	
Play with language? *Imaginative* (word game, tell a story, sing a song, recite a poem, etc.)	
Communicate factual information? *Representational*	

the basis of observations of an individual child's use of different language functions. These observations can be carried out over a period ranging from two days to a week, as the child is interacting with other children in the class. You can also create circumstances that require using language for different purposes, and then observe how ably each child can perform under those circumstances. An activity could be set up where children must give directions for a procedure (regulatory language, in Halliday's terms), tell a story (imaginative language), share a personal feeling (personal language), request a favor (instrumental language), inquire about how something works (heuristic language), or report on some happening (representational language), and you observe the child's language use during those activities.

These categorizations are not always easy to make, and the frequency of a given child's use of certain language functions may depend on classroom circumstances, such as what the children nearby are doing. Over a period of two days or more, however, significant patterns are likely to emerge. If certain children rarely ask questions during this period, or phrase them very poorly when they do, this should be a signal to you to set up activities that will give them additional exposure to and practice in using the unfamiliar functions.

Assessing Dialect Differences. It is important to note that speaking a dialectical variation of English is not a language problem per se. Dialect speakers have not improperly learned standard English, but rather they have properly learned a nonstandard dialect. Dialects, as we are told by Labov (1970) and other sociolinguists, are perfectly workable forms of language *within the setting in which they are learned.* Children who speak nonstandard dialects should learn the language of the school and the greater community, in our view, but they should be given credit for having learned to talk in *some* form and not be treated as if they were ignorant because they haven't yet learned standard English.

There are no specific procedures in general use for the assessment of dialects. Teachers can virtually always tell whether a child is using a dialect from listening to the child, though they may need some practice in order to understand the dialect. Within the dialect, however, a child may or may not have a well-developed command of language. Also, there is the problem of which grammatical forms of standard English a child *understands,* even if he or she does not use exactly the same forms in dialectal speech. Thus the same procedures just presented for assessing delayed language development can be used to test those who speak nonstandard dialects: not to see to what extent they speak dialects but to see (a) how fluent they are within the dialect (the MLU measure and the assessment of language functions will shed light on this) and (b) what important features of standard English sentences they understand and do not understand (the sentence-modeling task will be informative here). This assessment is important because, although the children may have dialectal variations of many standard grammatical constructions that are intelligible within their own dialects, without comprehension of the standard forms they may encounter difficulty in following classroom discussions and in reading.

Assessing Bilingual Students. Several testing procedures have been developed to determine the *language dominance* of children — that is, the relative fluency they have in whatever languages they speak. This is often an important issue, since it is generally recommended that children be taught to read in their dominant language (Office of Bilingual Education, 1978). Nevertheless, for the overwhelming majority of American classroom teachers who are monolingual speakers of English and who have only limited bilingual services available for their students or no such services, the question of bilingualism is not so much one of language dominance but of how much English the child knows.

Thus you will have to ascertain the English-speaking ability of your bilingual students. Again, the procedures described above will be helpful. If, however, bilingual services are available, then children should be referred for the testing of language dominance if a less-than-fluent command of English is suspected. Such testing usually requires that the examiner be fluent in the child's native language, so we will not describe these tests here.

Assessing Articulation Problems. Articulation means the production of speech sounds. Problems in this area stem from several sources. Some result from late language development: A child may not yet be able to make the "sh" sound, for example. Other sounds may be normal pronunciation for some dialect or another language. Spanish, for example, makes no phonemic distinction between the sound "ch" and "sh"; thus *shoes* and *choose* are often pronounced interchangeably. A small number of articulation problems are caused by hearing problems or a physical deformity of a child's mouth.

Most articulation problems can be successfully treated by speech therapy, and many therapists devote a majority of their time to the correction of articulation problems. Nonetheless, it is a good idea to take an inventory of the sounds a child can and cannot produce when articulation problems are suspected. In cases where speech therapy is not available, there are steps you yourself can take to help the child.

Note also that in the course of normal speech development, certain sounds emerge before others, and some do not develop in many children until second grade or later, even under normal circumstances. Susanna Pflaum (1978) has devised a checklist for recording the emergence of phonemes in young children (see Table 3.2). This checklist can be used by the classroom teacher either for making a detailed referral of a child to a speech therapist or as a basis for the correction of specific sound deficits.

Assessing Voice Problems. Problems of voice, including excessively nasal or harsh tones and excessively loud or low speech, arise from a range of different causes. An overly harsh, boisterous, or soft tone of voice may indicate strong emotions a child is experiencing at a particular time. Feelings of anxiety, insecurity, or frustration may be behind any of these tones of voice. On the other hand, hearing impairment is another possible cause of unusually loud or soft speech. Physiological impairments in the throat and nasal cavities can lead to a voice that is excessively shrill or harsh. According to Petty and Jensen (1980), lack of awareness of how they sound to others and emotional insecurity are the most prevalent causes of voice problems.

In order to offer appropriate help to the child, it is necessary to determine what the nature of the voice problem is and also, insofar as possible, what its source is. To make such an assessment, you should watch the child closely in as many different situations as possible and record answers to these questions:

1. Is the child's voice shrill or excessively nasal?
   a. Under what circumstances?
   b. Under what circumstances is it *not* shrill or nasal?
2. Is the child's voice excessively loud?
   a. Under what circumstances?
   b. Under what circumstances is it *not* excessively loud?
3. Is the child's voice excessively soft?
   a. Under what circumstances?
   b. Under what circumstances is it *not* excessively soft?
4. Is there any evidence in the child's behavior to suggest that he or she is insecure, anxious, or hostile?
5. Is there any evidence to suggest that the child has a hearing impairment? (Such evidence may be manifested in persistent behaviors such as frequent requests to have statements repeated, frequent confusion of simple oral directions, complaints of ringing, buzzing, or pain in ears, turning or

Table 3.2 Checklist for assessing phonemic acquistions

Name _____

		PHONEME OBSERVED	DATE	AGE
THREE- AND FOUR-YEAR-OLDS				
/n/				
/t/	*Often lost in final position*[a]			
/g/				
/m/				
/b/	*May be lost in final position*			
/d/	*May be lost in final position*			
/w/				
/h/				
/p/	*May be lost in final position*			
/k/	*In /ks/ for x only /k/ is realized*			
/f/	*May alternate with /v/*			
/ŋ/				
FIVE- AND SIX-YEAR-OLDS				
/v/	*May alternate with /f/*			
/ǰ/				
/θ/	*Occasionally changed to /f/*			
/š/[b]	*In consonant clusters, next phoneme altered; often lost in final position*			
/l/	*Often lost or reduced in medial or final position*			
/r/[b]	*Often lost in medial or final position*			
/s/[b]				
/z/[b]				
/ž/[b]				
/č/[b]				
/ð/[b]	*Occasionally changed to /d/*			
/hw/[b]				

[a] Italic type indicates adaptations to be made for some Black English–speaking children.
[b] These phonemes may not develop until after age six.
From Susanna Phlaum-Connor, *The Development of Language and Reading in the Young Child*, 2nd ed., Columbus, Ohio: Merrill, 1978, p. 93. Reprinted by permission.

> tilting head toward the speaker, strained posture in listening, cupping of ear(s) toward speaker, or chronic upper respiratory infections or allergies.)
>
> — Gillet and Temple, 1981, p. 311

Instruction for Children with Language Problems

The same language development activities we have described elsewhere in this chapter and in this book will be of help to children with language problems. In particular, exposure to a good, articulate adult speech model is of the utmost importance. Exposure to other children who speak standard English fluently will also advance the nonfluent ones more quickly than isolating them from the fluent children. Additionally, they need plentiful opportunities to converse about interesting subjects, both concrete things in the here-and-now and ideas abstracted from these things, as well as subjects they have read about. Creative dramatics, storytelling, puppet shows, and the other activities discussed in this chapter are of great worth.

In addition, children with language problems respond best to organized, systematic, and extensive language encounters. In order for these students to make all the progress they can, we must decide what their needs are, choose the activities as well as the classroom conditions that will be of most benefit, and schedule these activities so that they can participate in them for large amounts of time every day. This does not mean planning wholly new activities for these children but rather adapting, varying, and timing ongoing activities with their special needs in mind.

Activities for Language-Delayed Children. Some activities for helping language-delayed children develop spoken fluency are as follows:

1. *Conversation.* A teacher, an aide, or an adult volunteer takes one or two children aside for fifteen to twenty minutes a day for conversation. Dialogues work best if there is a story read, a picture viewed, or an object manipulated to start a discussion. Conversation should take what the child talks about as the lead. Extend what the child says, don't just repeat it back, so that the conversation moves forward. Speak distinctly and use complete sentences.

2. *Talking about pictures.* Show a series of pictures to a small group of children. Start by modeling a sentence that could be said about a picture: "The boy is riding his bike." Then, as a new picture is introduced, ask each child to say a sentence of the same form: "They are picking up trash," "She is buying groceries," and so forth.

3. *Describing actions.* With the teacher and a group of younger children seated in a circle, one child stands up in the middle and pantomimes an action. The teacher first models a guess as to the activity with a complete sentence: "He combed his hair," then the children take turns offering guesses, using the structure of the teacher's sentence as a model. The teacher can put the sentence in the past tense, present progressive tense, and so on.

4. *What if?* Model and practice certain verb forms by asking questions that require certain verb forms as a response — "What would you buy if I gave you ten dollars?" "What would you do if I handed you a snake?" "What will you do after school today?" "Where will you live when you grow up?"

5. *Negatives: the cow doesn't fly.* With a small group of children, say, "I have a cow. The cow doesn't fly." Then, "I have a horse. _____" (child might say, "The horse doesn't bark" and so on) (Pflaum, 1978).

6. *Repeating sentences in rhythm.* Rhythm helps children repeat sentences. With a small group, form patterned sentences, such as:

TEACHER: "Who can say, 'You are nice'?"
JOHN: "I can say, 'You are nice.'"
TEACHER: "John can say, 'You are nice.' Who can say, 'I like you'?"
AMY: "I can say, 'I like you.'"

— Pflaum, 1978, p. 87

7. *Repeating Rhymes.* Simple rhythmic rhymes and songs that can quickly be memorized help children speak whole sentences when they repeat them. "This Old Man," "Baa Baa Black Sheep," and any number of others are good.

8. *Skits.* Skits that have stock phrases like "Little Pig, Little Pig, let me come in" can be acted out over and over again with the speaking parts rotated to different children.

Much of the most important language instruction in school is the informal sort children receive through routine interaction with their peers. With those who are late developers of speech, however, their natural reticence and their lack of contributions to normal classroom discussions often mean that they will not benefit from the same class time as much as other children who are more active. To ensure that these children do not simply get lost in classroom activities, Cohen and Plaskon (1980) recommend that you pay special attention to the seating arrangements in the class and to the pattern of classroom activities, in a deliberate effort to see that language-delayed children are included as much as possible.

A conventional seating arrangement with rows of individual desks can prevent the language-delayed child from choosing classmates with whom to interact, limit the child's opportunities for peer dialogues, and perhaps isolate the child from others. In addition, many classmates will not be free to converse with the language-delayed child, and most of his or her verbal interactions may be with the teacher. A seating arrangement with groups of pupils around tables can help in this regard because the language-delayed children will be more able to choose as work partners those to whom they relate most easily and to do so naturally and unobtrusively. Perhaps most important, such an arrangement allows you to adapt and modify ongoing activities and materials to fit the needs of special children without singling them out.

Activities for Developing Use of the Functions of Language. Role plays and other language activities should be developed to give children practice in each of the functions of language. They should practice using language in those functions that assessment indicates they use very little, as well as developing more variety in the language functions they already use. The activities listed below are starter ideas. You should be able to think of others that are suited to your own situation.

1. *Instrumental Function.* Role-play shopping at a hardware store, persuading a millionaire to give you a thousand dollars, talking the principal into giving

the students a day off, talking a mugger out of stealing your lunch money, or asking your little sister or brother not to eat the goldfish.

2. *Regulatory Function.* Teach someone else how to play a game; tell others how to form a certain design out of a tangram without letting them see yours; tell someone else how to draw a picture of the ugliest or best-looking person you ever saw; give people directions to find your house; play Simon Says or discuss and formulate rules for conduct in the classroom.

3. *Heuristic Function.* Use a discovery lesson in science; bring an animal to class and have the class ask questions about it; play "mystery person"; interview a classmate and tell the rest of the class about what you learned; have a guest come to class and invite questions about his or her hobby or specialty.

4. *Personal Function.* Participate in Show and Tell; look at pictures or highly imagistic films or listen to music and tell how it made you feel and what it resembled; take part in a group discussion of such topics as "What makes you afraid (happy, proud, furious, etc.)?"

5. *Interactional Function.* Conduct interviews or small group discussions to decide "What are the five best things in the world?", "How should we stage a class skit?", "What should we write to a pupil who is out sick?" Role-play various interpersonal encounters, such as a lost child asking directions home from a passerby, a tired parent taking a young child to a restaurant, or a youngster mistakenly accused of misbehavior by a parent or teacher.

6. *Imaginative Function.* Make up a chain story, a group poem, or a song; listen to stories; tell stories; choral-read poetry; move to music or a poem; invent a skit or puppet show for a story.

7. *Representational Function.* Participate in Show and Tell; describe your neighborhood; report verbally on an experience, such as a field trip; reach inside a closed bag and describe what a hidden object feels like so that others can guess what it is; close your eyes and say out loud every sound you can hear; close your eyes and walk around the room touching things, describing them to a guide walking with you.

Activities for Children with Articulation Problems. Children should be screened every year for speech problems and when problems are detected, they should be given whatever special instruction is needed. In recent years, legislatures and the courts have taken the position that such instruction is the child's right under the law. "Appropriate instruction" does not always require a speech therapist, although a qualified person should determine just what is required. In many cases, the teachers themselves can be of real help to children with articulation problems. In a general way, you can help by

1. serving as a good speech model for the class;
2. stressing the importance of clear speech, whenever appropriate;
3. ensuring that all children are screened for speech problems every year;

4. ensuring that children who need it have corrective speech instruction;
5. seeking guidance from a qualified speech therapist before attempting to correct serious speech problems in children, or attempting to give parents advice with respect to these problems.

— Petty and Jensen, 1980

When you do find it necessary to provide corrective instruction to a child who has articulation problems, Petty and Jensen suggested that these steps be taken:

1. Illustrate and demonstrate for the child how to make the sound correctly.
2. Form the sound clearly while the child observes the action of the lips and tongue.
3. Have the pupil examine his or her imitative attempts by use of a mirror.
4. Follow this procedure in practice exercises that require the child to:
   a. Repeat the sound several times
   b. Speak syllables that include the sound
   c. Speak short sentences in which the sound is used with some repetition, including sentences containing words of high social utility that children actually use in their own expression
   d. Utilize exercises that facilitate breathing and using lips and tongue

— Petty and Jensen, 1980, pp. 334–335

Activities for Children with Voice Problems. Problems of voice quality include speech that is too shrill and nasal, too harsh, too loud, or too soft. These problems stem from a number of causes. Since hearing impairment or physiological abnormality are sometimes implicated, children who are suspected of having such problems should always be referred to a qualified speech therapist for appraisal and possible treatment. More frequently, emotional insecurity or simply a lack of awareness of how they are coming across is the cause of these problems (Petty and Jensen, 1980). In these cases, it will fall within the teacher's and the class's responsibility to help the child or children in question.

Calling attention to the issue of voice quality is one way of dealing with the problem. If you say, "Susan, please ask me that again in a soft voice," it can help — if you phrase the reminder in an affectionate and supportive tone of voice (Petty and Jensen, 1980). Along the same lines, you can inform the parents that you are working on this problem and ask for their help at home.

Using role plays and creative dramatics that require different tones of voice is another effective method. Give the quiet child a loud role; give the loud child soft lines. Ask for several volunteers to demonstrate the tone of voice that might be used for certain lines: "How would you say, 'Fee fie foe fum! I smell the blood of an Englishman!'?" "How would Baby Bear say, 'Someone's been eating my porridge, and ate it allllll up!'?"

Tape record different children's voices. Play the tapes back to them one at a time and ask them if they are pleased with the way they sound or if they would like to improve their voice quality.

If students' feelings about themselves or their emotional security seem to be involved in the voice problem, go out of your way to make them feel comfortable, accepted, and involved in activities with the other children.

Summary

Most children enter school as fluent speakers, but school requires fluency in both formal and informal language, using language for different purposes and with different audiences. Language arts instruction must provide systematic exposure to the full range of language functions.

Discussion and dialogue activities expose children to the various uses of social language. Suggested activities include using telephones, Show and Tell, small group brainstorming, consensus groups, panel discussions, and Grouptalk.

Classroom dramatics help children explore their feelings, interpret literature, and experience a wide variety of language forms. Dramatic play with simple costumes and props induces them to use drama spontaneously. Choral-speaking activities include fingerplays, choral verses, refrains, and antiphonal arrangements. Mime, acting without words, and improvisation, spontaneous role playing with impromptu dialogue, extend their interpretation skills. Role playing and puppetry offer many opportunities for creating dialogues and interpreting literature. Readers theater involves oral interpretation of literature with minimal acting.

Storytelling, both by adults and by children, is an important vehicle for exposing youngsters to stories and helping them develop speaking skills. Wordless picture books are good storytelling starters, and storytelling can also be combined with mime, role playing, puppetry, and other drama activities.

Listening activities should help children learn to listen to one another attentively and for a variety of purposes. In the classroom listening can be encouraged or discouraged by a number of physical conditions and speaker behaviors. Listening games can help students concentrate on following oral directions, remembering sequences, categorizing, and developing auditory discrimination. Directed listening-thinking activities use predictive questioning to help children form hypotheses about forthcoming events in stories they listen to. Listening and study skills are combined in activities calling for transcribing, summarizing, and outlining.

Problems with language may involve delays in syntactic development, articulation difficulties, and lack of fluency with a variety of language functions. Language divergence may be reflected in lack of fluency in standard English forms and in lack of familiarity with English. Sentence-modeling tasks and measurement of utterance length can be used in language assessment. Checklists are suggested for informal assessment of phoneme articulation and use of all language functions. For children with language problems, an environment rich in language exposure is of primary importance. Adult language modeling and plentiful opportunity for oral language use every day are required. Special opportunities must be made for these children to tell, describe, ask questions, explain, express feelings and opinions, and informally converse with adults and peers. Ongoing activities and classroom organization should be examined for ways to enhance these children's interaction with others. Most often this does not involve making up new activities but simply modifying and adapting ongoing ones for the benefit of those with language problems.

CHAPTER FOUR

Understanding Reading and Literature

CHAPTER OUTLINE

Of all the language arts, reading is the one that usually gets the lion's share of attention in the elementary school day. It is important to remember, however, that reading is a *language* skill, that it develops as a part of the child's overall language ability. Because of this factor, the following points about language ability apply to reading:

— Reading will not usually develop disproportionately faster than other language abilities. For children to grow as readers, they must also grow as talkers and listeners, as writers, and as spellers.

— Like other language skills, reading ability develops best when children are placed in situations where they see reading used in meaningful and exciting ways and when they are encouraged to begin reading themselves. Reading skill can be advanced by direct teaching, too, but teaching is most efficient only when the teacher understands the reading process and understands what children do when they go about learning to read.

— Reading ability develops through a series of stages, and children need somewhat different kinds of support from the teacher at each stage.

— Since reading is a language ability used for communication, the *type of material* we read demands different reading skills, just as different styles of speech place different demands on the speaker. Literature, including poetry, has special rewards but it also requires special approaches. In addition, readers must learn the structures of stories, explanations, descriptions, and arguments.

In this chapter we will describe in detail what the ability to read consists of, and how it develops through the elementary grades. We will begin with a careful observation of the reading act and try to describe what happens between eye, brain, and page as a scientist of perception would. Next we will examine reading behavior in prereaders, beginners, and early mature readers. The process of reading is the same in all stages, but the emphasis and required conditions change from the first approaches to print to the achievement of independent literacy. Where one is forming basic concepts about print, another is gaining advanced concepts and also collecting sight words, while another is reading in bigger chunks and is relating background knowledge *schemata* to the task of reading.

What is read is also important. The structure of the text must be taken into account by successful readers, and, hence, by successful teachers of reading. The structure and rewards of literature, one of the main reasons why we teach reading, are briefly outlined in the closing pages of this chapter.

What Do People Do When They Read?

If you position yourself so that you can closely watch another person's eyes as she reads, you will observe that the movement of the eyes as they follow a line of print is not smooth and continuous but abrupt and jerky. A closer look will show that the eyes make a series of jumps and pauses, which have been termed *saccades* (jumps) and *fixations* (pauses) (Huey, 1908/1968).

You may wonder at what points during the eye movement we are actually seeing print — during the saccades, or during the fixations? If you look at print through a paper tube while someone moves the page in front of you, the print becomes a gray blur. Thus when print moves vis-à-vis the eye, we cannot focus on it. But why, then, are we not aware of this movement of eye vis-à-vis page when we read? The answer is complicated, but it sheds important light on the reading process.

When readers make a fixation, they take in a portion of visual information from the page. At first this information goes into *short-term memory*, a sort of mental viewing and holding area, where it can be processed by the brain. If the brain can make sense of the visual information and relate it to something already known, the information is transferred into *long-term memory*, where it can stay indefinitely. If the information in short-term memory is not transferred into long-term memory within five to seven seconds it is lost and forgotten.

For the eye to take in visual information and place it into short-term memory takes about *fifty milliseconds (one-thousandth of a second)*. For the brain to scan the information and either transfer it into long-term memory or reject it takes another two hundred milliseconds. Now during this second stage, the time that the brain is considering the information for long-term memory storage, the reader is in effect blind: No new visual information is being taken in. The reader has the sensation of still seeing whatever information is being processed at that moment, but in fact what is before the eyes may be quite different, such as text moving before the eyes as they pass to the next point of fixation.

The reader's eyes take in visual information during a fixation, and then simultaneously one's vision "shuts down," the brain processes the information, and the eyes move on to the next fixation. The combination of processes takes about a quarter of a second. The amount of time involved is fixed by nature and is the same for everyone. How is it, then, that some people read so much faster than others?

The answer lies in the amount of information taken in during a fixation. Psychologists have discovered that our perceptual apparatus is constructed to handle five to seven items per fixation. Note, however, that an *item* may be very small or very large, depending on a phenomenon called *chunking*. As far as perception is concerned, an item is anything the mind can meaningfully group or chunk together. Graphic marks can be chunked together if we can recognize that they constitute letters. Letters can be chunked together if syllable-based spelling patterns can be discerned in them; otherwise there is a limit of about five on the random letters we remember. Words can be chunked if we can find relationships of grammar or meaning between them; otherwise there is a limit on the number of isolated words we can perceive in one fixation.

Though our ability to chunk visual information depends on what is on the page, it also depends on what is in our heads. We need prior knowledge of the letters before we can use them as the basis for chunking. We have to have some representation of words stored in memory before we can use them as a basis for chunking. Before we can chunk on the basis of grammar and meaning, for example, we must have some idea of the grammar of sentences and of possible meanings of sentences.

In a real sense, what we can read depends on what we already know, but it also depends on our willingness to look beyond minutiae and go for the larger picture. Active readers who bring questions to what they read, make mental predictions about what they will encounter, and mentally confirm or refute their own predictions as they find significant information in the text are far more efficient than those who set their sights only on recognizing the words and rendering them accurately out loud.

This last point is an important one for teachers, since there are children who are so preoccupied with pronouncing each word correctly that they fail to get the sense of what they read. They may plod along very slowly, and when someone is not prodding them to read, they give up. There are other children who bring to the task an expectation that the reading will make sense. They think and read in units larger than single words. They tend to read more rapidly and sustain their reading even when by themselves. There are also a few readers at the other extreme. They predict *too much*: They skip along giving a fanciful reading that is only occasionally connected to the words the author wrote. They seem to have little way of knowing when their reading is not in step with the text.

The kinds of reading done by children in each of these groups are called *strategies*, because they are the means of dealing with reading tasks that youngsters usually employ. Thus children who are not reading efficiently are not merely reading inefficiently: They are still practicing some strategy, some approach to reading, that is not so efficient as another strategy might be. How they come by their strategies is partly through their own invention and partly through our influences on them as teachers.

It is important that we be able to think clearly about the strategies we hope to impart through our instruction. And it is equally important to be able to recognize the strategies that children are actually using, so we can offer effective help.

Before we can go further with our description of what readers do and how they learn to do it, we must distinguish between the different *stages* of reading.

The Stages of Reading

It is useful to divide elementary reading development into the stages of *prereading*, *beginning reading*, and *early and later mature reading*.

Prereading

By *prereading* we mean roughly what other writers have meant by the term *reading readiness*. Both terms have to do with certain concepts and abilities that children must develop before they can be taught to read. One month our best efforts to teach a certain youngster to read may seem to fall on stony ground; three months later the child may take easily to reading instruction and begin to make rapid progress. Clearly, there are factors other than our instruction that make this child begin to learn to read. These factors are *prereading concepts*.

We can identify several areas of specific abilities and concepts that children must develop in order to begin to read. These insights are important for teachers because they suggest definite steps we can take to help students who are not yet profiting from beginning reading instruction. The most important prereading competencies are: *elaborated oral language, story language, cognitive clarity, the concept of a word in print, the ability to segment phonemes*, and a certain amount of *cognitive and emotional maturity*.

Elaborated Oral Language. In Chapter Two we described in some detail what children know when they are able to talk. That entire discussion is relevant here, because comprehension of stories that are either read or listened to requires that children understand the language in which the stories are written. Three aspects of language development deserve special mention.

One of these aspects is *word meaning*. Children must know the meaning of most of the words they encounter in beginning reading. Not every child who enters kindergarten has seen snow, or a church bell, or leaves changing color dramatically, or a tiger, or many of the other things and events that correspond to basic vocabulary. Not all of them have accurate concepts for terms like "bigger/smaller," "more than/less than," "before/after," or "because of." Reading is a step removed from talking, which itself is a step removed from direct experience. Before neophyte readers encounter these words and concepts in reading instruction, it is essential that they have easy verbal command of them. An important responsibility of the teacher's is to find out when children have deficits in essential vocabulary items and concepts and to step in with helpful activities when problems are spotted. Moreover, teachers must be alert to these problems at whatever level they occur and be ready to offer help.

Another aspect of language that is important for learning to read is *grammar*. Here we are not talking about "correct grammar," such as not saying *ain't* or not splitting infinitives. We are concerned instead with *syntax* — whether or not a child understands the particular meaning conveyed by word order or word inflections in sentences. Sometimes an exact understanding of grammar is not necessary for us to understand an utterance. "Lion . . . attack" or "Attack . . . lion" would make adequate sense to us if we heard either expression uttered by a battered lion tamer, but there are far more instances where grammar is necessary for correct understanding. Consider "The lion's attack" versus "The lions attack," or "The lion tamer" versus "The tamer lion." Especially in reading, an adequate level of grammatical development is necessary to understand the meaning of sentences.

A third important aspect involves the expressiveness of language, reflected in *restricted and elaborated codes* (Bernstein, 1966). These codes have to do with the amount of explicit meaning children tend to encode in their language. As we saw in Chapter Two, most speakers have a range of codes (or registers) they can use, ranging from intimate to formal to ceremonial. On the intimate end, many vague, nonspecific terms are used, since the common experience of close friends makes the use of more explicit terms unnecessary. On the formal end, however, we do not assume that this shared experience exists, and we must convey our meanings in more explicit words.

Bernstein's observation has been that some children do not have adequate control over the whole range of language codes. He has observed that many of them have been accustomed to speak only in the restricted code at home. Although they may have normal intelligence, and even know word meanings and grammatical structures, they are not used to hearing language that "spells things out." They are not accustomed to the precise use of words, or the sentence structures that go along with elaborated meanings.

When it comes to learning to read, these youngsters are at a particular disadvantage, because the language of print is elaborated language. Writers use complete, elaborate sentences and precise referents. Children whose language experience has consisted entirely of informal conversations with people who share their understandings and interests will find printed material somewhat foreign to them.

From the foregoing discussion of the three main aspects of language, one theme is repeated: Children must have a good command of spoken language before learning to read is a possibility. This command includes vocabulary, grammar, and the use of elaborated expression, and it is not a one-time requirement that students meet and are done with. Throughout the primary grades, they must continue to be given oral language enrichment to support their reading development because the language demands of reading itself increase.

Story Language. Children who come to school with a fluent command of elaborated language typically come from families where they are talked to and listened to, and where they are taken seriously as communicators from a very early age. In such families, the children are usually read to as well. Because those who come to school using elaborated language are usually familiar with many books and stories, it is easy for us to overlook another somewhat separate aspect of language development that is important: *Children must be familiar with the language of stories.*

Although stories use elaborated language, they do not merely spell things out; they spell them out in a certain way. Stories have their own conventions for using language. "Once upon a time . . ." is a phrase that signals several things to the experienced listener or reader. It means that what follows will be a story, a fanciful story, not literally true, but interesting, and with particular predictable structures. The audience knows that immediately following the phrase, a place will be mentioned and that this place will be the setting of the story. People or animals will be named, and they will be the main characters. The choice of words, the rhythm and repetition, the fancy of stories are delightful to most youngsters, but to a few they are unfamiliar, and, like the other aspects of language we just described, they can cause difficulty for children who are translating their usual ways of thinking into a new way. If this translation must be done at the same time they are just coming to grips with letters and sounds and print directionality such as left-to-right and top-to-bottom, then unfamiliarity with story language can be troubling to some beginning readers and prereaders.

The remedy for this is simple and pleasant: Read to the children often. Reading aloud offers many benefits, and one important one is to familiarize students with the language of stories before they have to take on the task of extracting this language from print.

Cognitive Clarity. More directly related to the act of learning to read is the idea of *cognitive clarity*. What this term refers to is the extent to which children understand what reading is, know what they must do in order to learn to read, and understand the meanings of terms commonly used by teachers in reading instruction. Downing and Thackray (1975) cite studies showing that when measures of cognitive clarity about the task of learning to read were taken, those children who seemed early on to know what they were about showed greater progress in learning to read than those who were unclear.

One thing children should be clear about is what reading is for. Many youngsters, when asked, seem unaware that reading is for getting messages — stories, letters, directions, and the like — that have been written in print. Another is how print works. From Marie Clay (1975) we get an example of what happens between teacher and class when the children do not firmly understand how print works or what teachers mean by the words they use when they teach reading:

> Suppose a teacher has placed an attractive picture on the wall and asked her children for a story which she will record under it. They offer the text "Mother is cooking" which the teacher alters slightly to introduce some features she wishes to teach. She writes.
>
> Mother said,
> "I am baking."
>
> If she says, "Now look at our *story*," 30 percent of the new entrant group will attend to the *picture*.
>
> If she says, "Look at the words and find some you know," between 50 and 90 percent will be searching for *letters*. If she says, "Can you see Mother?" most will agree that they can but some *see* her in the picture, some can locate "M" and others will locate the word "Mother."
>
> Perhaps the children read in unison "Mother is . . ." and the teacher tries to sort this out. Pointing to *said* she asks, "Does this say *is*?" Half agree it does because it has an "s" in it. *"What letter does it start with?"* Now the teacher is really in trouble. She assumes that the children *know* that a word is built out of letters but 50 percent of the children still confuse the verbal labels "word" and "letter" after six months of instruction. She also assumes that the children know that the left-hand letter following a space is the "start" of a word. Often they do not.
>
> — Clay, 1975, pp. 3–4

Clay's own *Concepts About Print Test* (1972) is constructed to discover which important principles a particular child knows and doesn't know about written language and learning to read. Whether or not you use such an instrument, if you are teaching beginners you should constantly examine the tasks you give the children, determine what they must understand to be able to carry them out, and find out which children have and which have not acquired the prerequisite understandings.

The Concept of Written Words. One concept about print is thorny enough to warrant separate treatment: the *concept of word*, which really contains two concepts. The first is that we realize language comes to us in units of words and that we recognize where the boundaries between words occur. This concept is involved in recognizing that

"Whuzapnin, man?"

or

"Kanchaseeum doinuh bestahkin?"

can be divided into

"What is happening, man?"
"Can't you see I'm doing the best I can?"

The second aspect of the concept of word is recognizing how written words are marked off as units in a line of print. Words are left-to-right–oriented clusters of letters separated from each other by spaces on either end. A potential reader must realize that these spaces mark the boundaries of written words and that these configurations correspond to spoken words. A potential reader must also be aware that words are not individual letters either; nor are they necessarily the same as single beats of stress (syllables). Only when the reader's concept of a word as a unit of language meshes exactly with the word units on the page can he or she attend to words, find associations between words in the mind and words on the page, or study the parts of words. While it is not a sufficient condition, developing a concept of words is a necessary condition for children to begin to learn to read (Morris, 1980).

So the concept of word turns out to be an important one for beginning reading. In most children it develops naturally; in fact, many teachers are probably not even aware that such a thing is developing at all. For those students who have not developed the concept of word there are many things we can do to help them along. Labeling things in the room, taking dictation from them and pointing to the words as we read the lines back, giving them exercises in cutting apart familiar sentences and matching the words back together are helpful. These techniques and others are described in detail in Chapter Five.

Beginning Reading

Beginning reading is like the first solo runs on a bicycle: They tend to be short and uncertain, but at least nobody is running alongside holding us up. In bicycling, a coordination of balance, pedaling, and steering has been achieved. In beginning reading, a knowledge of sight words, some skill in word analysis, and some sort of notion of fluent reading have come together to enable the child to read through the line unaided.

Sight Words. Words that can be recognized immediately without analysis are called *sight words*. Having amassed a large body of sight words is important for several reasons. First, as the number of sight words approaches the total collection of words that must be read, a large portion of the task of reading — that of word recognition — is taken care of. Second, even when readers have fewer sight words than the total number of words they encounter in their reading, the words they *do* know help them guess the words they don't know. Third, for children who are still consolidating the concept of word, sight words serve as "anchors"; that is, when they find words they know in a line of print, these can help them correct themselves if they have read, say, a preceding two-syllable word as two words.

The term sight word has another meaning, which refers to the selected lists of words such as the Dolch Sight Words or other collections of "basic words." Because these words occur with great frequency in all written material [some two hundred of them account for 80 percent of the words found in elementary grade level reading matter (Ekwall, 1976)], they are often taught to children by memorization. Unfortunately, these high-frequency words tend to be lacking in concrete referents; sometimes they are meaningless grammatical "function" words like *the*, *is*, *and*, *for*, and *of*. Because they have no vivid associations for children, they are more difficult to remember and recognize in print than other words. Moreover, if youngsters recognize basic sight words and nothing else, they are not much closer to the meaning of the text. Consider, for example, the following passage from a children's story. In the first version of it we have omitted the words that Ekwall does not consider "basic" for preprimer, primer, and first-grade reading levels:

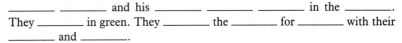

— Ekwall, 1976, p. 70

Got that? Now here is the same with only the "basic" words taken out:

— Manning-Sanders, 1977, p. 1

It is surely easier to guess the basic words given the low-frequency words than to guess the low-frequency words given the basic words. Thus, even though the basic sight word lists do offer some advantages, their low appeal to memory and low information content don't make them much of a bargain.

Incidentally, children do learn many of the basic sight words on their own without resorting to flash cards. Henderson, et al. (1972) compared the words beginning readers had in the word banks in a language experience program with the words on a basic sight list and found that about half of the word bank words were on the basic sight word lists, even without any special effort to "drill them in."

Word Analysis. Sight words also help in giving students sound and spelling patterns of known words to which they can relate similar unknown words. Children who have "kick" and "trick" as sight words have some basis for figuring out "thick," although they may need guidance in formulating such generalizations: "*k + ick = kick*; *tr + ick = trick*; therefore the unknown *th + ick* must be *thick*." As Henderson (1984) has noted, in order to reach such a generalization, a child must realize that a word is divisible into a beginning consonant + the spelling pattern that comes after it (see Chapter Six). At the same time the child should know the sounds of beginning consonants and vowel spelling patterns: vowel + consonant + silent *e*, vowel + silent vowel + consonant, and so forth.

Stauffer (1979) and others have noted that children are best able to make headway in these matters after first having accumulated at least fifty sight words. Then they can discover the generalizations at work in words they already know, a somewhat easier approach than to begin by memorizing letter-to-sound correspondences and then applying them to the unknown words. In our discussion of the word sorting procedure in Chapter Five we demonstrate an approach for helping beginning readers with word analysis.

A Conception of Fluent Reading. In the section on prereading, we discussed the notion of cognitive clarity: the idea that the understanding of what reading is, why it is done, and how it is done can make a critical difference in how efficiently children set about learning to read. In at least one specific sense, the question of how they think about reading is still important when they are beginning readers too. The burdensome business of word recognition and word decoding can loom so large that they can easily forget that the purpose of reading is to get sense from print. When most of the children in the class give halting and labored renderings of the lines they are assigned to read, it is natural for the other students to assume that this stuttered, inflectionless word calling is what they are *supposed* to do.

Some children really do have difficulty reading words, of course, and thus they read in a halting, disfluent fashion. Nevertheless, it is always a good idea for you to provide a model fluent reading for them and make sure they understand that fluent, natural, sense-making reading is their ultimate goal. The method of repeated reading, described in Chapter Five, was developed with precisely this end in mind. See also the discussion of readers' theater in Chapter Three, since this is also a good way to convey the idea to beginning and more mature readers that fluent, inflected reading is what they should be after.

Reading by Grammar and Meaning. Beginning readers are understandably preoccupied with accurate word recognition and pronunciation. Yet fluent

readers also rely on the grammatical and meaning-related context of sentences in order to read more quickly and with greater understanding than they could with word recognition alone.

As Frank Smith (1978) has noted, attending to grammatical and semantic information aids readers in two ways. First, it enables them to chunk more information into each fixation (see the beginning of this chapter); that is, they can detect grammatical clusters such as *in the woods*, *would have been*, and *a great, big truck* as they read them, thus reading them as units rather than as individual words.

Second, using grammatical and meaning-related information helps readers identify words they might not otherwise be sure of. Students who do not know the word *mother* are nevertheless likely to guess it if they know the other words and are guided by the grammar and meaning in the sentence "The boy kissed his *mother* good night."

In beginning reading, children should be encouraged from the first to utilize what they already know of the grammar and meaning of the sentence to help them identify what is coming next.

There are several procedures that encourage youngsters to be sensitive to grammatical and meaningful (or *semantic*) information as they read. One is simply to ask them when they come to an unknown word to wonder "what would make sense" there. Others are the techniques that stress predicting outcomes, such as the Directed Listening-Thinking Activity (see Chapter Three) and the Directed Reading-Thinking Activity (see Chapter Five). Still another helpful activity is the *cloze procedure*, which is normally used as an informal test of reading comprehension. Used as an instructional device, it can be helpful in getting children to consider grammatical and semantic information in recognizing words. The cloze procedure will be explained in more detail in Chapter Five.

Early Mature Reading

Between second and fourth grade, the context of reading changes dramatically. As Jeanne Chall puts it, in the early grades, children learn to read; in the later grades they read to learn (Chall, 1979). The differences between the two show up in many ways. Table 4.1 summarizes some of the most important ones.

Teachers must realize that there are significant changes in the demands placed on students between the early and later grades, because many children who succeed fairly well in beginning reading face serious difficulty and sometimes even failure when faced with later reading tasks. In the present section, we will highlight two characteristic tasks of later reading that are not included in Table 4.1: *learning vocabulary from text* and *thinking in larger information structures*.

Learning Vocabulary from Text. In beginning reading, word recognition is a matter of recognizing printed versions of words that are already in one's spoken vocabulary. In later reading, children are faced with the task of learning new words from text, words they do not already know. Hence, the problem of vocabulary in later reading is not only one of deciding on the pronunciation of a written word but also deciding on its meaning. It is estimated that, beyond third grade, *a majority of the new words children learn they learn from reading.* An important part of later reading skill, then, involves the ability to discern word meanings from text.

When authors use unfamiliar vocabulary, it is not always possible to determine the meaning directly from context. Hittleman (1978) suggests that the best strategy in such cases is to formulate a hypothesis as to what the word might mean and then test that hypothesis against the other occurrences of the word in the text. To do this, readers must be aware of the structural devices

Table 4.1 Some differences between beginning reading and later reading

	BEGINNING READING (PRIMARY GRADES)	LATER READING (MIDDLE ELEMENTARY GRADES AND UP)
FOCUS ON:	Learning to read	Reading to learn
MATERIAL IS:	Mostly fiction	Mostly nonfiction
	Short passages, changing topics	Long sections, continuous topics
PURPOSES FOR READING ARE:	Explicitly set by teacher and short term ["Read this sentence (perhaps aloud) and tell me what it says"]	Generally set by teacher or by student and long term ("Study pages 140–158 for a quiz on Friday")
RESPONSE TO THE READER IS:	Immediate and directly related to the act of reading ("You missed three words, Richard")	Delayed and indirectly related to reading ("You didn't know the material, Linda")
EVALUATION OF THE READING FOCUSES ON:	Oral reading, comprehension of short, explicit questions	Silent reading and *learning* of longer material; the ability to *use* information

SOURCE: From Jean Wallace Gillet and Charles Temple, *Understanding Reading Problems: Assessment and Instruction*. Copyright © by Jean Wallace Gillet and Charles Temple. Reprinted by permission of Little, Brown and Company.

authors use to signal meaning. According to Deighton (1959) and Hittleman (1978), writers generally use five types of signals:

1. *Definition.* These take the form "*X* is (or "is called") *Y*," and communicate an explicit definition of the word: *An iconoclast is a person who deliberately violates other people's traditions. A person who deliberately violates traditions is called an iconoclast.*

2. *Example.* Not recognizing the term itself, the reader can narrow down its meaning from the examples given. Look for telltale words or phrases like *for example, such as, like,* and *especially: Venomous snakes, such as the rattlesnake, the copperhead, or the coral snake, are to be avoided.*

3. *Modifiers.* Modifiers used to describe an unknown word may give an indication of what it is: *The minaret that the Moslems built stood tall, slender, and graceful above the other buildings in the town.*

4. *Restatement.* Unknown terms are sometimes stated a second time using other, more familiar words. One such device is an appositive, a group of words following the word defined and set off by commas or dashes. Restatement is also done by using key words or phrases like *or, that is,* and *in other words: Chauvinism, an aggressive loyalty to one's own group, originally applied to national patriotism only. They fired the attendant because of her indolence; in other words, she was lazy.*

5. *Inference*
    a. *Parallel Sentence Structure.* As in 2 above, we can often get an idea of

the nature of an unknown word by recognizing a known word in the same series: *Each office contained some type of medical specialist. In one was a family practitioner; in another, an obstetrician; in another, a radiologist; and in another, a hematologist.*

b. *Repetition of Key Words.* If an unknown word is repeated in different contexts we can narrow down its meaning: *It is sometimes said that only primitive people have taboos. That is not so. Even advanced cultures like ours have them. In America, for example, it is taboo to speak directly about death, or about a grown person's age or weight.*

c. *Familiar Connectives.* Some familiar connectives, especially subordinating or coordinating conjunctions, show us the relationship between ideas and thus allow us to associate an unknown idea with a known one: *John was very excited about the award, but Judith seemed indifferent.*

Bringing Prior Knowledge to Reading: Schema Theory. In our discussion of the chunking phenomenon at the beginning of this chapter we noted that what we derive from print depends very much on what we bring to it. At that point we were talking about concepts of letters, words, and grammar. Now, however, we can talk about the more general levels of background knowledge that we use to understand written text. Cognitive psychologists have recently come up with what they call *schema theory*, which offers one way of explaining what some of these larger units of knowledge might be like (Adams and Collins, 1979; Anderson, 1977; Bartlett, 1932; Minsky, 1975).

The theory can be summarized as follows. When authors write about some topic, they put their ideas about that topic in written form. Now the authors' ideas about the topic are organized into mental frameworks called *schemata* (the singular form is *schema*). Schemata are complex idea structures existing in the mind, which relate ideas, things, and events bound together in a person's experience. An individual could, for example, have a "birthday party" schema. This schema might include the ideas of guests coming together, a one-way giving of gifts, a birthday cake with a certain number of candles, singing of "Happy Birthday to You," and so on. Now if that person who had the birthday schema heard about a particular birthday party, the birthday party schema would serve as a framework for making sense of details he or she encountered. The people mentioned would be interpreted as guests or hosts, objects named interpreted as gifts, and so on.

When authors write about their ideas they do not write out their entire schemata; that is, they do not express *everything* they know about the topic or the relationship among all of the ideas. They usually write out only those aspects of the schemata that they judge to be most informative to readers. They expect the readers to supply the rest for themselves, from their own schemata.

It follows that readers must summon up appropriate schemata in order to comprehend the text. If all goes well, the experience of reading will enable them to add details to these schemata, or to forge connections among schemata that they had not made previously. In this way readers learn from reading.

But things don't always go well. Sometimes readers don't have the appropriate schemata in their experience. Such would be the case if a particular person had never seen or heard about an American birthday party. What is far more typical, however, is for readers to have the schemata but to fail to summon them up, fail to make connections between what they already know and what the text is telling them. In other words, they do not read *actively* — they have what we call "comprehension problems." They can identify many words correctly, calling them aloud in a sing-song voice, with little comprehension of the meaning. If we ask them for a recall of what they have read, they give us a very literal account, giving back a few phrases or sentences verbatim, without apparently knowing their significance.

In order to prevent or eliminate comprehension problems, our strategies should be those that lead children to read with the mind actively engaged: raising questions, making predictions, and expecting the text to make sense. In Chapter Five we present several teaching methods that are geared to this end, especially the Directed Reading-Thinking Activity, since this device addresses more closely than any other the task of making children active readers.

Sensing the Structure of Written Text

Psychological studies of the reading process have shown us another dimension of the importance of readers' prior knowledge — what they bring with them to the act of reading. This dimension has to do with their sensitivity to different structures and purposes of written text: what a particular written passage is intended to do, and how it is organized.

To read efficiently, we must be able to distinguish among and respond appropriately to many varieties of fiction and nonfiction. This means that the predictions we make, and the questions and expectations of meaning we bring to each act of reading, should be appropriate to the specific kind of matter we are reading at that time.

In the following pages we will describe some of these varieties of fiction and nonfiction, and the ways they affect our responses to them. We begin with nonfiction.

Taxonomy

What pattern of organization do you perceive in this passage?

THE GUITAR

The guitar is one of the most popular stringed instruments. Because it has a fretboard, and strings stretched across a soundbox that are played by plucking, it is considered a member of the lute family.

For centuries the guitar had a rather small wooden body with soft strings fashioned of animal gut. In the present century, however, several distinct classes of this instrument have emerged. The traditional version has lived on as the "classical" guitar, but there now exist steel-string guitars and electric guitars.

The steel-string guitar has a long, narrow neck and an enlarged body. It makes a louder, more piercing sound than the classical guitar. The electric model, an off-shoot of the steel-string guitar, has its sounds amplified and its tones modified by electronic devices. It can make sounds loud enough to deafen a rock musician. It can also make a variety of tones, many of which do not sound "guitarlike" at all.

This piece of text is organized by classifying. The author is listing and defining the different instruments collected together under the label "guitar" and showing their relationships to one another.

If readers are to understand this passage they must perceive the taxonomic, or classificatory, structure. If you asked them to recall what the passage said, you would expect them to remember the kinds of guitars discussed, what made them different from one another, and how they were related within the "family." Taxonomic text structures are frequently encountered in science materials, especially in life sciences.

Chronology

What pattern of organization do you perceive in this passage?

BURTON

The town of Burton, in the Midlands of England, has a history that is typical of trading villages of the region. Nothing of the town existed before the ninth century A.D. The hill overlooking the Avon River where the town now sits was covered with thick forest.

At about 870 A.D., Northumbrian knights cleared the hillside and erected a rude fortress as an outpost against the South Saxons lurking across the Avon, which then served as a southern frontier of Northumbria. By the time peace was established some thirty years later, a stone castle had been built, surrounded by about thirty dwellings, and some crops had been grown nearby.

With the peace and political stability of the tenth century, Burton grew in earnest. Pastures were cleared for five miles around during the first half of the century, and fine manor houses erected from the timber with the profits made from sheep raising. Trails that crisscrossed the settlement grew to well-traveled roads, and by the middle of the eleventh century Burton served as the chief market center for the surrounding thirty- or forty-mile area. The town grew comparatively wealthy.

But prosperity came to an end when Cromwell and his Roundheads burned the town in the seventeenth century. They marched the residents of Burton off into captivity, and few ever returned.

This account is arranged according to a sequence of events. Its chief organizational feature is *chronological*. In order to fully understand this passage, one must picture the unfolding of events in time. If you asked readers to recall this passage you would expect them to remember the events that were described, the time they occurred, and the order in which they took place. Chronological text structures are frequently used in historical material.

Cause and Effect

The passage about the town of Burton also used cause and effect as an aspect of the organization. In the following passage this pattern is more pronounced.

BLACK ROBES IN THE DESERT

Scientists sometimes question the wisdom of "folk wisdom." The case of the Tuaregs' robes is a case in point. These nomadic people live in the area of the southern Sahara desert, the hottest terrain on earth. For centuries they have worn the same head-to-toe black wool robes. Since black absorbs more heat from the sun than any other color, scientists wonder why they've kept them through the years. Some people speculated that they had only black sheep as a source of wool, but an inspection of their herds dispelled that notion. Others speculated that black might have been chosen for its protection against the nightly desert cold, but scientific tests showed that black robes held heat no better than white ones.

Finally, through a series of experiments it was discovered that the black robes are actually cooler than white ones. The explanation is that the sun heats the upper part of the robe, which causes air to rise up through the loose-fitting robe and out through the open neck. Thus a constant draft is maintained through the robes, and this draft evaporates perspiration, which cools the wearer.

To comprehend this passage readers must operate on at least two levels: They must recognize the larger cause-and-effect question. "Why do the Tuaregs wear black robes in the desert?" and recognize its answer: "Because their black robes keep them cool." They must also recognize the other cause-and-effect relations that together explain the seemingly contradictory statement that black is cooler in the desert. Cause-effect writing is found in many content subjects, including health, social studies, the sciences, and home economics.

Written Directions

Some written materials give instructions for carrying out a procedure or performing some action.

HOW TO START YOUR NEW CAR

Making sure the emergency break is fully engaged, depress the clutch and move the gear shift lever to NEUTRAL. Pull the choke out all the way. Push the throttle to the floor, release it, then push it halfway down. Now, insert the key in the ignition and rotate the key forward to the START position. After the car has started and warmed up, push the choke in fully.

To grasp this passage adequately, readers must attend to the steps described and to the order in which they are presented. They could show they understand by getting into the car and following the steps. Short of that, they could write a list of the steps in the proper order, or properly arrange a set of pictures detailing each step. Material in the form of written directions is used most frequently in math and science, and in many places outside of school.

Comparison and Contrast

In trying to understand what something *is*, it is often helpful to know what it *is not*. Comparison and contrast goes beyond simple description by describing two or more things simultaneously, pointing out their likenesses and differences.

WILL THE REAL COWBOY PLEASE STAND UP?

So many people pretend to be cowboys these days that it is getting harder and harder to tell the real cowboys from the dudes. Dudes and cowboys both wear western hats, wide tooled-leather belts with ornate buckles, jeans, and boots. The jeans of both dudes and cowboys may be worn and faded, in contrast to their boots; both dudes and cowboys are likely to wear shiny, expensive-looking boots. But the real cowboy's belt is usually sweat-stained around the top edge, and he often tucks his jeans into the tops of his boots. The brim of the cowboy's hat is sometimes tipped at a rakish angle, but so is that of the experienced dude. Neither is particularly bowlegged anymore, although this used to be one way to differentiate between the two. Today, both dudes and cowboys are apt to drive pickups or jeeps instead of riding horses.

The surest way to tell a real cowboy from a dude is to look at the eyes. The cowboy's eyes are clear and steady, and his gaze holds yours. The dude's eyes flicker this way and that, as if to see what impression he is making on others.

To understand this passage, one must recognize which aspects of description are related to which of the things being compared, and which aspects are related to each other; that is, hats compared with hats, eyes with eyes, and so forth.

When a description is formulated for one of the things being compared but not the other, the reader must mentally supply its opposite to the things not described; that is, if one man's belt is sweat-stained, the other's belt must not be so.

The ultimate test of a reader's comprehension of this passage would be to distinguish between actual people, one of which was a real cowboy and the other a dude. Comparison-contrast structures are found in many content subjects, especially social studies and science.

Explanation or Exposition

Much text material in schools is used to describe or explain. Since organization of such material varies widely, it is hard to describe concisely. The material may be entirely verbal as in the example below, or it may include numbers and formulas, charts, graphs, and pictures.

THE DEADLY COBRA

The cobra is one of the most deadly snakes in the world. Many wildlife experts consider it *the* deadliest animal. Its venom, its mobility, and its behavior are legendary.

The cobra's venom is more deadly even than that of the rattlesnake. Its large fangs do not inject the venom as do the fangs of other poisonous snakes; instead the fangs are used to pierce deep wounds in the victim's flesh, and the cobra releases venom from sacs in its mouth into these punctures. The deadly venom is carried by the bloodstream and attacks the victim's central nervous system. One African variety spits its venom at its victim's eyes; it can "spit" up to 8 feet with almost pinpoint accuracy, and the highly corrosive venom blinds the victim unless it is immediately washed away.

The cobra may be the only snake that seeks out humans to attack. Most snakes and other animals avoid contact with humans at all costs, and attack them only when escape is blocked or in defense of their young. Cobras, however, seem to have no such avoidance instinct; rather, they have been known to seek out and follow humans before attacking them and doing so without provocation. Their actions are those of a predator hunting, and the prey is human.

The reader's main task in understanding expository material is to recognize main ideas and supporting details, to grasp the information that is being explained. Expository writing is encountered in virtually every subject in the curriculum.

The nonfiction reading materials found in textbooks from elementary school through college employ a wide variety of patterns for organizing information. The mental activity involved in comprehending a passage written in one pattern is different from the activity involved in comprehending a passage written in a different pattern.

We can demonstrate this point by considering the questions we should ask for each pattern. See Table 4.2.

Research has shown that good readers are aware of differences in the way text is structured and that they respond to these differences appropriately. Poorer readers tend to treat all kinds of text the same (Marshall and Glock, 1978–1979; Danner, 1975; Meyer, 1975; Taylor, 1980).

Teachers can do their students a real service by helping them recognize text structures and adjust their reading to each one. More specifically, teachers should (a) make sure children have regular exposure to a variety of text structures as early as second grade on up and (b) call their attention to the organization of prose and guide their response to different kinds of organization by asking appropriate questions (see Chapter Five for relevant procedures).

The Structure of Stories

Stories have structures, too. In fact, the structure of stories is more complex than any nonfiction. Let's look at this structure in more detail in the following story:

Table 4.2 Questions used to discern organizational patterns of text

ORGANIZATIONAL PATTERN	TYPE OF QUESTIONS
Taxonomy	What kind of thing is X? What defines it as such? What varieties of X exist?
Chronological	What happened first? What happened next? What did these events lead to?
Cause-Effect	What caused X? What were the effects of X?
Comparison-Contrast	How are X and Y alike? How are they different? How are X and Y related to Z?
Direction Sequences	What do I do first? How do I do it? What do I do next?
Expository-Explanatory	What is the main idea? What supports that idea?

SOURCE: From Jean Wallace Gillet and Charles Temple, *Understanding Reading Problems: Assessment and Instruction*. Copyright © by Jean Wallace Gillet and Charles Temple. Reprinted by permission of Little, Brown and Company.

THE DOG AND HIS SHADOW

Once there was a big brown dog named Sam. One day Sam found a piece of meat and was carrying it home in his mouth to eat. Now on his way home, he had to cross a plank lying across a running brook. As he crossed the brook, he looked down and saw his own shadow reflected in the water beneath.

He thought it was another dog with another piece of meat and he made up his mind to have that piece also. So he made a snap at the shadow, but as he opened his mouth the piece of meat fell out. The meat dropped into the water and floated away. Sam never saw the meat again.

— McConaughy, 1980, p. 158

The story of Sam, short as it is, nonetheless has all of the structural elements we expect in a simple story, and it has them in the right order.

It begins with a *setting*, in which a character is introduced in some place at some time:

Once there was a big brown dog named Sam. One day, Sam found a piece of meat and was carrying it home in his mouth to eat. Now on his way home, he had to cross a plank lying across a running brook.

Next in the story comes an *initiating event*, which is either some occurrence or some idea that strikes someone and sets events in motion in the story, or that causes some important response in the main character:

. . . he looked down and saw his shadow reflected in the water beneath.

As a result of the initiating event, the main character has an *internal response*:

He thought it was another dog with another piece of meat . . .

He then sets a *goal*:

. . . and he made up his mind to have that piece also.

In order to achieve the goal the main character makes an *attempt*, some overt action to reach the goal:

So he made a snap at the shadow . . .

and this attempt has an *outcome*:

. . . but as he opened his mouth, the piece of meat fell out. The meat dropped into the water and floated away.

Following the attempt and outcome, there is a *consequence*; that is, some new action or situation results from the character's success or failure to achieve the goal:

Sam never saw the meat again.

There may be a *reaction* — an idea, an emotion, or some further action that indicates the main character's feelings about achieving or not achieving the goal, or a response that relates the events of the story to some larger set of concerns. *The Dog and His Shadow* did not include a reaction, but if it had, it might have looked like this:

(Sam was indeed a sadder and wiser dog!)

or like this:

(A steak in the mouth is worth two in the brook!)

Taken together, the elements of stories and the order in which they are presented are sometimes called a *story grammar*, because the elements in stories can be combined in some patterns but not others and in ways that remind us of sentence grammar, which also arranges words in certain orders but not others. A schematic rendering of the structure or grammar of stories like "The Dog and His Shadow" is found in Figure 4.1. The grammar we just saw might be made more elaborate by making provision for *episodes* in it.

Episodes exist when a story is made up of more than one series of attempts and outcomes, as when the main character tries first one method to achieve the goal, but fails; tries another method but also fails; then tries another method

Figure 4.1   A diagram of the structure of "The Dog and His Shadow"

Story = Setting + Initiating Event →

Goal → $\left\{ \begin{array}{l} \text{Attempt} \rightarrow \text{Outcome} \\ \text{Attempt} \rightarrow \text{Outcome} \\ \text{Etc.} \end{array} \right\}$ → Consequence (→ Reaction)

Key: = means "is made up of"
    → means "causes or leads to"
    { } mean "choose one or more of the enclosed elements"
    ( ) mean "you may choose or omit the enclosed element"

and finally succeeds. Such is not the pattern of *The Dog and His Shadow*, but it is the pattern of a great many other stories. When we consider the addition of episodes, and the interaction of more than one principal character, each having a goal, then even so-called simple stories like *Three Little Pigs* can be shown to have a fairly complicated structure. Most children come to school with an inner awareness of these structures — that is, they already have in their minds a very complicated and yet orderly idea of what stories should be like. Thus when they hear a reader or storyteller mention a time and place early in the story, they register these elements as comprising a setting. When a person or idealized animal is mentioned, they put this being down as the main character, and so on (Stein, 1978; Rumelhart, 1975; Thorndyke, 1977; Mandler and Johnson, 1977).

Where do they get this knowledge? Mostly from being read to, it would seem, although there is little research to inform us on this point. Television contributes some of this understanding but not very much. If we think of story grammar as the ability to recognize the story elements when they are stated *verbally*, then a glimpse at the TV shows children like will show that relatively few of these elements are developed in words. The focus is on plenty of action, with the internal response, the goal, and the reaction being communicated only by gestures or implied in actions.

There is more to stories than story grammar, just as there is more to language than sentence grammar. Without an appreciation of structure, however, readers cannot tell how all the elements fit together and they will miss the significance of much that goes on in stories.

It is therefore worthwhile to help develop an appreciation of story structure, especially if there are children in the class who have not been read to extensively. There are many ways to do this. Foremost, of course, is to read to them frequently, using rich and interesting stories (as well as text with other kinds of structures). Questioning techniques that require them to make predictions about outcomes are valuable. See particularly the Directed Listening-Thinking Activity described in Chapter Three. Writing stories, and discussing each draft as children write them, is another way to approach the question of story structure (see Chapter Seven). Making up new endings for stories, or changing early events and discussing how later portions of the story would likewise change, are also good activities (see Chapter Five).

Children's Literature

Before we close this discussion of the process of reading and the structure of text, we should make a few comments to balance our approach to literature. What we have said thus far has been derived mainly from psychological and linguistic studies, which are interesting and important, but they leave us wanting more: Neither psychology nor linguistics offers a sufficient account of what we enjoy about literature, or what its value is to the human soul and mind. Both can answer technical explanations of what happens when we read, but they stop well short of explaining *why* we read, and what reading does for us on the broader scale of human values.

The Development of Children's Literary Habits

Not all societies in the world have written literature, but in those that do, literature holds a special fascination for people from toddlerhood to old age. Little ones enjoy the reading session as a time of closeness with a parent or older brother or sister. They are comforted by the sound of the reader's voice and fascinated by the rise and fall of it, the speeding up and slowing down, the rhythm and drama of the story or poem being read. Children who cannot yet talk or understand much in the way of speech will sit enthralled as a story is read — but they will not hold still if you read the newspaper! There is some very fundamental attraction in the sound of stories and in the meeting of a book and a reader that takes hold very early on.

Before they are even out of the babbling stage, these budding readers will open a book, turn the pages with the palms of their hands, and chant sing-song nonsense at each page. By ages three and four they have favorite books that they delight in hearing again and again (woe be unto the reader who leaves out a word!). In kindergarten, where the teacher reads to the children, they have the opportunity to act out scenes from the stories in skits or in puppet shows. For many children these are not new experiences, though they are delightful ones. Youngsters of three or four who have favorite stories like to act them out in skits or perform them in puppet shows at home. This is spontaneous activity; parents usually don't have to instigate it, though they are called upon to be the audience. (When after much persuading the parents drop what they are doing and sit down to watch the play, the children become convulsed with giggles and run around the room in very active disorganization. Imagining and planning the play are valuable activities for children, but performing it for others is beyond them and need not be insisted upon.)

For some children, the books read to them in kindergarten will be their first. When we compare the hundreds of hours of literary exposure other youngsters have had to these children's lack of it, we see that this group is at a serious disadvantage. Kindergarten and first-grade teachers can and do have an enormous influence in the development of reading habits. In a very real sense, they can save those who would be indifferent to reading otherwise.

In first grade, children are faced with the task of learning to read for themselves what they used to rely on others to read for them. This is a time of both reward and frustration. The sense of competence and independence that comes with being able to read is exhilarating, but the gap in substance between the books they are accustomed to hearing and those that they are able to read for themselves is frustrating. If adults stop reading to children at this point, then the children, cut off from hearing good literature and mocked by their inability to read interesting works for themselves, may lose interest in literature altogether. The best course of action is to continue involving them in literature by reading to them, while seeing to it that the material they are given to read is as substantive and real as their reading skills permit. Trade books they have already had read to them, highly predictable books like Bill Martin's *Instant Readers*, and books that they and their classmates have dictated are good bets. For children whose interest in literature has been nurtured right along, it is astonishing how rapidly they can become able to read substantive books in which they are interested. It is not unusual to find an enthusiastic child in the latter part of first grade charging through a book that is considered sixth-grade level.

Many authors have noted a fairly predictable progression in the kinds of literature that appeal to children of increasing age. Sara Lundsteen has observed that as children mature, they are attracted first to literature that encourages them to fantasize, then to explore, then to identify with animals, then to identify with heroes, then to have models, and finally to have vicarious experiences (1978, p. 184). She further suggests that teachers accommodate children's developing abilities, needs, and interests in the following ways:

1. When children are developing a sense of humor, you should introduce them to books with incongruous situations, slapstick, surprise endings, and play on words (such as Sesyle Joslin's *What Do You Say, Dear?* (San Francisco: Addison-Wesley, 1958) and *What Do You Do, Dear?* (San Francisco: Addison-Wesley, 1961), two books that provide great fun by telling children how they should behave in outrageous situations; or *The King Who Rained*, by Fred Gwynne (New York: Messner, 1981), whose illustrations show how children might interpret some adult expressions: "Mommy's playing bridge" has a picture of Mommy stretched out stiff between two sofas with people walking across her.

2. As children become able to sustain attention in a book for longer periods of time, the teacher should set aside some time for independent reading and also see to it that each child has a book handy to read during the moments of free time between activities — even students who rarely finish other activities early. For this reason the whole class reading time, sometimes called USSR (Uninterrupted Sustained Silent Reading), is a good idea.

3. By third grade, children begin to form intense — if ephemeral — friendships and are very much subject to influence by their peers. This is a good time to have them discuss their favorite books in class, to read selected passages from them, and to act out some of the plots as a group enterprise. Sharing books in this way capitalizes on peer influences to encourage reading and also makes reading something less of a solitary exercise.

4. After age seven or eight, children become less egocentric in their interests and points of view. They begin to take more notice of other people's lives and not just theirs and their parents'. They also achieve a more realistic perspective on where their lives fit in time and space in relation to people who live in other countries or have lived in other periods of history. This is a suitable time to introduce biographies, stories with strong central characters, and existing stories from other times and places.

5. In the upper elementary grades, children become able to approach the same problem in different ways and recognize that a piece of literature they are reading could have begun or ended another way, or have been written in another form, such as a newspaper article or a play or a poem. When this stage is reached, they can begin to examine literature from different points of view and begin to notice why authors have characters do what they do, why they use certain images and certain words. They can practice rewriting a story as a play, or a news article as a story. They can read several biographies of the same person and decide why one is more effective than others. If they are writing extensively themselves, they may begin to recognize choices authors make and conventions authors use.

Qualities of Literature That Appeal to Children

As children grow in reading ability the variety of books available to them widens considerably, and there is a phenomenal variety available these days. Fictional and nonfictional works abound on a multitude of topics. Books not often seen in previous generations include folk tales from African and Latin-American cultures, as well as realistic stories about the problems of young people — especially of urban children, children who are members of minorities, and children who are coping with sobering problems such as confrontations with drugs or the divorce of their parents. In Chapter Five we list sources of reviews of books for children and discuss ways of staying current with the available literature. For now, we can list a handful of qualities that seem to keep students reading in general and coming back to certain authors in particular.

Broadening and Deepening Experience. Children and adults read literature because it enables them to have experiences in their imaginations that they

could rarely have in real life. What comes immediately to mind here are books about children in magical circumstances such as the Oz books or about children who are heroes in what are normally adult ways, such as the young detectives in the Nancy Drew stories, the Hardy Boys, or Encyclopedia Brown. If children read only to indulge in fantasies or to get momentary excitement, however, most of us begin to suspect that they are underusing their reading ability. As parents and teachers, we want at least some of their recreational reading to teach them something too. Perhaps their reading can introduce them to characters who come to understand themselves better in the course of the book and hence help the readers to understand themselves better too. Perhaps it can show them characters who are suffering undue hardship and yet find the resources to triumph over them. Perhaps it can present characters who learn important moral lessons about love and devotion, about courage, and right and wrong.

"Reading helps you get to know people better. People are *clearer* in books than they are in real life. Books tell you what other people are thinking, so later you can kind of tell what people you meet must be thinking, too." Thus says Anna Brooke, one very good fourth-grade reader. She likes E. Nesbitt's works, C. S. Lewis' Narnia books, the Moomintroll books, and books by Madeleine L'Engle. She has read all of them several times. She likes the stories and the exotic goings-on, but she also wants to understand and appreciate the people and events in her own life more fully. When we say that literature broadens the experience of children, we should not forget that it can deepen their experience too.

Readers seek not only the novel and exotic but also those works that will give them insights they can use in their own lives. Perhaps this explains the popularity of books like *Tales of a Fourth Grade Nothing* by Judy Blume (New York: Dell, 1981) or *The Cat Ate My Gym Suit* by Paula Danziger (New York: Delacorte, 1974) and other currently popular books that describe with insight and humor the lives of typical modern children. In fact, stories that are too far removed from a child's own experiences have little appeal. If children are to get to know other times, other lands (or other neighborhoods) through reading, then such stories must have a young protagonist in the story with whom they can identify. Even then, however, they might pass over such books on their own, if the teacher or librarian did not first arouse their interest by reading them the beginnings of these works aloud in class or in the library.

Getting to Know Interesting People. Despite the appeal of the current wave of realistic books for children, many young readers are still drawn to such old standbys like *Jane Eyre*, *Treasure Island*, and *The Secret Garden* and are often willing to put up with intimidatingly strange vocabulary in order to get through them. Why? Anna Brooke, our fourth grader, says it is because she finds the characters in them interesting. They are richly drawn. They face debilitating problems and overcome them by cultivating and relying on qualities of strength, courage, intelligence, and steadfastness. Anna Brooke and other children admire these characters and want to be more like them. Reading books with solid, admirable characters is like knowing good people — people who by their examples show youngsters ways to act and qualities to strive for in their own lives.

Appreciating Rich Language. The language of books is strangely transparent to children. It is rare to hear them say they like a certain book because of the words the author uses, or even to comment on the language at all. Nevertheless, the language of literature certainly has an effect on children. Sometimes it shows up in their speech: "Mother, I'm *dreadfully* hungry!," says a third grader. Sometimes it shows up in their own writing (see Figure 4.2).

Figure 4.2   The language of books shows up in children's writing

---

FUR SEALS

Black and brown like Ebony,
Flippers like Dragon wings,
Claws hidden ingeniusly,
that very seldom sting.
  Eyes so large and innocent,
Disarming, seem to say,
"May I have your kind consent
to go on out to play?"

— Anna Brooke, Grade 4

PINK

The inside of a bunny's ear
  Happy
The tip of a strawberry
A carnation
A spring rose
Pink
Happiness glows

— Jessica, Grade 3

At the same time, the language children acquire from their reading has a sort of cumulative effect: It enables them to read and enjoy more and more sophisticated literature. It is another prime benefit that they gain from reading well-written books. Like the substance, and the characters, literary language is something children must become accustomed to. Teachers and parents should take the initiative in introducing children to books with rich language so as to arouse their interest and induce them to read on their own.

Literature Study in the Elementary School

Literature in the high school is serious business. Students read selected works and learn to subject them to painstaking analysis. Should our approach to literature in the elementary school become more like this? A review by Sloan (1976) of expert writing on this question found that most authorities on elementary school literature recommend exposing children to literature and encouraging them to read it but not studying it systematically. Other authorities have observed that elementary-aged children learn much that is of a serious nature and wonder if a more systematic and serious approach could be taken to literature in the elementary years.

There are some problems, however, with the idea that serious literature study can be pushed down into the elementary years. These problems lie primarily in the nature of a child's thinking in the elementary years. Arthur Applebee (1978) has found that children think about literature in a manner quite different from older students. Probably the most fundamental difference is the way they understand fiction. When Applebee asked groups of six- and nine-year-old children if it were possible to go and visit Cinderella, some two-thirds of the six-year-olds agreed that, provided transportation could be found, it could be done. One nine-year-old in ten still agreed. Certainly in order to conduct any analysis of literature we would have to be able to assume that our students firmly sensed the difference between fact and fiction.

Even when children do recognize that Cinderella and similar characters never existed, they may not approach a piece of literature the same way older students do. We asked a third grader to think of a different ending for a book she had read several times. Although she had long since demonstrated that she knew the story was not literally true, she was horrified at the suggestion that it was made up, that it could be changed around by someone else. To her this was like suggesting that she redesign a friend. Surely any analysis of literature must presuppose that the students recognize that literature is the product of an author's imagination and craft.

Clearly, if the goal of literature is to have children analyze works of fiction, then it seems that at least until fifth or sixth grade this effort is not going to be very successful.

A more realistic goal is to expose children somewhat systematically to different kinds of literature. This approach takes its impetus from the work of Northrup Frye, a Canadian literary critic. Frye has addressed himself to the large question of what literature is, and what it contributes to human life, and he has also written about approaches to literature in the elementary and high school.

Frye's thesis is that experience with literature can be cumulative — that is, what we read this year can enable us to get more out of what we read next year. This is so, Frye believes, because all of literature is actually one large fabric, constituting the great story of humanity. This story begins with humankind in a position of wholeness and tranquility, and a spirit of unity with one another and with nature. Then comes a fall from this idyllic state, followed by the struggle to regain the lost state of serenity. The story has more details, of course, but the point is that some aspect of the story seems to be the theme of most literature, according to Frye. Christians and Jews will recognize this as the story of the Bible, though as Frye points out, versions of the story appear in non-Judeo-Christian cultures as well.

Frye's theory is sometimes called the theory of the *archetypal plot*, since he believes that all literature is a set of variations on one central story. While for pedagogical reasons Frye acknowledges that it can be instructive to read bad or mediocre literature as well as good, he does maintain that certain works are essential for a reader to know in order to understand not only the archetypal plot but also many of the allusions and references that are repeated throughout much of literature. Features of the archetypal plot in some literary works come closer to the surface than in others, and hence these works can be especially helpful in interpreting other works of literature. At the top of Frye's recommended list for reading in elementary school are stories from the Bible, followed by Greek, Roman, and the Norse mythology, then folk tales. Frye feels that English and German folk tales are most central to the western literary tradition, but we would certainly suggest using African, Hispanic, Oriental, and other folk tales because of their contribution to an appreciation of other cultures as well as for their literary benefits. For more on Frye's theory, see the listings of his works and also of a book by Sloan at the end of this chapter.

When we consider literature as a unified whole and appreciate the cumulative quality of reading, then it becomes apparent that elementary teachers can make an important contribution to children's literary growth by exposing them to folk tales, myths, and perhaps to Bible stories in the course of their other reading. Specific techniques for working literature into the elementary school language arts program are found in Chapter Five.

Poetry as Literature

Poetry is a form of literature that appeals naturally to children. There is a directness and expressiveness about it that is close to their own language. An appreciation of poetry is worth nurturing and maintaining for its own sake. Moreover, as we shall see, it can carry over both to an appreciation of other forms of literature and to the ability to write clearly.

Rhythm and Movement

The sound of poetry, the rat-a-tat-boom-boom-boom probably accounts for much of its initial charm to children and its lingering popularity with adults. You can move to it: You can skip rope, move your body, and tap your feet. It is more memorable for the rhythm: Think how much more quickly we can memorize a verse from a song or poem than we can a paragraph of prose. Poetry is more pronounceable too. We once taught a first-grade child who was very late in developing language. Her dictation was two or three words per utterance and she could not echo-read successfully; that is, she could not repeat lines after the reader. Her greatest success was in echo reading with lines of verse from Bill Martin, Jr.: "Brown bear, brown bear, what do you see? I see a redbird looking at me" (Martin, 1970, pp. 1–3). She could not fit in all of the words, however, until she was told to clap her hands to the rhythm of the poem; then she got the whole thing.

The rhythm of poetry helps us when we write prose, since good prose has a rhythm to it too. Even if we do not write poetry, our prose can be made more readable if we develop an ear for sounds in language, and the ear is developed most directly by listening to poetry.

Assonance and Consonance

The same also goes for the other sound qualities of poetry. Aside from rhyme, which modern poetry may not have, the device of matching up consonant sounds (called *consonance*) and matching up vowel sounds (called *assonance*) is another often-used means of manipulating sound to good effect. It is used by prose writers, sometimes without their even being aware of it. Note how T. H. White has used both in this passage from *The Once and Future King*:

> The boy slept well in the woodland nest where he had laid himself down.
>
> . . . At first he only dipped below the surface of sleep, and skimmed along like a salmon in shallow water, so close to the surface that he fancied himself in the air.
>
> — 1966, p. 27

Concrete Language

Poets favor concrete and simple words, and they would rather conjure up a vivid image of real things than to express an abstraction in words. In prose writing too an image conveyed in concrete words is often an effective way of expressing an abstraction. Note these lines by Henry David Thoreau, introducing his book, *Walden*:

> I do not propose to write an ode to dejection, but to brag as lustily as chanticleer in the morning, standing on his roost, if only to wake my neighbors up.
>
> — 1854/1962, p. xvii

In fact, many style manuals for writers make this point deliberately. Note this advice from Strunk and White:

> 16. *Use definite, specific, concrete language.* Prefer the specific to the general, the definite to the vague, the concrete to the abstract.

A period of unfavorable weather set in.	It rained every day for a week.
He showed satisfaction as he took possession of his well-earned reward.	He grinned as he pocketed the coin.

> — Strunk and White, 1979, p. 21

Children and poets agree on this point: Both prefer images and concrete language to abstractions and vague concepts.

Metaphor and Simile

The logic of poetry is not very difficult, Frye notes. *A is like B*; *A is B*. These are the two common propositions made in poems. They are comparisons of one thing to another, sometimes proposing that one is like the other, sometimes saying that one *is* another. The first is a *simile* and the second is a *metaphor*. Both give poetry much of their power, and they too come naturally to children. Children, especially young ones, often find the need to make up a new term for a novel thing or event. The three-year-old daughter of one of the authors had been around woodcutters most of her life but not motorcycles. The first motorcycle she heard underway she named a "chainsaw bicycle." It is only a small jump from there to see what Carl Sandburg meant when he wrote, "The fog comes in on little cat feet."

Metaphors and similes are two of the means through which language can grow and stretch. When Nixon's men decided to "stonewall it," their term was a metaphor meaning that they would form a barrier around the president as uncommunicative as a stone wall. Even the word "barrier" in the previous sentence is a metaphor, because the men were not physicially obstructing access to the president but only figuratively denying access to his secrets. Our appreciation of metaphors and similes in the newspaper, on television, and in everyday speech can be deepened by our experience with poetry.

Summary

Thoughtful teaching begins with a clear idea of what we want students to learn. Before considering methods for teaching children to read (the subject of Chapter Five) we have considered in this chapter what the process of reading and the materials of reading are like.

To begin, we find that the act of reading itself consists of moving the eyes across the page in a staccatto fashion comprised of *saccades* (jumps) and *fixations* (rests). We perceive text during the fixations. The eye transfers visual data to *short-term memory storage*, from where it is either transferred to *long-term memory* or lost. Curiously, the human perceptual system can accommodate about five items per fixation, but the amount of information in a single item can be enlarged greatly through the process of *chunking*: clustering data together into meaningful groups. Speed and efficiency in reading depend in part on past experience, which is what provides the basis for chunking, and partly on a willingness to seek larger bites of information as we read.

Although reading is a unified process, there are at least four identifiable *stages of reading development*: *prereading, beginning reading, early mature reading,* and *later mature reading.* This stage is the province of well-developed readers in late high school and adulthood and is outside the focus of this book (see Adler and Van Doren, 1972, for an illuminating discussion of this stage). Prereading, sometimes called reading readiness, is the stage where children develop prerequisites for learning to read. Those that we discussed in this chapter were *elaborated oral language* (including knowledge of word meanings, developed syntax, and a familiarity with what Basil Bernstein calls the elaborated code), *story language* (familiarity with the language, conventions, and structure of stories), *cognitive clarity* (an understanding of what reading is for, and of the meaning of the terms used in reading instruction), and the *concept of written words* (which includes both the realization that words are divisible units of language and that words are represented in print as left-to-right configurations of letters bounded by spaces on either end).

Beginning reading, the next stage, usually begins in late first grade and has its own set of requisite achievements. Among these are the acquisition of *sight words* (words that have become so familiar to children that they can recognize them instantly — not to be confused with *basic sight words*, which are lists of high-frequency words that some authors recommend for rote teaching), skill in *word analysis* (the ability to recognize structural similarities between words and to use this knowledge to recognize unknown words), a *conception of fluent reading* (the understanding that reading should not be a labored word-by-word process but a more relaxed, meaning-oriented activity), and *reading by grammar and meaning* (in which children use the syntax and meaningful or semantic context of a passage to help them read more efficiently).

The next stage, the last to be discussed in this book, is *early mature reading*, which usually begins between second and fourth grade and lasts through the rest of the elementary years. Early mature reading marks a turning point in children's education, since it is here that they stop focusing so much on learning to read and begin to use reading to learn other subjects and for recreation. Two important achievements of this stage are *learning vocabulary from text* and *learning to think in larger information structures*. Because students learn most of their new vocabulary from reading, it is essential that they develop effective strategies for identifying the meanings of new words from the explicit or implicit cues supplied by authors. A number of these cues were described in the chapter. The other important ability that develops during this stage, thinking in larger information structures, means that children can use their own experiences (stored in *schemata*) to interpret the meaning of text. Most schemata relate to the nature of things and events in the world, but another important set consists of a familiarity with different structures of text: *taxonomy, chronology, cause and effect, written directions, explanation or exposition,* and *stories*. Each of these structures requires different kinds of comprehension on the reader's part; students who can accommodate themselves successfully to these text structures are better readers.

The process of reading and the structure of text do not explain why people read or what literature means to people. A discussion of *literature* itself is needed to understand these issues.

Children who are read to become fascinated with literature at a very early age — often before they can talk — and continue to grow in their awareness and appreciation. Learning to read, however, can interrupt their aural appreciation of literature unless teachers keep reading to them aloud.

The kinds of literature that appeal to children and the qualities they look for in books and stories change as they develop, but in general they benefit from *vicarious experience, well-drawn characters,* and *rich language*.

Approaches to the study of literature in the elementary school usually center on focusing fluent reading exposure to and appreciation of literature. Northrup Frye's recommendation, however, is that children be systematically exposed to works that shed the most light on our literary traditions, among them Bible stories, myths, and folk tales.

Finally, *poetry* has a special appeal to children and can be appreciated for its *rhythm and movement*, its *sound* (especially *assonance* and *consonance*), its concrete language, and its comparisons (*metaphors* and *similes*).

In the next chapter we will put these concepts to work in a discussion of methods for teaching reading and literature.

CHAPTER FIVE

Teaching Reading
and Literature

CHAPTER OUTLINE

In this chapter we discuss a wide variety of practices and procedures for teaching reading and literature in language arts: teacher-directed and student-directed activities; strategies for group and independent work; methods of using basal readers, content-area materials, student-selected trade literature and non–book materials like newspapers, magazines, catalogs, and brochures; and projects involving writing, art, dramatics, and role playing.

We also discuss principles and methods of assessing progress and diagnosing problem areas, supporting poor readers in the classroom, integrating children's literature into the reading program, and finding sources of information about children's literature and non–book materials.

Our primary goal in this chapter is to help you develop practical strategies for integrating literature into the reading program, deepen your students' understanding and appreciation of literature, and extend reading instruction into content-area subjects with a wide variety of methods and materials. We believe that children should read widely and use many types of text, not just commercial reading materials; that they should be challenged to think critically and respond sensitively to literature as well as to master reading skills; that they should read self-selected materials for pleasure as a routine part of the language arts program; and that they should be actively involved in writing, speaking, and listening in reading instruction.

This chapter begins with discussions of the basic aspects of reading ability treated in Chapter Four — word recognition, word analysis, comprehension, and reading fluency — and then describes activities and procedures to help your students develop and refine these skills. Because group discussions are typical activities in every language arts program and classroom, several types of group discussion procedures are addressed, followed by activities to help your students develop specific comprehension skills in groups and independently. The use of trade literature, prose, and poetry is treated in sections that deal with individualized reading programs, as well as ways to help children respond to literature critically and aesthetically and to share their reading interests, tastes, and discoveries with others.

Issues involving assessment of progress and diagnosis of common reading problems are discussed, along with methods and materials useful in determining students' strengths and weaknesses. Ways to provide extra support and involvement for poor readers are detailed. Then the discussion turns to ideas for using everyday reading materials such as newspapers, magazines, and other non–book written materials, and the chapter ends with a list of resources for locating these types of materials.

Developing Word Recognition

Word recognition is an important aspect of reading, because without it we cannot grasp a writer's message. Recognizing the words makes it possible to understand written language and is thus an important step toward comprehension, the real goal of reading.

We recognize some written words immediately without having to figure them out. Immediate recognition is called *sight recognition*, and the words we can recognize at sight make up our *sight vocabulary*. Words encountered during reading that are not recognized at sight must be figured out in some way, and this process is called *word analysis*. There are several ways we can help children become skilled in word analysis. Some techniques focus on analyzing words individually. Others are intended to help students polish their word recognition skills so that they can read text fluently and focus on the meaning of what they read rather than getting bogged down in analyzing one word after another.

Developing Sight Vocabulary

Many children can already recognize some words in print before they begin school. Without direct instruction or drill, they often come to recognize several dozen or more individual words. Often these words are their own names, common brand names, and words seen on traffic signs, grocery containers, and labels. Experiences like being read the same storybooks many times, looking

through magazines and newspapers with an adult, going grocery shopping and having attention drawn to words on signs, labels, and the like help make these words memorable because they are seen *frequently* and *in meaningful contexts*.

There are several classroom activities that can help children recognize words at sight by providing both frequency and meaningful context.

Dictated Experience Stories. Dictated stories are a part of the language experience approach to beginning reading (Allen, 1976; Hall, 1981; Stauffer, 1980). The stories are told by the children to an adult, who writes down the children's words verbatim. They can be dictated by individuals or small groups in collaboration. The completed stories are read aloud many times until they are memorized and individual words and phrases can be identified at sight both in and out of story context.

In a dictated story a child's natural language is preserved by verbatim transcription. You can add a word here or there to complete thoughts or sentences, but extensive modification implies that the children's language was incorrect or inferior and quickly stifles their desire to participate. The greatest value of dictated stories lies in the repeated rereading, which enables children to immediately recognize their own words when they see them in print.

Box 5.1 shows the steps in producing a group dictated story. Here are two example stories:

BOX 5.1
Using a Dictated Experience Story

1. Provide a concrete stimulus or topic: an interesting object, photograph, storybook or poem, a guest speaker, field trip, etc. Encourage students to bring things that they can talk about.
2. Guide the children in discussing and describing the topic, so they have plenty to say about it.
3. Tell students you will help them write the story.
4. Ask volunteers to provide sentences about the topic; ask questions if necessary to help them structure sentences.
5. Print what they say verbatim on a chart tablet or sheet of newsprint so all can see it. You can add a word here or there, but preserve their vocabulary and syntax.
6. Read the completed story aloud once, pointing to the words as you read. Read at a natural rate.
7. Lead the children in choral reading three or four times through. Continue pointing to words as you do this.
8. Ask volunteers to read and point to words and sentences they know. Continue choral and individual readings over several sessions until the story is memorized.
9. Give each child a duplicated copy of the story to illustrate, reread, and collect in individual folders.

THE FIRE STATION

Tonya said, "We went downtown to the fire house."
Mike said, "We got to climb on the engines."
Marylou said, "They turned on the siren and we had to cover our ears!"
Tommy said, "They lined up their boots and raincoats by the engines."
Sherman said, "We saw where they sleep and they have a big pool table."

GOING TO THE FIRE STATION

It was a fun trip. They showed us how they slide down the pole. They put out fires and do first aid. They have a thing that pulls smashed cars apart. The new engines are yellow instead of red.

In the first story the teacher repeatedly wrote the phrase "_____ said" and used quotation marks. This format will help the students learn to read one another's names and to recognize dialogue. After they have mastered this format, the second story format can be used to illustrate written narrative.

The following independent activities will help them practice reading the dictated stories.

1. Provide the students with another duplicated copy of the story, cut into strips. Have them put the strips in order using the intact copy as a model. When it can be done easily, cut the story into phrase strips, then into

individual words, so that they can practice visual discrimination and matching as they complete the story.

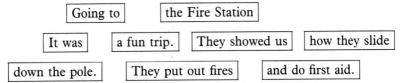

2. Use dictated stories for handwriting practice. For work on specific letter formation, have students select words containing that letter from their stories to practice writing.
3. Provide copies of dictated stories with words or phrases omitted. Students complete them by remembering the original story, or making up new elements, and writing in the blanks as well as they can.
4. Have students reread stories independently to a partner or aide.

Word Banks. Word banks are children's individual collections of words, from dictated stories and other sources, that they can recognize at sight. The word bank is the tangible representation of their growing sight vocabulary. Words recognized at sight are written on small cards and collected in recipe boxes or other durable containers. As new words are mastered they are included in the word bank. To help in remembering these words, children can:

1. Reread stories and underline words they recognize at sight. Give them blank cards to copy mastered words for their word banks. A partner or aide can check spelling.
2. Review word bank words, lay aside those not recognized quickly, and then find all those words in the stories and review them.
3. Make copies of words with letters made of sandpaper, wallpaper scraps, string glued to paper, clay, or other materials.
4. Make words with Link Letters, plastic letters, or alphabet cards.
5. Cut out different sizes of letters from newspapers or magazines and glue them on paper to form words.
6. Find sight words in newspapers or magazines, cut them out, and paste them on the back of the word bank cards.
7. Cut out magazine pictures representing word bank words, paste them on paper, and label the pictures.

Pattern Books and Rhymes. Many simple children's books have a patterned rhyming or repetitious element. These are easy to read because the pattern makes it easy to remember what comes next. There are hundreds of such books; a list of some is included in this section.

Pattern books can be treated just like dictated stories, by choral rereading, selecting words learned at sight, and rereading independently for practice.

Nursery rhymes, jingles, short poems, and song lyrics are all easy to read and are rich sources of potential sight words. They also make a nice change from dictated stories. Here are some suggested activities.

1. Use a poem as you would a dictated story: Write it on chart paper, choral-read it, and provide a duplicated copy for illustration, rereading, and word identification.

2. Use song lyrics as poetry, singing instead of reciting. Singing lends itself to fluent, rhythmic rereading.

3. Make up simple rhymes or sets of sentences containing words children should learn to recognize, such as color words, names of days and months, or cardinal and ordinal numbers. Use traditional rhymes that all children will be familiar with, like

   One little, two little, three little Indians . . .

   One, two, buckle my shoe . . .

   or make up your own like

   Red is the color of apples and stop signs.
   Yellow is the color of school buses and butter.
   Blue is the color of the sky and blue jays.
   Green is the color of grass and pickles.

   On Monday it rained all day.
   On Tuesday it was sunny again.
   On Wednesday we had a fire drill.
   On Thursday we went to the library.
   On Friday . . .

   September means going back to school.
   October means trick-or-treating.
   November means the coming of winter.
   December means holidays and giving gifts.

4. Make up new books, together with your children, by innovating on a pattern book they have read or poem they have learned. Help them supply new words following the pattern, illustrate their pages, and staple them into a book for the class library. Write the pattern on duplicated sheets or the board. For example:

   Red is the color of _____ and _____.
   Purple is the color of _____ and _____.

   or

   On Monday . . .
   On Tuesday . . .

Here are some books with patterned structures. Your librarian can help you find more.

SOME BOOKS ON PATTERNED STRUCTURES

Abisch, Roy. *Around the House that Jack Built*. New York: Parents Magazine Press, 1972.

Barry, Katherine. *A Bug to Hug*. New York: Young Scott, 1964.

Bodecker, N. M. *Let's Marry Said the Cherry*: And Other Nonsense Poems. New York: Atheneum, 1974.

——. *It's Raining, Said John Twaining*. New York: Atheneum, 1973.

Charlip, Remy. *Fortunately*. New York: Parents Magazine Press, 1964.

de Regniers, Beatrice. *May I Bring a Friend?* New York: Atheneum, 1964.

Domanska, Janina. *If All the Seas Were One Sea*. New York: Macmillan, 1971.

Einsel, Walter. *Did You Ever See?* New York: Scholastic Books, 1972.

Emberley, Ed. *Drummer Hoff*. Englewood Cliffs, N.J.: Prentice-Hall, 1967.

Frasconi, Antonio. *The House that Jack Built*. New York: Harcourt, 1958.

Joslin, Sesyle. *What Do You Say, Dear?* Reading, Mass.: Addison-Wesley, 1958.

——. *What Do You Do, Dear?* Reading, Mass.: Addison-Wesley, 1961.

Keats, Ezra Jack. *Over the Meadow*. New York: Four Winds, 1971.

Krauss, Ruth. *What a Fine Day*. New York: Parents Magazine Press, 1967.

Langstaff, John. *Soldier, Soldier, Won't You Marry Me?* New York: Doubleday, 1972.

Martin, Bill, Jr. *Brown Bear, Brown Bear, What Do You See?* New York: Holt, Rinehart & Winston, 1970.

Martin, Bill, Jr. and Peggy Brogan. *Bill Martin's Instant Readers*. New York: Holt, Rinehart & Winston, 1971.

Mayer, Mercer. *What Do You Do with a Kangaroo?* New York: Scholastic Books, 1973.

McGinn, Maureen. *I Used to Be an Artichoke*. St. Louis: Concordia, 1973.

Nolan, Dennis. *Big Pig*. Englewood Cliffs, N.J.: Prentice-Hall, 1976.

Pomerantz, Charlotte. *The Piggy in the Puddle*. New York: Macmillan, 1974.

Quackenbush, Robert. *She'll Be Comin' Round the Mountain*. New York: Lippincott, 1973.

Schultz, Charles. *Happiness Is; Security Is; Love Is*. New York: Determined Productions, undated.

Sendak, Maurice. *Chicken Soup with Rice*. New York: Scholastic Books, 1962.

Shulevitz, Uri. *One Monday Morning*. New York: Charles Scribner's, 1967.

Supraner, Robyn. *Would You Rather Be a Tiger?* Boston: Houghton Mifflin, 1976.

Sutton, Eve. *My Cat Likes to Hide in Boxes*. New York: Parents Magazine Press, 1973.

Zemach, Harve. *The Judge*. New York: Farrar, Strauss, 1969.

Zolotow, Charlotte. *Someday*. New York: Harper & Row, 1965.

Voice Pointing. This term refers to the beginning reader's ability to recite a memorized sentence, rhyme, story, or the like and accurately point to the written words as they are spoken. This skill is an important one in developing a sight vocabulary, for it helps the children to physically match spoken words and their written counterparts. Learning to voice point helps them learn what the words they are saying look like in print and where they occur on the page. It helps them become aware of the spaces between printed words, spaces that are not discernible to the ear when we say a phrase or sentence aloud. It helps students become aware of and familiar with distinctive features of printed words, such as length and component letters.

As you read dictated stories, rhymes, and other written material, you should quickly point to each word or run your hand along under the line you are reading to model matching spoken and written words. As the children choral-read, continue to do this in order to show them where they are in the writing. As they reread their own material they should practice pointing to each word, while reading at a natural speed. Be careful not to read yourself in an unnaturally slow, word-by-word fashion but rather at a natural speaking rate. As students practice voice pointing, make sure they also keep their speed up. It is very important to avoid word-by-word reading at the early stages, because it quickly becomes a bad habit.

Labels and Signs. Label items in your classroom and refer to the labels frequently. By putting labels on things rather than in lists or on flashcards, you provide the meaningful context children need to learn to recognize them.

To begin, make printed tagboard labels such as *clock, wastebasket, window, light switch, pencil sharpener,* and so forth. Read them aloud and help the children point out the named objects and then attach labels to them. Every few days, review the labels by asking, "Who can show us the sign that says *window?*" or "Who can show us the sign that tells us where we throw away scrap paper?" When the labels are learned, take some down and let the children identify the words and reattach them. Then mix them up and make a game of finding the misplaced labels and returning them to their proper places.

Have the children make bulletin board displays by cutting out magazine pictures for labeling; they name the objects as you label them. Help them group related things: Halloween items, supermarket products, colors, things that are round, and so on. Such displays help them associate names with objects, categorize things, and learn to recognize and spell words. Display them prominently, review them frequently, and add to or change them periodically.

Developing Word Analysis

Word analysis strategies are used to figure out words that are not recognized at sight. There are three strategies that can be used to identify an unknown word:

1. Context analysis, or the meaning of the surrounding words and phrases; in effect, the reader asks, "What would make sense here?"

2. Structural analysis, or the use of word parts like affixes and base words.
3. Phonic analysis, or the use of letter sounds within words.

Good readers use all three types of analysis. When reading for meaning, especially during silent reading, good readers use context and structural analysis frequently and phonic analysis less often. Unfortunately, some teachers and many reading instruction programs emphasize phonic analysis at the expense of other strategies, but all three should be taught systematically. There are a number of activities that can help develop facility with word analysis.

Context Activities. Right from the beginning children should be encouraged to ask themselves "What would make sense here?" when they encounter unfamiliar words in text. The following context activities can help them learn to use context and the sense conveyed by phrases and sentences to figure out unfamiliar words in text:

1. Read familiar material aloud to children; nursery rhymes and folk and fairy tales are good. Pause before important words or familiar phrases and allow volunteers to complete the phrases aloud.
2. Write familiar sentence patterns with pairs of predictable elements, like "Please pass the salt and _____" or "We had birthday cake and _____," on the board. Let volunteers complete the pairs aloud, then make up new, absurd pairs like "salt and scissors" or "cake and spinach."
3. Provide passages from previously read basal stories, dictated stories, and other text that is easy to read. Delete some important words and replace them with blanks. Let the students work together or alone to complete passages with words that make sense in the passage.
4. Underline descriptive words in story passages. Let students work alone or together to substitute words or phrases with similar meanings, or change the meaning by substituting opposites.
5. Ask volunteers to supply words that can have more than one meaning. Have the students work alone or together to write sentences to show the different meanings and illustrate them. Pages can be collected and bound as a book.
6. Let the children use their word banks to make up sentences by placing word cards in a row. Let them try making up rhymes and absurd or very long sentences. Have pairs select ten or so cards from their word banks and try to compose a story using all of the words, either writing or dictating.

Phonics and Structural Analysis Activities. Letter sounds and word parts can help in decoding unfamiliar words. Most commercial language arts programs put great emphasis on these word analysis skills, and they provide detailed, sequenced activities. A list of helpful books to which you may refer is included in this section.

It is important to remember that phonics is based on the sounds of letters in words. Phonics activities should be primarily oral so that sounds are clearly identifiable. Too many phonics activities are paper-and-pencil tasks, which makes them too abstract; we cannot always tell what sounds will be in words by looking only at the letters of words in print. The following activities may be helpful:

1. Introduce a new phonics skill by using auditory discrimination. Pronounce pairs of words and ask volunteers whether they have the same phonic feature: Do *pin* and *pal* have the same beginning sound? Do *salt* and *milk* rhyme?

2. Extend auditory discrimination to identifying one element in three or four that does not have a similar element: Which word does *not* begin with the same sound: *milk, boy, monster, monkey?*

3. Introduce a new letter sound by asking volunteers to supply words beginning with the same sound. (At this stage, don't confuse *letters* used with *sounds* they represent; *fox, father,* and *phone* all start with the same sound, for example, as do *cat* and *kittens.*)

4. Name an animal and make a game of finding words with the same initial sound for things the animal might eat, wear, or use: A *fat fox* might eat *french fries, frog's* legs, and *fish* and wear *flippers, feathers,* and a *football* helmet. These responses can be illustrated and posted around the room.

5. Let the students search their word banks for any words that have the same phonic feature as an example word, like the beginning sound in *hand,* the vowel sound in *pick,* or the final sound in *hot.* (Again sound, not spelling, counts here.)

6. Practice sound substitution by deleting the initial (or final) sound in a word and have volunteers supply another sound to make a new word: *Hat–cat–fat–mat* or *had–has–ham–hack.*

7. Let teams search books, magazines, and the like for as many words as they can find with a particular phonic or structural feature (like the initial sound in *man* or the same ending as *running*) in a specific amount of time. The team finding the most examples wins.

8. Give several examples of words with a particular sound feature, then have the children find and cut out magazine or catalogue pictures of things with the same feature, glue them on paper, and label them.

FURTHER READINGS ON WORD RECOGNITION AND ANALYSIS

Brogan, Peggy and Lorene Fox. *Helping Children Read: Some Proven Approaches.* Huntington, N.Y.: Krieger, 1979.

Buckley, Lillian A. and Albert Cullum. *Picnic of Sounds: A Playful Approach to Reading.* New York: Scholastic Books, 1975.

Burmeister, Lou E. *Words: From Print to Meaning.* Reading, Mass.: Addison-Wesley, 1975.

Ehri, Linnea C., Roderick W. Barron, and Jeffrey M. Feldman. *Recognition of Words.* Newark, Del.: IRA, 1978.

Forgan, Harry and Bonnie Striebel. *Phorgan's Phonics*. Glenview, Ill.: Scott Foresman, 1978.

Heilman, Arthur W. *Phonics in Proper Perspective*, 4th ed. Columbus, Ohio: Charles Merrill, 1981.

Holmes, Paul C. *Phonics Guidelines: An Introduction*. Dubuque, Iowa: Kendall-Hunt, 1980.

Hull, Marion. *Phonics for the Teacher of Reading*, 2d ed. Columbus, Ohio: Charles Merrill, 1976.

Pearson, P. David and Dale D. Johnson. *Teaching Reading Vocabulary*. New York: Holt, Rinehart & Winston, 1978.

Scott, Louise B. *Developing Phonics Skills: Listening, Reading and Writing*. New York: Columbia University Press, 1982.

Developing Reading Fluency

Because of the limits of short-term memory, reading must be fluent and fairly rapid. Comprehension of word and phrase units is impossible when the reader reads haltingly, pondering one word after another. Several classroom procedures can be used to help children read fluently and confidently, thus avoiding the habit of word-by-word reading.

Choral and Echo Reading. These are methods of *support reading*, by which youngsters practice oral reading in a more supportive setting than reading aloud alone.

Choral reading is reading aloud in unison. It helps alleviate the anxiety many children feel, and many adults can remember, about making mistakes during solo oral reading. Choral reading and rereading were discussed in relation to dictated experience stories and pattern books, but it is also an effective alternative to solo oral reading of basal stories and other text. Instead of just one student reading, several read together. The best results are achieved when you join in the choral reading and then the students reread the same passage by themselves. You have an opportunity to model fluent reading and support the students through the passage, and the students also practice rereading the material. This procedure may not be useful for long stories, but is useful for shorter prose material and poetry.

Individual oral reading has another drawback besides causing anxiety. It frequently wastes the time of those not reading. Few children "follow along" as one reads; more often they read ahead, try to figure out where their part will begin, or daydream. In a group of eight, one reading and seven waiting is a waste of precious group instruction time, but with choral reading all eight read. In fact, in such a group an individual might spend eight times as much time actually reading! If you fear that the sound of a whole group reading aloud will disturb your other students, show them how to read aloud softly.

Although at all levels oral reading should be balanced with much silent reading practice, some written material deserves to be real aloud for the beauty of its sound. Poetry and evocative descriptive material are examples of such material, and choral reading is an excellent procedure here. It can be an enjoyable experience for youngsters who would ordinarily shun it or avoid oral reading alone. Numerous choral-reading activities are detailed in the section, "Responding to Literature," later in this chapter.

Echo reading, wherein one person reads aloud a short passage and a partner echoes the reading, is useful for short passages and some poetry. The first reader must be a fluent model; the teacher, an aide or adult volunteer, or an older good reader can do this. Echoing can be done by a single student, a pair, or a small group. Thus the first reader literally shows the others how to read the material fluently. Because it can be tedious, it should not be overused, but it is useful in short sessions with difficult material or very unfluent readers.

Repeated Reading. This method (Samuels, 1979) involves reading the same material aloud a number of times to practice smooth, fluent oral reading. Each student keeps a personal chart of reading speed and accuracy over a selected passage, with the goal of reaching a particular criterion.

Repeated reading helps students develop sight recognition of words, oral reading fluency, and confidence in their reading abilities. It is not intended to directly aid comprehension, nor is it useful for children who can already read fairly fluently. It is particularly intended for unfluent readers who have small sight vocabularies and spend little time reading at all. Box 5.2 lists the steps in using repeated reading. Figure 5.1 shows a model chart, partially filled in.

The greatest value of repeated reading is not that the rate of reading a rehearsed passage improves, although this can be very motivating to the reader.

BOX 5.2
Steps in Using Repeated Reading

1. Choose, or help each student choose, a fairly comfortable, interesting selection to practice reading. It should be too long to memorize: 100 or so words for younger children, 200 or more words for older ones. Trade books and previously read basal stories are good.

2. Make up a duplicated chart for each pupil (see Figure 5.1). Omit the accuracy axis if you want to simplify the task.

3. Time each reader's first, *unrehearsed* oral reading of the passage. Mark the chart for Timed Reading 1.

4. Instruct the readers to practice the passage aloud as many times as possible for the next day or two. Let them practice in pairs, independently, and at home.

5. Time the reading again and mark the chart for Timed Reading 2, and show the students how to mark their own charts.

6. Continue timing at intervals of several days. As the rate increases for the first passage, help each child set a rate goal, say, twice as fast as the unrehearsed reading.

7. When the reader reaches the goal set, begin a new passage of equal (*not* greater) difficulty. Successive portions of a long story are perfect. Repeat steps 3 through 6.

Figure 5.1   Sample repeated reading chart

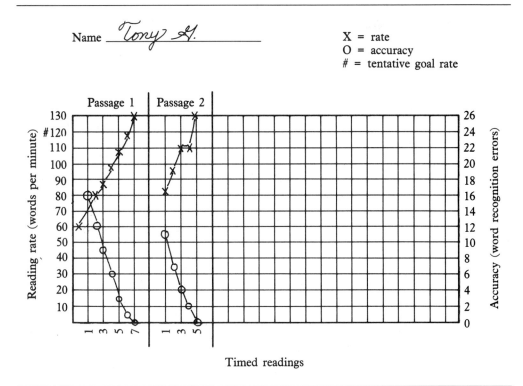

Timed readings

The real value lies in the practice youngsters get in fluent oral reading. What usually happens is that each time a child begins a new passage, the unrehearsed reading rate increases from that of the previous passage (see Figure 5.1). This improvement is likely due to practice in reading and to increased confidence.

Developing Comprehension

Comprehension, understanding what we read, is the most basic and important aspect of reading. Reading is a process of getting meaning from print, and getting meaning is comprehension. We read to understand, to get information, to share the author's ideas and experiences. Word recognition, decoding, and all other skills only *serve* comprehension, which is the ultimate goal of all reading instruction.

Comprehension instruction can take many forms, and most teachers use a variety of methods and materials. Group discussion activities and specific skill activities, which may be done individually or in groups, are widely used.

Group Discussion Activities

Probably the most common classroom comprehension activity involves a group of students who read the same material and answer teacher-initiated questions after they have read. Basal reader manuals provide directions for this type of activity and also a list of comprehension questions from which teachers can choose. Such questions should be evaluated rather than being used automatically, to ensure a proper blend of open-ended questions and evaluative information as well as closed-ended questions and factual information. Several read-and-discuss formats are available.

Directed Reading Activity (DRA). The DRA format, first described by Betts (1946), is used most often in the typical basal reader lesson plan. The DRA has five components, which can be modified to provide variety and fit students' particular needs. They are shown in Box 5.3.

A typical directed reading lesson is comprised of these steps:

1. *Readiness.* Help students to *develop concept background* by using maps, pictures, films, or realia to familiarize them with the story; examine titles and pictures for clues to the story events. *Encourage motivation* to read by discussing the author or illustrator, telling children about the story's setting, and reading an interesting passage to them and letting them share prior experiences with the group. *Preteach vocabulary* that is likely to cause difficulty by pronouncing, spelling, defining, and illustrating new words in the story. *Set reading purposes* by forming questions or statements that will guide the reading to follow.

2. *Directed Silent Reading.* Break up reading of long stories into sections; read shorter stories without breaks. Provide individual help with difficult words so that the students can focus on reading for meaning.

3. *Comprehension Check.* Guide understanding and appreciation of the story by discussion. Encourage readers to retell and summarize the story as well as

---

BOX 5.3
Directed Reading Activity (DRA) Components

Readiness for reading: prereading questioning or narrative introduction to arouse interest in story

Directed silent reading: reading successive portions of story in entirety to gain information

Discussion: teacher-initiated questions to check for comprehension

Oral rereading: rereading selected portions or locating passages conveying specific information

Follow-up: any of a variety of composition, art, word study, or further reading activities to reinforce and practice learned skills or for enrichment

to answer questions about it. Choose questions from the teacher's manual judiciously; *don't* ask them all. Use questions calling for inference, conclusions, judgments, and opinions as well as factual recall and detail. Discuss the feelings and attitudes of the characters as well as the story events. Locate and discuss pretaught vocabulary and other new words.

4. *Oral Rereading.* Instruct students to reread particular passages aloud; avoid having them reread the entire story. Have them locate and reread portions to answer comprehension questions above, and to justify their answers and illustrate their points. Encourage oral rereading of dialogues and colorful descriptive passages.

5. *Follow-Up.* Help the children to *extend and practice comprehension skills* by writing synopses or summaries, putting events in sequential order, dramatizing parts illustrating scenes, or composing alternative story outcomes. *Reinforce word recognition skills* by locating and categorizing similar words from the story, substituting synonyms or antonyms in sentences, locating base words or affixes in words, or finding words in the story that share a specified sound, spelling, or meaning feature. *Extend appreciation and enrichment* with creative writing, dramatics, cooking, art, music, or extended reading activities. Introduce related stories and poetry for pleasure reading, other works by the same author or illustrator, or other works about the same place or time period. Enrichment activities should include speaking, listening, and writing as well as reading.

Typically teachers do steps 1 through 4 in groups and step 5 as independent work, using teacher-made or commercial worksheets, workbooks, and learning centers for seatwork. With such a plan, if you had three reading groups it would take two days to complete a DRA. You would meet with each reading group each day; while you work with one group the other two groups work independently, following a cyclical plan. Thus each reading group has direct group instruction, independent practice work, and independent enrichment activities including creative writing, pleasure reading, and listening.

Table 5.1 shows a sample two-day lesson plan for a complete DRA lesson with three reading groups. In this plan, each of the groups begins a new story cycle on Monday. Group 1 begins the day by meeting with the teacher and completes the cycle Tuesday; while Group 1 meets with the teacher on Monday, Groups 2 and 3 complete independent work from the previous story and begin independent work based on the new story after they have had their group session. This staggered plan ensures that each group meets with the teacher for instruction and assignments *before* proceeding to independent work and that each group has different tasks each day. It also provides a good balance of activities and is manageable for the teacher, but it is only a skeleton: Specific types of activities for each group would necessarily take into account the strengths and needs of individual children and groups as well as general or specific curriculum goals.

Table 5.1   Sample two-day lesson plan for a DRA with three reading groups

MONDAY	GROUP 1	GROUP 2	GROUP 3
FIRST PERIOD	*Group* (new story) Readiness Silent reading Comprehension check	*Independent* (previous story) Skills follow-up activities	*Independent* (previous story) Projects Pleasure reading
SECOND PERIOD	*Independent* Skills follow-up activities	*Independent* Projects Pleasure reading	*Group* (new story) Readiness Silent reading Comprehension check
THIRD PERIOD	*Independent* Projects Pleasure reading	*Group* (new story) Readiness Silent reading Comprehension check	*Independent* Skills follow-up activities

TUESDAY	GROUP 1	GROUP 2	GROUP 3
FIRST PERIOD	*Group* Oral rereading Additional discussion Check skills work	*Independent* Additional skills follow-up Creative writing	*Independent* Complete projects Listening Pleasure reading
SECOND PERIOD	*Independent* Additional skills follow-up Creative writing	*Independent* Complete projects Listening Pleasure reading	*Group* Oral rereading Additional discussion Check skills work
THIRD PERIOD	*Independent* Complete projects Listening Pleasure reading	*Group* Oral rereading Additional discussion Check skills work	*Independent* Additional skills follow-up Creative writing

Directed Reading–Thinking Activity (DRTA). Developed by Stauffer (1975, 1980), the DRTA is a group comprehension activity that features prediction of the story events prior to reading, reading to prove or modify predictions, and the use of divergent thinking. Before reading and at selected points in the story the students are encouraged to predict possible outcomes based on prior information and what has been revealed to that point, and to use logic, induction, and knowledge of the story structures. The DRTA can increase children's motivation to read because it arouses their curiosity and involves them actively in the discussion. The Directed Listening-Thinking Activity, described in Chapter Three, is a variation of this activity.

The DRTA can be effectively used as an alternative to a DRA and also within the DRA as an alternative to the traditional directed silent reading and comprehension checking steps. This latter way of using a DRTA is particularly effective. The components of the DRTA are shown in Box 5.4.

BOX 5.4
Directed
Reading–Thinking
Activity (DRTA)
Components

Surveying and purpose setting: examining title, first illustrations, or first portion of a selection to elicit predictions about topic or plot

Silent reading of first portion of selection, stopping at a preselected place just prior to some important event, to confirm or modify first predictions

Prediction of upcoming events and reevaluation of prior predictions based on revealed information

Repetition of silent reading and prediction steps to end of selection; may be omitted if selection is short

Postreading discussion, including summary of story events and students' self-evaluation of their use of story clues and predictions

Here are the steps to follow in conducting a group DRTA with fiction:

1. Show or read the title, first illustrations, or opening part of the story. Ask questions like "What might this story be about?" or "What might happen in this story?" to elicit first predictions. Accept each one noncommittally and jot it on the board. When you have two or more different ideas, review them and direct students to silently read to the first stopping point (selected beforehand) to see if any of the predictions are confirmed.

2. During silent reading help the children with difficult words. As they reach the stopping point they should close or turn over books and *not* read ahead.

3. Ask volunteers to summarize the section just read and to point out predictions that no longer seem probable; erase them or change them on the board as students suggest new ideas. Avoid using terms like *wrong, right,* or *true*; instead use terms like *possible* or *likely*. Elicit predictions about events in the next section and press for justification of predictions. Begin reading the next section with the new predictions in mind.

4. Repeat the predict-read-prove cycle to the story's end.

5. When the story is completed, ask volunteers to summarize the whole story, put events in order, discuss the characters' motives and feelings, and review the ways the group used story information to make predictions. Add any additional comprehension questions or follow-up activities you wish.

A DRTA with nonfiction material differs in several ways from a fiction DRTA. With nonfiction, we would not ask what might happen next, since nonfiction text may be lacking in events while conveying much factual information. Instead, we would ask students to predict what information a text selection might convey and have them describe, before the reading, what they already know about the topic. These general steps can be followed:

1. Prepare your prereading questions beforehand by determining what types of information the passage contains and how it is organized. Develop a set of general questions that will help children determine what they already know (or think they know) about the topic. If you were going to read about the building of the first transcontinental railroad, for example, you might begin by asking:

— What do you think was special about the Union Pacific railway?
— Where did it begin? Where did it end?
— How long do you think it was?
— How long do you think it took to complete?
— What might the Golden Spike be? Why do you think it was important?
— What problems do you think the railway builders encountered?
— In what ways might the railway have changed the area in which it was built?

2. Have the class quickly scan the material or look at illustrations and headings if you wish. Pose your prereading questions, encouraging the students to disagree with one another and provide as much specific detail as they can. Jot their guesses on the board, accepting all noncommittally. Review predictions and begin silent reading; direct the children to watch for information they had predicted.

3. After reading have volunteers point out confirmed predictions; modify those that were not confirmed and add new information not predicted. Ask other comprehension questions and use follow-up activities as you desire.

Whether you use a DRTA with fiction or nonfiction material, you will find that it has these attractive features:

— Students themselves set reading purposes by making predictions and reading to prove or refute them.
— They generally read more actively and enthusiastically because they are more interested in finding out what happened.
— They often remember more information, even after much time has passed, after a DRTA (Hammond, 1979). One reason for this accomplishment may be their increased curiosity.

Box 5.5 lists some guidelines that will help ensure your success with DRTAs.

Guided Reading Procedure (GRP). Developed by Manzo (1975), the GRP is an intensive group discussion technique aimed at helping students develop unaided recall of text information, inferential thinking, and the ability to organize information. According to Tierney, Readence, and Dishner (1980), the GRP is most appropriate for the middle grades and above. Both fiction and nonfiction material can be used, but it is particularly useful for dealing with nonfiction text.

BOX 5.5
Guidelines for
Successful DRTAs

Accept predictions without evaluation. Predicting does not mean "guessing right," but rather coming up with possible alternatives.

Don't break up passages with too many stopping points. Three or four stops is plenty and one or two may be fine.

Have students mark stops in advance and firmly enforce the rule of not reading ahead; nobody will want to predict if one already "knows" the answers.

Encourage participation by letting students choose which of several different predictions they think is most probable if they can't think of a new prediction.

Focus on predictions rather than who offered them; comments like "Arthur's idea . . ." focus attention on Arthur rather than his idea.

Strictly avoid value terms like *right* and *wrong*; use *likely, unlikely, confirmed* instead.

Respond positively to all students' efforts to predict; predicting is risk-taking.

In this activity students read a text passage silently, then close their books and orally recall everything they can while you note the items remembered, accurate or inaccurate, on the board. Do not probe or otherwise aid recall at this point. When everything anyone can remember has been elicited, students look back to the passage to search out unrecalled information and to correct inaccuracies. Selective oral rereading can be done at this stage, and both the teacher and the class can pose questions to help find information. Then help the students organize the information they have gathered using graphic means such as outlines, charts, time lines, trees, or other ways of showing how the text is organized. Then ask comprehension questions that do not require recall of facts but rather drawing conclusions and inferences, making judgments, and applying facts to new situations. A short quiz and appropriate follow-up or extension activities complete the GRP. Box 5.6 shows the components and steps in using this procedure. Steps 1 through 5 should be done in one period as a group, steps 6 and 7 can be done independently, with step 6 following the group activity on the same day. Step 7 can extend over more than one day.

Since the GRP is an intense activity, it is most effective if used no more often than once weekly (Manzo, 1975) and only with material that is appropriate for such concentrated study. Particularly important material densely written (containing much critical information in a fairly short passage) may be appropriate. It is essential that the GRP be conducted in a supportive, positive way, with students encouraged to attempt the recall even if what they recall is later disconfirmed by the text. Otherwise, the GRP could become a task to be dreaded.

A structured approach to concept development and purpose setting can feature activities like *structured overviews* and *expectation schemes* to help students organize the old information and incorporate the new.

BOX 5.6
The Guided Reading Procedure (GRP)

1. *Preparation for reading:* Students quickly scan material, make predictions about topic, or read first few sentences to set purposes for reading.
2. *Reading and unaided recall:* Students read passage silently and close books. Volunteers provide as much information as can be recalled; teacher jots recalled items on board without evaluation or probes.
3. *Aided recall:* Students search text for un- recalled information and anything inaccur-

ately recalled. Teacher makes changes and additions to board.
4. *Organization:* Teacher and students orga- nize recalled information focusing on how text was structured. Outlines, charts, etc. are completed.
5. *Comprehension questioning:* Teacher poses questions calling for higher-level compre- hension skills such as synthesis, judgment, inference, and application.
6. *Comprehension testing:* Teacher gives a short quiz in which recall, organization, and higher-level understanding (steps 2–5) can be assessed.
7. *Application and manipulation:* This is an optional step utilizing follow-up and ex- tension activities.

Structured overviews (Barron, 1969) are diagrams that show graphically how a selection is structured and organized. They may also contain new vo- cabulary and key concepts and show visually how concepts and terms are related. These diagrams are usually made up by the teacher, who can leave blank spaces to incorporate prior information with new hypotheses. Discussion of a structured overview prior to reading can help students see the overall organization of the material and develop expectations about what they will read.

Expectation schemes (Hall, Ribovich, and Ramig, 1979) are student-pro- duced outlines or visual representations of concepts and information students expect to read about in a selection. After briefly surveying the material, they jot key ideas or statements on cards and arrange them hierarchically or in some appropriate classification scheme. Since the resulting classifications represent their prior information and tentative expectations about what they will read, there are many ways these expectation schemes can be organized. After the reading, they are rechecked and modified by adding, deleting, correcting, or changing the position of idea cards to fit the new information gathered.

Specific Comprehension Skill Activities

There are many types of activities for refining and deepening comprehension abilities and extending group discussions of the material read. They usually focus on the use of one aspect of comprehension, such as locating main ideas or placing story events in sequence rather than on developing more global understanding or appreciation of a story. Most often they are completed indi- vidually instead of in groups and are done without teacher supervision. These activities come from many sources, such as basal reader workbooks and duplicating masters, skills management systems, and commercial skills materials purchased separately from a language arts program. Basal manuals also provide numerous suggestions, and teachers make up many such activities themselves.

Used appropriately, they are valuable instructional aids, but there are two important cautions that must be observed:

1. For maximum learning, students need both teacher guidance and group interaction. If independent skill activities are overused as a management technique, students are left to work alone too much. Learning or practicing skills in isolation can deprive youngsters of the exchange of ideas and the challenge of using their skills productively for some immediate result.

2. Specific skill activities tend to partition reading-thinking processes into discrete parts, but how much can complex, interrelated processes be partitioned? Are aspects of comprehension truly separable? Probably not. Focusing too much on discrete acts can create distorted ideas of what the goal of reading is in the minds of young readers and can also contribute to their confusion or ignorance of what they are supposed to be doing or why. Such confusion certainly reduces effective performance.

Specific skill activities should never be used primarily to keep children busy or as a substitute for spirited discussion and inquiry. They should be used only to give students additional practice in areas where they need it, and to extend direct instruction and group interaction. The goal of practicing skills is always to help readers incorporate specific strategies into the integrated reading process. The following sections describe some activities that help to develop comprehension skills in specific areas.

Getting and Organizing Information. Comprehending ideas and information explicitly stated in text is sometimes referred to as *literal* comprehension, but too often literal activities call merely for rote recall. Activities that call for more than recall include:

1. selecting the best title for a passage from several choices
2. making up original titles for stories
3. locating main idea sentences and paraphrasing them
4. condensing stories or passages by rewriting them as "news items" for a newspaper
5. composing "telegrams" conveying the most important information in a passage
6. composing headlines for newspaper stories
7. putting events in proper sequence by drawing a series of pictures showing the sequence
8. putting events in proper sequence by composing a "police report," as a detective might in recording events leading up to a crime

9. rearranging scrambled sentences to create a coherent, logically ordered paragraph or summary
10. composing a written (or dictated) description (of an object, scene, or event from a story) that is detailed enough so others who haven't read about it could draw it accurately
11. composing written (or dictated) causes for effects in a passage, or the reverse.

Forming Inferences and Judgments. Comprehension of ideas that are *inferred or implied* in text requires higher-level thinking skills than literal comprehension. At this level students practice more divergent thinking, use of logic, and critical thinking skills. Some activities might include:

1. providing introductory or conclusion sentences or paragraphs for passages without them
2. predicting effects that might result from stated causes in a passage (Possible effects may be illustrated or dramatized as well as written or dictated.)
3. composing "what if . . ." situations and consequent results of them
4. predicting upcoming events from information contained in a story portion that has been read (as in a DRTA)
5. composing alternative endings for a story (including acting them out)
6. writing or dictating detailed descriptions of characters, settings, objects, or events in a passage, focusing on aspects inferred but not spelled out in the passage
7. composing "stories" describing what might happen after the conclusion of a story just read, or what might have happened before a story began
8. composing dialogue between or among characters from a story or description in which little or no dialogue occurred (This activity resembles changing a narrative to a "radio play.")
9. classifying text elements or portions as reality or fantasy, fact or opinion (Advertisements and newspaper articles can be used to introduce this process.)
10. changing a "real-life" story or passage to "fantasy" by changing human characters to talking animals, changing realistic settings to outer space or magic castles, endowing characters with magical or superhuman powers
11. writing a factual description of some real process or event (such as a sunrise, the blooming of a flower, or change of seasons), composing a fairy tale or folk tale that "explains" how or why such things happen
12. following a series of "clues" to the solution of a mystery prior to reading the solution ("Minute mysteries" are excellent for this.)
13. constructing a series of "clues" or pieces of "evidence," in writing, art, or dramatics, for other students to use in solving a mystery

Responding and Evaluating. Children learn to read critically and sensitively when they are encouraged to use their senses, emotional responses, and background experiences. They should use and develop these abilities in beginning reading as well as in upper grades. Some activities include:

1. locating specific words and phrases that communicate mood
2. elaborating brief factual descriptions by inserting descriptive words and mood-setting language
3. selecting music to accompany a story that adds to and develops the mood (Students may choose to mime story portions or prepare dramatic oral readings accompanied by music they select.)
4. illustrating text (or composing new illustrations) using abstract painting techniques, paper tearing, crayon rubbings, block prints, or other art that does not focus on representational drawing
5. representing mood or events in a descriptive passage or story using movement or mime
6. locating words and phrases that show the author's positive or negative opinions about a character or event and discussing the connotative power of certain words
7. revising a passage or description by changing words with positive connotations to negative, or the reverse (for example, changing descriptive phrases, or adding them, to make a pleasant character unpleasant or a spooky setting cheery)
8. locating and classifying words and phrases that convey sensory images in stories, descriptions, and advertisements
9. brainstorming about connotations of various brand names in advertisements and listing mental and sensory images they evoke (for example, cosmetics, toiletries, and automobile ads); experimenting with the connotative power of words by making up positive and negative new names for products; writing ads for existing products and inventing new ones
10. comparing and contrasting two or more accounts of the same material; looking for positively and negatively loaded phrases and impressions of the author's position (for example, articles from different magazines or newspapers, letters to the editor, campaign speeches, political reporting, and interviews or biographies)
11. composing fictional biographies or obituaries of story characters, people in the news, or superheroes; experimenting with ways to make the accounts sympathetic or unsympathetic toward the subject
12. listening to a story with the eyes closed and forming a mental image of a central character: describing in words or art details of the character's appearance, expressions, dress, body language, and gestures, striving for as much detail as possible
13. locating a point in a story at which a character had to choose an action, position, or belief, and then revising the story from that point on, with the character making a different choice resulting in different outcomes
14. composing a review of a book or story, with a summary of the story and specific evaluations of style, characters, plot, and dialogue

15. writing (or dictating) a letter to a story character evaluating his or her actions in the story (If the students would have acted differently, have them tell how, and what might have resulted.)
16. writing (or dictating) a letter to the author(s) or illustrator(s) of a story or book telling your opinions or feelings about the work (If the addressee is living, the students should mail their letters to the publisher.)

Additional activities for responding to trade literature are included in the next section.

Responding to Literature

Comprehension of literature involves more than the sentence-by-sentence understanding that so often passes as the aim of elementary reading instruction. Good literature consists of thoughts, images, the turn of a phrase, and glimpses of real or imaginary life. These elements speak to us when we first read them, and they return to us again and again in new clothing as our experiences in living and reading call to mind what we have read in the past. Adults who habitually read literature tell us that it gives their thoughts more interesting forms and ties the experiences of day-to-day living together with larger patterns of human and natural history. It offers counsel and encouragement to those who wonder what people were put on earth to do, and how it is to live inside someone else's skin; literature can show the way to reach out to others.

Children who make a habit of reading find companions in books. But they also find people and things that they dread. They run into some situations that are pleasant and some that are the stuff of nightmares, and in all these encounters they learn about the nature of good and evil, love and hatred, courage and cowardice, peace and violence. Youngsters who acquire the habit of reading become schooled in the story of humanity.

The highest form of response to literature is criticism, by which we mean *disciplined responding*. In young children a valid form of criticism is to listen intently to a story, giving the imagination over to it, while in an older student, criticism may be to wonder why an author chose to make a certain character do or say a particular thing.

Criticism does not mean to determine whether a work is good or bad. Criticism strives instead to find out whether or not a work can evoke a response. As Sloan (1975) suggested, it is not relevant to the study of literature to ask children whether they *liked* something they read, because most often they like what is most familiar to them. Thus the works that they read or that we read to them in order to broaden their experience with different kinds of literature often will not be works they like, simply because these works are less familiar than stories, television shows, or comic books.

Criticism does not seek to explain what a selection means. When we are teaching poetry, or stories that seem to intend to do more than entertain us, it is tempting to ask students to explain what the work means. Often what we really want the reader to do is restate some main idea or theme in explanatory language. This implies that the writer began with the message, then clothed it in another form — a story or poem, perhaps — to disguise it. Youngsters have a hard time understanding why writers would do this, instead of saying what they intended simply and plainly. Their puzzlement makes sense, since writers of course don't create stories and poetry in this way. A writer at work thinks up a poem as a poem, or a story as a story. When we want to get at the meaning of a work, we must consider its effect on us in its present form, not as a disguised restatement of a belief or message.

Criticism does not mean putting yourself into a story. When we ask students what they might have done if they were characters in a story, we invite them to react from their own frame of reference, not from that of the characters. Characters in stories act in particular ways because of their own traits, values, and circumstances. How another might have acted in a character's place takes us away from the important point: whether the character's actions were consistent with the ways the author portrayed him or her. Such questions also invite further digression from the story, as one student after another offers an anecdote from personal experience. In a very short time, the story line may be forgotten because one anecdote calls forth another, and you are faced with trying to wrestle the group back to the story.

Instead, we should focus on the story itself with questions that encourage students to discuss the characters rather than themselves, like "What kind of a person do you think So-and-So is? How do you think he or she would react to temptation? What kind of a friend do you think he or she would be?" These kinds of questions help readers stay within a story, lead them back to the story to find support for their answers, and lead to deeper, more careful reading.

Responding to Stories

Children of different ages go about the process of criticizing, or making a disciplined response to stories, in very different ways, depending on their maturity, experience, and prior exposure to literature. Across the grades, we can help children respond to stories critically if we:

1. Approach a work as a coherent whole; that is, avoid tearing a story or a poem apart in discussion or analysis.
2. Keep all questions focused on what is in the work and avoid focusing on personal feelings or real world logic.
3. Especially in the earlier grades, encourage children to respond creatively to a story or poem, rather than translating it into everyday speech.

Here, then, are several modes of responding to stories, listed approximately in the order of the ages of children for which they are suggested.

Listening Attentively to Stories. The first and most basic response children make to literature is to listen carefully when a work is read, to sway their bodies to the rhythm of the language in the story, to study eagerly the pictures that accompany it. As Henderson (1981) has observed, we can often tell which children enter school with good past experiences with literature: They are the ones who come quickly and enthusiastically to take their places when the teacher announces story time. Those who lag behind and seem disinterested need extra attention from the very beginning. We take those children in our laps, if they are still small enough, and read them a story by ourselves. We also can *tell* them a story, taking extra care to include details that they will like, and even to put them into the story as characters in order to engage their attention. All youngsters deserve to be read to at least daily, and those who do not at first respond enthusiastically challenge us to tailor special experiences with stories that will captivate them.

With most of the stories that we read, especially to young children, simply listening to the story attentively is all the response that we should seek. The natural thing is to hear or read stories and comment on them inwardly as we experience them. Being led to discuss or otherwise respond further to them is valuable only if it is done occasionally; if it is overdone it puts an unnecessary burden on the experience of hearing or reading a story. We adult readers enjoy talking over a provocative book with a friend from time to time, but if we knew we had to find something interesting to say about *every* book we read, most of us would soon get out of the habit. So it is with children. The occasional requirement to make some overt response to a story can be both enjoyable and instructive, but to do so too often detracts from the experience of reading or hearing stories.

Predicting Story Events and Outcomes. An excellent way of encouraging children to respond to a story is to stop reading or storytelling at a critical point in the story and ask for predictions of what might happen next. (Look back to the description of the Directed Listening-Thinking Activity in Chapter Three.)

Making predictions encourages children to utilize their sense of how stories work. This is not always the same as how things work in real life. In stories, most problems have solutions; such solutions may come from unlikely sources, especially in classical tales involving magic and enchantment. Students who are unable to use predictable story structures can benefit by hearing the predictions of others more familiar with stories.

Predictions are based on what is presented in the story, supplemented by the listeners' prior knowledge and experiences, thus helping them to focus on the story itself. Stating a prediction, or stating agreement or disagreement with another's prediction, helps listeners make a commitment to the story, and their curiosity and interest are enhanced. Predicting helps children develop the habits of listening attentively, using logic and reasoning, and responding actively to stories.

Illustrating Stories. A response that is both simple and creative is to draw a picture of some character or some event from a story. If you encourage students to think about what they want to put into their picture before they begin, a picture can require them to think with their "mind's eye" and translate the author's words into visual images.

Individual pictures can be done quickly. A more elaborate variation would involve a group of three to five students collaborating on a collage, montage, or diorama that depicts the story by means of its important events.

Another idea is to have each student choose a character and create a coat of arms for that character. Of course, you must begin by explaining that a coat of arms is a sort of heraldic picture with pictorial symbols of a family's heritage. The coat of arms is divided into three or four sections, each with a picture that symbolizes something important about the character or family in a story. After they have read or heard a story about a character, the children can decide what three or four symbols could show the most important things about that character, and then draw them into a coat of arms. Figure 5.2 shows an example of a coat of arms developed for Jess in Katherine Paterson's *Bridge to Terabithia*.

Students can also draw a map of the scene of a story, showing where the important events took place. Or they can design a house that a favorite character would live in, or a suit of clothes that he or she would wear. Additional activities of this type are listed in the section, "Alternatives for Sharing Books," later in this chapter.

Acting Out Stories. Acting out a story or part of it is a form of critical response. If the students can act out a sequence of a story, they demonstrate that they have internalized its events. If they can portray a character in a scene in such a way that their gestures, tone of voice, facial expression, and body language show what that character thinks and feels, then they demonstrate an understanding of the character that is more eloquent than words.

For most students, the easiest scenes to act out are the most active ones. Portrayal of actions involves an understanding of actions and sequences, but the more subtle psychological dimensions of a story can be acted out only if the students have previously learned how body movements, tone of voice, and facial expression can be used to portray a character's feelings from previous experience with creative dramatics.

Remember that the purpose of using dramatics as a response to literature is to offer children a chance to act out an interpretation of a story they have read or listened to. This purpose should set limits on the teacher's urge to tell the class how to act it out. It should also keep the skit from necessarily becoming a full-blown performance for the class next door or for Parents' Night. The point is to let the students concentrate on how the story can be portrayed, without overburdening them with the technical details of production.

Children should discuss and find alternative solutions to questions of how characters should be cast and portrayed, how much of the action should be acted out, whether dialogue or a narrator would add to the portrayals, and whether dramatic efforts must be viewed by an audience. Questions like, "How

Figure 5.2   Coat of arms for Jess, *Bridge to Terabithia*

would you act out this scene?" are fine. Children can briefly discuss their ideas, then push back the desks and try a piece of a skit without fully developing it. Of course they should often have the opportunity to take more time with a skit — once every two weeks or more often — but as a response to literature, discussing how they *would* stage a story or a scene can be a good device for criticism. Such a discussion could include the costumes the actors would wear, the best setting for the skit, the props that would be needed, and the music and sound effects that should be used. All these points require the students to think hard and imagine in detail the story they have been studying — just what criticism is for. And if a really good idea for a skit or a play should come out of such a discussion, then the class can take the time to put it on.

Dramatic Reading. When children are able to read a story without help from an adult, dramatic reading can be an excellent responding activity. Dramatic reading is oral reading that renders the dramatic potential of a story through the inflection of the voice. Such inflection includes rate (speeding the reading up or dragging it out), volume (soft or loud), tone of voice (shrill, booming, jubilant, harsh, angry, soothing, authoritative), pitch (a high voice, a low voice, a falling tone, or a rising tone), and phrasing (pronouncing each word distinctly or running them together). Dramatic reading can also include variations from formal to informal tone, as well as regional and dialectal variations of English.

The possible variations may seem daunting, but most of these features we control without realizing it. A good warm-up experience is to listen to a record of a trained reader. School and public libraries have phonograph records of professional actors reading stories, as well as films of trained persons reading favorite children's books. Children won't be able to bring all the flavor these professionals do to their reading, but such records and films serve as a model for how dramatic reading is done. Of course, you should make a point of reading with expression when you read to the children so they can gradually absorb a wider range of ways to render stories orally.

Dramatic reading can be done with key passages, dialogues between characters, or whole scenes, and parts of dialogues can be assigned to different readers. It is best if children get the opportunity to experiment with different ways to read a passage or a line before settling on a best version. You might ask several students to read the line the way they think it should sound and follow up with a discussion of ways that seem most appropriate. Groups can be asked to prepare a scene or a dialogue, and then take turns presenting their different versions to the class.

Dramatic reading requires children to respond to a work of literature while keeping them in touch with it. It invites them to sense and to portray the emotional contour of a story and render it aloud, without requiring them to find words to *describe* the tone, an abstract and difficult procedure. The more they experience dramatic reading the more meaningful an activity it becomes.

Characters' Internal Dialogues. Youngsters often seem to have troubles with the covert psychological aspects of stories, such as motives, feelings, and inner reactions to events (Mandler and Johnson, 1977). As we saw in our discussion of story grammar in Chapter Four, these psychological phenomena are important, integral parts of all stories. One way to call attention to them is through a character's internal dialogue, a private conversation a character might have with himself or herself.

All of us have "inner speech"; that is, when we are thinking over something important, we frequently put our thoughts silently into words and "say" them to ourselves mentally. Children's language is less internalized than that of adults, however; children, especially primary graders, commonly talk to themselves when faced with a dilemma or problem. To help them respond to the feelings, beliefs, and motives of a story's characters we can ask them to say out loud or to write down a conversation that a character may be having with himself or herself at that time. Such a "conversation" may take the form of a soliloquy, a letter to another, or a diary entry. Wordless picture books are a good stimulus for this activity, since interpretations depend entirely on the illustrations. Storybooks that deal particularly with facing problems and dilemmas are also good. In Madeleine L'Engle's *A Ring of Endless Light* (NY: Farrar, Strauss & Giroux, 1980), for example, how might Vicki talk out with herself her ambivalent feelings about Zach? When she discovers she can communicate telepathically with dolphins, how might she describe her feelings about her gift in a letter or diary? In Roy Ronald's *A Thousand Pails of Water*, a picture book, what internal dialogue might the young boy have as he grows more exhausted trying to keep the beached whale alive and, as he finally collapses, fearing his efforts have failed?

The conversation should be imaginative; it should be put into the words the character might really have used. Otherwise, the students are likely to find a few words that oversimplify the character's response. People are rarely just "happy" or "mad," but this is the answer many children give when we ask them to tell us how such-and-such a character was feeling at some spot in the story. The "conversation with oneself" is intended to get beyond these one-word abstractions and help students to experience and communicate some of the richness and complexity of human motives and feelings.

Writing About Stories. A number of composition activities can be used to help students respond to stories. One way to do this is to take the part of a character and write a letter to another character.

As in internal dialogues, this activity encourages children to try to use both the language and thinking a character might have used, which is a useful role-taking activity. Young children can dictate their "letters." Students of any age can use familiar folk and fairy tales to begin with: Papa Bear could write a letter to Goldilocks' parents complaining about her trespassing; Cinderella's stepmother could write a letter to her new son-in-law explaining her reasons for her harsh treatment of Cinderella. Another student could take the part of the letter's recipient and write a letter in response. Such letters involve elements of explanation, persuasion, and many other purposes for writing, many of which are discussed in detail in Chapters Six and Seven.

Another way to write about stories is to create new stories based on those already heard or read. This type of writing activity focuses more on imaginative writing. It helps children to think critically and responsively about the nature of the story's characters and the ways authors present and relate events. Two such activities are (a) to change one critical event in a story and see how things may be altered by such a change, and (b) to write a new and different outcome to a story.

Critical Discussion of Literature. All of the foregoing activities involved students in making disciplined responses to literature without requiring them to come up with abstract language to describe a work. While children can show quite a sophisticated understanding of a story through a dramatic reading, a skit, or a drawing, they may be surprisingly mute, however, when we ask them to tell us what a story is about, or what it means. We can all do a number of things well without being able to talk about them. We can dance, make up poems, and appreciate something beautiful, but if we are asked to explain exactly how we do these things we may be at a loss for words. So it can be with responding to literature.

Yet eventually we do want children to be able to talk about what they read. Most elementary school children will not advance very far in this ability, but by late elementary school they can make a beginning, and their doing so will make their experiences with literature in secondary school much more enjoyable and rewarding.

At the beginning of this section we mentioned some types of critical questions that are best to avoid — questions that deal with personal evaluations of the story or that relate the story to concerns that are outside of the story itself. Glenna Davis Sloan (1975) maintained that the best kinds of literary questions are those that call children's attention to the structure of stories while drawing on their imaginations but avoid requiring them to memorize definitions or violate a story's wholeness.

Literary questions that center on form and structure are like the following:

— Did the story end as you expected it to? How did the author prepare you to expect the ending?
— Suppose we thought of a different ending for the story. How would the rest of the story have to be changed for the new ending?
— What does the author do to get the story going? Suppose that opening were changed or removed; how would the rest of the story be changed?
— What kind of person was the principal character? Did he or she seem to change during the course of the story? How? What caused such change?
— If a particular character were removed from the story, how would the whole be changed?
— If the order of events were changed, what would happen to the story?
— If the story took place somewhere else, or in a different time, how would it be changed?
— What does the author do to create suspense, to make you want to read on to find out what happens?
— Every story writer creates a make-believe world and peoples it with characters. Even where the world is far different from your own (as in fantasy), how does the author make the story seem possible and probable?
— What signs and signals indicate that a particular story will be fanciful rather than realistic? Humorous rather than serious? Spooky or scary?
— In what ways is this story and its characters like others you know?

— Sloan, 1975, p. 78

One of the thrusts of Sloan's questions is to encourage children to begin to see works of fiction as the result of deliberate choices made by authors. This in itself calls for a certain amount of maturity. Indeed, many first and even second graders have not yet come to recognize differences between fact and fiction in what they read (Applebee, 1978). Young children may have difficulty responding to these kinds of questions, since they may believe that story characters and the things they do are real and that the stories are true accounts. Older children, however, can begin to deal thoughtfully with this type of story analysis.

Responding to Poetry

Poetry is a condensed form of literature in which thought, image, and sound come together in combinations that demand the very best from a writer's style. Since poetry may be either ignored or overly dissected in school, good experiences with poetry may be rare, but it has a timeless appeal that keeps us coming back to it. Its sound and rhythm have enormous appeal for young children, who make up verse spontaneously in their play. Literature with rhyming or rhythmic elements, one kind of poetry, is perennially popular with children. Some commercial language arts materials that capitalize on the sound and rhythm of poetry and verse are Bill Martin, Jr. and Peggy Brogan's *Sounds of Language* basal reader series (1974) and the same authors' *Instant Readers* storybook sets (1971). In these books, children's earliest encounters with reading involve them in highly rhythmic verse — verse that is either very familiar, like:

> "Happy birthday to you
> Happy birthday to you
> Happy birthday, dear Henry
> Happy birthday to you!"
>
> — Martin and Brogan, 1974, p. 10

or else verse that, through repetition and well-placed pictures, soon becomes familiar:

> "Brown bear, brown bear
> What do you see?
> I see a redbird
> Looking at me.
> Redbird, redbird
> What do you see?
> I see a yellow duck
> Looking at me."
>
> — Martin, 1970, pp. 1–5

Older children continue to enjoy the rhythm and sound of poetry, and they also begin to respond to the capacity of a poem to convey a deeply felt meaning through images, symbols, and sounds. Poems can express the shock of loss:

DARK GIRL

Easy on your drums,
Easy wind and rain,
And softer on your horns,
She will not dance again.

Come easy little leaves
Without a ghost of sound
From the China trees
To the fallow ground.

Easy, easy drum
And sweet leaves overhead,
Easy wind and rain;
Your dancing girl is dead.

— Arna Bontemps, 1963

Poem can express the lightness of gaiety:

HEAVEN

Heaven is
The place where
Happiness is
Everywhere.

Animals
And birds sing —
As does
Everything.

To each stone,
"How-do-you-do?"
Stone answers back,
"Well! And you?"

— Langston Hughes, 1947

Poems can express humor and irony:

CHESTER

Chester come to school and said,
"Durn, I growed another head."
Teacher said, "It's time you knowed
The word is 'grew' instead of 'growed.'"★

— Shel Silverstein, 1974

★ "Chester" (p. 147) from *Where the Sidewalk Ends*, The Poems and Drawings of Shel Silverstein. Copyright © 1974 by Shel Silverstein. Reprinted by permission of Harper & Row, Publishers, Inc.

Children should be surrounded with poetry and have some contact with it daily. There are as many kinds of poems as there are kinds of prose for children: straightforward and metaphoric, sad and humorous, serious and nonsensical, bitter and sentimental, predictable and startling. Poetry, like prose, should be integrated into units and topics in language arts and the content areas. Some poetry should be thought over and discussed; some should be enjoyed purely for fun; some should be read silently and some aloud in unison or in voice choirs. Poetry can add a new dimension to the study of just about anything.

Read poetry to your students at story time, just as you would prose, and sample widely from the whole range of types of poetry; only through wide exposure do children develop literary tastes and preferences. Include poetry collections in your classroom library and select from them when you read aloud. You will also want to have some comprehensive poetry anthologies and collections on hand; lists of some representative books are included at the end of this section.

We can help students enjoy and profit from poetry without necessarily analyzing a poem's meaning or structure. It is not necessary or even desirable to study most of the poetry we share with children. Much of it should be shared purely for enjoyment. When we do want to delve more deeply into a poem we can do so without enjoying it any less.

Reading Poetry Aloud. Most poems deserve to be read aloud, because they are designed to be spoken and heard in order to fully savor their qualities. Choral reading of poetry in unison, in dialogues, and in voice choirs can be challenging and effective for children.

Choral reading in unison is a very supportive activity; all can participate without the fear of making mistakes and drawing attention to themselves. Youngsters should be familiar with the sound of a poem before they try to choral-read it, so you should first read the poem aloud with good, but not exaggerated, expression. (You may want to read it aloud more than once.) Then the children should practice the poem a number of times until they can really read together. After they can read in unison they can practice using their voices to interpret the poem. This involves varying pitch, volume, and rate to create effects that augment the poem. This Mother Goose rhyme, for example, is enhanced by a rhythmic marching beat and could be read with emphasis on the "up" and "down" lines, or by beginning softly, growing louder, and then softer again as though a corps of soldiers had marched by:

> The Grand Old Duke of York
>   He had ten thousand men,
> He marched them up a very high hill
>   And he marched them down again.
> And when he was up he was up
>   And when he was down he was down
> And when he was only halfway up
>   He was neither up nor down.

Some poems and verses are effectively read aloud as *dialogues*, which means that individuals or groups take turns reading parts that respond to each other. Many familiar nursery rhymes and verses for children are framed as dialogues, and youngsters will enjoy responding to each other chorally, as in this Mother Goose rhyme:

> How many miles to Babylon?
> Threescore miles and ten.
> Can I get there by candle-light?
> Yes, and back again.
> If your heels are nimble and light
> You may get there by candle-light.

Here is a poem for older students that lends itself to oral reading in dialogue:

> One day I went out walking
> and met a ghost behind the barn.
> "Hello, hello," the ghost did say,
> "I am hungry and far from warm."
> But the ghost looked sad and timid
> and said, "Please don't go away."
> So I was brave and stood quite still
> to hear what the ghost would tell.
> The ghost said, "I've been lost for days
> since from high heaven down I fell."
> "And do you want to go home again?"
> I asked the ghost to let me know.
> "Oh yes," the ghost said, "help me please,
> for I don't like the wind and snow."
> "First I'll share my apple with you,"
> I told the ghost and then it smiled.
> "I haven't eaten in three whole days.
> Thank you, thank you," the ghost replied.
> And then I had a good idea
> and ran into the tall red barn.
> "Oh please don't go," the ghost cried out,
> "for I am still not warm."
> "Look here," I pointed for the ghost,
> "a ladder taller than I've ever seen."
> "What good is that?" the poor ghost sighed,
> "What does a ladder mean?"
> I dragged it out the big barn door
> and leaned it up against the wall.

The ghost was scared to see it then
and said "I'll surely fall."

But I told the ghost to climb way up
and look for heaven wide and long.

The ghost said, "Bless you," and "Farewell,"
and then the ghost was gone.

— Deborah Tall, 1983

Yet another way of interpreting poetry aloud is to use *voice choirs*, children divided into groups by their tone of voice: high, middle range, or deep. Groups in voice choirs respond by saying parts aloud, and their voices are used to interpret dialogues, descriptions, and phrases that help set moods.

Children should be assigned to high and low voice groups (or, if you wish, high, middle, and low voice groups) not simply by placing boys in one and girls in another but by having tryouts. The simplest procedure is to have all the children memorize a line of poetry and then recite it, one after another. You can usually tell from one runthrough whose voice is high and whose is low. In fact, the children themselves can help you make the judgments. Invariably there will be some boys and some girls in both groups.

Once you add the dimension of high and low voices, you have many different ways to match the sound of the reading to the content of a poem. You can balance high and low voices, as well as group and individual readers. You can vary the rate of reading from slow to fast, the volume from whispers to near shouts, the phrasing from words individually articulated to words run together.

The following poem has been adapted for a voice choir with four elements: high voices, low voices, an individual reader ("one"), and the group as a whole ("all").

(High)   What do you think the leaves are thinking
(High)   when autumn comes and they must fall?
(One)   I bet they like the colors they turn
(All)   and how many people come to call.

(One)   But after they turn red and yellow
 (High)   Orange, (Low) gold, (All) or scarlet bright
(One)   soon they wither, dry, and fall
(Low)   and that means they must die.

 (High)   But leaves don't mind (One) I don't think
(High)   that they must die and disappear
(High)   cause every spring they come back
(All)   bright green to greet another year.

— Deborah Tall, 1983

Writing Poetry. Another way for students to respond to poetry is to write some themselves. In recent years teachers have become increasingly interested in the poems school children can produce. Wide exposure to the poetry and verse of others is the beginning; writing their own, individually or as a group effort, follows naturally when children have daily contact with poetry. Specific ways to help them write their own verse are given in Chapter Seven.

As mentioned earlier in this section, you may find these or other poetry collections helpful:

POETRY ANTHOLOGIES

Abdul, Raoul, ed. *The Magic of Black Poetry.* New York: Dodd, Mead, 1972.

Adams, Adrienne. *Poetry of Earth.* New York: Charles Scribner's, 1972.

Arbuthnot, May Hill and Sheldon L. Root, Jr. *Time for Poetry,* 3rd ed. Glenview, Ill.: Scott Foresman, 1968.

Belting, Natalia Maree. *Our Fathers Had Powerful Songs.* New York: Dutton, 1974.

Bennett, Jill. *Roger Was a Razor Fish and Other Poems.* New York: Lothrop, Lee & Shepard, 1981.

Bernikow, Louise, ed. *The World Split Open: Four Centuries of Women Poets in England and America, 1552–1950.* New York: Random House, 1974.

Brewton, Sara and John Brewton. *Laughable Limericks.* New York: Thomas Crowell, 1965.

Clymer, Theodore, ed. *Four Corners of the Sky: Poems, Chants and Oratory.* Boston: Little, Brown, 1975.

Cole, William, ed. *Poem Stew.* New York: Harper & Row, 1981.

———. *A Book of Animal Poems.* New York: Viking Press, 1973.

———. *Pick Me Up; A Book of Short Short Poems.* New York: Macmillan, 1972.

———. *The Poet's Tales: A New Book of Story Poems.* Cleveland: World, 1971.

de Regniers, Beatrice S., Eva Moore, and Mary Michaels White, compilers. *Poems Children Will Sit Still For.* New York: Scholastic Books, 1969.

Fleming, Alice. *Hosannah the Home Run! Poems About Sports.* Boston: Little, Brown, 1972.

Hill, Helen and Agnes Perkins, eds. *New Coasts and Strange Harbors: Discovering Poems.* New York: Thomas Crowell, 1974.

Larrick, Nancy, ed. *I Heard a Scream in the Streets: Poems by Young People in the City.* New York: Evans, 1970.

———. *Room for Me and a Mountain Lion; Poetry of Open Space.* New York: Evans, 1974.

Livingston, Myra Cohn, ed. *Listen, Children, Listen.* New York: Atheneum, 1972.

———. *One Little Room, An Everywhere.* New York: Atheneum, 1975.

Miner, Earl and Hiroko Odagiri, trans. *The Monkey's Straw Raincoat and Other Poetry of the Basho School.* New Haven: Princeton University Press, 1981.

Moore, Lilian and Judith Thurman, eds. *To See the World Afresh*. New York: Atheneum, 1974.

Morton, Miriam, ed. *The Moon Is Like a Silver Sickle: A Celebration of Poetry by Russian Children*. New York: Simon & Schuster, 1972.

Ness, Evaline. *Amelia Mixed the Mustard and Other Poems*. New York: Charles Scribner's, 1975.

Opie, Jona and Peter Opie, eds. *The Oxford Book of Children's Verse*. New York: Oxford, 1973.

Parkhurst, Ted, ed. *Fruitbowl Rhinos: Little Poems by Little People*. Little Rock, Ark.: August House, 1980.

Plotz, Helen. *Gladly Learn and Gladly Teach: Poems of the School Experience*. New York: Greenwillow Press, 1981.

Townsend, John Rowe. *Modern Poetry*. Philadelphia: Lippincott, 1974.

Tripp, Wallace. *A Great Big Ugly Man Came Up and Tied His Horse to Me: A Book of Nonsense Verse*. Boston: Little, Brown, 1973.

POETRY COLLECTIONS BY INDIVIDUAL POETS

Barnstone, Willis. *A Day in the Country*. New York: Harper & Row, 1971.

Bodecker, N. M. *Let's Marry Said the Cherry: And Other Nonsense Poems*. New York: Atheneum, 1974.

Carroll, Lewis. *Poems of Lewis Carroll*, compiled by Myra Cohn Livingston. New York: Thomas Crowell, 1973.

Causley, Charles. *Figgie Hobbin*. New York: Walker, 1974.

Chaucer, Geoffrey. *A Taste of Chaucer*, ed. Anne Malcolmson. New York: Harcourt, 1964.

Ciardi, John. *Fast and Slow*. Boston: Houghton Mifflin, 1974.

Dickinson, Emily. *Letter to the World*, ed. Rumer Godden. New York: Macmillan, 1969.

Fisher, Aileen. *Like Nothing at All*. New York: Harper & Row, 1979.

———. *Feathered Ones and Furry*. New York: Harper & Row, 1979.

Fox, Cedering-Siv. *The Blue Horse and Other Night Poems*. Boston: Houghton Mifflin, 1979.

Frost, Robert. *Complete Poems of Robert Frost*. New York: Holt, Rinehart & Winston, 1949.

———. *In the Clearing*. New York: Holt, Rinehart & Winston, 1962.

Giovanni, Nikki. *Ego-Tripping and Other Poems for Young People*. New York: Lawrence Hill, 1974.

Hardy, Thomas. *The Pinnacled Tower: Selected Poems of Thomas Hardy*. New York: Macmillan, 1975.

Holman, Felice. *I Hear You Smiling and Other Poems*. New York: Charles Scribner's, 1973.

Hughes, Langston. *Don't You Turn Back*. New York: Knopf, 1969.

Hughes, Ted. *Season Songs*. New York: Viking Press, 1975.

Kuskin, Karla. *Near the Window Tree*. New York: Harper & Row, 1975.

Lear, Edward. *Whizz!* New York: Macmillan, 1973.

Lee, Dennis. *Alligator Pie*. Boston: Houghton Mifflin, 1975.

Livingston, Myra Cohn. *The Way Things Are and Other Poems*. New York: Atheneum, 1974.

McCord, David. *One at a Time*. Boston: Little, Brown, 1977.

Merriam, Eve. *Finding a Poem*. New York: Atheneum, 1970.

————. *Out Loud*. New York: Atheneum, 1973.

Moore, Lilian. *See My Lovely Poison Ivy and Other Verses About Witches, Ghosts and Things*. New York: Atheneum, 1975.

O'Neill, Mary. *Hailstones and Halibut Bones*. New York: Doubleday, 1961.

Riley, James Whitcomb. *The Gobble-Uns'll Git You Ef You Don't Watch Out*. Philadelphia: Lippincott, 1975.

Rimanelli, Geose and Paul Pinsleur. *Poems Make Pictures, Pictures Make Poems*. New York: Pantheon Books, 1971.

Roethke, Theodore. *Dirty Dinky and Other Creatures*; *Poems for Children*. New York: Doubleday, 1973.

Rossetti, Christina. *Goblin Market*. New York: Dutton, 1970.

Sandburg, Carl. *The Sandburg Treasury*; *Prose and Poetry for Young People*. New York: Harcourt, 1970.

Silverstein, Shel. *Where the Sidewalk Ends*; *Poems and Drawings of Shel Silverstein*. New York: Harper & Row, 1974.

Stevenson, Robert Louis. *A Child's Garden of Verses*, multiple editions: ill. Jesse Wilcox Smith (New York: Charles Scribner's, 1969); ill. Tasha Tudor (Chicago: Rand McNally, 1981); ill. Brian Wildsmith (New York: Watts, 1966).

Wilbur, Richard. *Opposites*. New York: Harcourt, 1973.

Reading for Enjoyment

Almost everyone believes that reading should be enjoyable for children and that they should read interesting, well-written stories in school, but there are several influences that seem to prevent this from happening. What are some of these influences?

First, widespread use of commercial language arts programs that emphasize skills mastery rather than reading of literature influences the language arts curriculum. We should remember that specific reading skills are a means to an end, not the end itself. Mastery of skills is intended to make the process of reading fluent, meaningful, and enjoyable. If, however, students spend more instructional time practicing isolated skills, completing worksheets, and playing skills games than they spend reading connected text, or if those who can read basal material at a particular level comfortably and successfully are not allowed to work at that level because they cannot complete the accompanying skills materials, then the tail is wagging the dog.

Second, basal texts are written primarily to appeal to large audiences. Many states still have statewide text adoption committees, and the impact of a company's being "listed" or not on a statewide adoption approval list can be measured in millions of dollars. Many other considerations besides the quality of the literature are important in such decisions. What is considered desirable in one state or area may cause a series to be rejected in another. Publishers cannot be blamed if they tend to "play it safe" in materials, because a product sells only if it offers what the public wants, but materials that are utterly uncontroversial, containing a smattering of everything and little of substance or literary worth, may be the result. Until the public demands something different, publishing companies will continue to produce relatively bland materials that are engaging but rarely memorable or thought-provoking.

Third, adults may not be very good at predicting what kinds of literature youngsters will like. Because adults and children think and experience things differently, what appeals to adults may not appeal to children — and language arts materials are written by adults for children, as well as by adults for the approval of other adults. What the teachers and administrators on an adoption committee think is appealing may miss the mark with the students who will have to read it.

Fourth, what reading students do in language arts is assigned. Much of the time they read because they have to, not because they choose to. And regardless of the nature of the task itself, most of us do what we must with less enjoyment and commitment than when we do what we want. There is no way around our requiring students to practice what they are learning and to experience many literary forms, but we should not forget that being required to do something probably does not enhance one's enjoyment of the task.

These influences are not ones we can readily change, and many would not wish to. We can, however, be aware that for students to "read for life," making reading a lifetime skill rather than only something done in school, they must find reading a pleasure, a practical and useful process, and a process over which they can exercise their right to choose. A language arts program should therefore provide a rich environment for self-selection of literature, reading for pleasure, and reading to satisfy the students' own purposes.

Individualized Reading

An individualized reading approach is most often used as a supplement to a basal reading–language arts program. The term "individualized reading" may be confused with "individualized instruction," but the terms are not synonymous. The latter term refers to an overall instructional plan where students are given pretests that purport to reveal individual skill weaknesses. Then each pupil is assigned work to develop those skills. In theory, each student in a group or class may be working on a different skill at a given time.

Individualized reading, however, is a structured approach that focuses on the reading and discussion of self-selected, nonbasal materials. Such an approach has these features:

— Students select their own reading material from a wide variety of trade books and are given guidance and suggestions to help extend their interests and tastes.
— They participate in regularly scheduled pupil-teacher conferences, which may include one or more students who are reading the same book or material on the same topic.
— They use trade books, magazines, and other popular materials rather than basals.
— Skills needs are noted during the conferences and instruction provided then or later in regular group instruction time.

Implementing an individualized reading program may be somewhat intimidating to neophyte teachers who fear that, without the pacing and sequences of skills of a basal program, they may not be able to provide enough guidance and instruction. They may also fear that such a program will take too much time from other areas, but, as an adjunct to a sequenced basal program, individualized reading has many benefits and need not take large amounts of instructional or planning time. Teachers need the following:

— reading materials for self-selection, including a classroom library of books and magazines
— a simple form of record keeping to note the materials read, pupils' progress, and outcomes of the conferences
— some time set aside daily for conferences and reading

Here is an example of how you might organize such a program. First, a classroom library is established, and, if possible, comfortable reading areas set up. Such facilities can be very simple. If book storage is a problem, the librarian can provide a rolling shelf and an assortment of books from the school library to be kept in the classroom for, say, a month at a time. A few floor pillows, an area rug, and some low shelves grouped in a corner can create an appealing reading area. (Some teachers have used large appliance cartons, beanbag chairs, even an old bathtub as places for children to curl up and read.)

About thirty minutes a day is set aside for reading and conferencing. During that time all students read their self-selected materials and the teacher schedules five- to ten-minute individual conferences. Students come to the teacher's desk or another area for private conferences, bringing what they are currently reading.

During the conference you choose from these general activities, or others:

1. The student briefly summarizes what has been read since the last conference.
2. You ask questions to check the student's general comprehension, such as:
   a. What kind of person is the main character?
   b. What is he or she trying to accomplish in this story?
   c. Where and when does the story take place?
   d. What was the main event in the story?
   e. What did the main character learn from his or her experience?
   f. What might happen in the next part of the story?
3. The student reads aloud a short portion of previously read material. You or the student selects what is read aloud. A passage to be read aloud in the next conference is also selected.
4. You ask specific vocabulary or word analysis questions from words in the material. The student is asked to find words or phrases that were unfamiliar and then explain how they were figured out.
5. You note problems or potential problems in word attack, vocabulary, or comprehension that should be dealt with during the basal lesson or direct instruction time and also suggest skill strategies or activities for the student to complete before the next conference.
6. If a new book will be needed soon, you might suggest and describe possible choices and discuss with the student new topics to explore or further reading on the same subject.

You will want to devise your own conference record forms. Figure 5.3 is a sample form showing the outcomes of two successive conferences with one student. It shows how a teacher used the self-selection process to help one reader focus on the feelings and attitudes of story characters, compare and contrast characters, reread to locate specific information, use context clues to reveal meanings of unfamiliar words, use art activities and dramatic readings to share a book with others, relate story events to personal experiences, predict upcoming events and read to confirm or revise predictions, locate and classify factual information, and develop research skills. In addition, the student's reading tastes and interests were broadened, and the teacher noted the child's growing excitement and pleasure in reading fine literature.

Anecdotal records like these are also excellent vehicles for sharing information during parent-teacher conferences. They show parents in concrete terms how their children are progressing in the development of reading tastes and habits and provide a way for parents to help their children develop positive attitudes toward reading out of school.

An individualized reading program can be used as more than a supplement to a basal program. We know some teachers who have found that basal placement tests given in the spring of the previous year frequently do not result in accurate placement in a basal the following fall. These teachers prefer to do

Figure 5.3 Sample reading conference record

Name *Monica L.*

Material read: *Island of Blue Dolphins* Date: *10-8*

Conference activities: M. read aloud section describing Rontu's death. Discussed Karana's feelings toward dog, located & reread K's description of her loneliness (p. 101). Went over M's list of things K. had to build for herself. Models of house & tools almost completed.

Observations: Should complete book before next conference. M. is deeply involved w/story & characters, wants to learn more about wolves & read more survival stories. Comprehension is excellent; sensitive to Karana's feelings — related K's grief to her own when her dog died.

Recommendations: Suggested Call it Courage, Tirka Liktat, Julie of the Wolves, & Swiss Family Robinson for next book. Planned for M. to share her models of Karana's house & tools and a dramatic reading with class next Monday.

Material read: *Julie of the Wolves* Date: *10-16*

Conference activities: M. read orally section describing tundra. Answered ques. comparing feelings of Karana & Julie (Miyax) when they each realize they are on their own. Located 5 Eskimo words w/context clues showing meanings. Predicted ways Miyax might try to make friends w/wolves. M. will make a list of them for next conference.

Observations: M. is reading at every possible moment! Excitement high, enjoying reading about these resourceful females. Interest in wolves growing — I must locate nonfiction on wolves for her.

Recommendations: Use list of predictions as she reads to confirm her guesses; also check w/nonfiction sources. Begin listing factual info about wolves' behavior from book — use as beginning of research for report on wolf. Begin planning an art activity to share w/class.

their own placement and diagnostic assessment as soon as school begins. Instead of immediately beginning basal instruction, they start with individualized reading for the first two to three weeks. During the language arts period students select their materials, read, participate in conferences, and work on activities and projects suggested during the conferences. The teachers plan and conduct the conferences, evaluate work, and do diagnostic testing individually. They have reported that their students are subsequently placed in basal levels more accurately, they get to know their students' interests, abilities, and work habits faster, and the students begin the year by reading widely and enjoyably. After the first few weeks the free reading period is shortened to allow time for reading groups and basal instruction, but the individualized reading continues as a regular part of language arts.

Other teachers have found that as the end of the school year approaches, many children complete a basal level but may be unready to begin a new one, or teachers may be averse to beginning a new level with little time left before school ends. Individualized reading provides an alternative that rewards students for completing a level and sends them into the summer with a habit of reading for pleasure. It is relatively easy to help them pick books for summer reading when they are accustomed to doing it in school.

We know of a district that planned to change to a new basal system one fall, but unforeseen events prevented the delivery of books and manuals by September. Teachers didn't want to begin the year with the old series and switch to the new within weeks, nor did they want to "mark time" with kits and duplicator sheets until the books arrived. So they began the year with individualized reading, and by the time the series arrived their students were well into reading for pleasure.

You might find some of these sources helpful in learning more about an individualized reading program:

Coody, Betty. *Using Literature with Young Children*, 2d ed. Dubuque, Iowa: Wm. C. Brown, 1978.

Coody, Betty and David Nelson. *Teaching Elementary Language Arts: A Literature Approach*. Belmont, Calif.: Wadsworth, 1982.

Forgan, Harry W. *The Reading Corner*. Santa Monica, Calif.: Goodyear, 1977.

Harris, Larry A. and Carl B. Smith. *Individualizing Reading Instruction: A Reader*. New York: Holt, Rinehart & Winston, 1972.

Musgrave, Ray G. *Individualized Instruction: Teaching Strategies Focusing on the Learner*. Boston: Allyn & Bacon, 1975.

Raymond, Dorothy. *Individualizing Reading in the Elementary School*. West Nyack, N.Y.: Parker, 1973.

Veatch, Jeannette. *Reading in the Elementary School*, 2d ed. New York: Wiley, 1978.

A more general list of sources for children's literature and annotated bibliographies is included at the end of this chapter.

Alternatives for Sharing Books

One of the best ways to encourage children to read widely and to use their reading, writing, and oral communication skills is to have them share their favorite books with others. Book sharing need not mean book reports, which frequently degenerate into mindless summaries delivered to disinterested audiences or, worse, to the teacher only. Such "sharing" is a sham; it does nothing to encourage others to explore the same material and usually causes students to *avoid* reading if they can. Book sharing should be an active, creative process that helps children practice their language and artistic abilities for some real purpose.

A word of caution is needed, though. It is unnecessary, even undesirable, for students to share every book they read. Not all books one reads are equally enjoyable or thought-provoking. Even students who enjoy most of the books they select will be put off by the demand of doing something after each one. After all, how many books do you read for pleasure that you'd want to share with others? You may enjoy telling friends about your favorites or recommending books to them, but not every one you read.

Children should be allowed to choose which books they will put effort into sharing. They can keep track of all their reading by completing a card file or a very brief summary, as well as by sharing with the teacher during the conferences, but only their favorites deserve the thought and effort that book sharing requires and deserves. You might suggest that a student do a project on about one of three or four books read for pleasure.

There are countless ways of sharing books. Here are a few general suggestions, grouped roughly by type.

ART-BASED ACTIVITIES

1. Create a large, colorful poster "advertising" your book. Include the title, author, and illustrator and a few sentences describing the story or what you liked the best about it. Illustrate your poster with drawing, painting, glued-on real materials, cut-out magazine pictures, or fancy lettering. The posters can be hung in the classroom or library.

2. Using paper or tagboard strips about 2″ x 6″, make colorful book marks and leave them on the library table or circulation desk for others to pick up. (This is a favorite activity for holidays, Book Week, and other special events.)

3. Create a bulletin board illustrating or describing your book. Make a dimensional display by using inflated balloons with felt-pen faces or features glued on, each one representing characters. Tape the tied-off base of the balloon securely to the board, then make bodies and costumes to scale from paper, cloth, cotton, or whatever. You can even add dialogue in cartoon-style "bubbles" from the characters' mouths. Balloon heads can be made more durable by covering inflated balloons with a layer of papier mâché (newspaper strips, wallpaper paste, and water), then painting and decorating them after they have dried completely.

4. For a story with characters who have unusual styles of dress, like historical tales, science fiction, or stories from other lands, create a display of costumes. Use scraps of fabric, cotton, fur, beads, foil, feathers, wallpaper, ribbon, lace, and fringe to make authentic costumes for clay or wire models or male and female "action figures."

5. Make an advertisement "selling" your book just as magazine and TV ads sell cars, cosmetics, and other products. Make up "testimonials" by famous people, catchy slogans, and colorful descriptions.

6. Make a display of masks representing characters, accompanied by written descriptions, or use the masks to role-play part of a story. Masks can be made with sheets of duplicator paper, paper plates, papier mâché, grocery bags, or similar materials. (Teachers: Be sure eye holes are large if masks are to be worn.) Mask instructions are given in the section, "Classroom Dramatics," in Chapter Three.

7. Use blank transparencies or a continuous roll of overhead projector film to create a "filmstrip" about your book. (Divide the continuous film into frames.) Use china markers, wax pencils, or other markers to draw and color scenes. Project the film or transparencies in order on an overhead projector, with narration.

8. Create a set of puppets you can use to act out scenes from, or a summary of, your book. Puppets can be as simple as paper circles or small paper plates glued to tongue depressors, or much more elaborate hand puppets with stuffed heads, sock or bag puppets, or even simple marionettes. (If you have puppets at home, dress them differently or disguise their original .appearance for this activity.) See "Classroom Dramatics" in Chapter Three for many examples of puppet types.

DRAMATICS ACTIVITIES

1. Dress up in a costume worn by a major character in your book. Improvise with pieces of clothing, hats, wigs, or masks, and include small hand props that your character would carry or use. Tell your classmates about your experiences in the book, your life before or after the book's events, or your feelings about the way you were characterized in the story. If someone were to write another story about you, what would you like to have happen in it?

2. Write a script for a radio play describing parts of your book and summarizing it or describing your feelings about it. Include dialogue between characters as well as your narration. Experiment with different voices or ask friends to read different parts. Experiment with sound effects and/or music too. Tape record your script or ask if you can read it to your class over the PA system.

3. If you read a book that taught you how to do something, collect materials, or make models of them, give a demonstration showing others how to do it too, or show how a character made, discovered, or invented something in a story.

4. Role-play a part of your story, with friends playing other parts. Write a script and read from it while acting (as in readers theater) rather than trying to memorize lines.

5. Make some puppets, and a simple puppet theater from a large carton or movable screen. Write a script and put on a puppet show, reading your script from behind the scenes and using different voices.

6. With some friends (especially others who read the same book), put on a mock trial. This is especially good for mysteries and suspense stories. Create characters (defendants, prosecutors, defense lawyers, judge, witnesses, and jury) and a script showing how events unfolded through testimony, evidence, and arguments. Poll the jury to see who wins the trial. "Reporters" can write news stories about the trial for the class newspaper.

WRITING ACTIVITIES

1. By yourself or with others, produce a classroom newspaper in which story events are treated as news stories. Duplicator masters can be used if the newspaper will be distributed; large newsprint sheets can be used for a display or bulletin board. Rule your paper into columns, with room for headlines and illustrations (use a real front page as an example). Mix types of articles: news items, interviews with the author or characters, a travel item about the setting, even a weather forecast. Write or type your stories in narrow columns, draw pictures for illustrations, and write eye-catching headlines in large print.

2. Write a telegram summarizing story events in short sentences. You can make up realistic telegram forms and run them off on a duplicator. For 1 above, reporters can send details of news items to the editor before they write their stories.

3. Write a letter to a friend or pen pal describing your book, or to a story character describing your reactions to a story, or write a real letter to an author or illustrator, if living, reacting to his or her work. Send your letter to the publishing company and see if you get a letter back!

4. Imagine that you are a character in a story. Keep a diary to record events, your feelings about them, and your hopes and plans for the future. Date your entries from the beginning to the end of the story.

5. Select one or two quotations from a book that represent the feelings, attitudes, or personality of a character. Copy the quotations, write a short essay telling why those quotes represent that character, and then write a short summary of how the character's actions showed what kind of person he or she was. You might include a drawing of the character or some important story action.

6. If you read a biography or a historical fiction story about a famous person or historical figure, try the Who Am I? game. Using information from what you read, write clues to the person's identity such as place and date of birth, a description of some physical characteristics, likes and dislikes, hobbies, and important things the person did during his or her lifetime. Make your clues clear and accurate but don't give away too much information — make your classmates guess who the person might be.

7. Try writing a summary of a book or story as a song or poem. Look at some examples of poems that tell a story, such as Robert Nathan's *Dunkirk*, James Tippett's *I Spend the Summer* or songs like "The Ballad of John Henry."

8. Think of an object that represents the main action, setting, or character of a book you've read. Draw and cut out a large outline of the object from construction paper. You can use an outline map of the country where a story took place, a spaceship or robot for a science fiction story, an animal shape, an article of clothing, a building, or even an invention.

Write a short summary of the story including how you felt about it. Paste it in the middle of your cut-out shape and decorate or add detail as you wish. (Teachers: This is a good, simple activity for young readers and reluctant writers and makes for some attractive displays too.) Here are some examples: *Davy Crockett* — coonskin cap; *King Arthur* — armor helmet; *Miss Hickory* — hickory nut; *Paddle-to-the-Sea* — birchbark canoe.

Dealing with Reading Problems

Evaluating children's progress in language arts and reading is a critical component of every teacher's responsibilities. Every school and school division has required evaluation procedures and instruments: Commercial reading program tests, standardized achievement tests, and criterion-referenced objectives and mastery tests are common. All teachers develop their own ways of evaluating progress and abilities in day-to-day teaching, however, and in this section we describe some general concepts and procedures for ongoing student evaluation as well as methods of supporting poorer readers in the classroom.

Box 5.7 lists some important principles of evaluation, which means much more than the administration of tests. There are many ways that teachers can gather information without giving tests. Many involve analyzing reading qualitatively; that is, determining what strategies students use even when they make errors.

Functional Reading Levels

Most readers who are beyond the beginning stages of learning to read can read some kinds and levels of material more successfully than others. We can categorize these varying levels of difficulty by referring to *functional reading levels:*

BOX 5.7
Principles of Evaluation

Evaluation Is:

Positive; strengths and mastered skills are as important as weaknesses and needs.

Continuous; strengths and needs change quickly as children gain new experiences and strategies.

Practical; all evaluation is for the purpose of instructional improvement, not to classify or label students' difficulties.

Qualitative; tests can yield results, but results must be weighed and a teacher's insight used to make them meaningful.

Independent Reading Level — the highest grade level of material that is *easy* for the student to read. Little or no aid is needed while reading; comprehension of what is read is very good to excellent; most words are recognized at sight, and few must be decoded, so reading is generally rapid, fluent, and accurate. The independent level is best for pleasure reading, independent activities, homework, and other activities where children are expected to work successfully without help.

Instructional Reading Level — the highest grade level of material that is *comfortable* for the student to read, although it is harder than independent level material. Here the student has sufficient prior information about the topic so

that comprehension is good, but teacher guidance is needed to develop new skills and refine comprehension. More unfamiliar words may be encountered at this level and word analysis skills are needed. Readers may make word recognition errors, but the errors rarely change the meaning of the text or cause confusion. The reading rate may be slower than at the independent level but is still comfortably rapid for good comprehension. Instructional level material is best for school texts, basal readers, and other material used for direct instruction and for reading where help is available.

Frustration Reading Level — material that is more difficult than the highest instruction level, where the text is *too difficult* for successful reading. Comprehension is poor; reading is usually slow, with frequent pauses to analyze unfamiliar words. Word recognition errors are frequent, often changing the meaning of the text and causing misunderstanding and confusion. Reading at this level is a frustrating, exhausting experience and must be avoided if students are to have positive attitudes about reading. They must never be required to read frustration level material except for the specific diagnostic purpose of determining what their frustration level is. They may occasionally self-select material we know is too difficult for them, and when their intrinsic motivation is high they may be able to get through such text, but other than these two conditions, frustration level reading should not be assigned.

Table 5.2 shows the various characteristics of the functional reading levels in summary form.

Table 5.2 Functional reading levels

	CHARACTERISTICS	TYPICAL READING
FRUSTRATION LEVEL TOO HARD	Poor comprehension Slow, stumbling rate Much word analysis necessary	No assigned material Diagnostic purposes Self-selected material where student's interest is very high in spite of difficulty
INSTRUCTIONAL LEVEL COMFORTABLE	Good comprehension Good accuracy in word recognition Fairly rapid rate Some word analysis needed	School textbooks & basal reader Guided classroom reading assignments Study guides and other work done with guidance Forms and applications
INDEPENDENT LEVEL EASY	Excellent comprehension Excellent word recognition accuracy Very little word analysis needed Rapid, smooth rate Very few errors of any kind	All pleasure reading All self-selected reading for information Homework, tests, seatwork, learning centers, and all other assigned work to be done alone

General Diagnostic Strategies

In day-to-day teaching, systematic informal observation of a student's reading strategies, responses, and interests is the best source of information for instructional planning. Informal procedures, which are not related to norms (average performances of large groups) and require no strict administration procedures, are very useful because they allow the teacher to observe reading of everyday text in normal reading situations, they allow qualitative as well as quantitative analysis, and they can be fitted into the normal teaching routine without setting aside instructional time for testing.

Most teachers use informal procedures to determine appropriate reading levels and to identify areas of strengths and weaknesses in word recognition and reading comprehension skills.

Finding Instructional Levels. Since students cannot derive maximum benefit from instruction unless they are placed in basals and other textbook materials that represent their instructional levels, determining these levels is an important responsibility. Most basal reading series have placement tests, but because they usually have a multiple-choice format and require students to read both questions and answers, they may not be very accurate in indicating at what level of material a youngster can read comfortably. Teachers need other devices for placing students more accurately. *Cloze* and *maze procedures* and *informal reading inventories* are useful alternatives.

Cloze Procedures. A *cloze* (Taylor, 1953) is a reading passage with words systematically deleted. Students use context and comprehension of the intact text portions to supply the missing words, thus creating "closure" or completeness. When a cloze is made up from a book or other material students have not yet read, their degree of success in completing the passage can show whether the text represents their independent, instructional, or frustration level. These results facilitate grouping students for instruction and help in making appropriate reading assignments (Bormuth, 1966, 1968a, 1968b; Jones and Pikulski, 1974; Rankin and Culhane, 1969).

A cloze procedure is easy to make up and score and can be administered to groups or a whole class at once if desired. Box 5.8 lists the steps in preparing and administering the cloze.

A cloze score of 40–60 percent correct shows that the text represents a student's instructional level. Scores of above 60 percent represent the independent level; those below 40 percent indicate the frustration level (Bormuth, 1968a, 1968b; Rankin and Culhane, 1969).

Once the reading level has been established, you should draw up three lists, of students with scores well above 60 percent, those close to or between 40 percent and 60 percent, and those well below 40 percent. The first group can be assigned independent reading and homework from the text, and it should be easy reading for them. The second group can be assigned supervised

BOX 5.8
Using the Cloze Procedure as a Placement Test

Preparation

1. Select a 275–300 word passage that students have not read before. It should be fairly complete in itself; a story or chapter beginning is good.
2. Leave the first sentence intact, then delete every *fifth* word and replace it with a blank. If the fifth word is a proper noun, date, or numeral, leave it in and delete the next word, then continue counting as before. Stop when you have deleted fifty words. Leave the final sentences intact.
3. Type the story on a duplicator master. Double space it and use the same length blank every time. Run off a copy for each student. Use of a separate answer sheet is optional.

Administration

1. Teach the procedure using example sentences on the board or on exercise handouts. Be sure that students know how to use surrounding context to figure out what a deleted word might be.
2. Explain the scoring criteria. Be sure students understand that no one will get all items right and that even 50 percent correct is a good score.
3. Distribute the papers. Students should work alone and not use books to help them. Give them plenty of time; encourage them to take their time.
4. Collect and score the papers. For placement purposes only exact replacements (not synonyms) are scored correct.

reading in class and given direct instruction and guidance in reading it, since it should be fairly comfortable reading for them. The third group should be given easier material and they should use the book primarily as a reference for the time being. If they *must* use that book, as in classes where only one textbook is required for all pupils regardless of their reading ability, they must be given much support by listening to the text read aloud or on tapes, echo and/or choral reading, and the use of films, demonstrations, summaries, and so forth to supplement the text and help in concept development.

You may find a cloze helpful:

— at the beginning of a year for whole groups or classes
— when a new student enters a class
— when a new textbook or similar material is introduced
— when making text adoption decisions, to see if present students can comfortably read material being considered
— if a trade book or supplementary text is being considered for use with a group already placed in graded materials

Maze Procedures. A *maze* (Guthrie et al., 1974) is a cousin of the cloze. It has a multiple-choice format instead of blanks, so it is considerably easier to complete. It may be preferable to the cloze for young students, very poor readers, and hesitant children who are intimidated by all the blanks in a cloze. Criteria for the reading levels are higher than for the cloze. Box 5.9 lists the steps in using a maze, and Figure 5.4 shows a portion of a maze as an example.

BOX 5.9
Preparing and Using a Maze Procedure for Placement

Preparation

1. Select a passage students have not read before, as for a cloze (see Box 5.8). A passage about 150 words long yields twenty-five items; one about 275–300 words long yields fifty items.
2. Leave the first sentence intact. Count off every fifth word as for the cloze, skipping any proper nouns, dates, and numerals for deletion.
3. Instead of substituting blanks for words, create a three-item multiple choice for each item (see Figure 5.4 for an example). One choice will be the correct word; one will

be the same part of speech but different in meaning; one will be different both in grammatical function and meaning. All three choices should be fairly similar in appearance and sound.

4. Order the choices randomly so the correct word occurs in a different position each time.
5. Type the story on a duplicator master, allowing plenty of room between lines. No answer sheet is necessary, as students will circle or underline their answers.

Administration

1. Follow the same steps as for the cloze administration (Box 5.8).
2. Students should have practice beforehand in selecting choices and should know that no one will get every item correct. The maze procedure is not timed.

Figure 5.4 A portion of a maze procedure

Mandy Mouse peered out from under the thick hedge. Her shiny black eyes

listened		another		these	
looked	first one way, then	antler	as she searched for	thing	dreaded
books		under		the	

	whiskers		asks	
cat. Her long	whisper	twitched in tiny jerks	as	she sniff, sniff, sniffed
	winters		if	

forest
from   the cat's scent.
for

Score criteria for the maze are as follows (Guthrie et al., 1974): 85–100 percent accuracy represents the independent level; 65–85 percent, the instructional level; below 65 percent, the frustration level. You can group your students as previously described for use of the selected material.

Informal Reading Inventories. These devices, often called IRIs, are sets of story passages of increasing difficulty, representing graded school reading material from primer through upper grades, with comprehension questions accompanying each passage. Some teachers construct their own IRIs from basal readers and similar graded materials. There are also commercially published IRIs, and a list of them is included in this section. IRIs are individually administered, either in one sitting or in several shorter sessions.

Usually a student reads one passage orally and one passage silently at each grade level, answering orally administered comprehension questions after each passage is completed. Listening comprehension can also be assessed at various grade levels of difficulty by having the student listen to another passage read aloud by the examiner and then answering comprehension questions after each passage is completed.

IRIs can be used to assess strengths and needs in:

— silent and oral reading comprehension, by analyzing responses to comprehension questions after the student has read the passages
— oral reading fluency, by observing oral reading of passages
— use of context, structural, and phonic analysis in word recognition, by observation and analysis of oral reading *miscues* (divergences from the written text)
— silent and oral reading rates, by timing the reading of passages
— listening comprehension, by analyzing responses to comprehension questions after the examiner has read the passages

IRIs are also very useful in determining a student's independent, instructional, and frustration levels.

Many IRIs include other components, such as word recognition inventories and phonics inventories. A word recognition inventory (WRI) is made up of graded lists of individual words which typically occur in text material at various grade levels. Students are asked to pronounce as many words as they can, using word recognition strategies to figure out any that are unfamiliar. They are not asked to define or explain the meanings of the words, nor do they read connected text on these inventories. WRIs are useful in assessing sight recognition and decoding strategies (phonic and structural analysis) applied to individual words in isolation. They are not used to assess comprehension or the use of context in word recognition, since the words appear in isolation rather than in meaningful context. By rating the degree of accuracy and the strategies students use when they make errors, judgments can be made about specific word recognition skills. Phonics inventories are usually made up of lists of unfamiliar or nonsense words that require the student to apply decoding strategies to pronounce them. Analysis of their attempts and successes can provide information about which decoding strategies they can use reliably and which they need to work on.

Commercial IRIs contain detailed directions for administration, scoring, and analysis. The scores on comprehension questions at each level and the accuracy scores on oral reading are used to determine the functional reading levels. The widely accepted practice for many years has been that if students can answer about 70 percent of the comprehension questions correctly and read orally with 90–95 percent accuracy at a given level, that level of material represents the instructional level; if they can answer about 90 percent or more of the questions correctly and read aloud with 95 percent or better accuracy, it represents the independent level; and if comprehension is well below about 70 percent and oral reading accuracy is well below 90 percent, it represents a frustration level. Oral reading miscues, WRI responses, patterns of comprehension, and reading rate are used diagnostically to determine what needs to be taught or practiced and what skills have been mastered.

Commercial informal reading inventories are listed below.

Bader, Lois A. *Bader Reading and Language Inventory*. New York: Macmillan, 1983.

Burns, Paul C. and Betty D. Roe. *Informal Reading Assessment*. Chicago: Rand McNally, 1980.

Ekwall, Eldon E. *Ekwall Reading Inventory*. Boston: Allyn & Bacon, 1979.

Johns, Jerry L. *Basic Reading Inventory*, 2d ed. Dubuque, Iowa: Kendall-Hunt, 1981.

Silvaroli, Nicholas J. *Classroom Reading Inventory*, 4th ed. Dubuque, Iowa: Wm. C. Brown, 1982.

Woods, Mary Lynn and Alden J. Moe. *Analytical Reading Inventory*, 2d ed. Columbus, Ohio: Charles Merrill, 1981.

Spotting Comprehension Problems. Since understanding what we read is essential, problems in comprehension can be devastating to a child's reading growth. All of us have difficulty understanding some of the things we read. Children occasionally misunderstand or fail to understand what they read for the same reasons that we may have occasional problems: because they lack familiarity with a particular topic, because sometimes text is poorly organized or heavily dependent on unfamiliar or unusual language structures, because a particular text may introduce many new concepts one after another without much elaboration, or because they are not particularly interested in a topic. Inasmuch as reading materials differ widely, even when written for a particular grade level, and since everyone has unique interests, motives, and prior experiences, a reader's comprehension will vary from day to day and from text to text. When, however, students have problems understanding much of what they read, especially when they are trying hard and are motivated to succeed, comprehension problems assume considerable importance.

Many children have difficulty understanding what they read because their reading is slow and dysfluent. Those who have small sight vocabularies must depend heavily on word analysis, and as they read they have to stop repeatedly to try to figure out unrecognized words. When they must stop to figure out a word, they have to "shift gears" mentally; they must try to remember the sense of what they read up to that point while they apply word attack strategies, which requires them to think of two or more things at once. Ideas can be stored in short-term memory for only about five or six seconds, and if new words can be figured out and made sense of quickly, their memory of those ideas may be relatively unaffected. If, however, students take longer than a few seconds to figure out a new word, or if such stops occur frequently, the limits of short-term memory will work against them. Thus they may lose the sense of the reading as they repeatedly stop to decode or analyze.

Fluent reading requires sight recognition of most of the words in the text. Poor sight recognition and overdependence on word analysis make reading for meaning difficult, and sometimes impossible. Students *must* read materials in which they can recognize most (about 90 percent or more) of the words at sight, a basic characteristic of the instructional level. Halting, dysfluent readers must be placed in easier materials so they can focus on comprehending what they read, and they must be given instruction that facilitates their sight recognition of words and deemphasizes the need for decoding during reading.

Some students have almost the opposite problem: They read rapidly, with excellent word recognition but still do not understand what they read. Such students frequently prefer to read aloud rather than silently; they may mutter half-aloud as they read "silently," and may lose their places frequently and show signs of frustration when they have to read without subvocalizing. On an IRI, their oral comprehension scores are usually higher than their silent comprehension scores at the same levels, although both scores may be relatively low.

These students are often referred to as "word callers"; that is, when they read they tend to focus on *pronouncing* words rather than *understanding* them. In fact they may confess that they need to "hear themselves say the words" in order to understand much (which is why they prefer oral reading and habitually subvocalize). They are not processing print directly, but recoding it to speech, and the effort and concentration they expend on pronunciation and rapid decoding prevents them from being able to grasp the meaning behind the words.

Word callers essentially conceive of reading as a process of pronouncing words rather than a process of getting meaning. Their reading strategies are superficial, and their mental involvement with print is limited. Their reading behavior may look and sound a lot like real reading, but it is not. Real reading is sense making, not sound making, and fundamental instructional change is required in order to help such students develop a whole new conception of what reading is.

Word callers should do very little oral reading, if any, because their dependence on hearing the words must be replaced by the ability to process print directly into meaning. It may be painful for them to have to do what they do least well, so they must be supported in silent reading until they become fluent in it. Passages must be kept short, to minimize frustration and losing one's place. Stories may be broken up into numerous segments; reading of short articles, paragraphs, and summaries should be emphasized. After silently reading a passage, students should immediately summarize or paraphrase what they read, orally at first and later in writing as well. Comprehension questioning should be kept brief, and it should not be done until *after* the summarizing step so that the students can pick up information they did not include spontaneously. Reading instruction should focus, at least for a time, entirely on comprehension; word analysis activities can be suspended or greatly deemphasized during this period.

Simple cloze and maze procedures are excellent devices for helping to focus on meaning. You may choose to delete words as you think best, perhaps leaving out only every tenth or twelfth word, or leaving out only nouns or verbs for a time. Any word that makes sense should be accepted as correct. Cloze or maze passages can be made up from stories already read as well as from the students' own compositions or everyday material. Spelling and grammar errors can be ignored for a time, until the youngsters develop greater facility with making an "educated guess" and using sense-making strategies to reconstruct text.

DRTAs, DLTAs, and related prediction activities are excellent for getting word callers to focus on meaning and engage their interest and curiosity in story events. DRTAs should be read silently with fairly frequent stops for prediction and oral rereading should be done selectively. Be sure to praise your students for risking a guess and encourage them to participate as actively as they can.

Spotting Word Recognition Problems. As we described in the previous section, word recognition and comprehension problems frequently interact. One of the most common causes of poor comprehension is a lack of sufficient sight recognition to move through text rapidly and smoothly so that attention can be focused on meaning rather than on identifying words.

Oral reading fluency should be observed in a variety of kinds of materials, and for a variety of purposes. Students will read *least* well when they have not rehearsed or previewed the material, so they should routinely preview what is to be read aloud. This may be all that is necessary to really improve oral reading fluency.

We should remember too that all readers, regardless of their skill, make *miscues*, or oral divergences from written text, when they read aloud. Even adult fluent readers commonly make slip-of-the-tongue errors or minor rewordings of the text. If such miscues do not significantly alter the tone or message of the print, they are unimportant. Young readers miscue too, and not all miscues are significant. Here is an example of two students reading aloud the same text sentence:

> *Text:*   *City dwellers like a quiet place of green, of grass and trees, as much as anyone does.*

Reader 1: City people like a quiet place of green grass and trees as much as anyone.

Reader 2: City dealers like a quite place of green, of grass and trees, as much as animal does.

Each reader made three miscues: Reader 1 substituted *people* for *dwellers*, omitted *of*, and omitted *does*; Reader 2 substituted *dealers* for *dwellers*, *quite* for *quiet*, and *animal* for *anyone*. Though each made three miscues, the results of their miscues were very different. Reader 1 conveyed the ideas of the text sentence in a somewhat simplified, more natural-sounding sentence. Reader 2 made miscues that significantly altered the meaning of the sentence; although the substitutions look and sound somewhat like the intended words, they do not make sense.

Informal analysis of miscues can be done by having a student read aloud to you while you mark the miscues on a copy of the text. You can devise your own "shorthand" for marking miscues or you can use a widely used set of marks and notations:

— *Substitution* of one word for another: Write the miscue above the text word.

The big ~~brown~~ *black* dog barked.

— *Insertion* of a word or phrase not in text: Write the miscue above a caret where the insertion was made.

Chris drives a red ^*pickup* truck.

— *Omission* of a word, part of a word, or a phrase: Circle the omitted elements.

The doll fell (down) from the shelf.

— *Correction* of miscue without help or direction: Put a check mark next to the original marking.

The doll fell (down)✓ from the shelf.

Using such a coding system will help you keep up with the oral reading as it proceeds. After you have marked the miscues you can analyze each one to learn what strategies the reader depends on by asking three questions about each:

1. Does the miscue *mean* about the same as the text word?
2. Does the miscue have the same grammatical *function* as the text word? (For example, did the reader use a noun for a noun, a modifier for a modifier, or preserve plural or verb tense markers like *-s* and *-ed*?)
3. Does the miscue *look* and/or *sound* like the intended word? (Does it have the same beginning or ending sound, vowel sound, affix, or number of syllables?)

To determine preferred strategies, make a list of the uncorrected miscues with the text word for each one after it. Make three columns for checking off strategies and mark them Meaning, Function, and Appearance/Sound. Compare each miscue to the text word, including the phrase in which the miscue happened and check off which strategies were used.

Figure 5.5 is an example of a girl who used grammatical function as a cue in all her miscues. She also produced miscues with high sound similarity in four instances, but only three of her five miscues made good sense. She appears to have a good grasp of the syntax of written language; greater focus on what would *make sense* where an unrecognized word occurred would help her understand more of what she reads. Cloze passages would be beneficial in this case.

If you are more concerned with whether a student's miscues make sense than in what caused them, simply classify the miscues according to whether or not the author's meaning was generally preserved.

Figure 5.6 is an example of a reader who made seven uncorrected miscues, but only two resulted in a significant change of meaning. (It may be argued that *any* change in the author's wording causes meaning change. The question is, How drastically is the overall message affected? Your own good judgment is the best criterion.) Of those two, *about them* for *above them* is really a

Figure 5.5 Sample miscue strategy checklist

Cathy slipped *slid* into the crowded classroom just as Mr. Burton reached *raked* out and pulled the door shut. Hugging the wall, she moved carefully through the crowd to the *toward* very back of the room. As she edged toward the rear, she prayed no one *played nobody* would notice her.

TEXT	MISCUE	MEANING	FUNCTION	SOUND/APPEARANCE
slipped	slid	√	√	√
reached	raked		√	√
to	toward	√	√	
prayed	played		√	√
no one	nobody	√	√	√

Figure 5.6   Sample meaning-change checklist for miscues

threw theirselves

The children flung themselves down in the tall deep grass under the trees. They

flopped   *pointing*   *dampness*

lolled like broken dolls, panting a little and rubbing their faces against the cool damp

about

of the earth. Above them the leaves hung down like limp green flags, their edges

curled

curling gently inwards.

		MEANING CHANGE	
TEXT	MISCUE	SIGNIFICANT	INSIGNIFICANT
flung	threw		✓
themselves	theirselves		✓
lolled	flopped		✓
panting	pointing	✓	
damp	dampness		✓
above	about	✓	
curling	curled		✓

"judgment call"; you may or may not find the miscue acceptable. It is less important than *pointing* for *panting*, an obvious meaning change.

Many teachers wonder how often, and when, they should correct miscues. Some feel compelled to correct every one, believing that no error can possibly be unimportant. Others don't want to jump in every time but are uncertain when they should intervene.

Our best advice is: When a student reads aloud, listen to the reading but don't follow along in your copy of the text. If you can detect a miscue by listening, the miscue probably caused a significant meaning change or violated the syntax in an important way. Insignificant miscues will not be perceived by listening and need not be corrected, but important ones should be corrected.

You may find some of the following sources helpful in learning more about diagnosing reading problems:

Bader, Lois A. *Reading Diagnosis and Remediation in Classroom and Clinic.* New York: Macmillan, 1980.

Cheek, Martha and Earl Cheek. *Diagnostic and Prescriptive Reading Instruction.* Dubuque, Iowa: Wm. C. Brown, 1980.

Clay, Marie. *Early Detection of Reading Difficulties*, 2d ed. Exeter, N.H.: Heinemann Educational Books, 1980.

Ekwall, Eldon E. *Diagnosis and Remediation of the Disabled Reader.* Boston: Allyn & Bacon, 1976.

Gillet, Jean Wallace and Charles Temple. *Understanding Reading Problems: Assessment and Instruction.* Boston: Little, Brown, 1982.

Harris, Albert J. and Edward R. Sipay. *How to Increase Reading Ability*, 7th ed. New York: Longman, 1980.

Johns, Jerry, Sharon Garton, Paula Schoenfelder, and Patricia Skriba. *Assessing Reading Behavior: Informal Reading Inventories.* Newark, Del.: IRA, 1977.

Rupley, William H. and Timothy R. Blair. *Reading Diagnosis and Remediation.* Boston: Houghton Miffin, 1979.

Stauffer, Russell G., Jules C. Abrams, and John J. Pikulski. *Diagnosis, Correction and Prevention of Reading Disabilities.* New York: Harper & Row, 1978.

Wilson, Robert M. *Diagnostic and Remedial Reading for Classroom and Clinic*, 4th ed. Columbus, Ohio: Charles Merrill, 1981.

Support Measures for Poor Readers

The best way to support poor readers in language arts is to be certain that they are placed at their instructional levels, regardless of their grade level. They learn best from materials in which they can work comfortably. If the text is too difficult, they don't learn new skills to apply; instead, they learn how dreadful reading can be and how incapable they can be made to look. Both children and adults learn to avoid things they do poorly and that seem too difficult to ever master. A diet of frustration-level reading can cause a student to avoid reading and books forever onward.

Poor readers should be encouraged in every way possible to read for pleasure. Because it is hard for them, they usually avoid every contact with reading, and because they spend less time reading than others, their progress is slower than their peers. Yet they must read in order to become better readers. Self-selected reading of any materials they will use is a must for poor readers. They have to be actively "sold" on the idea, by hearing others share books they've enjoyed, by hearing book talks and selected parts of good books read aloud, and by attractive displays of a wide variety of books and non–book materials.

Many poor readers can participate fully and productively in classroom activities where reading and writing are deemphasized, such as discussions, demonstrations, role playing, simulations, hands-on projects, and speaking-listening activities. They should be drawn into these activities as fully as possible. Students frequently believe that if they read poorly, they will do poorly in other activities too and may not volunteer or call attention to themselves. The more their language is activated, however, and the more fully they participate in ongoing activities, the more their limited reading abilities will be used and extended. If they cannot write an article for a class newspaper, they should be involved in illustrating, typing prepared copy, or duplicating and distributing the final copy. Those who cannot read a script well enough to play a part in readers theater or a puppet show should be involved in creating scenery or costumes, making puppets, directing action, and making up programs or advertisements. The more actively they participate in contributing what they can, the more they will be drawn into reading and writing, and the more they will be accepted and valued by their peers.

Echo reading and choral reading are excellent support measures. They provide poorer readers with a way of getting through material that is too difficult to read alone. These measures, discussed previously in this chapter, are like life preservers to those floundering in difficult text.

Whatever ways you use to support the efforts of less able readers and writers, all students of all abilities should be included. If echo and choral reading are used only with poorer readers, they shun these activities. Any measures that are taken only with less able students can become a kind of ghetto, as can the inflexible "low reading group." Groups should be changed and activities varied so that everyone, regardless of present performance levels, does different things and works with different peers. Sometimes students need to work with others of similar abilities; at other times groups should be formed on the basis of shared interests or need for instruction in a particular skill. These groups tend to be more heterogeneous and are more likely to overcome some of the social stratification that affects every classroom.

Using Non-Book Materials and Resources

If we want children to read widely for pleasure, to acquire information by being exposed to many types of printed materials, and to make reading a lifetime habit, then we must provide them with a wide variety of materials and activities to foster these goals. Since we depend heavily on the use of books in the classroom, we may overlook the many non-book materials that are readily available and extremely useful.

Newspapers are a perfect place to start. They are part of everyday life for most adults and should become so for children too. They are probably the most inexpensive and readily available form of printed material around, and they belong in every classroom. Daniel Fader, who has long advocated the use of newspapers, magazines, and paperbacks in teaching reluctant readers, wrote, "The newspaper is no more the answer to a teacher's prayer than any other inanimate teaching tool. But it is a superior tool when coupled with the animating force of the teacher's confident use, because it contains within its pages something to engage and reward the interest of every student" (1976, p. 82).

Most newspaper publishers are delighted to help you get started using newspapers in your classroom, because they too have a vested interest in helping children acquire the newspaper habit. Many larger newspapers employ education specialists who create classroom materials, work with teachers, and facilitate getting copies to your school. Smaller papers may not have such a specialist, but someone will be responsible for school services. Call your local paper and inquire.

In many areas the local paper may be a weekly, and many residents may rely on a daily paper from a big city some distance away. Which paper is more useful? We prefer the regular use of the most local paper, even if it lacks features the larger papers have, because by using it students get to know more about their own community and its businesses, resources, issues, and attitudes. You may choose to supplement the local paper with copies of the larger daily once or twice a week. In fact, having more than one paper available makes it possible for students to compare different coverage of the same event in news stories, editorials, and letters to the editor.

Because most comprehensive newspapers contain something for just about everyone, newspaper activities can include math, social studies, science, health, and other content areas as well as reading. The newspaper is an invaluable resource in integrating reading and language study with all the subject areas.

Magazines are another excellent source. Parents may be willing to donate copies of their favorites when they are finished reading them, especially weekly news magazines, which tend to pile up rather quickly, and the parent-teacher organization may be willing to buy subscriptions for classroom use. Before you make such a request, check with your librarian who subscribes to magazines for the library. He or she can tell you which offer special rates or incentives to schools. Also, contact your local magazine retailers or newsstand owners. Some may be willing to donate the leftover copies that must be replaced as soon as a new issue appears. Since such "leftovers" are usually destroyed anyway, retailers may be happy to let you have them if you carry them away. (Before you distribute those copies, be sure all are appropriate for children!)

MAGAZINES FOR CHILDREN

Boys Life Magazine. Irving, Tex.: Boy Scouts of America.

Cobblestone. Peterborough, N.H.: Cobblestone Publishing.

Cricket. La Salle, Ill.: Open Court Publishing Co.

Dynamite. Marion, Ohio: Scholastic Magazines.

Ebony Jr. Chicago: Johnson Publishing.

Electric Company Magazine. New York: Children's Television Workshop.

Highlights for Children. Columbus, Ohio: Highlights for Children, Inc.

National Geographic World. Washington, D.C.: National Geographic Society.

Odyssey. Milwaukee: Astro-Media Corp.

Ranger Rick. Washington, D.C.: National Wildlife Federation.

Sesame Street Magazine. New York: Children's Television Workshop.

Stone Soup. Santa Cruz, Calif.: Children's Art Foundation.

3-2-1 Contact. New York: Children's Television Workshop.

Your Big Backyard. Washington, D.C.: National Wildlife Federation.

A third source of reading material for classroom use is a mixed bag of catalogues and pamphlets. Catalogues of all sorts, which stuff the mailboxes of parents and teachers everywhere especially between September and December, are great sources of pictures, labels, descriptions, prices, and order forms. They are good for browsing as well as for the more structured activities discussed below. Pamphlets are a largely ignored source of limitless information. The U.S. Government Printing Office (Washington, D.C. 20402) is probably the largest source of free and inexpensive materials on just about any topic you can think of. The GPO publishes the *Monthly Catalog of United States Government Publications*, which are collected into a cumulative index for each year. It also produces subject bibliographies listing all their recent publications on a given topic, and you can write the GPO for copies of these bibliographies. Public and university libraries routinely receive copies of the *Monthly Catalogs*.

There are numerous other sources of free or inexpensive materials your students will enjoy writing for and receiving. (A list of such sources is given at the end of this chapter.) Local, state, and national tourism bureaus will provide booklets, maps, and all kinds of materials on written request, which will give students a chance to practice their letter-writing skills. Also, travel agents will often give all sorts of attractive booklets, brochures, maps, and posters to schools as they are replaced by newer materials. Such materials are much more visually attractive than typical geography and social studies materials, since they are intended to seduce people into spending their vacation dollars there and are usually packed with factual information about the climate, historical sites, culture, arts, traditional dress, and holidays.

Activities for Non-Book Materials

What can you and your students do with newspapers, magazines, and brochures? Here are some ideas to get you started.

1. Using newspaper advertisements or catalogues, locate and list (or cut out pictures and descriptions) of things you'd like to buy if you had only a certain amount of money to spend, say $100. Keep track of what you'd spend; no going into debt!

a. If you had to buy a used car and had only, say, $1000, what would be your best buy?

b. If you wanted to buy a new car, what would be the best buy? What kinds of cars cost the least? The most? What are the advantages and disadvantages of each?

c. Use supermarket ads to construct a "shopping list" of groceries for a week for your family. How much would you have to spend? How could you cut your costs?

   d. If you had, say, $100 to buy whatever you wanted for yourself, what would you buy? Cut out pictures and prices and make a Wish Book for yourself.
   e. If you had, say, $100 to buy gifts for everyone in your family, what would you choose? Make a Wish Book as above.

   2. Compare the horoscope columns from two or more newspapers for the same date, and a weekly or monthly magazine for the same period. Do they "forecast" the same things? If not, how do they differ? What is your "sign"? Use other sources to find out all you can about the characteristics of people with your sign. How are you similar or different to those predictions? Do horoscopes ever seem to come true?

   3. Find an interesting photo or cartoon. Cut it out and cut the caption off. Write a story about the picture making up as many details as you can. Or exchange pictures with a friend and write a story about his or her picture, then compare your stories.

   4. Try to write a summary of a news event in as few words as possible. Can you do it in one sentence? In "25 words or less"? Why do you think news stories are longer than this?

   5. Use the weather forecast and a weather map to figure out what the weather will be like tomorrow, or next week. What will the weather be like in another city? In another country?

   6. Cut out a wordless cartoon strip and write a description of the action or a dialogue for the characters. Or use one with words, cutting off the words. Write your own in the "balloons."

   7. Use sports pages and magazines to find out as much as you can about a favorite team or athlete. Write a biography of the team or athlete, illustrating it with magazine and newspaper pictures.

   8. If you have a favorite sport, find and cut out as many pictures as you can and glue them together to make a photo montage. Cut out words and phrases from headlines, articles, and ads to add to your montage. If you wish, add a short written summary of facts about the sport, scores of recent contests, or biographical information about a popular athlete. Display your montage.

   9. Find an interesting letter in an advice column and cut it out. Write a response to the letter as though you were the advice columnist.

   10. Using travel brochures, plan a "dream vacation" for yourself or your family. How would you get there? Where would you stay? What would you do and see? What souvenirs would you bring back? What would the weather be like, and what clothes would you need to take along? How much would you have to save for your vacation? Make up an itinerary for your trip and a budget of expenses.

   11. Use travel brochures and related materials to find out as much as you can about a place you're studying. Where could you write to get more information?

12. Cut out news stories without headlines and write new headlines for them. How do headline writers save space? Can you write a headline with the same number of letters and spaces as the original?

13. Select a printed recipe that sounds good to you and list all the ingredients you need. Then search the supermarket ads and find the lowest price available for each ingredient. Are there any ingredients you couldn't find advertised? Where would you buy them? Can you figure out about how much it would cost you to make the recipe if you had none of the ingredients on hand?

14. Cut out a cartoon strip and cut off the last frame. Now write an ending to the cartoon's "story" and draw a final frame to the cartoon.

15. Think of something you have that you'd like to sell. Write a want ad for the article. Use the newspaper's classified ad guide to figure out how much it would cost to run your ad. How could you save money by rewriting your ad?

SOURCES OF NON-BOOK MATERIALS

A list of a variety of materials for classroom use follows:

Selected Free Materials for Classroom Teachers, edited by Ruth Aubrey. Fearon Publishing Co., 2165 Park Blvd., Palo Alto, Calif. 94306.

Free Learning Materials for Classroom Use. The Extension Service, State College of Iowa, Cedar Falls, Iowa 50613.

Sources of Free Teaching Aids. Bruce Miller Publications, Box 369, Riverside, Calif. 92502.

Catalog of Free Teaching Materials. Rubidoux Printing Co., P.O. Box 1075, Ventura, Calif. 93001.

Over 2,000 Free Publications, Yours for the Asking, by Frederick J. O'Hara. New American Library, Inc., P.O. Box 2310, Grand Central Station, New York, N.Y. 10017.

Free and Inexpensive Learning Materials, edited by Joe L. Jackson. George Peabody College for Teachers, Division of Surveys and Field Services, Nashville, Tenn. 37203.

Sources of Teaching Materials, by Catherine Williams, Ohio University Press, Columbus, Ohio 43210.

1001 Valuable Things You Can Get Free, by Mort Weisinger. Bantam Books, Inc., 666 Fifth Ave., New York, N.Y. 10019.

The Whole Kids Catalog, section titled "Free or Almost Free," by Peter Cardozo. Bantam Books, Inc., 666 Fifth Ave., New York, N.Y. 10019.

Free Stuff for Kids: The Second Rainbow Book, edited by Barbara Haislet and Judith Hentges. Meadowbrook Press, 15235 Minnetonka Blvd., Minnetonka, Minn. 55343.

SOURCES OF INFORMATION ON CHILDREN'S BOOKS

Numerous professional organizations publish annotated bibliographies, book-lists, and other types of information about children's literature. The following organizations will provide you with information on what they produce.

National Council of Teachers of English, 1111 Kenyon Road, Urbana, Ill. 60801.

International Reading Association, 800 Barksdale Road, Newark, Del. 19711.

Association for Childhood Education International, 3615 Wisconsin Ave. N.W., Washington, D.C. 20016.

American Library Association, 50 East Huron St., Chicago, Ill. 60611.

Education Services Division, Scholastic Magazines, Inc., 904 Sylvan Avenue, Englewood Cliffs, N.J. 07632.

Superintendent of Documents, U.S. Government Printing Office, Washington, D.C. 20402.

The Horn Book Magazine, 585 Boylston St., Boston, Mass. 02116.

The American Council of Education, 1785 Massachusetts Ave., Washington, D.C. 20036.

American Association for the Advancement of Science, 1515 Massachusetts Ave., Washington, D.C. 20005.

New York Public Library, Office of Branch Libraries, 8 East 40th St., New York, N.Y. 10016.

American Friends Service Committee, 160 N. 15th St., Philadelphia, Pa. 19102.

Children's Book Council, 67 Irving Place, New York, N.Y. 10003.

Reading Is Fundamental, Room 2407, Arts and Industries Bldg., Smithsonian Institution, Washington, D.C. 20560.

Summary

A variety of methods and activities for teaching reading and using literature have been described in this chapter.

Teaching reading includes aspects of word recognition and comprehension. Word recognition is basic to getting meaning from print. Recognizing words at sight means immediate recognition without word analysis. Sight vocabulary is developed by seeing the same words frequently and in meaningful context. Dictated experience stories, word banks, pattern books and rhymes, matching speech and print through voice pointing, and using labels and signs help children acquire sight words. Word analysis includes using context, phonics, and structural analysis to decode words. Reading fluency is developed by choral reading, echo reading, and repeated reading activities.

Comprehension instruction includes both group and independent activities. Most common group activities are the Directed Reading Activity (DRA), Directed Reading-Thinking Activity (DRTA), and Guided Reading Procedure (GRP). Structured overviews and expectation schemes help students organize prior information and form expectations about what they will read. Independent skill activities focusing on specific comprehension skills should be used for practice and reinforcement. Activities include getting and organizing information, forming inferences and judgments, and responding to and evaluating what is read.

Comprehension involves responding to what is read as well as understanding it. Even young children are capable of literary criticism, or disciplined responding. Children can respond to stories and poetry by listening attentively, predicting story events and outcomes, illustrating, acting out stories, dramatic reading, composing internal dialogues for characters, writing about stories, critically discussing literature, reading poetry aloud chorally in dialogues and in voice choirs, and writing original poetry.

An important part of reading instruction is reading for pleasure. Individualized reading programs use trade literature in conjunction with school materials to teach reading. Book sharing through a wide variety of art, dramatics, and writing activities encourages wide pleasure reading.

Dealing with children's reading problems means assessing their strengths and weaknesses in all aspects of reading. Determining a reader's functional reading levels (independent, instructional, and frustration levels) is necessary for appropriate placement and instruction. Cloze and maze procedures and informal reading inventories (IRIs) are useful for this. Informal reading inventories include graded passages for silent and oral reading, questions for assessing comprehension, and sometimes word recognition, phonics, and spelling inventories. IRIs can help you spot comprehension and word recognition difficulties and deal with them instructionally. Inadequate sight vocabulary and/or poor decoding can cause slow, halting reading and poor comprehension. Concentrating on fluent word recognition, or word calling, can also cause comprehension problems. Appropriate activities are needed to build up weaknesses while supporting readers' strengths.

Non–book materials should also be a part of reading in language arts. Newspapers, magazines, brochures, and catalogues are all good sources. Many reading activities can be developed by using such sources, and they all help youngsters to extend and refine their reading skills.

CHAPTER SIX

Understanding
Written Expression

CHAPTER OUTLINE

The teaching of writing is the true test of any language arts program. Reading, talking, listening, and usage are all of fundamental importance in children's education. In their writing, however, we see revealed the color and complexity of their thought, the range of their reading, and the breadth of what they have experienced and talked about — in short, all of their intellectual and linguistic experience converge. But writing is more than the proof of what children know. The writing process itself provides them with the opportunity to sense more acutely, to think more deeply, and to express themselves more precisely than they could if they did not write. If humans have any actual means by which they can "lift themselves up by their own bootstraps," surely it is the gift of writing. When we write we can symbolize both the real and the imagined, and we can set the fruits of our thinking outside of ourselves where we can walk around them, consider them from all sides, go away from them and return to them, change them for the better, and share them with others. Is it any wonder that civilizations equate writing with human advancement and freedom?

Right now, writing instruction is undergoing a long-awaited renaissance in our elementary classrooms. Research is giving us a better idea of what it is that both old and young people do when they write. The better we understand the process that good writers use, the better able we are to set up conditions in classrooms and teach procedures that foster good writing.

First of all, we want to encourage children to write for "real" audiences, to consider topics before writing, and to critique and revise what they have written before considering the job complete. Second, we are beginning to recognize that even in the elementary school, children use a range of written forms that vary considerably from one another. They write stories, personal expressions, explanations, and arguments, and each of these forms calls upon a special aspect of writing ability. Teachers are beginning to recognize these differences and treat them systematically both in the topics they encourage children to write about and in the kind of help they give their students. Third, we are getting a better understanding of the way writing fits into a child's overall language development. We see the necessary role that talking, listening, reading, and being read to play in the child's development of writing ability.

In this chapter we will expand on these three areas of understanding writing —the writing process, the forms of writing and their requirements, and the development of writing in the context of other language skills. In Chapter Seven we will describe particular techniques for teaching writing, techniques that should make more sense to you after you have followed the background discussion presented in this chapter.

Our concern in these two chapters will center on *composition*, on what happens during the process whereby a writer first conceives of an idea, then goes through the business of shaping it up on paper, and, in the end, causes a similar idea to materialize in the mind of a reader.

Composition is not always the first thing that comes to mind when we think of writing and writing instruction. We may think first of handwriting, or spelling, or complete sentences, or punctuation, or neatness; that is, the *mechanics* of writing. We will deal with these aspects at length in Chapters Eight and Nine. To put them later is not to deny their importance; part of the task of learning to write is learning to express what we write in a form that will not distract the reader's attention from the message. Nonetheless, anyone who writes must first think of writing as the formulation and communication of a message. Otherwise there is no point in going to the trouble of polishing what we write (grappling with mechanics). So we ask you to concentrate with us first on composition — framing and expressing a message — and later on mechanics. Bear in mind, though, that as a teacher, you probably are now or shortly will be dealing with the issues of composition and mechanics at the same time rather than one after the other as we have the luxury of doing here.

The Process of Composing

If you had the job of training new employees at a large, diversified hospital, you might go about preparing for your work in the following way. You would carefully observe a competent person performing that job. You would analyze every task that that person carried out in the course of doing the job: all the steps that he or she performed as well as all the relevant knowledge that he or she used in order to perform each step. Then, when a new person was hired to do that job, you would know exactly what you had to tell and show that new employee. This procedure is called *task analysis*, and it is used as a part of industrial training programs everywhere.

Recently, the procedure of task analysis has been applied to the problem of teaching young people to write. Donald Murray (1980), who is both a Pulitzer Prize–winning author and a writing teacher, has carried out a detailed analysis of what accomplished writers actually do when they compose. What he found is directly relevant to writers of all ages.

Murray observed that the act of writing is not one act but four. It involves a complex mixture of *collecting* observations, *connecting* them to our previous experiences and to one another, *writing* them out, and *reading* them back as if we were someone else. Furthermore, Murray found the act of writing to be made up of not one stage but three: *rehearsing*, in which we plan what we have to say; *drafting*, in which we say it; and *revising*, in which we try to say it better. As we shall see, the forces of collecting, connecting, writing, and reading are played out during the stages of rehearsing, drafting, and revising. If we can understand these in detail, we can see clearly what it is we want children to be able to do when we teach them to write.

The Forces of Writing: Collecting, Connecting, Writing, and Reading

By collecting, Murray means gathering sensory observations from experience, or deriving insights from reflection. During every waking moment we are surrounded by sights, sounds, smells, and feelings that are potential fuel for writing. These sensations are not transferred onto paper verbatim, however, because there is another intellectual force at work that transforms them before we can articulate them on paper. This is what Murray calls the force of *connecting*: It consists of our constant acts of classifying, cataloguing, and associating every new sensation with past experience, which we must do if we are to negotiate the world successfully and not be overwhelmed by novelty. Yet for a writer, there is the possibility of doing too much connecting. This happens when, for example, we hear a new sound and say, "Oh, that's just a _____." We may miss the uniqueness of that sound, and we may let our past experience limit what we are able to learn from the new sensation. Murray concluded that the forces of collecting and connecting are thus somewhat at odds with each other. In order to make anything of the data our senses collect, we categorize them and connect them to our past experiences, but that act of connecting tends to make us ignore what is unique about what we have sensed. Novelists, naturalists, poets — in fact, all people who strive to experience the world deeply — must recognize the inbred tendency they have to treat everything as if they had seen it before and must avoid losing their sense of the unique in each new thing.

If people only collected and connected, they would not be writers. The next force at work is the force of *writing* itself. We gather impressions from the world and we stir them in our consciousness; we must now express them, put them outside of ourselves, write them down. The process of writing acts as a sort of filter for what we collect and connect. In our minds the mental experience of our sensations may consist of words and nonverbal memory traces. The sensations themselves may change, and our attention may fall on different sides of these impressions with each new reflection. When we write them down, however, our sense impressions are for now frozen in words, in "black and white." If we are not yet accomplished writers, the words may not have the color and the immediacy of our thoughts, but they are a beginning that we can build on.

As basic as the drive to express is the drive to criticize, or to evaluate. After the force of writing Murray listed this drive as the force of *reading*. When we write something down we read it back. Is it good? Did it capture the thoughts and images in our minds that prompted the writing? Like collecting and connecting, writing and reading are forces in opposition to each other, because our tendency to criticize can inhibit the act of expression. In other areas of experience we know that criticism can be devastating when we are in the first stages of doing something new, such as learning to dance or to play a guitar. We know if we have ever tried to teach anyone such skills that the criticism comes most often from the learners themselves, and when it does, it leads to a rigidity of thinking and acting that is inhospitable to learning something new. The force of reading can similarly restrict one's ability to transfer ideas into print if it comes to dominate expression. Nevertheless, complete disregard for criticism is not good either. Ideas sometimes chase themselves across the page, and it is our responsibility to see that they add up to something for the reader. Thus we must read what we have written as if we were someone else in order to see if we have achieved anything. The key is in the balance of writing and reading. Criticism must come but not before the writing has had a chance to take enough shape not to be obliterated by it.

The Stages of Writing: Rehearsing, Drafting, and Revising

By listing the intellectual forces at work in the process of writing we may have given the impression that this process begins with collecting and proceeds step by step through connecting and writing until it ends up with reading. Not so, according to Murray. When he describes the time sequence of writing, he lays out three stages: *rehearsing*, *drafting*, and *revising*. (All the intellectual forces may be at work in all three of these stages.)

Rehearsing, sometimes called "prewriting," is the beginning stage, the one in which writers think through the possibilities of what they might write. Of the intellectual forces, collecting and connecting predominate in the rehearsal stage, but there may be writing and reading too. We may write and review an outline, for example, or a set of notes to ourselves. Or, as in the method of "free writing" (see Chapter Seven), we may begin our efforts to write a paper by jotting down freely everything we can think of in connection with our topic, using what comes out not as the finished product but as raw material out of which we can create a finished product. We tend to forget when we give children writing assignments that they too need time for rehearsal, time to decide what they want to say about a topic. It is always advisable to give them opportunities to talk about their topic, to mull it over, perhaps to draw a picture first, before they get down to the writing stage.

The second of Murray's stages is drafting. Drafting is like writing except that the term is more tentative. This is because, as Murray insists, our first writing *is* tentative: We should expect that what we write out will be rewritten once, twice, or even more times. The translation from free-floating ideas to cold print can be immensely difficult to manage, and not even professionals expect to get it right the first time. Murray considers drafting an opportunity to get our thoughts onto paper, to see for ourselves what we have to say about our topic. Of the intellectual forces, not only writing comes into play but also the earlier ones of connecting and collecting. As we write out the early drafts, we discover new things from memory that we did not know were there, and we see new possibilities for connections between ideas that we did not suspect before we read them in print.

Professional writers lessen the sting of their own critiques by acknowledging from the outset that the first draft is tentative and that several others may well follow. They write these first drafts in the way that is easiest on themselves, not the way that looks best to the reader. They may use pencil or pen, they may make errors in penmanship or in spelling, they may cut their pages apart and tape them together in different orders. They know the final draft will have to be neat, but in the meantime they will not devote much attention to the visual appeal of pages that will eventually be thrown away in favor of a later draft.

Once our thoughts are in print we can read them and critique them. When the critiquing leads us to write portions over again, we have reached the stage of revision. First we study carefully what we have written and decide what it has to say. Then we go about shaping the writing so that it conveys its message most clearly and gracefully. Recalling the image of the sculptor removing granite from a block until the shape of the sculpture is fully revealed, Murray suggests that the process of revision is often one of removing any words, phrases, or paragraphs that may obscure the message. Sometimes revision leads us to take only one aspect of what we have written and to develop it fully, leaving in the wastebasket the parts that dealt with something else. Sometimes revision means that we rewrite the whole thing, taking off in a new direction entirely. At other times we may need to make only minor changes before our work is ready to stand on its own.

When we revise a piece of writing, it is important for us to put some distance between ourselves and the work so that we can see it as another reader might. When we read back at the same time we are writing, the thoughts in our minds that motivated the writing may speak to us as strongly as the words on the page. Thus we may think we have conveyed something clearly when we have only reminded ourselves of something we already knew.

Writers have different ways of achieving distance from their work. One way is to put a paper aside for a day or more after writing it and review it only when the thoughts that prompted the writing are no longer fresh in mind. Writers can also achieve distance by reading it aloud to someone else or by asking someone else to read the work, which is most successful when we realize what we expect of the reviewer. We do not want a grade. We do not want him or her to say "good" or "bad." We *do* want to be told what ideas the paper put into the reviewer's head. After all, the hardest part of writing is to put thoughts into words on paper. Thus the truest test of our success in writing is whether or not we put thoughts into a reader's head that are similar to the ones we had in ours when we did the writing.

The idea of revising the same paper many times can fill students with dread, but that threat of tedium goes away when they know that they will revise only those papers that they really care about. Calkins (1980a) writes of a third grader who voluntarily rewrote the same paper nine times before he was willing to let it stand on its own. Once the habit of drafting and revision is formed, writers receive the most important benefits that the act of writing offers: clear thinking, an appreciation of words and the turn of a phrase, a more critical reading style, and a sense of being more in touch with themselves and others.

The Approach of Children to the Writing Process

You may wonder at this point if the writing processes used by competent adult writers have anything to do with elementary aged children. Should we expect young neophytes and old masters to take the same steps when they create a composition? Essentially, the answer is yes. Some aspects of the process come naturally to children, while others need to be explicitly taught. The best evidence on this comes from Donald Graves and his associates Lucy Calkins and Susan Sowers, who conducted an intensive longitudinal study of elementary school children's writing.

Let's consider what Graves (1979) says about a child's approaches to each stage of the writing process: rehearsing, drafting, and revising. First of all, rehearsing: When children are allowed to take whatever approach they choose to a piece of writing, even the very young ones find it natural to start by rehearsing what they are going to say before writing. Six-year-old Toni, like many beginning writers whom Graves and his colleagues observed, chose to draw a picture before she wrote about her topic, an owl:

> Toni drew before she wrote, "I love super owl and I kiss him." When Toni drew, she chose the subject and gained control of the information as she sketched in the figure of a flying owl. . . . Drawing is the driving force behind much of Toni's writing. It serves as a rehearsal for the text as well as an important bridge from speech to print.
>
> — Graves, 1979, p. 19

Graves noted that the children used different approaches to rehearsing for writing. Some made repeated trips to the pencil sharpener or the bathroom as they thought about what they were going to say. Some talked out loud to themselves. Others talked about their ideas to nearby classmates. Still others started immediately to write, then examined and reflected on what they wrote before writing again. The findings pointed to the conclusion that young writers find it both natural and necessary to rehearse before writing.

What about drafting and revising? Do children view each draft of a paper as a tentative step toward a better product? Do they find rewriting necessary and natural? Apparently not. Editing and rewriting are tasks that do not come naturally to them. Instead, they are tasks that have to be modeled and taught. Unless children have seen serious adult writers creating several drafts to perfect a composition, they might easily believe that the flawless print they see in the books around them was written in one draft by flawless adult writers.

Graves therefore advises teachers to write in front of their students. If they see teachers talk aloud about the possibilities for a draft, then write, cross out, and rewrite, then consider aloud the merits and shortcomings of their works, and then again rewrite to make them clearer, they will see that editing and revising are necessary parts of the composing process.

Another impediment for children in doing revisions is their natural egocentrism. By this we do not mean that they are selfish. Rather, as we saw in Chapter Two, they have a cognitive tendency to assume that other people know what they know. They cannot easily take others' points of view or accurately judge others' needs for information. Assuming that a prime motive for revision is to make one's ideas clearer to an imagined audience, early elementary aged students may not be able to conceptualize this motive successfully.

Cognitive psychologists have observed that social experience helps children to overcome egocentrism in talking. Listeners grow impatient when egocentric speech leaves them guessing, and their complaints eventually teach children to take the audience into account. The experience of sharing their writing with others can help them overcome egocentrism in composition as well.

A third reason why drafting and revising may not come naturally to young children is simply that to small, unpracticed hands, writing is arduous. The task of writing even three sentences may tax a beginner to the limit. For this reason, many teachers do not begin to insist on revision until their students are able to turn out half a page or more at a sitting.

Moreover, even after they recognize the necessity of revising they will not automatically know how to do it. As Lucy Calkins has written, they usually need to be shown how to "make it messy to make it clear" (Calkins, 1980a). She and her colleagues in New Hampshire found that it was helpful to show children how to use editors' shortcuts and conventions for marking up their papers before revising them. Editors' marks include arrows to connect inserted sentences and paragraphs with their rightful locations in the text, carets to

Figure 6.1 Using editor's marks.

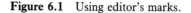

Robin When She Runs

When
Robin starts running. ~~Just then~~ her hair
starts flying. In a little while she
                          down
starts slowing ~~down~~. She starts
     panting
~~painting~~ like a dog. A few minutes
         takes some last big steps and she
later she Stops.

Robin is starting to run around the
track with some other ~~people.~~ people

show where new words should go, marks for reversing word order, and marks
to show when the spellings of words need to be looked up (see Figure 6.1).

As children become comfortable with the idea and practice of drafting,
they begin to vary the amount of attention paid to handwriting, mechanics,
and overall neatness, depending on whether they are writing an early, exploratory draft or a later one that is to be displayed or turned in. Graves, in the
study mentioned earlier, notes that when children are overly concerned with
handwriting, mechanics, and neatness in the first draft, they often lose track
of what they are trying to say. On the other hand, when they have taken the
trouble to follow the possibilities of a good idea through several drafts and they
have reason to take pride in what they have written and want to share it with
others, then they will have the motivation to write one more clean draft in
which the appearance and mechanics have been adjusted.

This suggests that in the same way that children learn to vary their spoken
language as the context shifts from home, to crowd, to schoolroom, a part of

learning to draft is learning to pay attention to handwriting and neatness in later drafts (Graves, 1979).

Revision is apparently a natural process for competent young, as it is for competent adult, writers. Like drafting, however, skill in revision does not come about all at once. Lucy Calkins (1980b) found in a study of third graders that they had no problem deciding whether to rewrite a piece. The difficulty came in knowing what to do when they rewrote. She noted that as they grew in their ability to improve papers by rewriting them, they seemed to employ similar strategies and to move from one up to another in the same sequence.

1. *Random Drafting.* The most primitive strategy Calkins observed was random drafting. Each new draft bore little or no relation to the one before it. Each new piece of writing took a new direction, as if the children had forgotten about the previous draft. Thus they were not revising their papers at all, though they wrote many papers on the same topic.

2. *Refining.* Refining was the strategy to which most children passed after they moved beyond random drafting. Their later drafts stuck very closely to their first ones; in fact they changed the first drafts only in superficial ways — mostly in spelling and handwriting. They did not elaborate the ideas in the first drafts or even rearrange them significantly. Calkins speculated that these children perhaps see writing as an unrevisable medium. They may be conceptually unable to look at a paper and imagine it a different way.

3. *Transitional Revision.* At a later time, many children who were first random drafters and then refiners entered a transitional stage. In this stage they would write one draft, then look it over critically, then begin another draft that was related to the first but which took a different approach to the topic. They would write many papers in succession in this way, but they rarely brought any into a final draft. This was a discouraging time for them, because it appeared that their expectations of their writing had suddenly been raised above their ability to produce. Their later drafts were not just refinements on early drafts but rather attempts to replace the previous drafts, which they themselves thought were poor.

4. *Interacting.* The most advanced revisers in the third-grade class Calkins studied used their first drafts to see what they had to say about their topic, then wrote later drafts to home in more closely on what they had decided was their central point. Here is a description of one student in this stage:

> "I don't think about titles for my piece until I've written enough drafts to find out what I'm writing about," nine-year-old Andrea says. Like professional writers, Andrea discovers what she has to say by seeing what she has said. She puts print onto the page in order to get her hand on it. "I don't know if this part's good, but I'll put it down so I can see," Andrea will say. She reads the section out loud, hearing and looking at her words as they lie on the desk in front of her. She may circle a line, saying, "This gives me an

idea for something better." The line is rewritten several times. As Andrea toys with the words at hand, she experiments with the direction and voice of her whole piece.

— Calkins, 1980b, p. 340

Interactors like Andrea have advanced along many fronts at once. They are mechanically fluent enough so that writing many drafts doesn't overwhelm them. They have developed a sufficiently critical eye and ear so that they can spot what is potentially good in a piece. And they have reached a flexible style of thinking about writing, so they can look at one piece and imagine it differently.

Calkins notes that it took time for the interactors to reach this advanced stage. Not only did they have to move through the more primitive stages first, but even within the last stage they did some growing. Andrea, for instance, had a very rigid and time-consuming approach to revision when she first reached the interactive stage. She would mark a sentence that needed to be changed, then redraft the whole piece to see how one change affected it. Only later was she able to try the same line several ways in a test draft before redrafting the whole paper. It was as if she had to learn the process of revision in an outward fashion—writing out each change to see how it looked — before it could become an inward process whereby she could imagine changes before they were thoroughly written out.

We will come back to the work of Graves, Calkins, and Sowers in Chapter Seven when we describe the specific techniques they recommend for teaching the writing process. Before we leave them, however, we should raise one question: Did the progress they observed in young children develop naturally or did their teachers teach them to write? The early work of Graves and his colleagues often conveyed the impression that children develop into fluent writers on their own; the teacher's instructional role was rarely put in the foreground of their report. However, the title of a later book by Graves on the subject sets the record straight: It is called *Writing: Teachers and Children at Work* (1983).

In essence, the work of Graves and his colleagues suggests that three conditions are necessary for children to make progress as writers. First, they must be allowed and encouraged to write on topics they really care about, with the expectation that their work will be read seriously for its content. After all, why should they sustain the effort of writing, marking up, and rewriting if they are not personally involved with their topics or expect what they write to be read with interest and care? Second, there is a developmental aspect to writing growth. Children need time and practice to get better at writing. The mentally mature child who has written extensively will do more interesting things with writing than the immature child who has written less. Third, children need sensitive guidance from adults in order to become good writers. What form this sensitive guidance might take is suggested in the following recommendations:

1. *Don't just talk about the writing process; get your students involved in tasks that will make them experience it.* You can't tell them they must learn to balance the forces of collecting, connecting, writing, and reading in the stages of rehearsal, drafting, and revision. It's important for *you* to know these things so you can understand what they're doing, but for children this sort of detail is overwhelming and unnecessary. Get them to write, and — little by little — make them plan what they are going to say, then think of other ways to develop or arrange their work, then rewrite to get closer to the ideas they feel could be more effectively expressed.

2. *Instruct them to write full papers, not fill-in-the-blanks as soon as they can do so.* They can make up the spelling (see Chapter Nine) at first and use spelling dictionaries later. They will learn from the beginning that the first priority in writing is formulating a message worth reading; the spelling and so forth can be taken care of in later drafts.

3. *Encourage them to rehearse before writing, but remember that they differ in the approach that works best for them.* Some need time to think about a writing task before they begin. Others find that drawing a picture first gets the ideas going. Some are helped by sounding out other students before they write. Others simply start right in writing, then see what they said, revise it, and go on from there. Be ready to suggest rehearsal methods to those students who need suggestions.

4. *Teach them to draft.* Point out that new ideas may occur to them after they have written a paper. Show them how they can mark up that paper, using arrows, taping on new pieces, and scratching out, in order to help them plan how the next draft will look. Point out that there are times when spelling and handwriting can be relaxed but other times when it must be right.

5. *Teach them to revise.* Through group and individual conferences, call their attention to what's good in their papers and to whatever needs further development. Ask questions that get them to think about ways to expand, redirect, and improve their papers. Teach them editing skills.

6. *Write in front of the children.* Write when they write. Demonstrate your own writing processes by composing on an overhead projector. Let them see all of the foregoing points in action.

7. *Share what they write.* Have them discuss their papers with other students. Post them on bulletin boards. Publish them in books and in classroom magazines and newspapers. When they write letters, mail them.

We will discuss in detail how to do these things in Chapter Seven.

The Issue of Balance:
Forms and Voices of Writing

Not long ago we joined with a group of teachers and school officials to design a playground for an elementary school. The physical education teacher said, "What we need is a balance. . . ." "A balance?" we asked, imagining an enormous painted steel balancing scale, large enough to accommodate 462 children at one time. "Yes," he continued, "a balance between devices that encourage upper body exercise, lower body exercise, coordination, social development, and imaginative play." We'd never thought of playgrounds in that way, but we could readily see that if we had been concerned with children's exercise to the extent that the physical education teacher was, the question of *balance* would have occurred to us too. After all, in health we promote a balanced diet, and in reading instruction a balance between fiction and non-fiction, decoding and comprehension, and so forth.

Suppose you heard someone suggest that children needed a *balance* in the kinds of writing they did. What kinds of writing would come to your mind? This is a serious question, because writing a poem is very little like writing an invitation for a guest speaker to visit the classroom: Each requires different writing skills.

Forms of Writing

If we wanted children to exercise all or most of their writing skills, what basic kinds of writing would we have them do?

This is not a new question. Students of rhetoric have dealt with it for thousands of years. In all that time, there has been general agreement that the kinds of writing boil down to half a dozen: *description, exposition, persuasion, expression, narration,* and *poetry.* Children, even first graders, are indeed capable of making recognizable efforts in all six of these categories. Below we will say a bit more about each category and immediately afterward discuss children's success at writing pieces that fit each one.

Description. Descriptive writing attempts to create a verbal portrait of its subject. Descriptive writers serve as the eyes and ears of their readers; they put us in the scene and allow us to experience what they experience. Here is an example:

> Deep in a jungle in South America, millions of cockroaches hide. When darkness comes, they will begin their nightly search for food. These tropical insects look just like miniature Darth Vaders. Each one has a shiny black head and a capelike shield. Scurrying about in the darkness, they nibble on fruits, dead animals, and decayed plants. Many are gobbled up by monkeys, birds, and lizards. These are *giant cockroaches.* Some grow to over four inches (10 cm) long. That makes them the largest cockroaches in the world!
>
> — Judy Braus, "Midnight Raiders and Other Invaders." In *Ranger Rick's Nature Magazine* 15, no. 11, November, 1981, p. 43.

Some writing is entirely descriptive, such as this example from a children's nature magazine. More often, however, descriptive writing is found imbedded in other kinds of writing:

> On this particular occasion the chair was taken by none other than the celebrated Miss Bianca, whose part in rescuing a prisoner from the Black Castle earned her the first Nils and Miss Bianca Medal ever struck.
>
> What a picture she made, as she stood modestly waiting on the platform for the applause to subside — her coat ermine-white, her long dark lashes fluttering over her huge brown eyes — round her neck a very fine silver chain — her whole tiny, exquisite figure thrown into graceful relief against a background of potted palms!
>
> — Margery Sharp, *Miss Bianca*. New York: Dell, 1962, p. 30.

Whether descriptive writing comes on its own or as a part of a longer work with a different purpose, its function is to convey exact images to us, what we would perceive ourselves if we had the writer's perspective.

Exposition. Expository writing explains. It may tell us how to do something or explain why something is the way it is. Here is an example of the first kind of expository writing, writing that explains how to do something:

> Use two long blocks from a block set or scrap lumber and go clippity-clop with them on a table to make the rhythm of a galloping horse. You can also hold one block in your hand and tap it with a pencil or spoon.
>
> — John Hawkinson and Martha Faulhaber, *Music and Instruments for Children to Make*. New York: Scholastic Book Services, 1969, p. 19.

For an example of the second kind of expository writing, that which explains how certain things are, just about all of this chapter should serve since it explains the process in a general way, without either describing one particular act of writing or giving explicit directions for writing or teaching writing (which is the topic of the next chapter).

Persuasion. Persuasive writing is intended to persuade the audience to take some action or to accept some belief. In adult writing, persuasion is used in newspaper editorials, in political campaign literature, in advertisements, and in religious writing. Here is an example:

> Tired of the same old drag? Summer's heat getting you down? Well, grab that someone special and get away from it all! Where?
>
> To sunny, colorful Martinique!
>
> To Martinique! Where miles of silver sandy beaches and aqua blue waters will have you relaxed and help you find the real you again in no time! Martinique! Where there's deep sea fishing, shell collecting, snorkeling, sailing, and lots of unspoilt beaches for soaking up the sun. Martinique! Where there are delicious meals, cooling drinks, and ultramodern hotels. Martinique! Where the friendly islanders say,
>
> "Come share paradise!"

Expression. Expressive writing tells others about one's own feelings, experiences, or point of view. People who write expressively usually are addressing readers who know them personally, and they use this type of writing much in the same way they use informal conversation. We rarely see expressive writing published; we most often see it in letters or in papers in which children write about their experiences.

Here is an example written by a six-year-old to a parent:

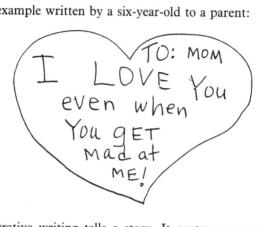

Narration. Narrative writing tells a story. It portrays an ongoing series of events that befall one person or several people, related by some motive, and leading up to some consequence or ultimate result. Narratives may be stories, in the familiar sense of tales such as *Peter Rabbit* or *Tom Sawyer* or *War and Peace*, but they need not always be fictional. We can have the "true story of the American flag" or "how Thomas Edison invented the light bulb" narrated as a sequence of events that develop a central theme.

Earlier in this book we presented a description of the structure of stories and also a sketch of story grammar, an approach that some psychologists have recently suggested as a reason for the similarities of the elements in stories and the relationships among them.

Poetry. Unlike the forms of writing previously discussed, poetry does not serve any one distinct purpose. It is usually expressive, but it may virtually serve all the other purposes as well. We can have narrative poetry, such as:

> Give us a tale, Grandfather Jones,
> Give us a tale, oh, do.
> I'll give you a tale, all right, I will
> But you must all stay quiet and still
> As I take you back to San Juan Hill
> And the charge of '92 . . .

There is also descriptive poetry, of which the Japanese haiku is a good example:

> In the shallows
> The fading sun abandons
> A lone heron.

There is even some expository poetry — lessons written in verse form that serve as mnemonics:

> Right is tight,
> Left is loose.
> (Describing screws, faucets, and so on)

> *I* before *e*
> Except after *c*
> Or when sounded like "a"
> As in "neighbor" or "weigh."
> (Describing a spelling rule)

> Red and yellow
> Kill a fellow.
> (Describing the bands on a coral snake)

The singing advertisement might qualify as persuasive poetry:

> If your snuff's too strong
> It's wrong.
> Get Tube Rose.
> Get Tube Rose.

> You'll wonder where the yellow went
> When you brush your teeth with ———.

Description, exposition, persuasion, narration, expression, and poetry are the basic sorts of writing that people do. Whether writing pleasant letters to friends, angry letters to uncooperative businesses, stories for publication, graffiti on subway walls, or scientific treatises — most of the writing people do conforms to one or another of these forms or some combination of them.

Children's Use of Different Writing Forms

"Write about elephants."

"Write about something that happened to you."

"Write about your family."

Assignments like these are common in elementary classrooms, but each one is incomplete. Even though they all specify topics, none tells the students what *purpose* and *form* their writing should take. Should they make up a story about elephants or describe them? Should they write a letter to a circus owner and ask for one? Should they write an argument against the extermination of elephants in East Africa? Whichever form the children elect, the task of writing will be quite different from what it would have been had they elected some other form. If the teacher pays no attention to forms of writing, the students are likely to gravitate toward some but then leave others unexplored.

Can children write in a range of forms? Yes. They find some forms more

difficult than others, but most of them are capable of differentiating their writing for different purposes, using different forms, even with their earliest writing experiences. In the following sections we will look at the ways they approach the various forms of composition.

Description. For their very first writing assignment, Ruth Nathan (Temple, Nathan, and Burris, 1982) asked a group of first graders to think of a member of their family or a pet, then to describe that person or pet in their papers so that a stranger could know something about him, her, or it from reading the paper.

Some of the children wrote:

MI DOG IS LOVABLE.
SHE IS BLAK.

MY PARIT IS OLWES CLRFL   ("My parrot is always colorful.
HE LICS TO FLI. HE LICS   He likes to fly. He likes
TO CRPE. HE OLWES LICS TO   to chirp. He always likes to
PLA.   play.")

MI MOM HAVE BRIN EYE AND   ("My mom has brown eyes and
A FAT TOME BECIS SHE IS   a fat tummy because she is
HAVEN A BABE.   having a baby.")

(In Chapter Eight we will discuss *invented spellings* such as those that appear in the above papers.) These fledgling efforts are clear in their purpose and clear in their form: They are pieces of descriptive writing. The very first time they wrote, these children were able to write for some purpose and use a definite form.

Older children, of course, handle descriptive writing more elaborately. The following piece by a third grader is in response to an assignment that asked her to write an item for the "lost and found" column in the newspaper:

Lost

A barbie doll white, white hair, blue eyes, blue jeans, pink sweater with barbie on it, pink boots with barbie on them and last seen walking into Leggets to get some jeans at River Ridge Mall. She is sixteen an if found call 863-0030, ext. 269 ask for Harold Hill. or come to 331 Jones Ferry Road apt. #5. Ask for mom or Wanda if not home go next door to apt. #6 and ask for Jean or Mrs. Ames and you will be given sixty-dollar reward.

— Wanda

A fourth-grade class went out on the playground where they divided into groups. One group sat on the ground with pencils and paper and observed as the other group ran in a circle around them. Each observer was asked to pick one classmate to watch and describe on paper. Before going inside, the students reversed roles so that everyone ran, everyone observed, and everyone wrote. Here are two papers that resulted:

Robin starts running. Just then her hair starts flying. In a little while she starts slowing down. She starts panting like a dog. A few minutes later she stops.

Jennifer H. when she runs

When she runs she picks her feet up high. Her feet
pat the ground hard.
She is huffing When she huffs she sounds like a train
Her clothes are flapping in
the wind. When she runs
her hair flopps up and down.
When she runs her heart beats fast. She look like
she is haveing fun because
she is smileing.

— Kelly

Descriptions can be challenging to write because the logic of description is not always easy. In the case of the "running" assignments, the children could describe what they saw in roughly the order that they saw it. With static objects, however, it is not always clear what kinds of elements should be mentioned, or in what order the elements should be listed. Description will thus remain a difficult form for children of all ages to master but a valuable one to attempt. We use elements of descriptive writing in nearly everything we write: letters, stories, poems, explanations, and arguments.

Exposition. Expository writing, as we noted earlier in this chapter, takes two forms. One form tells about something or explains it, while the other gives directions as to how to carry out some procedure. In one of their very first writing experiences, Ruth Nathan asked the group of first graders to explain in writing to others how to carry out a procedure — namely, "how to float on your back." Here is what two of them wrote:

HO 2 FOT N OR BAK I LAYA ON MI TOME AN STAN STEL FOR A YIL AN MUV VARE SLO. AN THE YOTR KEPS ME OP.	("How to float on your back I lay on my tummy and stand still for a while and move very slow. And the water keeps me up.")
YOU PRTAND THAT YOU ARE LAYING ON A BAD AN YOU JUS LAY BAK.	("You pretend that you are laying on a bed and you just lay back.")

Not surprisingly, older children usually put more into their expositions. These fourth graders were asked to write out directions for something they knew how to do:

How To Make a Cake

step 1: First get a sauce pan than after you get the sauce pan get the eggs, water, butter, and the flour.
step 2: After you have all of the supplies. Mix up the flour put in two or three eggs after you put the two or three eggs in put in a table spoon of butter after you have the butter stroke it 3,000,000 times if its to thick add a little more water if its not to thick don't add anything.

— Linda

Ingredients for being a Fast Runner

Step 1: Do exercises that make your legs develop such as deep knee bends (do at least 20 of them) and jumping jacks (do at least 20 of them). There's 7 days in a week so you should do these exercises 6 days a week.
Step 2: There is another thing you should do 6 days a week and thats run at least 1 mile.
Step 3: If you know how to run fast you should know how to fake people. except for your parents do not fake them.
Step 4: you can jump tree limbs that are 3 or 4 feet tall in height.

— William

The logic of expository writing is not difficult for children. The elements to be written out are the steps in a procedure. The order of the elements is the order in which the steps are performed. Of course, a number of things can go wrong. Children don't usually remember all the important details in a procedure or get them in the correct order. Also, their egocentrism may cause them to leave out or fail to explain a step that is clear to them but mystifying to the readers (what does William mean by "faking" people, for example?).

Persuasion. Persuasive or argumentative writing is used to coax others into believing or acting a certain way. Can elementary aged children use this form?

To find out, Ruth Nathan (Temple, Nathan, and Burris, 1982) and the present authors gave second and third graders the following assignment: *Think of something you would like to do but can't do because someone won't let you. Then write a letter to that person, trying to persuade her or him to let you do the thing you want to do.* Here are some of the papers we received:

Dear Mrs. Polino why won't you let us talk in the cafetearia: We have a right to! after all you talk in the longe. any way.

— Gail

Dear Debbie,
One day Debbie. Pow! Write in the ciser. O.K. Why is it allways we have to play baby. We never ride bikes.

Dear Dad,
Why can't I get a hourse? I would keep my room clean. I'd tak care of it. I'd be extra good I never would fight. Pleas! pleas! I would let my sisters ride it.

Sincerely,
Annie

Dear, Mom and dad. How come I can't ride into town on my bike. I'm careful enough around the block. If a car rides on the right and I'm on the right then I'll stop. And if a car rides on the left and I'm on the left I'll stop. And I'll ride on the side of the road.

Dear Mom, and Dad,
Mom I know we have Sam. But I'll chang the litter if we can have another cat. I'll take the litter out to the garbage. Please.

Sincerely yours,
Chad

Dear Mom and Dad,
I want a new stickerbook with new stickers. If you get it then I won't bug you about it any more. But maybe I will want more stickers. But not another sticker book.

Sincerely yours,
Megan

Dear Mom and Dad,
I want something real bad for my birthday. It's a puppy. I'll do anything for a puppy. If I don't get one I will die! Alot of people get animals for there birthday. If you get me one I'll paint my room. I'll feed the fish.

Love,
Nicole

Dear Mom,

I want castle grayskull because it could keep me occupied. And you would not have to listen to me saying I want castle grayskull. And I would play in my room.

Love,
Ricky

You can tell that all these children managed to write persuasively and that among them they used several different kinds of argument. If you were to consult a textbook on rhetoric, you would find that there are several basic persuasive strategies that writers can utilize. Young, Becker, and Pike (1970) describe four such strategies. Amazingly, the children whose papers we just presented used three of them. We will describe these strategies briefly, making up our own names for them.

1. *The Rational Strategy.* This one uses an appeal to reason or to a sense of fairness. "If other kids can do it, why can't I?"

Gail's letter to Mrs. Polino used this strategy: If teachers can talk in the lounge — their place to relax away from work — then children should be allowed to talk in the cafeteria — their place to relax away from work.

2. *The Reward/Punishment Strategy.* Another basic form of argument offers rewards to those who give in to the writer and punishment to those who don't. Automobile dealers advertise rebates on car prices, as an example of the first kind. Governments threaten litterers with stiff fines, as an example of the second.

Arguments that resorted both to rewards and to punishments turned up in the children's persuasive pieces. Annie promised rewards to her parents if they would get her a horse. Debbie's friend threatened punishments ("Pow! Write in the ciser.") if Debbie didn't let her choose the activity once in awhile. Megan and Ricky both offered to stop bothering their parents with requests if their wishes were granted.

3. *The Strategy of Overcoming Objections.* A strategy that is possibly more sophisticated than the first two is one that anticipates the reader's objections to the writer's argument and tries to undo those objections. Advertisements for life insurance companies often display the reasons why people claim that they don't need life insurance — they own farms or have a rich uncle who's a bachelor — and shoot these reasons down.

In the second graders' papers, the letter that requested permission to ride a bicycle into town used this kind of argument. The child anticipated that his parents would object to his request out of concern for his safety, so he tried to demonstrate that he knew how to ride safely and to stay out of the way of automobiles.

4. *The Strategy of Psychological Manipulation.* There is a fourth very subtle strategy frequently used by advertisers: manipulation. Advertisers use this strategy to make people feel ugly, unsuccessful, unwanted, and unclean if they don't buy certain products. Happily, no examples of this strategy appeared in the papers Ruth Nathan and we collected.

Expressive Writing. Left to choose their own approach to a topic, many children will write expressively. Expressive writing is centered on the self. It relates one's beliefs, likes, dislikes, and experiences. It is loosely structured and sounds more like spoken than written language. Even though the topic may be external to the writer, the writer's own feelings and beliefs stay clearly in focus.

Here are some examples:

i like disnee wolld. it is fun. i like spas mantin. the sumreens are fun to. oll the rides are fun. disnee wold is pllan fun. sum theing's are a maseing. like magic shoes and casles. you shod go thar sum time.

— Mosby, Grade 1

Nikia is my friend. I like him very much. He is my very best friend and is going to come to my house Wedsday. And I will be very happy. He will come this Monday and he is my best friend to.

— Grade 1

How I Feel About My Brothers Lukemia

These paragraphs are on how I feel about my brothers lukemia. Most of the time I feel like he could die anytime. I wonder what it would be like if he did die. Sometimes I wonder what my parents would do if he did and what I would do.

I act real nice to him most of the time, nicer than anyone Sometimes I do things with him when I'd rather be doing something else. Then I realize he's the same kind of person I am and I should treat him normally.

I go with him to Charlottesville when he has to go but I try not to miss any days from school. When he gets bone marrow needles in his backbone I hear him crying. I start crying so I have to go ride the elevators.

My brother has had lukemia since he was two and he's seven now. I guess I am real lucky not to have it.

— Kimberly, Grade 6

Narrative Writing. Children are often asked to write narratives but they sometimes find it difficult, which is surprising, because stories are the forms of writing they see most often. Note the following stories written by second and third graders. They were written in response to this assignment: *Everyone has a favorite vegetable. What is yours? Pretend that you have turned into your favorite vegetable. Write a story about your adventures.* Here is what some children wrote:

I am a carrot.

Hello, my name is carrot and I'm going to tell you a story. Once there was a boy and he planted me. And let me grow and until I got big. And got me out and he ate me up.

— No Name, Grade 2

The Carrot and The Rabbit.

Hi! Im a carrot and Im orange and Im crunchey and juisey. yum yum! said a rabbit hidding in the bushes as he came out. He chased me down the road and into the woods. We went all the way throuh the woods to a field. and finely he ate me.

— Mary, Grade 3

The Cucumber

Hi I'm a little cucumber. I'm in the refrigerraiter. Wait someone is taking me out. Now they are washing me off. Ouch! They are pealling me I wish they would stop Ouch! Finally they stoped. But after they stoped they got out a nife. My teeth started to chater. But just then I woke up and I found I was only dreaming.

— Bethany, Grade 3

My Carrit adventure

Once apon a time, a cupel years ago, I yust to be a carrit. It was a good life intil my life was in danged by five-hundred rabbits. And one of the rabbits cheased me into an open feild and then a hawk swoped down and carried the rabbit far far away, and that was the end of the rabbit, but it wasent the end of the hawk because I saw tons an tons of hawks and then all the hawks came down and looked over at me and they looked scared and I said this "What's a matter" and they said frightfully "take a look behind you" So what could I lose so I looked in back of me then I saw a lion, a wolf, a bear, a tiger, a rino and 15 cobras and I looked back at the hawks and all I saw thar was smoke so I ran as fast as I could and then I came to the Atlantic ocean and the ocean was howling and far far away came a great Whight Shark now what am I going to do with a shark in the ocean and fearce animals behind me. But to my relefe one of the hawk swoped down and picked me up veary carefully and carried me acrass the taribull ocean for seven day and seven nights and by the 8th mouning we arived in the middel a beuatiful garden and I made new friends and I lived happily ever after.

— Josh, Grade 2

Even though we asked for stories, the children wrote a remarkable variety of forms that were not all structured the way we expect stories to be structured. Let's examine some of the forms more closely.

The first three seem to qualify as stories. They begin by introducing a fictional character. They place that character in a problematic situation and they resolve the situation with an ending. What is it about them that makes them so easily recognizable as stories written by children? They seem to have a sort of "sliding board" structure to them. The situation at the beginning firmly sets the events that follow, and things swoop on predictably to their conclusion. "I am a carrot (carrots get eaten in this world). I run around. Somebody eats me. The end." Adult stories would have the protagonist set a goal (not get eaten), then present a series of attempts to reach the goal, followed by outcomes of the attempts, leading to some final resolution. Adult stories have an overall structure

CHARACTER + PROBLEM ⟶ RESOLUTION

containing smaller structures:

ATTEMPT ⟶ OUTCOME   ATTEMPT ⟶ OUTCOME

ATTEMPT ⟶ OUTCOME

Children's stories are more likely to have a single structure similar to the overall structure of adult stories, but lacking the related smaller structures.

Josh's story provides a fascinating contrast to the pattern of the first three stories. Far from the "sliding board" structure, he has a pattern we might describe as "one darn thing after another." Arthur Applebee (1978) calls this pattern a *focused chain* rather than a real narrative. The events are *chained* together one after another and they are *focused* on one protagonist (if the protagonist had been killed off early in the story and replaced by another, the result would have been an *unfocused chain*). Focused chains differ from more mature stories because the events do not develop one central theme; except for the very end, which is the conventional "I lived happily ever after," the character does not change from one scene to another. The order of the events themselves could be switched round without materially affecting the protagonist's development.

Focused chains give structure to continuing episodes on television. Think of the popular Saturday morning adventure cartoons with their unchanging heroes leaping from one peril to another, pausing only for station breaks and living happily ever after only at the end of the show, though their tranquility is sure to be shattered next Saturday, same time, same station. It would be wrong to assume that they were created by television, however. Focused chains have been present in children's stories for generations, and they are popular with storytellers all over the world.

Yet another difference between stories by children and those by adults is that children prefer to report action rather than motives. Characters in adult stories set goals. When things happen to them, they have psychological responses. At the end of the story, they are sadder and wiser or happier and wiser. The stories themselves may constitute a bit of wisdom: "So that goes to show you why it is foolish to expect to get something for nothing." Children's stories, however, are usually devoid of the psychological dimension, according to researchers (Mandler and Johnson, 1977). Even if we tell children stories with the psychological dimension — the goals, the internal responses, and the morals — left in, when we ask them to relate these same stories to others, they usually recount only the outward events and leave the psychological dimension out.

Nevertheless, children do not always omit goals and other psychological information, as the following story shows:

Me a Carrot

One morning when I woke up I was a carrit. I could hurdly belifeve it. I was ornge and green such a dull coler. I went to school. I did not want the kids to laufh at me but they did. My proublem was I did not know how to turn back into a purson. So I looked in evry magic Book. It was not in there. So I called the docker he gave me a Book and some aspbren. I turned back into a purson.

— Jennifer, Grade 2

The following stories were written for the same assignment:

Corn on the Cob

Now I have to do the dusting o-no Help Help some one Help me o-no please don't eat me plese. I tast like beans I can give you anything you want but me. If you like butter on me I don't have any. I have hot dogs and plenty of ketchup. Anything look there's some coffie over there it's folgers. Dont eat me. Help police. Ok I wont eat you I'll have a hot dot and some coffie. O thank you.

— David, Grade 2

I like cucumbers. And I like carits. Carits are good for you. Spench is good for you to. I dont like spench.

— Charlie, Grade 2

Unlike those we have discussed so far, these do not seem to have the form of stories at all. As it turns out, they are typical of a beginning writer's first stories. Applebee (1978) called them *heaps*, because the children seemed to heap together thoughts and observations without any attempt at creating a structure. Susan Sowers (1979), one of Donald Graves's colleagues in New Hampshire, called them *inventories*, because they struck her as inventories of everything that children knew or liked about the thing named in the topic. For Applebee, heaps and for Sowers, inventories were the earliest story forms children produced.

Yet a few of these stories do not seem to be heaps or inventories any more than they are real stories (narratives) or focused chains. David's piece, "Corn on the Cob," is a dialogue on the problem of being a vegetable that is about to be eaten. There were other dialogues in this set of papers too: using conversational language, including dialogue, instead of a strict story form with its characters and strict organization of certain kinds of elements. The reasons why many beginning writers make this choice have been explored in an interesting way by James Britton. His explanation is extensive, so we will devote the next section to it. First, however, let us make some concluding remarks about writing stories.

As writing assignments, stories have strong advantages and strong disadvantages. The advantages are that children are very familiar with them. They are surrounded by stories from infancy. They encounter them constantly both in school and out. Thus when they are asked to write a story, most of them plunge ahead enthusiastically as if they know what they are doing, but stories are by far the most complicated form of composition to handle because of their complicated structures. Most children can write expressive pieces far more easily than stories. Susan Sowers (1979) found that, given the opportunity to choose, children would write other forms of prose more frequently than they would stories. When they do try to write stories, they often write heaps or inventories or expressive pieces instead. While there is nothing wrong with this (with time and practice, their writings will get more storylike), they can get more of a balance of writing tasks and possibly experience more success if they are also encouraged to write in forms other than stories.

The Voices of Children's Writing

When children are asked to write stories or explanations or persuasive pieces, their works often come out sounding bouncy, loosely structured, and conversational. In other words, they sound like expressive writing.

James Britton (1970), a teacher and writing researcher in England, offered an explanation of why expressive writing keeps popping up in children's work. His explanation has to do with their language experience and their movement from talk into writing. It also has to do with their basic self-centeredness and the gradual process of realizing that their audience doesn't know the same things they do. Britton is worth taking the trouble to understand, but first we must come to terms with the labels he uses for the various forms of writing. Whereas we have been speaking here of six forms — description, exposition, persuasion, narration, poetry, and expression — Britton reduces these six forms to three basic *voices* of writing: the expressive voice, the transactional voice, and the poetic voice.

The Expressive Voice. The expressive voice is essentially the same as the expressive writing form we have already described in this chapter — the sharing

of one's personal feelings and observations. Writing in this voice has several distinctive characteristics. For one thing, it is very much like conversation: loosely structured, shifting in topic. For another, writers in the expressive voice write as if they knew their readers, as if the readers knew about the same things the writer knew about, and as if the readers were interested in the writer personally. Thus the writer is much in evidence in her or his own writing, both by the presence of the personal pronoun "I" and by the selection of topics and the treatment of them, which are of more concern to the writer than to anyone else.

The Transactional Voice. The transactional voice is a large category that includes the writing forms of description, exposition, and persuasion. What these three have in common, according to Britton, is that they are all intended to get something done in the real world, to conduct some sort of business between writer and audience. In the transactional voice the writer usually stays in the background. The focus is on the thing being described or explained, the process being elucidated, or the point of view being argued rather than on the author's personal feelings and experiences. If we are reading a nature book, we do not expect to read that spiders give the author the creeps. If we are reading a newspaper account of a train derailment, we do not expect to read about how early the reporter had to get out of bed to reach the scene or how the twisted wreckage made the reporter feel.

Transactional writing involves readers actively; it makes them do something. If it is descriptive, the readers can visualize the thing described and be able to deal knowledgeably with it should they ever encounter such a thing. If it is expository, they should understand the explanation or be able to carry out the procedure described. If it is persuasive, they should accept or reject the author's point of view. They should find themselves nodding their heads in agreement as they read the argument or shaking them in objection.

The Poetic Voice. Britton's poetic voice includes both prose and poetry. To qualify, a piece of writing must have been created as a verbal object meant to stand on its own and be enjoyed. Stories are not intended to conduct any business, as with transactional writing. We don't agree or disagree, believe or disbelieve stories. Instead, we appreciate them as wholes and are amused or moved by them as their authors intended.

Poetic writing differs from expressive writing in that it concentrates on events, their structure, and significance. Expressive writing focuses on the writer and his or her likes, dislikes, ideas, and experiences. Writers may put themselves into their own stories, but when they do so the focus is still on what happened, on the structure of events, more than on what the writer thought about them.

Britton has found that a child's earliest writing is done in the expressive voice. It usually keeps the writer in clear focus, so much so that to understand and appreciate much of children's early writing we must know them personally and be interested in their affairs. This may be caused largely by their egocentrism: They seem to assume that we see what they see, and they therefore neglect to explain things that we as readers do not know about.

A child's early writing tends to be chatty and loosely organized, very much like conversational speech. It is probably so for two reasons: first, because conversation is the language form with which children have had the most experience and with which they are most familiar; second, because it is easier for them to organize their ideas loosely than to set up and stay with a definite structure for their ideas, whether the structure be a story form, the steps in carrying out a procedure, or the reasons why the reader should accept some written argument.

The Transitional Voice. Beginning writers' preference for the expressive voice is so strong that expressive writing often crowds in when they write stories, explanations, arguments, or descriptions. Thus Britton has set up another more flexible category of writing, which he calls the transitional voice. This is a blend of either expressive and transactional or expressive and poetic voices.

Look again at this second grader's attempt to write a story about her favorite vegetable, a cucumber.

> I like a cucumber, because I am a cucumber. Do you know why I
> am a cucumber and we do not. Know why you are a cucumber.

This piece could be described as transitional between expressive and poetic writing. It has two expressive features. First, there is a consistent focus on the writer. We hear about what the writer likes. Second, the structure is conversational; in fact it is structured in the form of a dialogue. The child asks a question, and the audience actually enters the paper and answers it. The only poetic feature about this brief paper is that the child tried to imagine that he had turned into a vegetable.

Here is another piece, this one written by a second-grade boy doing a persuasive writing assignment:

> I want to drive a car.
> Dear Mom and Dad. Would you let me drive your car no-o-o! O.K.
> I want to. No-o. I'll drive the car tonight. They are asleep. I'll go
> get the car.

This transitional piece is a mixture of all three voices. It is persuasive to the extent that the boy thought of something he wanted and imagined an argument between himself and his parents to get it. It is expressive in both of the same ways the other paper was, namely, in the focus on the writer and his desires and actions and in the structure of the piece as a dialogue. Here again, the audience actually enters into the paper, uttering a firm "no-o-o-o!" The paper is also a little bit poetic, since the second part of it turns into a fictionalized account of events.

Elements of the expressive voice generally linger in children's poetic and transactional pieces because they have not yet learned to adhere to the structures of presentation demanded by the latter two voices. The remnants of the expressive voice that most often persist are the focus on the writer's self; a loose and somewhat rambling structure; and occasionally, but not always, a dialogue written into the paper.

Guidelines for Developing Children's Writing

Before leaving the use of different forms of writing, let us see what guidelines we can deduce from all this for those who teach children to write.

1. *Children can write in a wide range of compositional forms, but it may be necessary for you to suggest that they do so.* Left to their own devices, they will write in the form that is most natural for them, and, as we have seen, that form is expressive writing. It seems pedagogically sound for teachers to press for more of a balance in the forms of writing because children *can* write in these forms without suffering ill effects and because high school work and the demands of later day-to-day writing will require that they be able to write description, exposition, and persuasion as well as expression and narration.

We recognize, however, that they should be able to choose their own topic and direct their own approaches in much of the writing they do, in half of their papers at least. This is necessary because choosing and focusing a topic are tasks that require as much skill as other aspects of writing, and this skill can develop only if they have enough opportunities to exercise it. Also, as we noted earlier, in order for them to take the trouble to revise and refine their papers, they must have a strong stake in their topics, which comes more readily from self-selected topics than from the ones that have been assigned. The teacher's challenge, then, is to put enough variety in the writing assignments so that the students can learn to use a spectrum of writing forms, while at the same time giving them plenty of opportunities to choose and direct their own approaches.

2. *When you do give assignments, try specifying the purpose of the writing* (describe, explain, persuade, tell a story, create a poem, share a feeling or experience) *as well as the audience* (classmates, students in other classes, parents, other adults, teacher) *for whom the writing is done.* In our experience, children rarely have trouble sticking to the *topic* in writing, especially if it's one they have chosen themselves, but it is much more difficult for them to write for some purpose and to write with a particular audience in mind. They usually need practice in these latter two aspects, and thus your assignments should stipulate purpose and audience. Also, the purposes and audiences should be *real* as much as possible. The children should explain things that need explaining, and persuade about things that matter, for an audience that really has some reason to be interested in the writing.

3. *When your students create persuasive writing, call their attention to the kinds of arguments they and their classmates are using so they can learn to use different kinds.* You can have them practice persuasion in oral discussions and debates, or role-play persuasion in skits and puppet plays, or act out stories before they write. They can also use the format of letters to practice persuasive writing.

Is one persuasive strategy any better than the others? It depends on the content of the persuasion. Depending on the audience, it may be necessary to use all of the strategies at one time or another. David Ogilvy, a successful Madison Avenue advertiser, found this to be true when he was asked by the city of New York to design a new advertising campaign to combat the city's persistent problem with littering. When he accepted the assignment, he reviewed what his predecessor had done and found that previous advertisements pointing out how beautiful the city would look without litter, or showing how much tax money was spent to pick up trash, had already reduced littering by 75 percent. The remaining 25 percent of the litterers needed a different approach, Ogilvy reasoned. His new ads took the form of street signs that read: "No Littering. $200 Fine!" (Ogilvy, 1980).

Rather than tell the children to use any one persuasive strategy to the exclusion of others, we should take advantage of the diversity of strategies they are already using, make them more aware of the differences, and help them develop the ability to decide when circumstances justify the choice of each approach to persuasion. We can do this without resorting to pompous-sounding terms like "rational strategy" (although children actually enjoy knowing fancy names for concepts once they fully grasp the concepts). We instead can call their attention to the strategies of persuasion that they and their classmates have used in a particular assignment and ask how it would be to use a particular strategy with a different audience.

In regard to the persuasive papers we saw earlier in this chapter, for example, we might discuss the way the writer of the bicycle paper anticipated his parents' fears about his safety in waging his argument. How, we might then ask, could we use the same kind of argument to ask for a horse? In the same vein, we could discuss the reasonable approach used in the letter to Mrs. Polino and ask how we might shape the same argument to persuade Debbie to ride bikes once in a while. What makes a certain form of argument appropriate or not is the *context* in which it is used: who uses it, for whom it is used, what circumstances prompted it. Discussing the arguments children use can increase their realization not only of the range of possible types of arguments but also the kinds of contexts in which they are suitable.

4. *When children write stories, help them cope with the complexity of managing the numerous elements in their restrictive structures.* One way to do this is to have them practice thinking in terms of story structure. The Directed Listening-Thinking Activity does this with stories the teacher reads to the children (see Chapter Three). The Directed Reading-Thinking Activity does it with stories they read themselves (see Chapter Five). Both devices challenge them to predict outcomes of stories, given the evidence of the early passages they read. The basis for making the predictions in both exercises is usually the logic, or the structure, of stories.

We can call their attention to story structure by *talking them through* the writing of a story. In the case of the "vegetable assignment," for example, we could conduct a preliminary group discussion and have the class suggest a particular vegetable, then put it in a challenging situation. Then we could interject this suggestion: "Suppose the vegetable decided *not* to get eaten? What could it do? What would happen next?" In this way, using a group brainstorming format, we could help students manipulate those elements that make stories interesting: namely, the character's attempts to overcome a threatening situation and the conflict that results. Still another way to help them with the complexity of writing stories is to give them more guidance when we make the assignment itself. In making the vegetable assignment, for instance, we could say, "Pretend you are your favorite vegetable. You are growing in the garden, when a little bird tells you that one day you will be eaten. You decide you will *not* be eaten. How does your story go?" This assignment provides setting, protagonist, initiating event, and internal response plus goal and thus it sets the children up to finish the story in a way that gives it a more well-formed structure. Such an assignment, however, also limits their choices, so you must judge when and how often to use such a highly structured assignment. Limiting choices occasionally gives them an idea of a structural form that they can use later on, but it also limits the play of their imagination and it can inhibit the expressiveness of their writing.

5. *Don't pressure children into giving up expressive writing too soon.* Although heavy reliance on the expressive voice is the mark of the beginning writer, it does not follow that discouraging its use will encourage young writers to grow, any more than discouraging informal discussion will make them any better at giving speeches. The expressive voice is an important aspect of learning to write because it is a sort of laboratory where personal interests, experiences, imagination, and ideas come together. True, it is more concerned with self-discovery than with communication, often leaving readers out in the cold, but without the writer having made some self-discovery, little of interest can be communicated. Consider the science or social studies reports that third graders write. They go to the encyclopedia, copy down a few choice sentences, write a beginning and end, and produce a paper that shows no sign of their curiosity having been aroused or satisfied. Although such papers may be all transaction and no expression, excluding the expressive voice in an attempt to be objective and factual will result in papers that are barren and dull.

What we should encourage, then, is *parallel* development in all three voices: transactional, poetic, and expressive. We should give children plentiful opportunities to write expressively, to give vent to their feelings and experiences on paper, but at the same time we should challenge them to write descriptions, explanations, arguments, and stories and help them see how writing of these types is structured. If the various voices are mixed together for a time, so be it. More opportunities to write and discuss the effect of what is written will eventually give them control over the different modes of writing. Too much criticism in the meantime will inhibit effort, reduce fluency, and slow the rate of development.

6. *Surround children with models of good writing.* How do students learn story structure — what an interesting plot is like? How do they make a character come alive? Surely it is from reading and listening to other stories, written by people good enough to get published professionally. The same is certainly true about description, exposition, and persuasion. Children learn how these forms are handled by reading and appreciating good models of the forms.

The classroom should be filled with good examples of literature — and not just fiction but the other forms as well. There are two ways the teacher can encourage the children to take special note of the forms the pieces of writing have. One is to talk about the structure and encourage them to see how the writing is arranged. Another way, best suited for shorter and simpler pieces, is to have them write pieces that follow the same pattern.

In the next chapter we will describe techniques to put these and other suggestions into practice as we teach children to write.

Summary

Writing is in a sense the focal point of the language arts program. It is one skill that calls on all of the others for its development: Talking, listening, reading, grammar, spelling, and handwriting are all directly reflected in children's writing ability.

In this chapter, we suggested that the process of writing that adult professional writers use is applicable to child writers too. In Donald Murray's description of the writing process, there are three phases of writing: *rehearsal, drafting,* and *revising.* In rehearsal, writers explore their material and decide what they have to say. In *drafting,* they write out their material. Now that they can see what their material looks like on paper, they are ready for the phase of *revision* in which they read their work critically, as someone else might, and decide how they can convey their message more clearly and effectively.

Throughout these three phases, four intellectual *forces* are at work: *collecting* impressions and insights, *connecting* ideas into meaningful frameworks, *writing* out thoughts, and *reading* them back with a critical eye.

Children can be taught to use this three-phase process, and classroom practices should be geared accordingly. In particular, they should be encouraged to choose meaningful topics, to consider each draft of a paper tentative, and to critique and revise their writing. Revising is learned in stages: *random drafting, refining,* and *interacting,* which relate to the kinds of changes they are able to make in their previous work. Also of importance is to give them real purposes for writing and real audiences to read their papers.

The issue of balance in a writing program was discussed, and we suggested that students be encouraged to compose in all the forms of writing: *description, expression, exposition, persuasion,* and *narration.* Children as young as first graders can demonstrably use the nonnarrative forms of writing; in fact, we saw that stories are often the most difficult forms of writing for them.

When children try to produce stories and fail, the results are often *inventories*: lists of observations centered on a common topic. Many of their efforts to write more disciplined forms — be they stories or expositions — often come out as expressive writing. James Britton offers an explanation: *expressive writing,* the self-centered, bubbly, conversational kind, is close to the oral language beginning writers are most familiar with. The other voices, the *poetic voice* (fiction and poetry) and the *transactional voice* (description, exposition, and persuasion) are less like spoken language and are also more highly structured. Thus a child's early attempts to write in the poetic or transactional voice are quite often mixtures of expressive writing with one of the other two voices.

What should the teacher do about all this? The best course of action would be to assign writing in all three voices — expressive, poetic, and transactional. Unless the writing task requires children to use one of the other voices, they will write in the expressive voice. You will therefore need to encourage them to write descriptions, explanations, arguments, and stories from time to time but be sure to encourage their development in the expressive voice as well.

All this leads to a host of practical questions. What are some approaches to writing that enable children to write about meaningful subjects to a caring audience? In the next chapter we will describe several, including cultural journalism ("Foxfire writing"). How do children learn the various forms of written language? One good way is to use well-written model pieces as patterns to be imitated (we explain this in the next chapter). How exactly do you get children to revise a piece of writing and make it better? See the section on editing in the next chapter.

Also in the next chapter are many ideas for teaching children to write poetry, directions for binding their writing into book form so that it can be read to others, guidelines for evaluating their writing, and suggestions for helping the underachievers.

CHAPTER SEVEN

Teaching
Written Expression

CHAPTER OUTLINE

A tremendous variety of instruction goes on under the label of teaching writing, or composition. We teach handwriting, spelling, grammar, punctuation, situational conventions such as the parts of letters, and a whole set of concepts and techniques for generating ideas and setting them forth in writing. In this chapter, as in Chapter Six, we are dealing with composition and are concerned specifically with helping children express themselves in writing, getting ideas onto paper, and conveying messages to an audience. The teaching of mechanics such as spelling, grammar, and handwriting will be dealt with in Chapters Eight and Nine.

Even with mechanical aspects of writing considered separately, teaching composition is a complex process. In this chapter we deal first with the process of composing and ways to teach this process. Then we describe ways of working writing tasks into everyday settings and assignments, which we call functional writing, and follow it with a description of cultural journalism projects. Next we explore the writing of poetry and fiction and discuss ways of producing and publishing children's writing in the classroom, including the organization of a young authors' conference. The chapter closes with discussions of ways to evaluate children's writing and techniques for helping unfluent and reluctant writers.

Modeling and Teaching the Writing Cycle

Teaching writing means showing children how to work with their ideas and words so they can write what they mean effectively. To do so, you will have to not only *teach* the writing process but also *model* it.

The process of writing involves rehearsal, drafting, and revising. In rehearsal, or *prewriting*, the students discover and explore what they want to write about. In *drafting*, they create more than one rough draft of what they want to say about a topic. In *revision*, they craft their writing by adding, deleting, and moving sections, polish their writing and then produce a final version of it.

At each stage it is critically important for you to show them how these goals are accomplished by writing yourself and sharing your work with them. They have to *see* how a writer crafts his or her work rather than just *hearing* how it should be done. You should begin writing instruction by modeling the writing cycle, then continue to participate as a writer yourself throughout the year. Donald Graves (1983) demonstrates the writing cycle in this way:

1. Draw up a list of five topics you really want to write about, choosing topics that will interest your students; for example, a camping trip, a pet's death, an embarrassing school memory.
2. List your topics on the board, discuss each briefly, and tell how you came to choose one of them to write about at this time.
3. Begin a very rough draft on a transparency at the overhead projector so that students can *see* your writing begin to take shape. While you write, describe aloud your thoughts, word choices, and changes in focus or direction as they occur to you.
4. Begin revising on the transparency, using arrows to move or add parts, crossing out some parts and substituting others, making marginal notes, and asking students for suggestions. As in step 3, think aloud as you work.
5. At this point you can ask them to begin producing their own lists of possible topics, choosing one and beginning a rough draft. A few days later, as they get ready for further revisions, return to your transparency and revise and edit further as in step 4.

This kind of modeling shows students in concrete ways the steps writers go through in producing and crafting a piece of writing. When they actually see *you* mark up a rough draft, change directions during writing, struggle for the right word or image, and seek others' suggestions about your writing, they begin to realize that these are necessary and positive aspects of all writing.

BOX 7.1
The Writing Cycle

Stage I: Prewriting or Rehearsing

Discover what you have to write about by:

Keeping a list of topics in a work folder

Interviewing others and being interviewed

Writing alternative leads for a topic

Drawing before writing

"Free writing"

Stage II: Drafting

Make your writing more effective to others by:

Cutting drafts apart, changing and adding parts, and taping together

Using arrows and other marks to show changes

Using invented spellings for unfamiliar words

Using a dictionary, word bank, or other sources for correct spellings

Dictating a first draft to someone else

Stage III: Revising

Rework your early drafts and polish your writing by:

Sharing your work with others and seeking their suggestions in group conferences

Participating in teacher-student conferences

Editing your work for mechanical problems

Producing a final version of your writing

You should continue this modeling procedure regularly; once a week is good. Sometimes you should do some "uninterrupted free writing" on a transparency, during which time students can think about and begin a paper but cannot interrupt you for, say, ten minutes. After the time is up you can start circulating again. Graves (1983) noted that this practice has two positive effects: It shows young writers that everyone needs uninterrupted time in which to think and compose, and it helps them to develop self-reliance when they cannot always get immediate help from the teacher. Teaching the writing cycle involves making them aware of the need to undertake all three stages of writing and teaching them what to do at each stage (see Box 7.1).

Stage I: Prewriting or Rehearsing

There are many ways of helping children to explore what they are interested in and may have to write about. The goal of prewriting is to help them discover that they all have good ideas and much information in their heads, waiting to be written about, that others can share. Some effective prewriting activities are:

1. *Keep a list of topics.* All students should create lists of topics for future writing and keep them in their work folders, and they should periodically update their lists as their interests and store of information change. When they wonder, "What can I write about?" their lists will help them find a topic.

Discuss what makes a "good" topic. A third-grade class in New Hampshire came up with these guidelines:

Do	*Don't*
write about something you care about.	write about things that are boring to you.
start off with action, with here-and-now.	write about something you haven't done yet.
choose just one part or aspect of your topic.	keep going if it gets worse and worse.
	pick a topic that's too big for you to detail.

— Calkins, undated, p. 5

2. *Conduct interviews.* When one child interviews another, both may find a topic and a starting place. Interviews help the interviewer decide what questions need to be asked about a topic and help the interviewee discover what will interest others about the topic. One child might bring to class some significant object and be interviewed about it, as in this scene from a third grade:

> Andrea brought a bird's nest to school, intending to write about it. Her teacher suggested that a friend interview her about the bird's nest, "to find your story."
> The interview began with questions about the bird's nest. "Where did you find it?" "Did you see any feathers near it?" "Did you see it being made?" Each question deadended. No, Andrea hadn't climbed the tree to get it. No, she hadn't seen it being made, or found feathers near it.
> Eventually Diane found a question which worked. "Why did you bring the nest in?," she asked. Soon Andrea was telling her about her long-standing interest in birds, and about how she'd always wanted to fly when she was little. Andrea wrote the beginning of her piece. . . . Once when I was little I got a hank to fly. So I tried jumping off things and tried to float up and across. I tried and tried until my father made me and my sister cardboard wings. . . .
>
> — Graves, 1979, p. 572

3. *Write alternative "leads."* Leads are opening statements. Once a topic is chosen, children can be asked to write three different lead sentences and choose the one they like best before proceeding. This helps them discover a focus for their writing and avoid being "trapped" by their first idea. It also makes clear from the start that trying out new ideas and selecting some parts while crossing out others are routine practices in writing.

After Andrea wrote an opening sentence for her bird's nest paper, her teacher underlined it and suggested she write a different opening:

> Soon Andrea had written three different leads, each one more immediate than the one before it.
> lead 1: Once when I was little I got a hank to fly. So I tried jumping off things and tried to float up and across . . .
> lead 2: I always wanted to fly, but whenever I tried, I always fell Kaboom! on the ground . . .

lead 3: Kaboom! That hurt! Why can't I fly? Birds do. Whenever I try it, nothing happens . . .

Andrea chose her third lead. "It's happening now." She liked the active, present-tense voice she'd achieved through writing and rewriting her lead.

— Graves, 1979, p. 572

4. *Draw a picture first.* Traditionally we have allowed children to illustrate their completed written work as an embellishment, a reward for writing, or a time-filler for early finishers, but drawing first, then writing, is an effective way of helping them discover what they want to say about a topic first.

Drawing more than one picture may be helpful: a sequence of events, different characters, or alternative actions. Drawing as a rehearsal for writing is particularly effective for young or reluctant writers.

5. *Do "free writing."* Often we discover what we really want to say only after we've started writing on a new topic. According to Peter Elbow (1976), few writers plan firmly in advance but rather shift the focus, find new possibilities, or change points of view *during* the writing. This procedure can result in writing that lacks cohesion, or in giving up the attempt in frustration. Free writing, or writing without stopping in a stream-of-consciousness for a specified time period, helps writers make these discoveries before they have committed themselves to a particular direction for their work.

Free writing can be *unfocused*, with no predetermined topic, during which time a topic may be discovered; or it can be *focused*, in which writers jot down whatever comes to mind about a particular topic. The writer does not reread, make corrections, or stop to think; the writing must be *continuous*. Those who get stuck must put down something like "I'm stuck, I can't think of anything to write . . ." until a new idea pops to mind. Figure 7.1 is an example of a focused "free write" by an older student on the topic of her best friend. She has run sentences together, misspelled words, and "stalled" a little toward the middle; her focus changed several times as she let one idea trigger another. This written rehearsal, however, can help her select ideas, words, and images to include or discard when she begins drafting her composition. A conference with her teacher or a partner may help her find a "center of gravity" for her first draft if she has trouble choosing what to use from the free write.

Free writing for five minutes or longer is a good rehearsal for fairly fluent writers, those who write rather quickly and confidently. It is less effective for students in third grade and below than the rehearsal techniques discussed previously.

Stage II: Drafting

Prewriting and rehearsal activities pave the way for the process of drafting. The whole idea of creating additional drafts is to clarify meaning and to express more precisely what the writer has to say. It involves mentally stepping back from the work, considering what the reader might need to know, and developing objectivity about the writing. After meaning is clarified, the mechanical

Figure 7.1 A focused five-minute free write

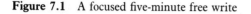

Okay what am I going to write about my best friend. my best friend is Helen, why do I like her so much? because mostly because she is kind to me she always is kind. What does that mean? She always seems so glad to see me she makes me feel like I'm very important to her. Its a wonderful feeling to be important to someone. She respects what I say about things but that sounds like we never argue. Oh we do, sometimes about little things that are so silly like what we should have done differently or why somebody is the way they are but even when we argue we are close to each other. I would rather argue with Helen than chat with anybody else. What else do I like about her? She always she always I'm spinning my wheels. why is it so hard to tell why you like somebody? It must be hard to talk about feeling like that usually we hide our feeling so nobody will laugh at us. Helen never laughs at me, never, that's one important thing I like about her so much. I can be myself just as silly or stupid as I am sometimes and She likes me anyway. She is a very easy to like person She has good taste in friends!

aspects can be polished in later drafts. Teaching the following procedures helps children develop drafts:

1. *Cutting and pasting.* Encourage them to write first drafts on large paper or with spaces left between lines, then to cut the papers apart and move sections or sentences around, taping or gluing sections together, until they find the most satisfactory arrangement of ideas.

2. *Using proofreaders' marks.* Show them how to use arrows, carets ($\wedge$), and other marks to indicate deletions, additions, and changes of wording.

3. *Using invented spellings.* In early drafts, not knowing how to spell a word can seriously inhibit the writer. Children should be encouraged, therefore, to attempt spellings of words they want to use and wait until later to check them with a spelling dictionary, word bank, or another person. As you will learn in Chapter Nine, allowing children to invent spellings for unfamiliar words helps them exercise their growing word knowledge and allows them to use the words they wish to use, not just those they can spell, in their composition.

4. *Using sources of correctly spelled words.* During the drafting stage they will need sources of words they can use in their writings so that they won't have to struggle over one word after another. When several children are writing about the same topic, let them suggest words they or others might need, then write them on the board for reference. Personal spelling dictionaries can be frequently updated, with new words copied into them, allowing a page for each alphabet letter. Bulletin boards and similar displays of common words should be available; one might feature pockets holding word cards, with a pocket for each beginning letter.

5. *Dictating to an older student or adult.* Most children, especially young ones, can think much faster than they can write. Their best ideas may never get into words unless they can occasionally dictate their thoughts to someone who can write quickly and accurately. Older students who can benefit from practice in transcribing speech (see Chapter Three) or adult aides or volunteers can help children construct a first draft from which the child can work to complete further drafts.

6. *Using guidelines for drafting.* Even young writers can discuss and suggest ways to make their early drafts more powerful and effective. You might begin by presenting a few suggestions by effective adult writers like Strunk and White (1978), Macrorie (1976), or Elbow (1981), and then eliciting suggestions from the children. Some general guidelines suggested by the foregoing writers are:

— Say what you mean directly.
— Be yourself; write in your own "voice."
— Describe sights, sounds, smells that put the reader into the scene.
— Write as though you were *telling* the reader about the topic.
— When you use descriptive words, choose vivid, precise ones.

Student-generated guidelines, with examples, can be made into posters or bulletin boards for frequent reference during the drafting process.

Stage III: Revising

Revising is the complex process of deciding what should be changed, deleted, added, or retained in a subsequent draft of a composition. Young writers need feedback from peers and from you to help them develop the ability to criticize and improve their own work. The cornerstone of the revision process is the *writing conference* (Calkins, 1980; Graves, 1983), an informal meeting in which you and one or more students discuss work in progress and offer suggestions Conferences are of two types: *scheduled* and *unscheduled*.

Scheduled conferences are planned in advance; all the students know when their conference with you will be and prepare for it by bringing a current composition-in-progress to discuss. Graves (1983) suggests a scheduled conference with each youngster once a week, always on the same day so that the conference is routine. If you have twenty-five students, five per day will allow you to meet with each one once a week. Scheduled conferences are short, although times vary depending on where the writer is in the composition process; four to five minutes is about average. During that time, most or all of these things will happen:

— The student shares a current composition in progress.
— You ask what is going well and receive an answer.
— You ask what is going badly and receive an answer.
— You ask where the student wants the writing to go next.
— You point out *one* skill or aspect of the writing to be developed or checked.

Some teachers keep a simple record of what transpired in the scheduled conference. After much experimentation, Graves (1983) and the teachers with whom he worked found that unless record keeping were extremely simple and fast, no records were kept. He suggested a notebook with a tabbed divider for each student's name and a few sheets of paper, each divided into a number of boxes as in the completed sample below:

Oct. 10	A Skunk I Saw
(date)	(title)
run-on sentences	+
(skill)	(rating)
good experience and involvement in piece	
(note)	

— Graves, 1983, pp. 144, 299

This form is simple enough to note what the students were working on, what skills the teacher drew to their attention or what needed further instruction, and any quick observation. It is short enough to prevent you from writing very much for each child, getting bogged down, and abandoning the effort.

Scheduled *group* conferences give children a chance to get feedback from peers and to provide it too. They are very important, because students should never become dependent only on *your* response to their writing. These conferences are held in groups of three to five, and the students share a work-in-progress and elicit help if it is needed. Sometimes a child will read a paper to a group and ask for help: "This beginning is boring but I don't know what to do" or "What else do you think I should put in?" Sometimes no help is sought, but just a chance to share: "I feel really proud of this." In a group conference of five children and the teacher, two can share and all provide comments in under ten minutes.

Unscheduled conferences take place as you move about the room speaking to individuals as they work. Such conferences are extremely informal and spontaneous; they usually consist of asking the students how the work is progressing, listening closely to the reply, and offering a word of praise or encouragement, a suggestion, or a way to get help. Like the scheduled conferences, these are chances for the writer to talk and you to listen and they rarely take more than two minutes. They are good for "base-touching," monitoring, and supporting; the student leads the way by indicating what, if any, problem may be occurring, and the teacher suggests a way of approaching it, offers a positive comment, and lets the student get back to work.

Graves found that in a daily sixty-minute writing period he used his time in this way:

5 min.   — once a week only writing with the class
10 min. — circulating around the class with individuals
20 min. — group conferences
5 min.   — circulating around the class
15 min. — individual conferences
10 min. — all-class share time

— Graves, 1983, p. 36

In any conference, the key to success lies in asking *questions that teach*: questions that lead children to discover what they have to say and want to communicate and that encourage them to talk about the work. Here are some suggestive types of questions:

To get started:
— How is it going?
— What are you writing about now?
— Where are you now in your draft?

To help explain and elaborate:
— Can you tell me more about that?
— How did you learn about this?
— Can you say more about . . .?

To help focus on the writing process:
— Where do you think you'll start?
— What do you think you'll do next?
— Where do you want this piece to go?
— If you put that idea in, where could it go?
— If you started again with that lead, what might come next?
— When you're not sure how to spell a word, what do you do?

To help writers see their own progress:
— What's the most important idea here?
— What's your favorite, or your strongest, part?
— How could you change _____ to include your new idea?
— How did you choose your subject?
— Why did you choose this lead?
— What problems might come up later?
— What do you think of your work so far?

Graves's book, *Writing: Teachers and Children at Work* (1983) is the definitive work on conferencing and guiding the writing process. We strongly urge you to use this source.

The guidelines for conducting writing conferences are listed in Box 7.2.

Peer Editing

Students should have extensive experience helping one another edit their work if they are ever to learn how to edit their own. It is generally easier for all of us to see what others have done well or poorly than to see those same aspects of our own work. Thus it is with children: They have an easier time editing the papers of others, because they can achieve more distance from them than they can from their own. Eventually, the skill they develop in editing others' papers can be applied to editing their own work.

Two effective approaches to peer editing are the group editing workshop (Cramer, 1978) and the teacherless writing group (Elbow, 1976).

The Editing Workshop. Cramer's (1978) editing workshop is a well-organized group procedure for teaching children how to edit their own writing. He recommends the procedure for the third or fourth grade and above and urges teachers to use group editing procedures systematically over a period of several years. Because children need sustained, frequent experience with editing before they develop the objectivity needed to fully edit their own work, it is a good practice to plan group editing about twice a week on a regular basis throughout the year.

BOX 7.2
Conducting Writing Conferences

Make conferences brief and frequent.

Let the writer read the work to you.

Let the writer talk; you listen. When you ask a question, allow enough time for a studied response.

Ask questions that lead students to tell you what they know, are doing, are confused about, or are proud of.

Focus on meaning until the final draft stage.

Take one thing at a time; suggest only one change or point to be considered in any conference.

The editing workshop follows a writing assignment in which individuals produce a draft or a composition beforehand. Cramer recommended that students have extensive experience editing nonfiction writing before they edit more imaginative work, and we concur. Until your students have had a number of these experiences, use factual or descriptive writing as the stimulus. Ask them to write a description of an object, scene, or event, a summary of a story heard or read or a film, a report of a science experiment, or a description of a real-life or story character. The writing of a draft for editing by each student who will participate should be completed the day before the editing activity. These drafts should be double or triple spaced. Here are the steps to follow in conducting this type of workshop:

1. Get permission to use a draft. Students can refuse but only with the understanding that they will submit a draft for editing at some time.
2. Prepare a transparency of the work. Omit the writer's name.
3. Project the transparency and allow sufficient time for all to read it. During this time *no* comments are allowed.
4. Ask, "What did the writer do *well?*" List on the board all comments and mark selected words or phrases on the transparency. *Only* positive comments are allowed.
5. If comments dwell on mechanics, lead the discussion to content by asking, "What sentence do you like best?" or "Who can point out a really effective word choice (lead, idea, and so on)?"
6. Then ask, "What could be *changed* in this paper?" (see Figure 7.2).
7. When three to six changes have been suggested, *stop*. Summarize the types of changes made on the bottom of the transparency.
8. Ask students to go through their own papers and check the areas noted, making necessary changes. Leave the transparency up for reference.

The Teacherless Writing Group. Peter Elbow's (1976) group activity focuses entirely on content and is most suitable for upper elementary students and advanced writers in middle grades.

In this activity each member of a group brings a composition to share and critique. If possible, copies are made for each group member; if not, a transparency of each paper can be used or the paper can just be read aloud. One person begins by reading (or displaying) his or her composition. Then every other group member responds in one of four specific ways to the writing:

— *pointing*, or stating what words, sections, or ideas the responder found most effective
— *summarizing*, or recapitulating in one sentence what the responder thought the main point, or "center of gravity," was
— *telling*, or saying what the paper made the responder feel or think about as it was read
— *showing*, or describing the paper metaphorically as if it were a season of the year, a tone of voice, an article of clothing, an animal, a kind of music, a place, or any other metaphor

Figure 7.2   An editing workshop sample

It's

A red maple tree live in the forest. Its a beautiful tree. It has many many

branches. Birds sit on it ~~and~~ animals come sit by it and little boys climb it. It *(It*
eats, drinks, and breathes through the roots.)
eats thrw the roots/and drinke thrw the roots/and breath thrw the roots. The

They are
leaves look like a crown. There red and yellow, the top of the tree is the corwn. *crown*

The roots are up under the ground to hold up the tree, the stem support the *T* *s*

A tree's
main part of the plant above the ground, a trees stem is called the trunk. In

Trees   their   don't   until
the winter the tree's lose there leaves and dont get them back intil spring of

weather   trees   leaves
the year. When the wether turns warm again the tree's get new leves again.

All summer the leaves are green.

Contractions: It's (it is), don't (do not), they're (they are).
Plurals: no apostrophe (trees).
Run-on sentences: period and capital letter.
Spelling: through, leaves, until, weather, their.

The writers do not comment in any way until everyone has finished responding; then they can respond to the comments. The process repeats itself with the next writer's paper. Before breaking up, the group should evaluate their work by taking turns commenting on the tone or helpfulness of the meeting.

In a teacherless writing group writers learn what their writing says to others, whether it communicates what they intended. Responding is focused, with readers or listeners reacting to the work without saying things like "This is good . . ." or "I didn't like . . . ." These groups yield the most productive responses when the children have already participated in group and individual conferences with you. In time, they learn how to respond helpfully and constructively to the writing of their classmates.

Teacherless writing groups of four to six members are best. The participants should change frequently so that they can experience a variety of audiences. This procedure is most effective for students in fourth grade and above, although primary graders can participate if they clearly understand what the group's purposes are and how to respond.

With teacherless writing groups in any grade you should model and discuss helpful responding and work closely with each group, but avoid dominating it.

Using Word Processors

Many schools are rapidly acquiring microcomputers for use in math, science, and other subjects. Word processing software makes the microcomputer a valuable tool in the writing program. Professional writers, including those in the newspaper industry, have been using computerized word processors for some years.

The great advantage of word processors lies in their capacity for revision and editing. Writers can produce one draft after another from the same base of words, expanding, deleting, moving sections, and rearranging at will without having to recopy. Cutting and pasting rough drafts is replaced by the use of editing features, which are generally simple for children to use.

During the process of revising, conferences with the teacher or with peers can take place around the word processor. You can demonstrate right at the keyboard how to add, delete, rearrange, or change lines or sections of the work.

If "hard copy," or a version of the work printed on paper, is desired the printer can produce flawless, attractive final drafts in minutes or less. Youngsters are delighted to see their work emerge in perfect form, with right-justified margins (each line ending directly below the preceding one, as in professionally published books). Publishing children's writing, for display or binding into books, can now be particularly attractive and professional looking.

Even young children can learn to use the computer keyboard for composing. In fact, active composing at the computer is easier for them than handwriting, since they are freed from the constraints of letter formation, spacing, and neatness. Since recognizing letters on the keyboard is easier than remembering and producing them, the composing process is faster, which is a great aid to young writers, whose thoughts and words run far ahead of their ability to write letters. As a result, their composing efforts are much less laborious and more rewarding (Richards, 1984). Children's enthusiasm for computer games extends into using personal computers for writing. We don't need to convince most children that the process will be fun; we need only to show them how to use today's technology efficiently.

Most word processor software in schools, however, was designed for adult users and is not always ideal for children. One software program, *The Bank Street Writer* (1982) is ideal for use in the classroom. It has a clear, simple, and readable tutorial (instruction) program; it is "menu driven," meaning that the editing functions of the program are continuously listed across the top of the video screen, and a single key press allows selection among them with no complicated editing controls; both lower- and upper-case letters are used; words are never divided at the end of a line of text; blocks of text being manipulated are highlighted on the screen to visually set them off; a "find-replace" function locates repeated instances of a word in text for spelling checks and wording change; and, it has the option to print exactly what appears on the screen in a 40-column display, or to convert to a standard 80-column printed format. This latter feature means that after children have edited and set up what they want on the screen, they can print out an identical copy. Almost all other word processors automatically convert a 40-column screen display to an 80-column printout. *The Bank Street Writer* is currently available for Apple and Atari computers. The school version, which has a teacher manual designed for self-instruction, is available through Scholastic Inc.

The field of word processing software is changing so rapidly that a review of available programs would be dated almost as soon as it appeared in print. Manufacturers are updating and improving their products, particularly for the student and school markets, and soon many programs will be available with the features *The Bank Street Writer* has. The best source of up-to-date reviews of word processors are the popular computer journals, like *Teaching and Computing* (Scholastic Inc.), *Personal Computing* (Hayden Publishing Co.), and *The Computing Teacher* (International Council for Computers in Education).

Word processors are having an enormous impact on the teaching of composition. Don't overlook these important tools for your classroom.

Functional Writing

Functional writing is expository material that meets an immediate need or a practical purpose in the classroom. These two characteristics make functional writing easy for most students to produce. It is also the type of writing most often done by adults in their everyday lives. For these reasons, children at all grades should have a great deal of experience doing functional writing, such as letters, reports, observations, summaries, and journals.

The functional writing adults do arises out of real need or usefulness. In the classroom, however, such writing is most often artificial, done for practice rather than for a real purpose. John Merritt (1978) used the terms *Gerbil* and *Mickey Mouse* to differentiate between real and artificial classroom activities. Gerbil activities, like their animal counterparts, are real; they may be unpredictable and at times messy, but they can yield real and sometimes unanticipated insights and experiences. Mickey Mouse is cute and clever, but unreal; activities resemble Mickey when they have some momentary appeal but are artificial and have no real-life outcomes. One learns little about real mice by observing Mickey.

How can you tell the difference between a Gerbil and a Mickey Mouse activity? One of the best ways is to consider the outcome or result of the activity. If students write something, is the writing used in the same way that it would be if someone had written it outside of school?

This point is best made by example. Writing letters is a fairly common activity in real life. When we write letters, we do so to communicate with others — friends, relatives, companies, charities, and so on. We write our

letters, mail them, and hope for some response. We don't hang them on bulletin boards or turn them over to another person for evaluation, although we may seek another's criticism before we mail them. Although we are concerned about the letter's appearance, including spelling and punctuation, we are at least equally concerned about how clearly we have expressed ourselves.

Children can write letters in school, and letter writing is often assigned as an activity to practice spelling, grammar, or handwriting. If, however, the letters are written to practice particular skills rather than to communicate with real people for real reasons, if they are evaluated and returned or displayed rather than being mailed, or if they are written for the teacher's purposes rather than for the children's, then letter writing is a Mickey Mouse activity. It is only when letters are written for real-life purposes — communicating with pen pals, seeking information from a company or government agency, or expressing opinions to a politician or school official — and when the letters are actually sent and replies studied that letter writing becomes a Gerbil activity. Spelling, handwriting, and other mechanics can be worked on and letters evaluated before mailing, but these purposes are secondary to the communication aspect.

Journals or diaries are another example. Outside of school, people write in journals to communicate with themselves, to preserve a record of their feelings and life's events; rarely is such personal writing done to communicate with others or to be criticized or evaluated by anyone other than the writer. In real-life journals, the writer retains absolute control over topic, length, and frequency of entries.

In school, journals are most often used to give children regular practice in free writing and self-communication. They can be asked to write at regular intervals, rather than writing at whim, so they can establish a "journal habit." This is a sound practice, but the journal's purpose should be free expression. If reading of journal entries is done privately by the writer and past entries are used to help the writer gain insight into his or her own emotions and behavior, the activity is a Gerbil. If, however, entries are graded or corrected by the teacher, if subject matter is censored to conform to the teacher's opinions or preferences, or if the journal is used only as a notebook for creative writing assignments, then the activity is a Mickey Mouse. People out of school don't keep or use journals for those purposes and neither will children.

Letters, journals, and every other form of functional writing must be real, or else children will simply not continue using them outside of school. If the purpose of the writing is to get a grade, they will not continue that writing out of school where grades are not given. Our greatest challenge is to develop functional writing activities that extend beyond the classroom walls and into the world outside of school.

The following sections describe some common types of functional writing that can be used to help meet this challenge.

Journals

Quite a few people like to keep diaries or journals. In form and content they are as unique as the writers who create them, but they are vehicles of personal expression and communication with oneself, because they are intensely private.

To many people, the greatest benefit comes from being able to reexamine the past, finding patterns in their own emotions and actions, reexamining their feelings and behavior with some objectivity, and putting things in perspective. They gain a sense of themselves in a larger context.

Journals kept over time can give children the same important insights, which may well be one of the best reasons for encouraging them to keep journals. Because they are more egocentric, more centered on themselves, than most adults, gaining objectivity about themselves is even harder for children than for adults. They are often less aware of their own motivations and the consequences of their actions than adults, but the act of writing them down, and the occasional thoughtful rereading of entries, can help them feel in control of their emotions and see evidence of their own growth and change.

One teacher we know has her students write something every day; once a month they take extra time to silently reread that month's entries, and in that day's writing they make a statement about what they have learned. Children are capable of great thoughtfulness, and some of their written statements reflect this:

— "I never should of had that fight with Natalie. I should of said I was sorry right away, and then maybe she wouldn't still be mad at me."
— "It was funny how scared I was about my report card. I thought my mom and dad would be really mad but they were not mad. My dad said math was hard when he was in school too."

— "The best day of the month was when we had Field Day and I won the 100 yard dash. I was really happy. My mom put my trophy on the mantel. I like to look at it sometimes."

Students can also be encouraged to review their journals for evidence of their own growth in writing. Because writing fluency often grows slowly, month-to-month evaluation may not be best. Evidence of growth is most striking when recent entries are compared with those written several months or a semester ago. Depending on their grade and writing ease, students can be encouraged to look for aspects such as increasing length of entries, fewer spelling problems, more complete sentences, better punctuation, use of more complex sentence forms, more precise or descriptive language, or whatever other criteria you believe show progress.

Remember that children may have more trouble than adults do in seeing evidence of their own progress, so talk to them about ways that such progress can be shown and elicit their own ideas. Also, they usually become so accustomed to and dependent on the evaluation of adults that they may find it hard to look at their work objectively or look for positive aspects rather than errors. Periodic journal review can become a powerful way of helping them develop objectivity, evaluate their own work, and see how they are growing in individual ways.

Since journal writing is a form of free writing, it should not be edited, corrected, or graded by the teacher. While children should be producing plenty of writing that *is* subject to editing, revising, and evaluation, journal writing does not serve that purpose.

There are two types of journals: *focused*, in which they are used to practice collecting ideas and sensory images for other writings and describing things, and *unfocused*, in which they are used for communication with oneself.

Focused Journal Writing. The processes of collecting and connecting, described in Chapter Six, can be practiced in journal writing.

Collecting, or gathering and recording sensory experiences to fuel thoughts and writing, is done by letting the children choose an object, a memory, or a mental scene and write about it in their journals. A few moments of silent reflection before writing will help them to focus their thoughts and words on the things being described. Those who get stuck without an idea can try describing a favorite object, a classroom or family scene, a recent event or conversation, or a scene outside the window.

Connecting, or describing how some things are like other things, is extremely useful. Children can be guided to connect experiences they write about to others by thinking and writing in response to questions like these:

— What does this remind you of?
— What other events made you feel nearly the same way?
— How was this event like another you remember?

— What other people or things have some of the same characteristics or features?

— When was the very first time you can remember you felt the same way?

Journal entries developed in these focused ways can be applied in other, more structured writings by using the journal as a sort of "warehouse" of ideas, descriptions, conversations, and characters. Many professional writers use this technique. Youngsters can use it to add to their other writing as well as to see some practical reason for free journal writing.

Unfocused Journal Writing. If children are already routinely using prewriting activities and keeping a folder of ideas for future writing, they might keep journals more for personal introspection and self-communication. Also, it may be easier to get reluctant writers, especially older students with negative attitudes about writing, to use journals for unfocused writing.

Unfocused journal writing is good for practice in sustained writing at regular intervals, just as sustained silent reading in self-selected materials is good for reading practice. In order to develop the journal habit, students should write in their journals routinely and regularly, but you must determine in advance *how often* you will want them to write in their journals, *how much* writing is a minimum standard, *when* the writing is to be done, *how to keep track* of journal writing, and *what will be unacceptable* in journals.

How often? For children in fourth grade and above, we prefer a daily schedule. Primary graders may do better with journals two or three times weekly and more structured writing on other days.

How much is enough? Decide on a minimum *quantity* of writing, not a minimum *time* to be spent, for the latter encourages dawdling. In our experience a one-page minimum works well; it can be completed in a few minutes and provides enough length to develop an idea without discouraging reluctant writers. The kind of paper used is a variable; primary graders can use paper with wide lines, and older children can start off using slightly smaller-than-usual paper, such as composition or shorthand notebook pages. Fifteen minutes is a reasonable amount of time for a one-page entry; anyone not finished then must complete the page during other periods of the day, perhaps instead of choosing an independent activity or before recess.

When should journals be used? We recommend early in the day, to allow time for later completion if necessary.

How should you keep track of journal entries? You needn't read each one, just see that it is done. As entries are completed children can bring their journals to you to check off, or they can be piled (opened) at a specified place. Scan each entry and initial it or mark it with a star, date, check, or whatever symbol you devise. As each entry is recorded, check off the child's name for that day. This system takes only a few minutes and ensures that you know who has completed the requirement for that day.

What's unacceptable? If we tell children they can write whatever they want, they will — and some may test your rules vigorously. Decide in advance what the minimal criteria are to be. Our rules may be helpful to you:

1. Use normal-sized handwriting only; every line must be used, from the margin to the right edge of the paper.
2. Don't use "socially unacceptable" language; if you couldn't *say* it to a teacher, don't *write* it.
3. You must be "checked off" daily; if you don't finish in the writing period you may have to forego other activities until you finish.

Letters

Writing letters is a natural outcome of conversation, since informal letters are one-sided conversations written down, and they make an excellent adjunct to many of the informal oral language activities in Chapter Three. Informal or "friendly" letters are the best place to start in helping children become letter writers.

More formal letters, to businesses, embassies, authors, and so forth are very worthwhile too. Writing formal or "business" letters is an important functional writing skill that adults use frequently, and such letters are easily incorporated into many classroom activities.

Letters of both types should be viewed first as *real* means of communication; that is, they should be written and actually mailed, and any replies received should be read and displayed. The letter format also has application for other types of writing, not intended for actual mailing but used as a framework for other expression, such as "letters" to a historical figure, a fictional character from a story, or an inanimate object. Specific suggestions for these types of letters follow.

Letters are excellent vehicles for practice in several of the basic writing forms described in Chapter Six, particularly descriptive, expository, persuasive, expressive, and narrative forms. (You may recall from Chapter Six that descriptive writing creates verbal pictures; expository writing explains something; persuasive writing employs argument and persuasion to take action or accept some point of view; expressive writing conveys the writer's feelings and beliefs; and narrative writing tells a story.) All of these written forms can be practiced in letters, whether intended for real use or not.

The National Council of Teachers of English (NCTE) publishes a delightful sixty-three page booklet called *P. S. Write Soon!* for students nine to fourteen years old. It encourages interest in letter writing with features such as creating your own stationery, stamp collecting, creating chain messages, inventing secret codes, and playing games by mail. *P. S. Write Soon!* is available for $2.50 from NCTE (1111 Kenyon Road, Urbana, Ill. 61801).

Informal Letters. Thank-you notes, "chatty" letters to classmates who are ill or have moved away, letters to pen pals, and informative notes to teachers, parents, and others personally known to the students are common types of informal letters used in the classroom. The following are a few activities for writing informal letters.

1. Help students generate lists of people whose work or special efforts help the class or school, then write individual or group thank-you letters to them; prereaders can dictate their letters. Guest speakers, storytellers, field trip hosts, parent volunteers, aides, older students and their teachers who have helped out in the classroom, librarians, and special teachers are good candidates. Don't overlook those whose work "behind the scenes" helps to keep a school going: janitors, secretaries, cooks, nurses, and others. Deliver or send the letters.

2. Descriptive and narrative writing can be practiced in writing letters to classmates who are ill or have recently moved away or to a teacher during an extended absence. These letters can describe classroom activities and events, stories and books read, and other matters of interest.

3. Expressive and persuasive writing can be practiced by writing informal letters to teachers, principal, parents, members of the community, and others expressing the students' views on community and school issues, program changes, conduct codes and rules, or other issues at home. Such letters can result from debates, group brainstorming, consensus groups, and other oral activities described in Chapter Three.

4. Students can use the letter format to write to story characters expressing reactions to the characters' actions or suggesting new outcomes. Likewise they can write to historical figures telling them what the world is like today or what innovations may have developed from a discovery or invention. This requires careful explanation of common things like cars, radio, TV, or plastics, which would be unfamiliar to someone from the past. (These are good writing activities for social studies and science as well as language arts.)

5. Alan Ziegler (in Zavatsky and Padgett, 1977) suggests asking children, especially young ones, to imagine they have a "magic stamp" that can transport their letters back into time or to objects, animals, even people of the future. A related art activity is to let children design magic stamps.

6. Pen pals are a wonderful way of using informal letters to learn more about other people and the places they live. Many children's magazines list pen pals. Organizations such as those listed below specialize in such contacts:

International Friendship League 22 Batterymarch St. Boston, MA 02109	Student Letter Exchange RFD No. 4 Waseca, MN 56093
League of Friendship P.O. Box 509 Mt. Vernon, OH 43050	World Pen Pals 1690 Como Ave. St. Paul, MN 55108
Letters Abroad 209 E. 56th St. New York, NY 10022	

Formal Letters. Writing formal letters is a truly functional skill, one that adults use frequently. There are a number of ways children can practice these skills and appreciate their usefulness.

1. Social studies offers many opportunities to request information by letter about different places. Your students can write to foreign embassies in the United States and American embassies in other countries as well as tourism bureaus in capitals of English-speaking countries for maps, guidebooks, brochures, and other information about places of interest. Other sources of such information that can be contacted by letter are Chambers of Commerce and tourism departments of the major American cities and state capitals, airlines, and travel agencies.

2. Don't overlook the U.S. government as a source of information on travel, agriculture, health care, consumer information, home management, personal finances, gardening, and a wealth of other information. Your students can write to the Superintendent of Documents, Government Printing Office, Washington, D.C. 20402 for the *Consumers Guide to Federal Publications* or check your library's *Monthly Catalog of United States Government Publications.*

3. Other government agencies or offices can be contacted for many types of information: for example, The Department of the Interior, Fish and Wildlife Service, Consumer Protection Agency, Smithsonian Institution, U.S. Postal Service, National Aeronautics and Space Administration, National Science Foundation, or the Nuclear Regulatory Commission. In addition many nonprofit organizations such as the National Geographic Society, National Wildlife Federation, or Sea Rescue Fund can provide information on a wide variety of topics. Check your public or university library's *Encyclopedia of Associations,* sixteenth edition, for names and addresses of associations, and *The United States Government Manual* (published yearly) or the *Encyclopedia of Governmental Advisory Organizations,* third edition, for addresses of government branches, agencies, commissions, task forces, and advisory groups.

4. If your students are interested in the work of a particular living author or illustrator, they can write in care of the publishing company.

5. They can also write to TV performers at the addresses below if they find out what network the person is with:

ABC (American Broadcasting Co.)
1300 Avenue of the Americas
New York, NY 10019

CBS (Columbia Broadcasting System)
51 West 52nd St.
New York, NY 10019

NBC (National Broadcasting Co.)
Rockefeller Plaza
New York, NY 10020

Mutual Broadcasting System
1755 S. Jefferson Davis
 Highway
Arlington, VA 22301

PBS (Public Broadcasting
 Service)
985 L'Enfant Plaza West
 S.W.
Washington, DC 20024

Motion picture companies' addresses can be found in the *International Motion Picture Almanac* in your public or university library reference section.

6. Students should practice life skills such as writing letters applying for jobs, making complaints, and requesting information. Many local businesses will supply your class with sample employment forms and the like upon request.

Notes, Summaries, and Reports

One of the traditions of many British and European schools is the notebook students compile of class notes, notes on what they have read, summaries of learning activities, and observations of experiments and ongoing processes. They compile compendia of information and observations in different subject areas, which serve as supplements to textbooks and related materials. Much more important, the notebooks force students to state concepts and ideas in their own terms, summarize and organize information, and write it down.

The British-style notebooks are ongoing rather than one-shot efforts, and they are worked on daily. Therein lies their greatest usefulness. Every day some time is spent summarizing a discussion, a story or passage read, an experiment; periodic observations of processes like plant growth, changes in weather, or development of tadpoles are recorded; reactions to what is read and done are included. The notebook requires *daily* writing as well as writing in one's own natural language.

Such an approach in language arts and in content areas, especially in science and social studies, could have several important benefits:

1. The class would have extended daily writing experience of a functional sort.
2. Writing would be integrated into all subjects rather than limited primarily to language arts.
3. The children would have daily practice in summarizing, putting events in order, separating main ideas from detail, and reacting critically.

We try to get our students to put information in their own words when we ask them to take notes and write reports, but these are usually dismal failures. Instead of taking *notes*, many students try to take *dictation* from the speaker; in their haste to catch every word, they stop processing the information they hear and become living tape recorders. Most get lost and give up the attempt or find they can't understand what follows because they heard but did not process what came before. A few, usually the best students anyway, succeed in this fashion, and their slavish verbatim encoding may persist into college and graduate school. They depend on reading and remembering later what they wrote down rather than on understanding material when it is presented.

Efficient note taking should be taught directly, beginning in late third or early fourth grade, in conjunction with the oral language skills of summarizing described in Chapter Three. Students should begin by creating a notebook with dividers for different subject areas. After practicing *oral* summarizing and stating of main ideas and important supporting details, they should practice writing these statements down as notes. Then they should have systematic practice in forming summary and main idea statements first orally, then in writing, until they are fairly adept at stating the most important information from a discussion, a film or demonstration, a sequence of steps, an article, or a story.

Another important functional writing skill in school is report writing. For too many students, "Write a report" means "Copy out of the encyclopedia." Why? One reason is the wide gap between what they read about a topic in textbooks and reference books and what they can write. Elementary children naturally fall short of being able to write like professional authors. Aware that "writing in their own words" will result in only a primitive imitation of such writing, they often forsake their own writing in favor of copying what a book says.

Another reason is that youngsters usually approach report writing with the firm belief that they know little, if anything, about the topic and that the books they use as sources "know" everything. When you believe you know nothing, relying on your own ideas and words is impossible.

We can take two concrete steps to remove these conditions. One is to supply only source materials that are easy to read. Children cannot paraphrase from an encyclopedia they cannot read and understand; they can only copy. Such reference materials are out of the range of most youngsters. What can be used instead? Encyclopedias truly appropriate for children like the *Golden Encyclopedias* are good; so are very simple how-to books, biographies, children's magazines like *Ranger Rick*, *Cricket*, or *National Geographic World*, and brochures collected from some of the sources mentioned previously regarding letter writing. (Travel and informational brochures, government bulletins for consumers, and the like are intended for use by the general public and are apt to be clearly, simply, and colorfully written.) Such appropriate materials should be collected and kept in the classroom or in a special place in the library while the reports are being prepared. Each type of source should be displayed and discussed with the children before beginning, because letting them loose in the library to forage for themselves will only make libraries intimidating and dissolve any self-reliance they have.

The other strategy concerns what we do before we set them to their tasks. After topics are chosen, a good practice is to brainstorm with students to elicit any and all information they already know, or think they know, about the topic. This procedure is closely related to the Directed Reading-Thinking Activity with nonfiction, a reading comprehension activity discussed in Chapter Five. The purpose of such brainstorming is to activate and bring to the front of the mind, so to speak, *prior knowledge*. Children choosing somewhat related topics can do this in a group, with the teacher asking general, leading questions that help them remember and tell what they already may know and helping them to write these ideas down.

In this process many children may find that they already know a good deal about their topics but that much of what they know may be fragmentary and disorganized. Their task, then, is to use sources to verify (or modify) their prior knowledge, organize it, and relate it to new information. Other children may find they have little prior information; some may go on to gather basic information from sources and organize it, while still others may choose to change topics if they have more prior information about another topic. In any case, when they turn to the actual "researching" of their topics, they will be armed with their own prior information rather than with the assumption of their own ignorance. They will be much more apt to synthesize what they read and write naturally instead of copying.

Reports can also focus on problem solving rather than strictly on reporting facts (Shaughnessy, 1977). This involves critical thinking, reaction, and interpretation, thinking skills that older elementary students need to practice. A problem solving approach could be applied to the traditional report by asking them to come up with, or presenting them with, a problem associated with their topic. Instead of just gathering and reporting facts about the crops grown in a region, for example, they could be asked to evaluate measures taken to increase crop yields such as irrigation, fertilization, or use of pesticides and propose an original solution based on what they learn about the region's people, climate, and other factors. They can also practice skills of persuasive writing by referring to evidence gathered to back up their positions rather than simply relying on flat statements of opinion.

Cultural Journalism

Cultural journalism means producing nonfiction writing by using the community and cultural heritage of students as a source. Instead of using just textbooks and library references to learn about and write about things, students use *people* as living references. Writing about what is learned is a natural extension of the learning, which itself is extended beyond the classroom into the home and community at large.

The parent of all cultural journalism efforts is *Foxfire*, a magazine published by rural Georgia high school students. Eliot Wigginton, a high school journalism teacher, sent his students into the community to learn about the "old ways" that were rapidly disappearing in southern Appalachia. What they learned they produced in magazine form, and the magazines became books, which became national bestsellers, and the approach gave birth to cultural journalism projects all over the country. Most of them are much too complex for elementary children to undertake, but the basic tenets are appropriate.

What are the most basic aspects of cultural journalism? What do these students do that might be productive for your students?

First, they write about things outside of school. They focus on people, places, and events in the community, which may also include aspects of school life and school people.

Second, they learn from other people, not just from books. They talk to people rather than primarily doing library research, and they learn that not all the world's knowledge lies between book covers, although they use books to help fill in the gaps.

Third, when they collect material about a topic they get involved in that topic. As they talk to people with special knowledge or skills, they often pick up part of that knowledge or expertise. So, they learn for themselves how to do things as well as learning how others do things.

Fourth, they write a great deal. They draft, revise, edit, and redraft in order to transfer what they have learned into forms others can read and learn from. In the meantime they learn how to accurately represent others' thoughts, actions, and words and to approach their own writing objectively.

Fifth, they work together in school to produce something they share with the people from whom they got their material as well as others. The outcome may be a magazine, a videotape, a TV or radio show, or a newspaper or community gathering. Whatever its form, the outcome of their work has an audience wider than the classroom, the school, or the parents' association.

It is not absolutely necessary to know in advance what the outcome will be; part way through, a new goal may suggest itself. A teacher we know began with the modest goal of helping her students learn more about their own families by conducting interviews with relatives and developing "family trees." They discovered that their relatives had experienced or could do so many fascinating things that the activity evolved first into a craft day, then into a local history fair. Your students' exploration of their many ethnic and national backgrounds may result in an ethnic pot-luck meal or a cookbook; becoming informed about local economic conditions may end up in a letter-writing campaign or in presentations to local governing bodies. Since neither you nor your students know in advance what will be learned in the process, the planned outcome can be scrapped or added to before it is finished. Be sure to let your class suggest outcomes too.

With elementary students, a good place to begin is with their own families. For most children, the 1960s are ancient history; their parents' school years and childhoods seem as unimaginably long ago as another century. With even older relatives, the past is more distant still. Their experiences during the Great Depression, World War II, and Korea, even the fifties and sixties, the ways things were done then, and the special, interesting things they know how to do now are the unseen backdrop to a child's life. They are fail-safe sources.

After your students start inquiring and really listening, they will uncover a whole world of things these older people know and can do: make musical instruments, identify edible plants, carve, weave baskets, quilt, make pottery, hunt, play bocci, make lamps, restore furniture or old cars, bake bread, or develop photographs. They can make history live through their own experiences: hurricanes, wars, emigration, unemployment, revivals, holidays, ethnic customs.

Interviewing is the most basic activity in cultural journalism. Grandparents and great-grandparents, uncles, aunts, parents, and relatives of friends are good people to begin interviewing.

Conducting Interviews

Interviewing means getting others to talk about what they know and keeping track of what they say so the interviewer can put it in writing. To begin, students should decide what people they should talk to, what to talk about, and how to conduct themselves.

Brainstorm with your students about people they know, especially relatives, who might have an interesting story to tell or an interesting skill or hobby. They can ask their parents to make suggestions too. Brainstorming helps them to remember stories they were told by relatives and things they remember older people doing or talking about, like grandparents reminiscing about the Great Depression, World War II, their school days, their own parents, or some other aspect of the "old days."

Some additional topics children could explore with older relatives, neighbors, and others are:

— what school used to be like
— a school graduation
— any of the "firsts": first car, date, job, best friend, and so on
— courtship and weddings
— long-ago family reunions, celebrations, holidays
— a terrifying experience or disaster
— death of a loved one, friend, or pet
— what work was like in the old days: factory, farm, shop, office, school, and so forth
— what *their* parents or grandparents were like: how they looked, talked, disciplined children, what they believed in, how they solved a problem
— how something was done before the advent of modern conveniences: farming, home remedies, cooking, sewing, building, furniture making, travel, games
— early memories of their home or neighborhood; how their family spent leisure time

After they have decided on a person or topic, help them prepare for the interview. Elementary children can profit from a "practice interview" with a friend, classmate, teacher, or other adult at school. Working in groups of three, they can "mock-interview" each other, one asking questions, one talking, and one recording. Each should have a question or topic prepared in advance to get the "interviewee" talking, such as:

— early school memories, like the first day of school
— a frightening experience
— an exciting experience: accident, trip, and the like

— how the family celebrates a holiday

— a hobby or interest: how these people got started, what they had to know

These "interviews" should be kept short; ten or fifteen minutes is quite long enough. Afterward group help can be sought to solve problems such as the conversation dragging, the interviewer talking too much or giving too little support, the recorder not being able to keep up. This dry run helps students anticipate problems and develops their poise and confidence.

An important point about questions: They should be *asked*, not *read*. That's why preparing more than one or two in advance is not a good idea. The questions, not the answers, become primary, and the whole interview falls apart. Students should know what to ask and not have to read from a piece of paper. If they run out of things to ask, they should end the conversation (gracefully) and talk to the person again later after reviewing what was said and coming up with new ideas. Several short, natural conversations are better than a single forced one that drags along or stalls out.

One of the most interesting things that can come out of interviews with older people are *oral histories*. Children and adults alike find these fascinating, as the popularity of books and films like the *Autobiography of Miss Jane Pittman* attest. The fascinating element in oral histories of older citizens is the interweaving of historical events and the drama of the everyday lives of ordinary people.

Developing oral histories helps children understand the ebb and flow of history from a very personal point of view. It puts history and social change in a human, rather than a textbook, context, and it brings them into sustained contact with the elderly, a contact that is missing today in the lives of most youngsters. Today, when few families care for their elderly in their homes, our contact with the past comes to us not from our own roots but from books, TV, and films. Your students may be far removed, both physically and emotionally, from their elderly relatives, but every community has the potential for developing such relationships. Contact your local volunteer organization to find out if there is a Foster Grandparents program in your area, or what senior citizens' groups exist. Or contact the administrator of a local nursing home; many such residents are there only because they have no families and are too frail to live alone, but they are well enough to talk with your students about their lives.

Writing Articles

Most cultural journalism projects culminate in a newspaper, magazine (even a dittoed one), or some similar written production, but not all: A craft fair, local history celebration, film, or some other outcome may result. Whatever the outcome, the students get a chance to do extended writing. What kinds of writing may be needed?

One general format often used is direct transcription of someone's words, which requires tape recording the conversation and later transcribing the tape directly into print. This format may be easier for some students than creating a narrative or expository article. It is best for conversations that do not involve demonstrations of something, such as someone describing a long-ago event or narrating a tall tale or scary story. It works less well with demonstrations of how something is done, because the tape often records apparently ambiguous statements like "You take this and put it under here and then turn it like this. . . ."

Direct transcriptions preserve the flavor of dialect, vocabulary, and tone and are best for speakers who are chatty and articulate, yet stick to the topic. If the speaker digresses, as most of us do, students should be taught how to use writing conventions like ellipses (. . .) and quotation marks to show that portions of the narrative were omitted.

Another general format is narrative created by the author about the speaker. This is the type of writing we see most often in magazines and newspapers: "Albert Herring is ninety-one years old. He has been making bluegrass music for eighty-six years. At the age of five he began picking out hymns his mother taught him on her dulcimer . . ." or "Two years ago while Jake Lamb was plowing near his home in Barboursville, his plow turned up some broken pieces of pottery. . . ." This type of nonfiction writing can be modeled for students by looking at news articles and descriptive passages that do not have dialogue, such as those in travel articles. It works well for summaries of events, biographies, and how-to articles, and for material gathered from an interviewee who did more "showing" than "telling," or whose speaking style was brief or undetailed.

The most common format is a combination of direct transcription and written narrative, which is extremely effective for almost every type of article, because it allows the writer to summarize and organize information while retaining the flavor and personal approach of the conversation.

Putting It Together

There are so many possible outcomes of a cultural journalism project that it is impossible for us to describe how it will turn out. Be it a magazine, a newspaper, a film, a radio program, a community gathering, a "museum," or whatever, there are a few guidelines that will maximize the experience for everyone involved.

1. *Take it as far as it can go.* Discuss with your students what to do and where to go after the articles or scripts are written, the displays arranged, the gathering organized. Are there still more stories to be explored? Begin another cycle. How could the people who helped them be helped by the children? Formulate plans and set them in motion. Remember that the project itself is not an end but a means to the end of tying school and community together. Build on what was begun.

2. *Make their work worth the effort.* When the community is their classroom, the community should be their audience. If a newspaper or magazine is produced, don't just distribute it within the classroom or at home; at the least, every person who was interviewed or contributed in any way should receive a copy of the work, delivered personally by the students. Talk to your principal or supervisor about informing the local newspaper of what your students have done. School administrators are usually delighted to receive such positive publicity for their programs and students. And the students themselves may not realize how important their efforts are until people from outside the school show their approval of what they accomplished.

3. *Give them real responsibility.* A cultural journalism project, like any Gerbil activity, is apt to be time-consuming, unpredictable, messy, and somewhat disorganized. You may be sorely tempted at times (probably at least once a day) to get control of the project. For teachers, that usually means "getting tough" in some way: using grades, privileges, or threats as a lever to get things done or taking responsibility away from the students and putting it on yourself. Sometimes it's just much easier to do something ourselves than to stand back and let a child do it. Whenever you possibly can, *squash that impulse.* Getting something done faster, more neatly, or more efficiently is not what's really important: What really counts is having students learn how to carry through on things, to persevere for the good of others, to feel the pride that comes only from *real* effort. Organizing pairs or triads of students helps, on the principle that "many hands lighten the load." Deadlines may have to be changed, or more realistic goals set, but don't make these changes unilaterally. Let the students work them out with you. The project will be truly theirs only if they have to take the final responsibility.

To learn more about cultural journalism, two excellent books are:

Wigginton, Eliot. *Moments: The Foxfire Book.* Washington, D.C.: Institutional Development and Economic Affairs Service, Inc. (IDEAS), 1975.

Wood, Pamela. *You and Aunt Arie.* Washington, D.C.: Institutional Development and Economic Affairs Service, Inc. (IDEAS), 1975.

Writing Poetry

Poetry should be an integral part of the language arts program in all grades. As discussed in Chapter Five, all children should have wide exposure to poetry as well as fiction and nonfiction prose. Writing poetry is a natural extension of reading it, and one that children enjoy, but the desire to write it requires an environment in which it is valued and enjoyed on a daily basis. Some guidelines for creating a positive environment for poetry are shown in Box 7.3.

Getting Started

Two simple techniques can be used to help children begin producing poetry easily, successfully, and enjoyably: *collaboration* and *innovation.*

Collaboration means working together, which is the easiest way to create a

---

BOX 7.3
Creating an Environment for Poetry

Share some poetry every day. Read to your students, let them read to one another, and invite guests to class to share poetry. Display poetry in the classroom and include it in the library.

Choose poetry you like. It if appeals to you, it will likely appeal to your students. Sample widely from the full range of poetry types.

Pair poetry with pleasure. Read or listen to poetry as a break from difficult subjects; do it while the children draw; use background music; darken the room and read by flashlight; go outdoors or open the windows; let them lie on the floor or curl up on a pillow to listen.

Encourage physical response. Let them sway, tap, rock, swing arms, or create appropriate sound effects; give them art materials to work with while they listen.

Bring poetry into the content areas. There are poems for every subject; seek them out. Try casting arithmetic word problems in verse; use verse as well as prose in handwriting practice, grammar exercises, and reading skill activities.

---

poem; nobody has to fear not producing a "good" poem or not knowing what to write. The simplest form is a group (or class) poem with everyone contributing a line. Young children can dictate their contributions for the teacher to write down; older ones can write their lines down and turn them in; all contributed lines are collected and read as one poem.

Kenneth Koch (1970) proposed gamelike rules for each line of his class collaborations; for example, if the theme were "I Wish . . ." each line should begin with the words "I wish" and include a color, a comic-strip character's or superhero's name, and the name of a place, as in the following:

> I wish I was Spiderman climbing up the
> Empire State Building in my blue
> Spider Suit.
> I wish I had Wonder Woman's gold bracelets
> and I would fly to Mexico.
> I wish that bad old green Hulk live in
> my basement.

Such "rules" help children focus their thinking without stifling their creativity. They support the child who fears not knowing "what to say" and give some cohesion to collaborations that are naturally rather disjointed. This type of structure should be loosened, however, as children become more experienced with poetry and lose their uncertainty about what to write.

Innovation means using the established pattern of a poem to write a different poem. For very young (or very hesitant) writers, highly structured verse like nursery rhymes, jingles, well-known lyrics like "Happy Birthday," and patterned rhyming storybooks like *Brown Bear, Brown Bear* or *Whistle, Mary,*

Whistle from the *Instant Readers* (Martin and Brogan, 1971), *Round Is a Pancake* (Sullivan, 1972), or *Hop on Pop* (Seuss, 1963) are good. Choral-read the verse until the pattern is well established, then write the basic pattern on the board or on a duplicating master and ask individuals or members of a group to complete one (or more) new lines or verses. These can be collected as collaborations or completed individually. A few examples, which may or may not rhyme, are given below.

Using *Round Is a Pancake* as the pattern:

> Round is a *circle*,
> Round is a *bowl*,
> Round is a *stone*
> *or a lump of coal.*
>
> Square is a *box*,
> Square is a *book*.
> Square is a *window*
> *and pictures on the wall.*

Using *Whistle, Mary, Whistle* as the pattern:

> *Dance*, Mary, *dance*
> And you shall *win a prize.*
> I can't *dance*, mother,
> Because *I closed my eyes.*
>
> *Fly*, bird, *fly*
> And you *can feel so free.*
> I can't *fly right now,*
> Because *I'm sitting in my tree.*

Innovation provides a structured outlet for original ideas. It is a much-maligned concept in school, often considered "copying," but this should not be the case. Using one's own ideas and words to reflect a theme or pattern used by another is a technique many successful writers have employed as they developed their skills and individual styles. It is a good way for youngsters to gain confidence in their own writing and experiment with words, patterns, and styles.

Poetry Themes and Activities

Although nearly any experience can form the basis of a poem, children who have not had a great deal of experience writing poetry may find the most success in activities that have some structure and provide a starting point. Poetry activities that suggest *repetition* of lines, phrases, sounds, or images, that encourage *expression of emotions,* and that foster *association and comparisons* are good (Koch, 1970, 1973; Larrick, 1973; Livingston, 1973).

Repetition. Repetition of lines, phrases, sounds, or images are attractive to children; most have a natural affinity for rhymes, rhythmic chants, and lines they know will be repeated over and over. These are elements of perennial favorites like nursery rhymes, fairy tales and fables, jump-rope rhymes, limericks, jingles, and Dr. Suess books. When a line or phrase is repeated over and over in a poetry writing activity, it gives the students a structure to hang onto and a vehicle for focusing thoughts. This predictable element allows them to concentrate most of the writing energy on developing images, selecting graphic words, and expressing feelings precisely.

A good way to start is to suggest, or let the children suggest, a phrase to begin each new line or verse (Koch, 1970). Some examples are:

> I wish . . .
> Sometimes I . . .
> Someday I'll . . .
> I used to be . . . but now . . .
> If I could . . . then I would . . .

Here are some poems fourth graders wrote using this technique:

Sometimes I wish that I had a brother or sister.
Sometimes I wish that I had someone to tease.
Sometimes I wish that I had someone to play with.
Sometimes I wish that I had someone to baby sit.
But best of all I wish I had someone littel to buy toys for.

> — Robyn

Sometimes I wish I had a brown convertible Rolls Royce.
Sometimes I wish I was in Hollywood.
Sometimes I wish I was a moviestar.
Sometimes I wish I was a kung-fu instructor.
Sometimes I wish I could visit Bruce Lee's grave.
Sometimes I wish I could visit Bruce Lee's museum.
Sometimes I wish I was an artist.
Sometimes I wish I could do flips.

> — William

If I were a queen I would buy a gold crown.
If I were a millionaire I would buy a bakery.
If I were a cat I would drink lots of milk.
If I were a butterfly I would be careful.
If I were a monkey I would live in Alaska.

> — Kelly

If I had a rollroyce I would drive all around town.
If I had a brother I could play all day.
If I had a Ferrari I could race everybody and win.

If I had a billion dollars I could buy all the
   Ferraris I wanted.
If I had all this I'd be happy.

— Jody

Senses and Emotions. Children respond immediately to poetry activities that
allow them to put into words their feelings and sensory images. Colors, tastes,
textures, smells, and sounds create powerful images, as do emotions like fear,
dread, excitement, grief, and joy.

One way to approach "sense poems" is to ask the children to include a
different color, taste, sound, or the like in each line. Here are some fourth
graders' color poems done in this way:

Blue makes me feel like a part of the sky.
Green makes me feel like a leaf.
White makes me feel like a soft cloud.

— Dennis

Brown makes me feel like I am a piece of dark
   brown toaste.
Red makes me feel like I am sitting in the hot
   sun all day long.
Black makes me feel like I am a dog.
Blue makes me feel like I am a Blueberry being squished.

— Jennifer

Pink makes me feel like a new born baby.
Black makes me feel all crumbley and hard.
Orange makes me feel like the sun going down.

— Robin

Aqua reminds me of the ocean below . . .
Yellow reminds me of bulldozers and road construction.
Red reminds me of bad marks on my papers.
Green reminds me of the chalk board and school.
Orange reminds me of bricks on the school wall.

— Dennis

One color, texture, shape, or other feature can be the focus of a poem, as
in these color poems patterned after those in Mary O'Neill's *Hailstones and
Halibut Bones* (NY: Doubleday, 1961).

What is Blue?

Blue is the color of a cold winter night.
Blue is the color of the flame of a torch.
Blue is the color of a big blue sky . . .

— Stacy

Red

What is red? A ball of fire from a dragon.
What is red? A red light when you suppose to stop.
What is red? Like a beating heart.
What is red? A nice juicy apple ready to eat.
What is red? A heart on Valentines Day.
What is red? A person with sleepy eyes.
What is red? The blood running through my head.

— Towanna

What is Green

Green is like a falling leaf.
Green is like lime icecream.
Green is like Popeyes spinch.
Green makes me think of jumpy frogs.
Green is nice for a friend.

— Freddie

Poetry that describes feelings and emotions is very effective. Some ideas to get your students started are:

When I'm mad . . .
I feel proud when . . .
Being afraid means . . .
Peace feels like . . .

Association and Comparison. Poetry that is alive and vivid has a freshness that comes from unique images and associations, but it takes effort to produce and express images and ideas that are fresh, startling, and memorable. One way to begin to help children tap these images is *free association*, the spontaneous pairing of unusual, unique elements (Koch, 1970). Try, for example, to associate sounds with colors: With eyes closed students might listen to a book being dropped, hands clapping, or a bird call, then immediately call out what color the sound suggested. They might try associating colors with numbers, sounds with shapes, textures with names of places, smells with sounds or fragments of music, variations of temperature with abstract, nontangible nouns. These pursuits help children to develop vivid imaginative images as well as a broad and precise vocabulary. For example, you might ask:

— What color is the number 4 (or what color does the number 4 remind you of)? What color is the number 87?
— What texture does Los Angeles make you think of? Rome? (Grainy, silky, smooth, furry, slick, raspy, gritty, are examples of texture words; also, like bark, rough cloth, feathers, sandpaper, wool, glass, or mud are comparisons.)

— What temperature (cool, icy, burning, and so on) or what color is jealousy?
Friendship? Anger? Worry?

— What sound would a large circle make? A tiny box? A long skinny rectangle? A perfect triangle?

Developing comparisons is another form of association. Beginners can practice forming comparisons with a single line for structure: "A _____ is like a _____." They can consider physical features like color, shape, or texture, then go on to consider more abstract or fanciful images:

A worm is like a wiggly toothpic.

— Paula

School is like a dull play.

— Joanna

Your hair is like spaghetti.
Your eyes are like meatballs.

— Youlanda

The globe is like a ball.
Africa is like a pork chop.

— Dennis

Your hair is braided
And looks like ropes.
Your hands are wiggling
And looks like spiders.
Your hair is loose
And looks like spaggetti.

— Lewanda

Comparing two things that seem on the surface to be completely dissimilar is an imaginative activity that expands children's awareness of words and meanings and helps make their poetry vivid. Try associating such dissimilar pairs as animals and places, feelings and concrete objects, flowers and sounds, colors and textures, or temperatures and smells. Here are some examples of responses to these kinds of questions:

San Diego is a green lizard sleeping on a rock in the sun. Its back is dusty and rough and it hangs on the rock with tiny toenails.

Dread means not wanting to do something you have to. Dread is like an enormous plate of cold mashed potatoes with lumps in it spreading all over a plate and looking cold and sticky.

If a violet could talk it would talk in a tiny whispery voice like a very old lady or a little chirpy bird. Its sound would be high and quivery.

A carnation makes a big brassy noise like a shiny trumpet. The noise it makes has sharp edges and it likes loud music like marches.

Form Poetry

After children have had extensive experience with poetry that focuses on expression rather than form, they may enjoy the challenge of writing poetry with stricter forms. By the time form poetry is introduced they should have had plenty of practice forming images, changing words, and engaging in free imagining. Then they will be able to express their ideas fairly easily while paying attention to form requirements like number of syllables, line length, rhyme, and meter. The following are some types of form poetry your students may enjoy trying.

Concrete Poetry. Since this is a playful form that makes a visual picture as well as a poetic statement, it is sometimes called "picture poetry." Styles of lettering, word choices, and visual configuration are aspects children enjoy playing with. They can begin by using just one word, playing around with visual ways of expressing ideas, and then extend their picture poems in length, as in Figure 7.3.

A good book to share with your students is Giose Rimanelli and Paul Pinsleur's *Poems Make Pictures, Pictures Make Poems* (1972).

Senryu. Senryu (SEN-roo) is a three-line Japanese form poem. It does not have a restriction on the number of syllables used, as does the more common haiku, but it does attempt to capture a single moment in descriptive language. Children can practice "capturing a moment" by looking at interesting photographs or by covering their eyes and uncovering them momentarily to take a "mental photograph." Here are some examples:

> I have a big dog
> As big as a pony
> I ride him to school

> — Tony
> Cramer, 1978, p. 145

> The last leaf trembles
> On a bare branch
> And falls to the ground.

> Icicles hanging from the roof
> Drip and shine in the sun.
> They shatter like glass when they fall.

Haiku. Pronounced HI-koo, this well-known form of Japanese verse has three lines of counted syllables: five in the first line, seven in the second, and five in the last. In addition it captures a momentary image and most often describes a scene from nature, setting a mood or creating a word picture. Although Japanese haiku in translation may not have the precise 5-7-5 pattern it has in Japanese, it should be shared with children as a pattern:

Figure 7.3   Picture poems

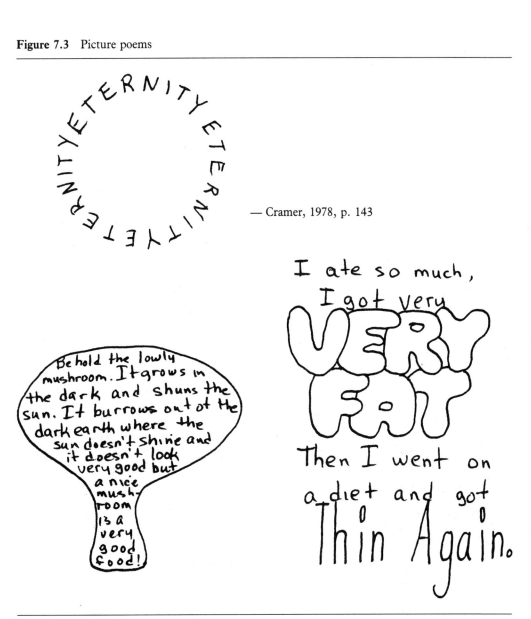

— Cramer, 1978, p. 143

Winter snowfall;
Branches of that fir tree.
Green bending under white.

Solitude;
One gray October afternoon
A towel on the sand.

Tanka. An extended haiku of five lines with a syllable-line pattern of 5-7-5-7-7 is called tanka. This Japanese form poem is not restricted to capturing a single moment or image, so it gives students a way of expressing a progression of ideas or events:

> Icicles on the eaves
> Dripping slowly in the sun
> Losing their life's blood
> Waiting to be saved by night
> Knowing their end is in sight

— Pat
Cramer, 1978, p. 145

> Fog drifts in patches
> Seeking to blanket the earth
> With its wet grayness
> The wind whimpers its sadness
> Waiting to reclaim glory

— Jimmy
Cramer, 1978, p. 146

Cinquain. Cinquain (SEEN-kain) is a five-line poetic form that traditionally features a 2-4-6-8-2 syllable pattern and constrains the number of words in each line: 1-2-3-4-1. In addition, the first and fifth lines are nouns that are synonyms; the second, third, and fourth lines are descriptive phrases. This is a very challenging form, and many teachers encourage children to follow one or the other constraints but not both simultaneously. For older students who relish the challenge, conforming to both constraints while developing a memorable image or idea is a real accomplishment. Here are examples of these forms:

Lines constrained (1-2-3-4-1 word pattern):

> seagull
> speckled, motion
> graceful wings dipping
> distance in your heart
> fisherman

— Cramer, 1978, p. 146

Syllables constrained (2-4-6-8-2 syllable pattern):

> warm wind
> stroking my skin
> sunlight dappled on leaves
> birds crying in the wind-swept trees
> summer

Both constraints:

> Kitten
> Crouching, pouncing,
> Flexing tiny catclaws,
> Eyes like amethysts glittering,
> Hunter.

Diamante. Pronounced dee-ah-MON-tay, this complex form poem has seven lines with constraints on the word classes and number of words used in each line. In addition, the lines are arranged in a diamond shape (hence its name), and a contrast evolves among the lines as the last line is the opposite of the first. The word-class constraints are as follows:

first line: one noun (subject)
second line: two adjectives describing subject
third line: three participles (*–ed, –ing*) describing action of subject
fourth line: four-word noun phrase related to subject
fifth line: three participles describing a different or opposite aspect of subject
sixth line: two adjectives
seventh line: one noun (opposite of subject)

Here are two examples:

> War
> death, sorrow
> fighting, killing, hating
> nightmare of all nations
> helping, healing, loving
> life, joy
> Peace

— David
Cramer, 1978, p. 147

(Note that David has made lines five, six, and seven opposites of the words used in lines three, two, and one.)

> winter
> icy-gray
> freezing blowing killing
> the season of death
> awakening stirring melting
> warm green
> spring

Responding to Children's Poetry

A child's own attempts at poetry must be responded to *first* and *most importantly* as a means of expression. Respond to content, and respond positively and constructively. Make your first comment positive: an image, a choice of words, a powerful phrase, a lilting combination of sounds, a thought or feeling conveyed. Let the child know directly what has reached you, with a comment such as "I really like the way this line sounds when you read it out loud" or "I especially like the way you described the rain here; it makes me feel as if I were there."

When children write anything, poetry included, much of what they write will be ordinary or uninspired; occasionally a thought or image will stand out from the rest with a special freshness or sincerity. Encourage them to identify the word, phrase, image, or other part of a poem *they* like best and to share those parts with others. As they rework and revise a first draft, those parts become the jumping-off point for further development.

We have had success with asking them to write a first draft of a poem, then put it away for a day or so. When they come back to it they gain a little objectivity, which they can use to mark in some way both the part they like best and the part they think "works" the least well. From there they begin further drafts, crafting a poem in the same way they would a prose composition.

Respond to a poem's form *only* after the student has worked at clarifying and developing the content. As with prose compositions, mechanical aspects like spelling, punctuation, and handwriting should not be considered until the final-draft stages; with poetry, aspects like rhyme, meter, and the like are important only in the structured form poems.

These books will help you learn more about teaching and writing poetry with children:

Arnstein, Flora J. *Poetry and the Child*. New York: Dover, n.d.

Cosman, Anna. *How to Read and Write Poetry*. New York: Watts, 1979.

Hayden, John O. *Inside Poetry Out: An Introduction to Poetry*. Chicago: Nelson-Hall, 1982.

Hopkins, Lee Bennett. *Pass the Poetry, Please*. New York: Scholastic Books, 1972.

Kennedy, X. J. and Dorothy M. Kennedy. *Knock at a Star: A Child's Introduction to Poetry*. Boston: Little, Brown, 1982.

King, Joyce and Carol Katzman. *Imagine That! Illustrated Poems and Creative Learning Experiences*. Glenview, Ill.: Scott Foresman, 1976.

Koch, Kenneth. *Wishes, Lies and Dreams*. New York: Random House, 1970.

————. *Rose, Where Did You Get That Red?* New York: Random House, 1973.

Kuskin, Karla. *Near the Window Tree: Poems and Notes*. New York: Harper & Row, 1975.

Larrick, Nancy, ed. *Somebody Turned on a Tap in These Kids: Poetry and Young People Today.* New York: Dell, 1973.

Livingston, Myra Cohn. *When You Are Alone It Keeps You Capone: An Approach to Creative Writing with Children.* New York: Atheneum, 1973.

Matthews, Dorothy, ed. *Producing Award Winning Student Poets: Tips from Successful Teachers.* Urbana, Ill.: NCTE, n.d.

Novak, Robert. *Writing Haiku from Photographs.* Fort Wayne: English Dept., Indiana University (Windless Orchard Series), 1977.

Shapiro, Jon E., ed. *Using Literature and Poetry Affectively.* Newark, Del.: IRA, 1979.

Tickle, Phyllis. *On Beyond Koch.* Memphis, Tenn.: St. Luke's Press, 1981.

Wood, James. *Poetry Is.* Boston: Houghton Mifflin, 1972.

Writing Fiction

Fiction writing is one of the most difficult composition tasks for children, because it places great demands on their imagination and description abilities and story sense. Yet fiction ("Write a story about . . .") dominates over other types of writing in many programs. Writing fiction is most successful when children have had extensive previous experience with functional, expository, and poetry writing. Writing activities should focus on helping them develop skill in capturing sensory images in words, describing actions and feelings precisely, writing dialogue, and developing believable story plots and characters.

Sensory Writing

Sensory writing (Moffett and Wagner, 1976) means focusing on the information we receive through one of our senses (sight, hearing, touch, smell, or taste) and trying to translate that information into writing. Such practice sharpens our awareness of the physical world and helps us learn how to use description to put our readers into a story. The following activities can help your students focus on perceiving through one sense at a time.

1. Sit down somewhere, close your eyes, and *listen* to the world around you. Think about using words to describe the sounds themselves, not what makes the sounds. Then describe what you heard in writing. Share your work and see if others can guess the sources of the sounds you described.

2. Take a "trust walk" with a partner. You wear a blindfold and are led around an area and touch the furniture, trees, ground, walls, or whatever is around you. Concentrate on your sense of *touch*, the textures of surfaces, shapes of objects, the air on your face. Write a description in prose or poetry of what your sense of touch told you.

3. Cut a "peephole" about the size of a quarter in a piece of paper. Go outside or to an unfamiliar area of the school, hold up your paper, and study what you can *see* in a restricted area. Concentrate on colors, shapes, light and shadow, and any movement you can see. Write down every detail, looking again if you need to.

4. Go to several different places around the school, your home, and outdoors. Sit quietly with eyes closed and let your *nose* tell you about your surroundings; concentrate on your much-neglected sense of smell. What odors are most noticeable near the kitchen? The art room? The janitor's supply closet? The gym, parking lot, and playground?

5. Bring objects from home to build a "sensorium" (Albert, 1981), a collection of objects to explore, classify, and describe using touch, smell, and your other senses. Look for things like empty cologne bottles, soap, candles, fabric and wallpaper scraps, bottle caps, small containers in different shapes, shells, stones, Leggo or Tinkertoys, doll house furniture and small toys, wind chimes, clean eggshells and nutshells, rubber stamps, and rhythm band instruments. Choose an object and list every detail of its shape, texture, color, sound, smell, and other characteristics.

6. Go outside and choose an area 2 or 3 feet square. Observe it closely and write down every detail of what is within the area. Draw a picture of it too. Then go back a week later and again a week after that. Repeat the same procedure each time, comparing your observations for changes.

7. Go outside with a magnifying glass and find a small insect or spider. Without disturbing it, watch its movement through the lens. Look closely at its body parts and the way it moves. Try to put yourself in the creature's place as it gets over obstacles like blades of grass, stones, twigs, and so forth. What would it feel like? What would your world be like? Describe what you observed and imagined in writing.

"Picture This!"

A good follow-up to sensory writing is to extend the observation of physical detail into experiences with stories by writing descriptive passages for stories so vividly that the reader can almost experience the setting through the writer's words.

1. Choose a familiar story that you know well: for example, *The Three Bears*. Then draw a picture of a scene from the story, like the bears' cottage when Goldilocks first visits it. Then write a description of your picture. Include every detail you can so that the reader will envision the scene: the stillness of the empty cottage, the smell from the bowls of porridge, the size and shape of the bears' chairs, the creak of the door as Goldilocks hesitantly pushes it open. . . .

2. Using a drawing as in 1 above, imagine that you are an eyewitness to the scene — you are actually *there*. Have a partner pretend to be a reporter interviewing you about what you observed. Then each of you write a description of the event as if for a newspaper article or TV news feature, putting in as much detail as you can.

3. Imagine that during the night someone came into your classroom and stole the teacher's desk (or some other object). In writing, describe your classroom as though you were writing the beginning of a mystery story about this theft. Imagine that you were the first on the scene and that the way the room looks now contains clues that may help you solve the mystery.

Writing from Drama

Drama activities in the classroom take ideas and events and present them in words, actions, and gestures that happen immediately in front of participants. Pairing writing and drama helps children to create a sense of immediacy and vividness with their writing. Here are some activities to get started:

1. Have them pantomime a scene involving some action: for example, a cat approaches a flock of resting birds and tries to single one out for capture, but the other birds attack the cat and drive it away. Using only gestures, let them try to convey the animals' feelings as well as actions.

2. Afterward, help them describe aloud how the characters *felt*, *looked*, and *moved*. Let them act out parts again if they are unsure.

3. List on the board the children's words, as in this example for the cat-and-birds scene:

Little Bird	Cat	Other Birds
lonesome	slinked	squatting down
feeling sorry for self	sneaky	preening themselves
scowling	stretched out one leg, then	ruffle their feathers
hunched shoulders	the other	stand up and down like a
frowning	eyes squinted	pump
trying not to look at the	licking its lips	angry faces
others	ducks its head	alarmed
	gets flat on the ground	swoop down
	tries to run without	pecking at the cat
	making noise	swatting with their wings
		flying in a circle

4. Choose two or three descriptive phrases and ask for alternative descriptions using more colorful, vivid, or active words, as in the following:

flying in a circle
- circling like hawks
- swarming like angry bees
- flying like a squadron of jet fighters

5. Ask the students to write a description of the scene using any of the phrases from the board and any others that occur to them.

6. Have one group pantomime a scene as above for another group. The second group then writes narratives of what they saw. Then the writers become actors for the first group.

7. Try writing narratives first, using as much descriptive language as possible and give the results to another group to act out as precisely as they can.

Show-ers and Tell-ers

Good writers don't *tell* a story in writing, they *show* it to the reader. They put their readers into the writing by using evocative description, action words, dialogue, and figurative language. Albert (1982) suggested using examples from prose and poetry to show how effective writers use these techniques and constructing short lessons that contrast dull and vivid word choices.

Working in threes, in pairs, and then alone, guide the students through comparisons of "telling" sentences that lack precise description and "showing" sentences that are highly descriptive in the following areas:

1. *Action Words*
   Telling: She walked down the hall, feeling angry.
   Showing: She stalked down the hall, banging her heels down hard with every step.
2. *Descriptions — Words and Phrases*
   Telling: The hikers felt hot and tired.
   Showing: The exhausted hikers dragged their boots a little with each slow step. Their sunburned faces were caked with gray dust and carved with streaks of sweat.
3. *Figures of Speech*
   Telling: The gypsy wore a bright red dress and lots of jewelry.
   Showing: The gypsy's dress was as red as freshly spilled blood, and her jewelry tinkled like a thousand tiny sleighbells.
4. *Dialogue*
   Telling: Mary thought of a solution.
   Showing: "Wait," whispered Mary. "I think I know how we can get out of this."

Watch for, and point out, well-constructed phrases and colorful word choices in everything the children read. Help them collect good descriptions and create a bulletin board or other display. Encourage them to share with the class any vivid and precise descriptions they find in their pleasure reading.

A word of caution: As children begin to experiment with evocative language, their writing may become quite florid at this stage. Keep in mind that while experimenting they may well overdo it and overuse descriptive or unusual words. This will pass as they write more and more, and they will eventually develop their own individual styles.

The Martian Observer

Good fiction writing demands not only a "mental eye" for details of the physical world and precision in choosing words. It also demands the ability to see the ordinary in fresh new ways. Everyday objects and events that are so common they are not even consciously perceived can become vehicles for helping children look at the world through fresh perspectives.

If a creature from another world visited Earth to learn all it could about our planet and its inhabitants, what would it see and think about? The device of the "Martian observer," developed in a novel by Vonnegut (1974), can successfully help children develop keen powers of observation.

You might introduce the Martian observer by sharing this poem with your class. The writer conceived of this poem while driving on the Garden State Parkway in New Jersey, imagining herself an alien from space looking down on the traffic and speculating about the nature of Earth's creatures.

> *Southbound on the Freeway*
>
> A tourist came in from Orbitville,
> parked in the air, and said:
>
> The creatures of this star
> are made of metal and glass.
>
> Through the transparent parts
> you can see their guts.
>
> Their feet are round and roll
> on diagrams — or long
>
> measuring tapes — dark
> with white lines.
>
> They have four eyes.
> The two in the back are red.
>
> Sometimes you can see a five-eyed
> one, with a red eye turning
>
> on the top of his head.
> He must be special —
>
> the others respect him,
> and go slow,
>
> when he passes, winding
> among them from behind.
>
> They all hiss as they glide,
> like inches, down the marked
>
> tapes. Those soft shapes,
> shadowy inside

the hard bodies — are they
their guts or their brains?

— Swenson, 1963, p. 59

After discussing how the poet compared familiar objects and events to what might be living creatures, have the children try considering other everyday scenes or things and figure out what a Martian might think they are or think is happening, such as the following events:

— a school bus delivering children to a school
— children playing ball or tag
— a teacher giving a lesson to a group
— a woman putting on makeup
— a child playing with a doll
— someone mowing a lawn
— people throwing litter out of a car
— vehicles going into and out of a car wash
— a family watching TV
— the Super Bowl

Writing Dialogues

Writing effective dialogue for fictional characters is a demanding task. It requires that the writer communicate to the reader what the character in the story is thinking about, feeling, trying to hide, and trying to get others to believe, without sounding artificial or stagey. The ability to write convincing dialogue develops from paying attention to what real people say and how they say it. First, use simple skits to produce spontaneous dialogues for students to observe and write down. Then have them listen to informal conversations at home, on the playground, and in class and write them down also. Finally, let them begin writing original dialogues, trying to make the language as natural as they can (Macrorie, 1976):

1. Observe a skit and listen to the characters' conversations. *Listen* first and try to mentally rehearse what was said, then begin writing after the skit is over. Write the characters' names, a colon or dash, and the words each said as if you were writing a script for a play.

2. Listen to conversations around you, then write them up as in 1 above, writing only the words actually spoken. From these "scripts," try writing a description of what was said, as in a story:

Script form —
HILDA: Know what happened last night?
GRACE: No, what?
HILDA: I had an accident on my bike . . .
Story form — Hilda leaned toward Grace and whispered, "Know what
happened last night?" Grace looked up from her work.
"No, what?" she asked curiously. . . .

3. Now try writing original dialogues. Can you convey the setting, the characters' feelings, and story events *only* through the characters' words? In the following example, how can you tell just from the dialogue where it takes place, what happens, and how everyone in the scene feels?

ELLEN: Hey Mark! Over here!

MARK: There you are. I've been looking all over for you.

ELLEN: Well, you found me. Here, get in line in front of me.

MARK: Oh! Sorry.

BILL: Whaddya mean, sorry? You made me spill my Coke.

MARK: I said I was sorry. I didn't mean to bump you.

BILL: Well, that ain't good enough. Look at this tray. My whole lunch is a mess. What am I supposed to do now?

MARK: It's not my fault. You had so much stuff on your tray. Why don't you try eating less?

ELLEN: Come on, you guys, cut it out.

BILL: Why don't you shut up?

MARK: Why don't you, big mouth?

BILL: Oh yeah? How do you like this? . . .

Translations

Translations entail recasting a piece of writing into another form; a folk tale can be rewritten as a newspaper story, or a story as a diary entry or a letter from one character to another (Moffett and Wagner, 1976). Translating different types of written forms into other forms is a good fiction-writing practice.

1. Find a newspaper account of an event like a fire, an election, or a hijacking. Rewrite the reported events as a story.
2. Rewrite a story or a folk or fairy tale in the form of a letter from a central character to someone else. In the letter, describe what happened to the character.
3. Take a familiar story and rewrite it in the form of a script for a play or puppet show.
4. Find a classified ad in the newspaper of something for sale. Write a story about how that thing came to be for sale.

Publishing Children's Writing

All students produce some work that is purely personal, such as prewriting exercises, first drafts that are never polished, and journal writing, but the purpose of most writing is to have others read it. As writers, children have something to look forward to and to work hard for when they know that the best of their writing will be published. They have a reason to take a piece of writing through several drafts and to work extra hard on spelling, punctuation, and handwriting. As readers, seeing the published work of their classmates gives them ideas for topics they themselves can write about, words they can use, and forms of poetry (such as the cinquain) or prose (such as a pattern story) with which they can experiment.

Classroom publication can take many forms. In this section we will describe some of the more popular ones: displays, bookbinding, and young authors' conferences.

Displays

Children's writing should be displayed around the room and in special displays in the hall, the library, or on the outside of your classroom door (see Box 7.4).

Traditionally teachers have displayed children's best work as a reward. There are two drawbacks to this practice: First, the teacher, not the student, does the selecting and second, some students may have work on display regularly while others rarely, if ever, get such a reward. These are good reasons to change our thinking. Instead of decorating the room or rewarding children, use displays to teach and reinforce writing skills. You can do this by letting them participate in selecting papers and by creating displays that demonstrate a skill they have been working on.

A display of "Work in Progress" is useful for demonstrating how rough drafts evolve into final drafts. Ask students to save their early drafts and post them in consecutive order. Another display might show how they wrote alternative leads for a composition, including a copy of their final drafts. A display of self-selected examples of their "best work" helps children learn to view their own work critically. Another way of practicing this is to let them mark their favorite part of a displayed paper. In these ways we use their work to demonstrate and reinforce what they are working at and help them develop judgment and objectivity about their own work.

Bound Books

Writing that children have labored over in order to produce the best work they can deserves to be made permanent. Helping them make their own bound

---

BOX 7.4
Displaying
Children's Writing

Change the papers frequently, every week or so.

Give the students opportunities to edit and polish their work before displaying it.

Ask permission to display any work. If a student says no, respect the refusal.

Make sure *every* child has work displayed regularly.

Use displays to demonstrate early drafts, editing, and other aspects as well as content.

Refer to displayed work; don't just post it and forget it.

Return all work to the writer when you take it down.

books is not difficult, it is extremely rewarding, and it is appropriate for children in all grades.

The simplest books are collections of individual papers stapled together with a simple cover of tagboard, construction paper, wallpaper, or fabric. These are fine for group efforts, especially in kindergarten or first grade, where all the children have contributed a page by writing or dictating and drawing a picture. For example, they could create a group book called "What Is Round?" Each may be given one or two pages with the sentence stub, "A ＿＿＿ is round" to copy. Each may cut out or draw a picture of a round object, then write or dictate its name to fill the blank space. Illustrated pages are collected and stapled together, creating a simple homemade "pattern book" in which each page has almost the same words, with the new words on each page illustrated, thus making each page easy to read. Books like these are excellent for reinforcing concepts like shapes, colors, textures, and other characteristics: What is red? Big? Square? Furry? Rough?

Group books need not be limited to such highly structured forms or be used only with young children. Older students can get excellent practice in collaborating and cooperating by agreeing on a topic, then contributing individual episodes in a long story like "The Saga of Supersquirrel" or researching and writing up different aspects of a nonfiction topic like "How to Care for

Your Dog" or "The History of Our Flag." Such group projects are excellent for science, social studies, and other content areas as well as for language arts.

From contributing to a group book children can move to producing individual books. First graders may have the most success by dictating their work, creating the illustrations first so that they are better able to stick to the topic when they dictate. Those who prefer to write their own can work with an older student or adult to change invented spellings into standard spellings and do some simple revision if desired.

Beyond first grade, they should work through the stages of drafting and revising so that the books they publish represent work that has been thoughtfully crafted. In this way they develop pride in their own work and in the effort necessary to produce good writing. Working with a partner or a small group is a good method for finding out if their writing really communicates to others. Likewise, small groups can work together on editing and proofreading, polishing the final drafts before they become books.

The types of books produced are limited only by your imagination and that of your students. Figure 7.4 suggests some imaginative ways of using covers and illustrations to make simple books.

The most durable and permanent books are made with sewn bindings and will last from one year to the next with moderately fair care in handling. They are perfect for work the students really want to preserve, as for a young authors' conference (next section), which could be contributed to the school library or another class or given as gifts.

When the final drafts are ready to be bound into a sewn binding, the children use sheets of unlined paper folded down the middle to create double pages. Then they copy or type their finished text onto the pages, include illustrations, and sew the double pages together down the fold. The sewn pages are then glued securely into separate covers made of cardboard covered with paper, wallpaper, fabric, or other materials. The steps in making a sewn book are shown in Figure 7.5. Older students can sew their own pages; younger ones will probably need adult help with this step. (Some teachers ask volunteers or an aide to sew together sets of three to six double pages and keep them on hand to give the children when they are needed.)

Every classroom library should contain a variety of books children have created themselves. They should be prominently displayed and readily available for pleasure reading. Sewn books, perhaps including a page of information "About the Author," should be displayed in the school library too. Many librarians will glue in a checkout card and pocket so these books can circulate. A "Local Authors" display of such bound books is attractive and highly motivating to youngsters.

Young Authors' Conferences

A young authors' conference is a writing project in which individuals, classrooms, grades, and even entire schools participate. Many weeks of sustained effort are spent writing, revising, editing, proofreading, and illustrating stories

Figure 7.4 Stapled books

Type	Sample	Cover	Binding	Elaborative Devices
Accordion Book Poems Patterns Sequence stories		Construction paper Contact paper over cardboard Posterboard	Fold pages accordion style. Staple or glue to cover.	Marbleizing art effect Photographs Shapes: triangles, squares, circles, etc. Tie-dye paper
Plank Book Poems Patterns Stories "How-to" directions		Thin plywood, 3/16" Wood sheets Balsam Woodburning sets	Drill hole in cover. Use key chain or notebook ring to bind together.	Newspaper cutouts Ink sketches Splattered paint Broken crayon drawing Corrugated cardboard pictures
Contact Books Poems Collections Group stories Individual stories		Cardboard covered with contact paper	Staple pages together. Glue to cover.	Typed stories on pages Typed stories, cut out and pasted on pages Creative art impressions with dropped candle wax and food coloring Potato prints Etchings Art materials: straws, buttons, etc.

Figure 7.5   Steps in making a sewn book (From Gillet and Temple, 1982, p. 359)

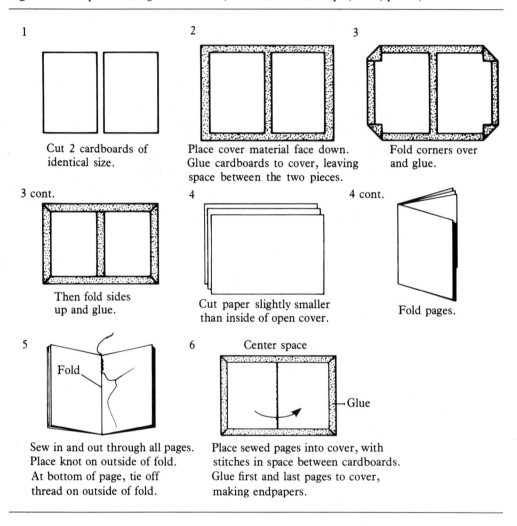

1

Cut 2 cardboards of
identical size.

2

Place cover material face down.
Glue cardboards to cover, leaving
space between the two pieces.

3

Fold corners over
and glue.

3 cont.

Then fold sides
up and glue.

4

Cut paper slightly smaller
than inside of open cover.

4 cont.

Fold pages.

5

Fold

Sew in and out through all pages.
Place knot on outside of fold.
At bottom of page, tie off
thread on outside of fold.

6

Center space

Glue

Place sewed pages into cover, with
stitches in space between cardboards.
Glue first and last pages to cover,
making endpapers.

or poetry, and binding books. Work can be evaluated by panels of judges and honors awarded. The effort culminates in a variety of ways such as a book fair, opportunities for children to share their work, or a visit from an author or illustrator of children's books. Young authors' conferences are held annually at schools and colleges across the country. They can be highly motivating experiences for student writers.

A young authors' conference is an exciting way to culminate a school year. Children in each participating classroom and grade begin producing compositions early in the spring and eventually choose which work will be polished for final production. Often categories are set up in advance, such as fiction, non-fiction, and poetry.

A young authors' conference can be organized into phases or units, corresponding to the stages in the writing cycle, so that each participating class is working in unison toward the final production. Unit One, which may run several weeks, is devoted to direct instruction and the production by each writer of a variety of rough drafts from which to choose. Unit Two is devoted to the actual production of final manuscripts and can be subdivided into units on editing, illustrating, and book binding. During this time period each student selects a composition for final work, revises and edits it, and produces it as an illustrated bound book. Unit Three, the culmination of the project, is devoted to evaluating the published works and sharing them.

Typically criteria for evaluating work are determined and agreed upon at the beginning of Unit One, often by students and teachers working together to determine what makes good writing. Both content and form are important; content aspects like story creativity, characterization and dialogues, organization and clarity of nonfiction writing, and form aspects like correct spelling and grammar, neat writing and binding, and illustrations are considered.

Some young authors' conferences are really writing competitions. In these conferences, each classroom selects its best work in each category to be evaluated with similar works from other classes of the same grade and a panel of evaluators is formed, perhaps including parents and personnel from neighboring schools. Other conferences focus less on competition than on sharing. Evaluation does not extend beyond the individual classroom, special awards are deemphasized and sharing activities like a book fair, poetry and story "read-ins," a visit from a children's author or illustrator, or a visit to a publishing house or bindery are planned.

Whether competition and awards are emphasized or deemphasized, it is important for every participant to be a winner in some fashion. An attractive certificate of participation, signed by the teacher and principal, is appropriate for every student. (These certificates can be inexpensively produced by the school division or a local printer and embellished with stick-on seals and ribbons.) Books that are judged to be outstanding in any category could be given a gold seal or a fancy bookplate inside. Every writer should participate in whatever sharing or culminating activities are planned. In any young authors' conference there may be special winners (and if there are, there should be *lots* of winners), but there must be *no* losers.

Evaluating Children's Composition

Evaluating is an important part of teaching writing, because it can help children become better writers. There are three basic types of evaluation: *reaction*, *analysis*, and *grading*. Each has different purposes and results, and each is appropriate for different tasks.

Reaction to writing means responding as a reader, not as an expert. It means telling the writer what you find most interesting or important, what communicates most effectively, or what confuses us. Reactions can be statements such as "I like this choice of words" or "This lead is especially effective," or they can be questions like "What do you think is the best part of this paper?" or "Can you tell us more about . . .?" Children should receive reaction from others at all points along the way, not just at the final draft stage, and they should react to their own work as well as the work of their classmates.

Analysis is usually undertaken by teachers for the purpose of determining how students are progressing and what they need to practice or be introduced to. Analysis is a sort of diagnosis of a child's writing progress.

Grading means assigning a composition to a particular place in a rank ordering from outstanding to unacceptable. Ideally, grades should be used to apprise students of what specific aspects of their work are strong or weak; criteria for grading should be developed and agreed upon before work is submitted for grading; and only a small portion of what children write should be graded at all.

Reaction was discussed previously in the section on teaching the writing cycle and treated even more fully in the section on conferences. Analysis and grading are discussed in the following sections.

Analysis

To determine a child's progress, work should be analyzed regularly and systematically, roughly at one-month intervals. Analysis should include consideration of the *process* of composition, *functions* of the writing, *qualities* of written style, writing *fluency*, use of *mechanics*, and the child's *attitude* toward writing.

Analysis of the writing *process* requires you to consider how the students come up with ideas for topics, what means they use to define a topic and set to work on it, how they approach creating drafts of a composition, and how drafts are revised. You must observe them at work, as well as considering the written work itself, to get answers to these questions.

Analysis of the *functions* of writing involves the range of topics and the range of purposes. Children cannot make progress unless they produce many types of compositions for a variety of purposes and audiences. They must also learn to take into consideration what the readers of a paper may know or not know, what is needed to get their message across, and how to stick to a topic without unnecessary digression or personal asides.

Analyzing writing *style* includes considering how the student organizes different types of writing, how the reader's attention is focused and sustained, how descriptions and dialogues are constructed, and how the writer involves the reader.

Aspects of writing *fluency* include how often children write, how much they write, and how complex their ideas are. Frequency of writing is controlled largely by the writing program, and we have stated before that every student should be writing every day in every grade. Although the quantity of writing can be judged by the length of the compositions or of sentences, these measures are sometimes misleading. Consider, for example, these two passages:

A: There was this rich man and he was dying but he didn't want anyone to know so he didn't call a doctor and he didn't go to the hospital and he just grew weaker.

B: There was a rich man who was dying but didn't want anyone to know. He didn't go to a doctor or to a hospital, but just grew weaker.

Passage A is longer than B, but B is more fluent; that is, the clauses are combined in more complex ways than in A. Some clauses are subordinate to others, and thus the same subject or verb is allowed to stand for more than one clause. To combine clauses in this way takes a more skillful command of the language than the kind of conjoining shown in passage A.

A measure called a *T-unit* (Hunt, 1965) can reveal the difference in complexity between these passages. A T-unit is a *minimum terminable unit,* or the shortest piece of a sentence that could make sense if it stood on its own. A T-unit, then, is a main clause, or a main clause plus any subordinate clauses. Passage A, by this definition, contains six T-units, since all of its clauses could stand on their own:

A: There was this rich man
    he was dying
    he didn't want anyone to know
    he didn't call a doctor
    he didn't go to the hospital
    he just got weaker

Passage B, though, contains two T-units, because more of its clauses are subordinated and could not stand on their own:

B: There was a rich man who was dying and didn't want anyone to know.

He didn't go to a doctor or to a hospital, but just grew weaker.

If we use as our index of sentence complexity the number of words per T-unit, we find that passage B contained roughly the same number of words as passage A but fewer T-units. The number of words per T-unit is therefore greater in B than in A:

	NUMBER OF WORDS	NUMBER OF T-UNITS	WORDS PER T-UNITS
PASSAGE A	34	6	5.6
PASSAGE B	28	2	14.0

Here, then, are some questions we can raise in the analysis of writing with regard to fluency:

— How long are the writing samples (in words per sample)?
— How long are the sentences in the writing samples?
— How many words per T-unit are there in the writing samples?

The T-unit is most useful as a measure of growth over time. Include a T-unit count in your monthly assessment and keep track of these figures from month to month. Youngsters whose writing is progressing in complexity will show fewer T-units and more words per T-unit over the school year.

Analysis of *mechanical* aspects involves handwriting, spelling, punctuation, capitalization, and grammar — in final drafts only. Since we encourage children to deal with content first and mechanics later, evaluating these aspects must be limited to final drafts. (The teaching of writing mechanics, handwriting, spelling, and grammar is discussed in Chapters Eight and Nine.)

A final consideration in analysis may be the most important of all: Does the writer *like* to write? If so, how do you know? If not, why not? Do we present writing to children in such a way that they *can* enjoy it? Do they write things they care about? Do they share and discuss what they write? Is classroom writing handled as the creative craft that it is — a form of expression that can be handled in many ways, a craft in which we can always become more skilled, more powerful? We cannot evaluate a child's attitude to composition, however, without taking a critical look at how we are teaching writing and how we are responding to what our students produce.

We have organized the questions we ask ourselves in analysis into the following checklist:

A WRITING ANALYSIS CHECKLIST

THE WRITING PROCESS
1. How often does the writer get ideas for writing
   — from the imagination?
   — from discussions with others?
   — by imitating a book, story, poem, TV show, and so on?
   — from the teacher's assignments?
   — from some other source? which?
2. When the writer means to rehearse what will be written, and narrow down the topic, does the writer
   — talk to classmates?
   — talk to the teacher?
   — draw a picture first?
   — think about it overnight?
   — start writing right away?
3. In drafting a paper, does the writer
   — write one draft only?
   — invent spellings, use a dictionary, or limit vocabulary to the words he or she can spell?

— scratch out words and lines, and cut and paste?
— seek comments from others about the way the drafting is going?
4. Does the writer revise a paper before it is considered finished? Do the drafts
   — all look like different papers, new beginnings?
   — look like mechanical refinements of earlier drafts?
   — interact with and build on the ideas of early drafts?
   — stop after one draft?

THE FUNCTIONS OF WRITING
5. What forms of writing has the writer produced?
   — stories?
   — poems?
   — expressive writing (personal experiences and opinions)?
   — persuasive writing?
   — descriptive writing?
   — expository writing (that which explains or gives directions)?
6. What kinds of topics has the writer written about?
   — topics about which the writer was an expert?
   — topics about which the writer had to learn more before writing?
   — topics about things that were present?
   — topics about things that were past or absent?
   — topics about abstract ideas?
7. What audiences has the child written for?
   — the teacher?
   — classmates?
   — other people known to the child? Whom?
   — other people unknown to the child? Whom?
8. In trying to stick to the topic, did the writer
   — limit the focus of the topic before starting to write?
   — stick to one thing or ramble?
   — focus more on the object of the writing or on the writer?
9. In trying to stick with the purpose of writing, does the writer
   — keep expressing personal feelings, although the topic and purpose suggest doing otherwise?
   — declare one purpose but pursue another (such as "The story about . . . ," which is expository, not narrative)?
   — shift from one purpose to another?
10. In trying to meet the audience's need for information
    — does the writer appear to assume the audience knows and is interested in the author?
    — is he or she careful to tell the audience things they will need to know in order to understand what is talked about?
    — does the writer address the same audience throughout?

QUALITIES OF WRITING STYLE
11. Does the writer use exact, well-chosen words?
12. Does the writer "paint pictures with words" — make the reader see what the writer saw?
    — is the focus on immediate, "here-and-now" images?
13. In regard to the organization of the papers:
    — does the writer keep the focus on one aspect of the topic at a time?
    — do the papers have identifiable openings?
    — are the details arranged in a reasonable order and do they relate reasonably to one another?
    — is there an identifiable ending to the papers?

FLUENCY OF WRITING
14. How long are the papers (in words or lines per paper)?
15. What is the average number of words per sentence?
16. What is the average number of words per T-unit?

MECHANICS OF WRITING
17. In handwriting, does the writer
    — have problems forming letters? Which ones?
    — have problems spacing between letters? Keeping vertical lines parallel? Keeping the writing even on the baseline?
    — write with uniform pressure? In smooth or in jerky lines?
18. In regard to spelling:
    — does the writer misspell words in the first draft?
    — does the writer correct the spellings of many words between the first and later drafts?
    — what does the writer do when uncertain of how to spell a word?
19. Does the writer have trouble with standard English usage?
    — does the writer write in complete sentences? If not, what are the units of writing like?
    — does the writer have problems with punctuation and capitalization? With which elements? In what circumstances?
    — are errors made in standard English grammar? If so, describe the errors.

ENJOYING WRITING
20. Does the writer take pleasure in writing?
    — how do you know?

Grading

Grades must go into the book, and children ultimately want to know how their work stacks up. They have a right to know, but we must be careful that our evaluation of their work does not stifle their own judgment. It is important that they be able to critique and improve their own work, and grading should not hinder them in developing this capability (see the guidelines in Box 7.5).

One global grade is rarely useful for responding to the various aspects of content and mechanics in a paper. It is better by far to either grade separately

> **BOX 7.5**
> **Guidelines for**
> **Grading Compositions**
>
> Allow students to select writing to be graded.
> Let them edit and revise work to be submitted for a grade.
>
> Use a grading method that shows what they did well.
>
> Let them suggest criteria for grading.
>
> Use a grading score sheet (Figure 7.6), written comments, or a conference to accompany a grade.

on content and mechanics or on various criteria so that the students can see what they did well, what needs further development, and how a global grade was determined.

Figure 7.6 shows a sample writing score sheet, adapted from one used by Jack Kates at the Kates Writing Workshop in Victoria, Texas, in October of 1979. Kates recommended handing out a copy to all the students while they are polishing up their papers so that they will know in advance the areas that will be evaluated and be able to pay particular attention to them. Each student completes the top box and staples the form to the composition handed in. The teacher completes the lower box, computes the grade, marks the paper with comments, plus or minus signs next to particular parts and so forth, and returns both score sheet and composition to the student. The score sheet can also be used if teacher and student confer about the paper.

Helping Reluctant Writers

Youngsters who doubt their own writing abilities are often reluctant to write very much, and what they do produce may bear out their worst fears about themselves. Often their handwriting is so illegible, their syntax so tangled, or their spelling so primitive that our attention is drawn first to these areas, away from their message. It is therefore most important that you respond *first* to the message, even if it means asking the student to read the paper to you or explain what was written. It is critical for reluctant writers to experience *communicating* despite their mechanical problems.

Characteristic Problems of Reluctant Writers

Every unfluent writer has individual areas of difficulty, but most also share a number of general problem areas. Understanding the common difficulties poor writers share helps us to approach these areas systematically.

1. *Anxiety and Negative Attitudes.* Poor writers fear making mistakes and revealing their ignorance, are anxious about being criticized, and believe that they can never produce good writing. These attitudes must be attacked head-on, because as long as they persist they will be crippling; they will prevent the repeated attempts that are necessary for any writer's success.

Figure 7.6   Writing score sheet

Students, please fill this in:

Your name: _____   Date: _____

Class period: _____

Title of your paper: _____

This is your score: _____

Here is how you earned it —

_____ 1. *Punch:* Right-sized topic
25   Focused on one idea, one thing, one happening
            Made the reader see what the writer saw
            Used colorful, descriptive words

_____ 2. *Plan:* Opening caught the reader's interest
25   Details, events, arguments in sensible order
            Ending left the reader with a thought

_____ 3. *Filling us in:* Seemed to have particular readers in mind
25   Told the readers what they needed to know

_____ 4. *Mechanics:* Spelling corrected before the paper was handed in
25   Handwriting and paper neat
                Punctuation corrected before the paper was handed in
                Capitalization corrected before the paper was handed in

_____ = Total
100

2. *Lack of Practice.* Whatever we do poorly, or believe we do poorly, we avoid doing. Unfluent writers are usually adept at avoiding writing assignments; they stall, lose their materials, find other things to do, fail to complete or turn in work, and sometimes overtly refuse to produce anything. The less they write, the less they progress.

3. *Preoccupation with Mechanics.* Many poor writers have the mistaken belief that good writing has to be correctly punctuated, free of spelling and grammatical errors, and neatly written. They often have more problems with these mechanical aspects than other children, and they try to grapple with these difficulties first. They concentrate more on mechanics than on expression, try to do too much at one time, and each attempt becomes more discouraging than the last.

4. *Lack of Support.* Most of the writing children do is individually produced, which is fine for the naturally talented child but leaves the poor writer out in the cold. Without the support of others, the unfluent writer becomes more and more discouraged and eventually gives up altogether. This is a sort of "survival of the fittest," which should *never* be a part of life in the classroom.

Dealing with Reluctant Writers' Problems

The most important principle in helping poor writers is to *take one thing at a time* and to concentrate on that single goal. Nobody, child or adult, can effectively tackle all problems at once. "One thing at a time" will lead to progress you can see, and that progress will be the impetus for further progress.

Tackling Anxiety. When you give the class examples of something well done, use the papers from the poor writers as well as those from the better writers. If, for example, you are demonstrating correctly structured sentences, search the poorer writers' papers and pull out every good sentence. You may find only one of them, but use it. Nothing turns on a poor writer's lights more than being shown as a good example to others!

As children write and you move about offering suggestions and corrections, carry a green pencil or marker. Use it to mark *good things*: properly spelled words, interesting comparisons, anything done well (content as well as mechanics). Develop as sharp an eye for the positive as for the negative. If you point out an error, point out something well done. Use praise *lavishly* and *sincerely*. Sincere comments like "I really like that sentence (or idea)," "When I read that I could almost see (hear, feel) it," or "This part clearly shows how you felt" helps unfluent writers see what they have done well and how they can do it again.

When correcting or pointing out errors, pick out just a few and ignore, for the time being, the rest. Calling attention to all of them overwhelms poor writers with the enormity of the correction task. It is up to you to keep the task manageable: "Find two words you're not sure you spelled correctly (or ideas you'd like to make clearer)" is a better direction than "Make sure you correct all your spelling (syntax, punctuation, and so on) errors."

Tackling Lack of Practice. Writing has to be made so necessary and so ordinary a process that the unfluent writer *can't* avoid it.

Make writing a part of every day. If we limited reading or talking to one period a week, or did it only when it rained during recess, or used it as a reward or a punishment, how rapidly would our students progress as readers or speakers? Writing must be as ordinary and as predictable a daily activity as reading or talking. A part of every single day must be spent doing free writing in journals, writing down observations, writing letters and summaries, working on a draft of a story or poem, or transcribing from a tape. If time is short, don't let writing be the activity that is omitted.

Make writing a part of every subject. Just as we don't read only in language arts, or solve problems only in math, we don't do writing only in one subject area. Children can use science experiments and observations as ideas for news articles and stories; social studies topics as starters for factual or fictional biographies, imaginative stories, and poems; health concepts as the beginnings of newspaper articles and reports. Even arithmetic problems can be written as "story problems."

Don't get annoyed at avoidance tactics, but don't allow them. If a child complains, "I can't write that much," respond with "Write down one sentence." When one is produced, one more can be coaxed out. Make sure the task is reasonable and that the unfluent writer actually *can* do it; "I won't" usually means "I can't," and your job is to be sure that they *can*.

Tackling Preoccupation with Mechanics. In this and the preceding chapter we have attempted to separate the process of composition into two manageable parts: first, the process of expressing ideas and second, the process of editing, revising, and polishing. Poor writers have much difficulty breaking composition into these two processes and often try to do both at once. As a result, neither is done very effectively.

Stress the importance of first drafts. Use them to focus on the expression of ideas and squelch the tendency to correct mechanical errors. They can wait until later.

Demonstrate the drafting-revision process. You might create a bulletin board that shows copies of several compositions from first effort through several revisions. First drafts will, of course, be messy and contain many mechanical errors. If you show your reluctant writers that *everyone's* early drafts are like that, they will be more apt to write drafts that focus on content rather than on mechanics.

Point out successes at every step of the way. If drafting means only correcting error after error, unfluent writers will strenuously resist revision.

Don't expect the final drafts to be finished products. No composition will ever be perfected, no matter who produces it or how many revisions it goes through. Aim for, and reinforce, *progress* rather than perfection. All that any writer can ever hope for is improvement.

Tackling Lack ·of Support. Although poor writers need more support than good ones, *every* writer needs support. How can you modify writing assignments so that the students are not left to struggle along individually every time?

Provide models that they can use as a starting point — for example, rewriting stories read or listened to in a summary or in another form, such as rewriting a play as a narrative or a story as a news article; rewriting a basic story plot but changing the characters or setting, such as casting humans as animal characters (or vice versa) or giving a modern story an "olden days" setting; writing fables, fairy tales, folk tales, and nursery rhymes as stories; and using patterned books and poems as the basis for innovations with the same or a similar pattern. Using one work as the model for another is *not* copying or plagiarism; on the contrary, it is, according to Cramer, ". . . a legitimate and useful way of developing and extending writing skill" (1978, p. 71). Many well-known professional writers have done this for years.

Use collaborative writing generously. Collaboration was discussed in the preceding section on poetry, and it is just as worthwhile for all other types of writing. For assignments that demand sustained effort, such as relatively detailed stories, or for work that is to be revised in subsequent drafts, children can be paired or work in groups of three. (Pairs and triads are more effective than larger groups.) You can let them select their own partners, but don't hesitate to assign partners too. Self-selection of partners often leads to pairs or triads of poor writers working together, and in this case they may contribute little to each other's progress. Mixed-ability groups are better, because the unfluent writer benefits from the skills of others. If triads are formed, a good plan is to group together a good writer, an average writer, and a poor writer. Then the group produces, together, one composition, which forces all three to cooperate and prevents two working together for their own benefit while excluding the third. The products of such efforts should be evaluated but not graded.

Use a tape recorder to capture the ideas and words of unfluent writers and let them transcribe from their tapes. This procedure separates the composition process into two manageable parts: (a) coming up with the ideas first and (b) writing down the words.

Use the "read-it-aloud" technique to avoid unnatural language. Some poor writers try to write in a very highflown, stilted, and artificial style, which they believe constitutes "good writing." In the attempt they get tangled up in twisted syntax and unfamiliar vocabulary, and what they produce may be nearly incomprehensible. Encourage all students, regardless of their skill, to read aloud what they have written. If it doesn't sound natural on the tongue, or make sense to the listener, it won't be understandable in writing.

Summary

The writing process consists of three stages: prewriting or rehearsal, drafting, and revision. In prewriting children discover what they know and can write about. In drafting they learn to approach the same topic in a number of ways and clarify what they mean to say. In revision they work toward producing a final draft of their work and participate in group and individual writing conferences. During drafting and revision, word processors can free them from mechanical constraints and allow them to focus on meaning until the final-draft stage. Structured activities like the group editing workshop and the teacherless writing group allow them to give and receive feedback on their writing.

Functional writing in the classroom includes writing letters, keeping journals, taking notes, writing summaries, and preparing reports. These activities must be made *real*, not artificial; letters should be mailed, for example. Children need extended practice in functional writing and should participate in it daily in every grade in the form of journals, notebooks, and summaries.

Nonfiction writing can be extended by using the local community and its residents, especially older people, as resources for learning about the past. This approach, called cultural journalism, involves children in interviewing others, transcribing interviews and writing articles about what their community "sources" have taught them, and presenting what they have learned to an audience wider than the classroom through a newspaper, displays, cookbook, or other means.

Poetry should be included in every writing program. Children enjoy writing poetry particularly when they are not constrained by typical poetry forms or conventions. Strict poetry forms should be experimented with only after they have had experience with free or experimental poetry.

Fiction writing, the mainstay of many "creative writing" programs, places particular burdens on youngsters. In creating fiction they need direct practice in making their writing vivid and conveying a sense of immediacy. Activities involving word choices, writing dialogues, and others are suggested.

Publishing children's writing is important to help them achieve a sense of audience and of pride in their work. Work should be prominently displayed, and finished works can be bound into books. Young authors' conferences are structured units in which students publish and share their best efforts.

Evaluating children's writing should include analysis of their progress over time, using a variety of means to assess growth. Only a portion of their writing should be graded; they should submit selected work for grading, and content and mechanics should be graded separately, with feedback provided on grades.

Reluctant writers need special support and guidance. They often suffer from great anxiety about any errors, are preoccupied with the mechanical rather than the expressive aspects of writing, and avoid writing whenever they can. Suggestions for dealing with reluctant writers' problems include consistently responding to meaning first, allowing collaboration with other writers, making writing a routine part of every subject, and tackling only one problem area at a time.

CHAPTER EIGHT

Understanding and Teaching Grammar

CHAPTER OUTLINE

Understanding Grammar

What can we do for students whose ideas are interesting but whose sentences are short and monotonous, barren of colorful adjectives or adverbs, and unclear in meaning because they don't use prepositional phrases and subordinate clauses? We can teach them to use grammar, that's what. The art of combining words effectively into sentences is a must in good communication, and all students need a rich repertoire of sentence structures in which to frame their ideas. Such a repertoire, in a word, is grammar. So long as they also have plentiful opportunities to talk, listen, read, and write, they can expand this repertoire by being taught grammar. What's more, instruction in grammar can be intellectually rich, it can involve imagination and creativity, and it can be related to experiences in literature, in creative writing, and even classroom dramatics.

You may be wondering if by *grammar* we mean the same tedious routine of labeling sentence parts and memorizing definitions of nouns, verbs, adjectives, and adverbs that have made grade school language classes so medicinal and miserable for so many. The answer is no. Recent development in linguistics and education have given us a whole new approach to grammar: a new way to define it, new goals that it can serve, and new techniques for involving students in teaching the subject. It is reasonable to say that modern grammar is a whole *new* subject. For those who are still skeptical, however, let us look back for a moment at what grammar teaching has meant historically so that we can clearly distinguish the new approaches from the old.

Grammar as a school subject has had a curious history. In ancient times it wasn't taught. Instead, schools in Greece and Rome offered instruction in rhetoric — the *use* of language to stir the hearts and minds of others. It was in medieval England that the forerunner of modern grammar first entered the curriculum, but this was Latin grammar, Latin being the language in which books were written. English-speaking students had to be initiated into Latin grammar before they could participate in academics. In Shakespeare's time, English replaced Latin as the language of schooling. The subject of grammar stayed on, however, like the fireman on a diesel train, long after its justification had disappeared.

English grammar has remained in the curriculum from Shakespeare's time to ours, and though it may have occurred to people to ask what the point was of teaching children the grammar of a language they already knew, it wasn't until scientific research methods were applied to educational issues at the beginning of this century that grammar instruction was seriously called into question. In short, if the purpose of teaching students grammar is to make them speak and write more "grammatical" sentences (according to some standard of grammaticality), teaching traditional grammar doesn't work. Studies that compare the sentences spoken and written by students who have been taught traditional grammar with those who have not show no differences in favor of those who have studied grammar (see Gleason, 1965, for a discussion).

These experimental findings have not succeeded in driving grammar out of the school curriculum, but they have inspired on the one hand an inquiry into what grammar and grammar skill are, and on the other hand they have led to a search for more effective methods for teaching the subject. Both efforts have met with some success. More careful and scientific accounts of English grammar have led in turn to more accurate measures of what school-aged children can and cannot do with grammar. With better accounts of the areas where they experience difficulty, educators have developed a handful of new methods for teaching grammar, and these — at last — can improve a child's facility with language.

In the pages that follow, we will investigate in some detail these newer approaches for describing grammatical concepts. We have two reasons for doing so. First, they are useful to know in order to understand children's developing power over grammar. Second, today's language arts textbooks employ modern linguistic terminology that may not have been in use when many of our readers were in elementary school. Following the discussion of grammatical concepts, we will describe the aspects of school-aged children's grammar that are strong, as well as those in which they should be encouraged to grow during the elementary school years. The entire second section of this chapter will be devoted to techniques for instruction in grammar.

Describing English Grammar

We might define grammar as a system of rules by which words are arranged into meaningful utterances. Now there is something odd about grammatical rules. All of us who speak and understand English know the rules, even though we might not be able to say them out loud. We know, for example, that *The dog gave the cat a wink* is a grammatical sentence, while *Wink cat dog the the a gave* is not. Similarly, we sense that there is something wrong with *Janie had a red, big ball* though we may not be able to put our finger on just what the problem is. Both of the latter two sentences violate rules of English grammar. The fact that we are aware of the violations indicates that, on some level, we know the rules that these sentences violate, even though most of us could not articulate them. Rules of the type we are describing here are subconscious psychological constructs. There is another kind of grammatical rule, however. That is the explicit kind, such as this:

> *When two or more adjectives precede a noun, adjectives of quantity come before adjectives of quality.*

or this:

> $S \rightarrow NP^{\star}$ *(subject)* $+$ *Verb* $+$ *NP (indirect object)* $+$ *NP (direct object)*

Explicit rules like these are made up by people who want to describe the first kind of rule, the deep-seated psychological constructs. Anyone can make up rules of this second type. The rules are good if they describe English grammar as it is actually used, bad if they don't. Either way they do not affect English grammar — the intuitive version that resides in people's minds — one way or another. A perfect set of explicit grammar rules would be one that described all of the sentences that most people would consider grammatical and failed to allow any that would not be considered grammatical. Such a set has never been invented, but linguists keep trying and in the process give us one kind of grammar after another. Aspects of two kinds of grammar — structural and generative-transformational — will be described here. Rather than describe either approach in its entirety (which neither space nor most readers' interest would allow) we will draw from each those elements that best serve the teaching and understanding of language arts. These elements will consist of:

— definitions of parts of speech, or form classes
— structures of common sentences
— transformations of sentences

Parts of Speech, or Form Classes. When we set out to encourage children to use a more interesting variety in the sentence structures they write and in the words they choose, it is helpful to establish some understanding of grammatical terms. These terms serve as labels that can direct a child's attention to the parts of a sentence that we want to improve.

The terms we mean are, of course, the ones like *noun, verb, adjective, adverb, preposition,* or *prepositional phrase.* As in most other areas of teaching grammar, however, considerable controversy has arisen in recent years between

---

* Throughout this chapter NP will be used to refer to a noun phrase.

advocates of traditional approaches and advocates of various new linguistic approaches over the definition of such terms. The traditionalists, for example, have customarily defined a noun as "a word that names a person, place, or thing," and a verb as "a word that names an action or state of being," but critics have charged that these definitions are too inexact to be of real service. The word "action" itself should be a verb by the traditional definition, yet it is a noun. The word "nothing" denotes "that which does not exist"; therefore it would not seem to fit the definition of a noun. Yet it clearly plays the role of a noun in a sentence such as "Nothing would make her change her mind."

The solution to the problem suggested by *structuralists* such as Fries (1940; 1952) lies in the premise just mentioned: the grammatical role played by words in sentences. What makes a word a noun is not what it means, as the traditional definition suggests, but rather the role it occupies in the grammatical structure of a sentence. The idea of *acting* may, for example, be expressed as a verb in sentence A, as a noun in sentence B, as an adjective in sentence C, and as an adverb in sentence D:

A. Juanita was *acting* strangely.
B. Juanita's *actions* were strange.
C. Juanita was strangely *active*.
D. Juanita was *actively* strange.

What makes us able to categorize each version of the idea of *acting* as either verb, noun, adjective, or adverb is not what each version means, because the meanings are roughly similar. We categorize each one, rather, because of the role it plays in relation to other words in the sentence. Since this approach to defining parts of speech is being adopted by more and more publishers of language arts books for children, we will take the time to acquaint you with the major ones now.

Structural linguistics uses the term *form classes* (Fries, 1952) to denote what traditional grammar means by *parts of speech*: nouns, verbs, adjectives, and so on. For the most part, structural linguistics employs the same terms for the traditional word classes, although there are one or two substitutions, as we will see below.

Words are usually assigned to form classes in three ways. Two of these ways have to do with the types of *affixes* that words of each class will accept. ("Affix" is a general word for both prefix and suffix.) There are two main classes of affixes: *derivational* and *inflectional*.

Derivational affixes have the effect of changing a word from one form class to another. The derivational affix *–ment*, for example, changes verbs to nouns, as in *govern/government, embarrass/embarrassment*. Thus, we can observe that the presence of the affix *–ment* at the end of a word identifies it as a noun. Other derivational affixes can be used to identify members of other form classes.

Inflectional affixes "adjust" some classes of words to work grammatically with other words in a sentence: *–s* is an inflectional affix signaling that a noun is plural; *–ed* is an inflectional affix showing that a verb is in the past tense. The inflections that a word accepts can be a clue to its membership in a particular form class. This method of identification is not foolproof, however, because what looks like the same inflectional affix can have different functions when it is attached to words of different classes.

A third means of assigning words to form classes is to observe the slots they fill in sentences. Since nouns, for example, tend to come after adjectives or *determiners* (words like *these, the, some, one,* and so forth), we can test for nouns by seeing if a word can fit a slot in a sentence that follows an adjective or determiner. To make this simpler, we have *test frames*, special sentences with slots left in them that only words of a certain class can fill. Here is a test frame for nouns:

One _____ was covered with _____.

Let us now consider the structural linguistic definitions for the most common form classes.

Nouns. Nouns can usually be identified by their inflectional and derivational affixes, as well as by the slots they can fill (see Box 8.1). Since words that follow adjectives, determiners (*this, that, these, those, some, any, my, your, a, the,* and so on), or prepositions are nouns, test frames for nouns can be constructed with slots left after words of those classes.

Verbs. Verbs are traditionally defined as "words that name actions or states of being." In structural linguistics, verbs are identified by the derivational affixes they accept, the inflectional affixes they accept, a telltale group of words called *auxiliaries* that accompany them, and the slots they occupy in a sentence. These features are outlined in Box 8.2.

Adjectives. Adjectives can be identified by means of their derivational affixes, their inflectional affixes, and the slots they will fill in a sentence test frame.

Three adjectival derivational affixes look like inflectional affixes on verbs, namely, *–en, –ed,* and *–ing.* If there is doubt about whether a particular word ending in one of these affixes is an adjective or a verb, try it out in an adjective test frame, which works very well. One form it frequently distinguishes from real adjectives is what is sometimes called an attributive noun, as with *telephone* in the example in Box 8.3.

Determiners. Another group of words that works very much like adjectives but is weeded out by this procedure is the group of *determiners,* a relatively new term that comes to us from structural linguistics. Determiners come in four varieties: There are *articles,* both definite and indefinite, such as *a* or *an* (indefinite) and *the* (definite). There are *demonstrative determiners,* such as *this, that, these,* and *those.* There are possessive determiners: *my, our, your, his, her, its, their.* Finally there are the *cardinal numbers,* one through ninety-nine (as Malmstrom notes, "*One hundred* begins over again by using *one* to signal that the noun *hundred* is coming up" [Malmstrom, 1968, p. 60]).

BOX 8.1
Nouns

I. *Derivational Affixes*

-age	coverage, silage
-ance	clearance, importance
-ee	trustee, employee
-er	employer, dancer
-ment	pavement, government
-ce	independence, insolence
-cy	democracy, lunacy
-ity	vanity, scarcity
-ness	stillness, silliness
(also:	-ster, -ism, -ist, -ship)

II. *Inflectional Affixes*

To make plurals:

-s	coats, pigs
-es	dishes, ditches

But note the irregular plural forms:

children, women, oxen, men, deer, geese, feet

Also, *mass nouns* are not commonly pluralized:

communism, milk

III. *Sentence Test Frames*

The _____ couldn't hide its _____.

One _____ had many _____.

Sharon was in _____.

Determiners often work in a fashion similar to adjectives. We can say "our popsicles" or "cold popsicles," and *our* and *cold* seem to have similar grammatical roles, but watch what happens when we try to insert *our* into the test frame for adjectives:

Our popsicles seem very *our*.

Cold, however, works fine:

Cold popsicles seem very *cold*.

All of the words that can be classified as determiners will similarly be rejected by the test frame for adjectives (see Box 8.3).

Adverbs. Adverbs are words like *suddenly, here, sloppily, then, quickly,* and *now.* Traditionally, adverbs were defined as "words that modify a verb or adverb." This definition often fails to make sense, however, especially when adverbs seem to bear no special relationship to the verb in a sentence. In a sentence like "Actually, I prefer tea," the adverb *actually* seems to comment

BOX 8.2
Verbs

I. *Derivational Affixes*

-ize	socialize, criticize
-ify	classify, mystify
-en	darken, lighten
-ate	hesitate, navigate
en-	enlist, enlarge
be-	belittle, bedazzle

II. *Inflectional Affixes*

-s	runs, moves
-ed	flagged, started
-ing	flagging, starting
to . . .	to run, to fall

III. *Auxiliary Verbs*

be/is/am/are/was/were	is going, was talking
have/has/had	have taken, has talked
might/may	might run, may rain
shall/should	shall fight, should speak
will/would	will run, would stall
can/could	can find, could lose
must	must begin

IV. *Sentence Test Frame*

$$(\text{The}) \text{ noun} \begin{Bmatrix} \text{may} \\ \text{will} \\ \text{must} \\ \text{can} \end{Bmatrix} \underline{\quad} (\text{the}) \text{ (noun)}.$$

Note that parentheses ( ) mean "may choose this element." Braces { } mean "must choose one of these elements."

Examples:
The aardvark *whistled* the tune.
Rain must *fall*.

on the whole phrase "I prefer tea" rather than on the verb alone, *prefer*. Similarly, in "Yesterday John was on top of the world," it is nonsense to say that the adverb *yesterday* "modifies" the verb *was*.

Structural linguistics uses no such definition for adverbs. Rather, this approach maintains that an adverb is a word that accepts certain derivational affixes and fits in certain grammatical slots in a sentence (see Box 8.4).

Prepositions. Prepositions belong to a larger class of what linguists call *function words*: words that may have little or no meaning in themselves but

BOX 8.3
Adjectives

I. *Derivational Affixes*

-y	funny, crazy
-ive	active, passive
-able	comfortable, agreeable
-ful	bashful, cheerful
-less	helpless, thoughtless
-ar	regular, circular
-ary	ordinary, legendary
-ic	civic, terrific
-ish	childish, fiendish
-ous	fabulous, hideous
-en[a]	wooden, woolen
-ed[a]	beloved, aged
-ing[a]	charming, interesting

II. *Inflectional Affixes*

-er	fuller, smaller
-est	biggest, tallest

III. *Sentence Test Frame*

A _____ noun seems very _____.

Examples:

A *stingy* person seems very *stingy*.

But not

A *telephone* man seems very *telephone*.

---

[a] Not to be confused with verb inflectional affixes.

which provide a sort of grammatical glue between the meaningful words in a sentence. Determiners are function words too.

There are approximately forty prepositions in English. Traditionally, children have been taught to identify them by memorizing the whole group, but it is doubtful that this serves any useful purpose. The device of the test frame can be used to identify them, and three frames can isolate the whole lot (see Box 8.5).

Prepositions come in groups of words, such as *in a hole, under suspicion,* and *with a tomato.* When we use prepositions to add detail and color to a sentence, we always use them in these groups, never alone. *P-groups* are the name structural linguists give to prepositions followed by noun phrases; you may know them as prepositional phrases. Thus when we are helping children to become aware of the advantages of prepositions, it is more useful to talk of these P-groups than to work on prepositions in isolation. P-groups can be used

---

BOX 8.4
Adverbs

I. *Derivational Affixes*

a-	ahead, away
-ly	slowly, happily
-ward	backward, skyward
-where	somewhere, nowhere
-wise	clockwise, likewise

II. *Sentence Test Frame*

_____ the noun _____ verbs the noun _____.

Examples:

Sometimes the clock disturbs the baby.
The clock *greatly* disturbs the baby.
The clock disturbs the baby *now*.

---

in sentence expansion exercises and in other creative work with grammar, as we will see in the second half of this chapter.

Basic Sentence Patterns. When asked to describe the difference between human language and, say, foghorns and bird calls linguists will tell you that human language is *creative*. Anyone who can talk with even modest fluency can utter an infinite variety of original sentences, few of which are exactly the same, or like sentences anyone else has ever spoken or will ever speak. This is true, and yet in another sense language is quite limited. Our expressions may be wonderfully unique and various, but the sentences we use are built around a surprisingly small set of patterns. In fact, many linguists list only about half a dozen *basic sentence patterns*. There is another set of a dozen or so *transformations* that can work on these basic sentence patterns. Mathematically, the possible combinations of basic sentence patterns and transformations make up quite a large set, but the number of basic sentence patterns and transformations is limited.

Research by Loban (1976) and Hunt (1965) suggests that the vast majority of children entering first grade can use all of the basic sentence patterns. Where they need to grow is in their use of transformations, many of which are not found in their sentence repertoire. Also, most teachers would add that children need to put vivid and definite words into their basic sentences. Quite successful teaching strategies can be built on the basic sentence patterns, first by means of slot-filling exercises such as *sentence expansion* and then by applying transformations to them, as in *sentence combining* (both are described later in this chapter). Basic sentence patterns are the forms of the simplest complete sentences we can utter or write. Malmstrom (1968) lists five of them.

BOX 8.5
Prepositions

Sentence Test Frames for Prepositions

The first frame identifies all but nine of the forty prepositions, according to Malmstrom (1968):

1. The ant crawled _____ the door.

   Those prepositions that will fit this slot are:

about	beneath	on
above	beside	opposite
across	beyond	over
after	by	round
against	down	through
along	for	to
around	from	toward
at	in	under
before	like	underneath
behind	near	up
below	off	with

   Prepositions that will not fit the slot are these:

among	during	regarding
but (meaning *except*)	except	since
concerning	of	until or till

Some of the second group will fit the slot in this test frame:

2. The old man was silent _____ the war.

The others — *among, but, except,* and *of* — fit the slot in this one:

3. No one was talking _____ the girls.

---

1. *Noun Phrase/Subject + Intransitive Verb + (Adverb).* This sentence pattern yields sentences such as

The football player sobbed uncontrollably.

Losers weep.

A noun phrase is a noun preceded by an optional determiner (see above): for example, "Those boys," "one hundred twenty-five aardvarks," "some astronauts," "a frozen yogurt," and so on.

The notation *noun phrase/subject* in the first basic sentence pattern refers to a noun phrase that is the subject of the sentence. *Intransitive verb* refers to a class of verb, sometimes called *intransitive complete,* that is more active than linking verbs like *is* or *seems,* yet does not take a direct object. *Walk, run, cry,*

brood, sleep, cavort, procrastinate, and *lie down* are all intransitive verbs. They all describe things that we can do, but not do to something or someone else. The notation +(Adverb) means this pattern may or may not take an adverb in this position.

Here are a few more sentences that follow this pattern:

Egbert slept peacefully.

Beatrice should have stayed there.

The smoke alarm buzzed annoyingly.

The second basic sentence pattern goes like this:

2. *Noun Phrase/Subject + Transitive Verb + Noun Phrase/Direct Object + (Adverb).* A *transitive verb* is an active verb that takes a direct object. Such a verb denotes some action that we do *to* someone or something else. That someone or something is the *noun phrase/direct object.* Whoever does the doing is the *noun phrase/subject.* This sentence pattern, like the one before it, allows for an optional adverb at the end.

Here are some sentences that follow this pattern:

Those parakeets are hurting my ears.

Amy tilled her garden all weekend.

Papa brought down two ducks right off.

Our team will beat your team decisively.

Note that some verbs can be transitive or intransitive. We can say

The player punted the ball *or The player punted.*

Papa shot two ducks *or Papa shot carefully.*

The only way to decide if a verb is transitive or not is to see if it has a direct object. If it does, it is transitive; if it doesn't, it is intransitive.

Here is the third basic sentence pattern:

3. *Noun Phrase/Subject + Transitive Verb + Noun Phrase/Indirect Object + Noun Phrase/Direct Object + (Adverb).* A *noun phrase/indirect object* is any noun phrase in front of which we could insert *to* or *for* without changing the sense of the sentence. For instance, in the sentence

The teller gave the two holdup men the money.

we could insert *to* in front of the noun phrase *the two holdup men* and the meaning of the sentence would not change:

The teller gave *to* the two holdup men the money.

Similarly in the sentence

Juanita bought her dog a new collar.

we could insert *for* before *her dog*:

Juanita bought *for* her dog a new collar.

Her dog is therefore a noun phrase/indirect object.

Both of the above sentences follow the third basic sentence pattern. Here are some more sentences that follow this pattern:

Herbert gives Shiela the creeps.

Herbert bought Shiela a pet boa constrictor the other day.

Shiela gave Herbert back his ring.

The fourth basic sentence pattern is arranged like this:

4. *Noun Phrase/Subject + Linking Verb + Noun Phrase/Predicate Noun + (Adverb).* Here are some sentences that follow this pattern:

Helen is a heartbreaker.

You may already be a winner.

Yolanda is a loner still.

The new elements in this sentence pattern are the *linking verb* and the *noun phrase/predicate noun*. Linking verbs are in English sentences what the "equals sign" (=) is in arithmetic equations. The various forms of the verb *to be* (*is, was, were, have been, will be, must be, may be,* and others) are linking verbs. So also are the following: *seems, appears to be, has become, remains,* and *turned into*. A noun phrase/predicate noun is a noun phrase that follows a linking verb and is equated with the noun phrase/subject by the linking verb.

Here are some more sentences that follow this pattern:

The witch turned into smoke right before our eyes.

Johnny was a junior at the time.

Many women become soldiers nowadays.

The fifth and final basic sentence pattern goes as follows:

5. *Noun Phrase/Subject + Linking Verb + Adjective/Predicate Adjective + (Adverb).* This pattern is identical to the pattern immediately preceding it except for the *predicate adjective,* which is substituted for the predicate noun. Thus instead of

Yolanda is a loner still.

this pattern gives us

Yolanda is lonely still.

Here is another sentence that follows this pattern:

The witch suddenly became furious.

Note in this sentence that we are taking the liberty of placing the adverb in one of the other slots it can properly occupy. We can also substitute in a P-group that has the effect of an adverb, as in the next sentence.

Yolanda seems lonely at parties.

In the morning the boxer felt much better.

In the section of this chapter on teaching applications, we will show how basic sentence patterns can be used in quasi-creative writing activities and in sentence expansion exercises.

Sentence Transformations. Having presented the five types of basic sentence patterns we come now to the bad news: Very few of the sentences written or spoken by fluent language users conform to these patterns. It's not that the patterns themselves are wrong. The problem is rather that although we use these basic patterns as the starting point for making our common sentences, we add *transformations* to change our basic sentences into more complex ones. Thus the basic sentence patterns are worth knowing, but we need to add to them an understanding of how sentence transformations work in order to get an explicit appreciation of grammar that is close to the complexity of the language that adults — and even schoolchildren — speak and write every day.

Malmstrom (1968) identifies three kinds of transformations:

— those that change one type of sentence into another, such as questions, negatives, and passive and elliptical sentences
— those that conjoin elements of several sentences into compounds
— those that reduce some sentences into fragments and insert them into other sentences

The first kind of transformation is readily used by almost all school-aged children, even though it is quite complex. Thus we will treat this group only briefly and devote more attention to the latter two kinds of transformations, since these are areas in which children need to grow and in which careful teaching has proved to be effective.

Transformations that Convert Sentences. Consider these sentences:

1. Herbert gave Sheila a boa constrictor for her birthday.
2. Did Herbert give Sheila a boa constrictor for her birthday?
3. What did Herbert give Sheila for her birthday?
4. To whom did Herbert give a boa constrictor?
5. Who gave Sheila a boa constrictor for her birthday?
6. Herbert did.
7. Give Sheila a boa constrictor for her birthday, Herbert.
8. Herbert didn't give Sheila a boa constrictor for her birthday.
9. Herbert didn't give Sheila a boa constrictor for her birthday, did he?
10. Herbert gave Sheila a boa constrictor for her birthday, didn't he?
11. Why did Herbert give Sheila a boa constrictor for her birthday?
12. When did Herbert give Sheila a boa constrictor?
13. A boa constrictor was given to Sheila for her birthday by Herbert.
14. What Herbert gave Sheila for her birthday was a boa constrictor.

Of the above fourteen sentences, only one, the first, follows any of the basic sentence patterns we presented in the previous section. The others demonstrate variations of six different kinds of transformations: a *passive*, a *negative*, an *imperative*, an *ellipsis*, three variations of *questions*, and a *cleft* transformation. After we explain each of these below we will look at one other: a *there* transformation.

1. *Passive Transformation.* *A boa constrictor was given to Sheila for her birthday by Herbert* is a passive version of the original basic sentence. Passive sentences take the form *Y was done to Z by X* instead of the normal order, *X did Y to Z*. Most school-aged children can understand passive sentences, but few can use them in speech or writing until the middle elementary grades.

2. *Negative Transformation.* With this kind of transformation, the basic sentence patterns are all taken to be positive. In order to make a sentence say that something didn't happen, it is necessary to subject the original positive sentence to the negative transformation. Thus, from the original basic sentence, we get *Herbert didn't give Sheila a boa constrictor for her birthday.* Negatives are understood and used by nearly all school-aged children.

3. *Imperative Transformation.* Another kind of transformation that was demonstrated in the boa constrictor sentences was the imperative. The sentence *Give Sheila a boa constrictor for her birthday, Herbert* was a command, an imperative form of the original sentence. Here again, we assume that a person would begin with a basic sentence in mind and subject it to the imperative transformation in order to derive the imperative form. Young children understand and use this form too.

4. *Ellipsis Transformation.* A fourth kind of transformation is the ellipsis, which simply means "leaving out." It starts with the original sentence and leaves out all but the part that is not understood by the context. The sentence, *Herbert did,* makes sense because it is offered as an answer to the question *Who gave Sheila a boa constrictor for her birthday?* A full response would have been *Herbert gave Sheila a boa constrictor for her birthday,* but that would sound silly, unless one said it in the course of giving testimony in a court of law. The ellipsis transformation is understood and used by school-aged children.

5. *Question Transformation.* Next, we come to the type of transformation in this set of sentences that has the largest variety of forms. This is the question transformation, and there are three kinds. A *yes/no question* turns the original sentence directly into a question: *Did Herbert give Sheila a boa constrictor for her birthday?* (The answer is yes or no). A variation is the *wh-question,* which isolates a particular aspect of the original sentence for investigation: *what* happened, *why* did it happen, *when* and *where* did it happen, *who* made it happen, and *how* did it happen? Since most of these query words begin with *wh-,* these letters give this type of question its name. The third kind is the *tag question,* where the communicator makes an assertion and then queries the audience as to whether the assertion is correct or not. *Herbert gave Sheila a boa constrictor for her birthday, didn't he?* is a tag question, and *didn't he* is the tag. All three of these forms of questions develop by school age.

6. *Cleft Transformation.* The sentence *What Herbert gave Sheila for her birthday was a boa constrictor* is the result of a cleft transformation. It started out as the basic sentence, *Herbert gave Sheila a boa constrictor for her birthday,* but was put through a mainly stylistic transformation that had the effect of stressing the idea of the *boa constrictor.* The cleft transformation gives emphasis by referring to something at the beginning of the sentence with the word *what* but withholding the identity of the thing referred to until the very end of the sentence.

The cleft transformation will work with verb phrases as well as noun phrases:

What Herbert did was give Sheila a boa constrictor for her birthday.

As Weaver (1979) points out, however, cleft transformations seem to work only when the thing to be stressed is nonhuman; that is, it will not work to call special attention to a person by means of the cleft transformation:

Who Herbert gave the boa constrictor to was Sheila.

Some children may not use the cleft transformation until the middle elementary years.

7. *There Transformation.* Here is an example of a sentence that is derived through the use of a there transformation.

Creepy things are in the barn.

There are creepy things in the barn.

There transformations are stylistic too. They often yield sentences that sound more natural than those without them. You will note that we couldn't use our Herbert and Sheila sentence to illustrate the there transformation, because there transformations normally work only when the basic sentence to which they are applied has some form of the verb *be* as its main verb. We can say *There are creepy things in the barn* but we cannot say *There gives Herbert Sheila a boa constrictor for her birthday.*

Before leaving this first group of transformations, we should note that they are not always handed out at the rate of just one per sentence. The sentence *Herbert didn't give Sheila a boa constrictor for her birthday, did he?* contains two transformations: a tag question and a negative. Many other combinations are possble. Questions can be combined with negatives, passives, and ellipses. Imperatives can be combined with ellipses, negatives, and passives, and so on. Thus we could easily end up with sentences like *Give her what? Was given what? By whom?* and others that would show an interesting trail of transformations if their derivatives were re-created explicitly.

Transformations that Combine Sentences. We have just looked at transformations that turn one sort of sentence into another: the kinds that ask questions, give commands, make active sentences passive, and the rest. Now we will consider transformations that combine two or more sentences into one. Here we confront a dimension of grammatical ability in which all elementary school-aged children need to grow. More than any other topic of grammar we have discussed thus far, this is one that can and should be converted into classroom instruction.

Consider these sentences.

Boa constrictors live in trees.

Boa constrictors get by on a diet of flying squirrels.

Boa constrictors give me the creeps.

We would not be surprised to see lines like these turned up in a third grader's paper. We *would* be surprised to see them in a paper written by a college student. How would college students write them differently? Certainly they would write them something like this:

> Boa constrictors live in trees and get by on a diet of flying squirrels. They give me the creeps.

or, if the writer were being playful, like this:

> Boa constrictors live in trees, get by on a diet of flying squirrels — and give me the creeps.

What the college students do is to combine the separate sentences in the youngster's composition into one or two sentences. They do it by leaving out the parts of the sentences that were repeated and then writing only those parts that contained new information, joining them together by using commas and the conjunction *and*.

Thus the noun phrase/subject *boa constrictors*, which was repeated three times in the original sentences, was used only once, its repetitions eliminated. Since the verb phrases contained new information, all three were included in the final sentence. Just about any part of a sentence can be eliminated or retained in this way. In the following sentences the words that occupy the noun phrase/subject slot change, while the remaining parts of the sentences are identical.

> Hoboes put their pants on one leg at a time.

> Presidents put their pants on one leg at a time.

> Priests put their pants on one leg at a time.

Thus they can be combined as:

> Hoboes, presidents, and priests put their pants on one leg at a time.

In these sentences, everything is identical except the prepositions:

> This is a government of the people.

> This is a government by the people.

> This is a government for the people.

Therefore we can eliminate everything that is repeated from the last two sentences and retain only their prepositions in the derived sentence:

> This is a government of, by, and for the people.

Although the above examples use only the conjunction *and* (the comma stands for the conjunction *and*), many others are possible. *But, or, nor, not, rather than, as well as* are all workable candidates for joining elements of sentences together. So too are the paired conjunctions *not only . . . but also, either . . . or, neither . . . nor*, and *both . . . and* (Malmstrom, 1968). Here are some of these other conjunctions at work:

Tweedledum will fit in the lifeboat.
Tweedledee will not fit in the lifeboat.
Tweedledum, not Tweedledee, will fit in the lifeboat.

Tweedledum will fit in the lifeboat.
Tweedledee will fit in the lifeboat.
Both Tweedledum and Tweedledee will fit in the lifeboat.

Tweedledum will fit in the lifeboat.
Tweedledee will fit in the lifeboat. (However, the lifeboat won't hold both
   of them.)
Either Tweedledum or Tweedledee will fit in the lifeboat.

Sheila doesn't like boa constrictors.
Herbert gave Sheila a boa constrictor.
Sheila doesn't like boa constrictors but Herbert gave her one.

Sheila doesn't like boa constrictors.
Herbert likes boa constrictors.
Sheila doesn't like boa constrictors but Herbert does.

The last set of sentences presents an interesting problem. Both *boa constrictor* and *Sheila* are used in both sentences; hence they are candidates for deletion in the derived sentence, but the derived sentence would not make sense if *Sheila* and *boa constrictor* were deleted entirely. Consider: *Sheila doesn't like boa constrictors but Herbert gave.* We still need to know what Herbert gave and to whom he gave it, even if the answers to both questions are terms that were used in the previous sentence. Because both *Sheila* and *boa constrictor* appeared in the earlier sentences, we need not repeat them *verbatim*. Instead, we can refer to them using, respectively, the pronouns *her* and *one*. Using pronouns like *her, him, he, one, them, they,* and *it* to stand for noun phrases that have already been named explicitly is called *pronominalization*.

A similar procedure can be applied to verbs. We noted above that the sentences

Sheila doesn't like boa constrictors.

Herbert likes boa constrictors.

can be combined into the sentence

Sheila doesn't like boa constrictors but Herbert does.

In the original two sentences, the verb phrase *like(s) boa constrictors* is repeated and is therefore eligible for deletion in the derived sentence. A complete deletion, however, won't work either, because the resulting sentence would not tell us enough:

Sheila doesn't like boa constrictors but Herbert.

Herbert what? To answer that question, we must insert *does*, which refers to the verb phrase *like(s) boa constrictors* from the earlier sentences. We can't really call this pronominalization, because *does* is an auxiliary verb, not a pronoun. Whether pronoun or verb, the point is that sometimes in combining sentences with repeated elements, it is necessary to insert either a pronoun or an auxiliary verb to stand for a noun phrase or verb phrase. Otherwise, the sentence would be unclear.

Transformations that Imbed Sentences. Transformations that result in sentences such as

Sheila played golf, but Henry went shopping.

leave both the original sentences,

Sheila played golf.

and

Henry went shopping.

on roughly equal footing. These are conjunction transformations. Consider this sentence, though:

Yours is like the shirt that I bought.

This was derived from

Yours is like a shirt.

and

I bought the shirt.

In the derived sentence, the two original sentences do not have equal footing. The second, *I bought the shirt,* was reduced and inserted into the first one.

There are many transformations of this type that reduce one or more sentences to fragments and insert them into another sentence. The sentence that is not reduced is properly called the *matrix* sentence ("matrix" means "framework"). It is the one that contributes the main verb to the derived sentence. The sentence that is reduced is called the *imbedded* sentence.

When a sentence is reduced and imbedded into a matrix sentence, the imbedded sentence plays the grammatical role of either a noun, an adjective, or an adverb in the second sentence. Hence the transformations are classified as *nominalizations, adjectivalizations,* or *adverbializations.*

In a later section, "Sentence Combining," we will outline the several varieties of each kind of transformation, so we will only briefly describe them here.

1. *Nominals.* Reduced sentences that function as nouns in the matrix sentences are called *nominals.* Here are some examples of nominals compared with ordinary nouns:

That you are leaving surprises me.
    nominal

For you to leave surprises me.
  nominal

Your *story* surprises me.
  noun

Nominals can occupy many of the same slots in a sentence that nouns can occupy.

I know *that you are leaving.*
   nominal

I want *you to leave.*
   nominal

I'm happy with *your leaving.*
    nominal

I'm happy with your *gift.*
    noun

Nominals typically occupy the role of NP/subject, NP/direct object, or NP/object of a preposition. They are most common in the role of NP/direct object, and this is the way children first use them (Loban, 1976).

2. *Adjectivals. Adjectivals* are reduced sentences that function as adjectives. Here are some examples of them compared with ordinary adjectives:

The fish *that bit the hook* tugged furiously.
  adjectival

The fish *caught by Sheila* was a small-mouth bass.
  adjectival

The trout, *the first one caught that day,* was puny.
   adjectival

The *trophy-winning* fish weighed six pounds.
  adjectival

The *biggest* fish had the least flavor.
 adjective

3. *Adverbials.* Reduced sentences that function as adverbs are *adverbials.* They can occupy the same slots in sentences that adverbs can. Here are some examples compared with ordinary adverbs.

When he saw the matador, the bull pawed the ground.
 adverbial

His feet churning the earth, the bull charged forth.
 adverbial

The bull charged forth, *his feet churning the earth.*
   adverbial

The bull, *when he saw the matador,* pawed the ground.
adverbial

The bull *heavily* pawed the ground.
adverb

Both conjunction transformations and imbedding transformations can operate on any of the five basic sentence patterns and in many combinations. These patterns and transformations together have the power to create very complex sentences:

> His face beaming with pride, Henry presented to Mrs. Shultz the frog that he had found the day before when he was exploring behind the house where the Johnsons lived before they moved to Canada.

This sentence could have been even longer, but more complex is not always better.

How Children Develop Skill with Sentence Patterns

How do children fare with the basic sentence patterns and transformations we have seen thus far? In a nutshell:

1. Nearly all school-age children can use the five basic sentence patterns (Hunt, 1965).
2. Nearly all of them can use all the transformations that convert sentences (passives, negatives, imperatives, ellipses, clefts, and *there* transformations).
3. In writing, many children (and adults) do not take advantage of the full range of possibilities offered by these basic patterns, the simple transformations, adverbs, and prepositional phrases. Their sentences are sometimes repetitive and dull (Fries, 1940).
4. Elementary school children are *just beginning* to use transformations that combine sentences.
5. There is much variability among children in the sentences they use (Loban, 1976).

The third and fourth points are fertile ground for teaching grammar. Children can be taught to use more varied and interesting sentences, and they can also be taught to combine short, choppy sentences into fewer complex sentences. Strategies for both aims are given in the next section.

On the fifth point, there may be several years' difference in development between the sentences that students in the same elementary classroom are able to use. We can pinpoint these differences more exactly by taking a look at a study of children's language development conducted by Walter Loban (1976). His study also shows more exactly which sentence structures typically emerge at which ages. Loban conducted a thirteen-year longitudinal study of 338 subjects, 211 of whom were still with him at the end of the study. He collected oral language samples (elicited through interviews) from the same subjects every year from kindergarten through grade twelve and written language samples from third grade through grade twelve. He made some general observations about children's language use at several stages of development (see Box 8.6).

Loban's estimates for the average age at which children reach developmental milestones in language use are quite helpful, but there are also striking differences that should not be overlooked. Using words per oral communication unit as an example, we find that *below-average* ten- to twelve-year-olds produce about the same number of words per sentence as the *average* seven- to eight-year-olds. Put another way, a verbally advanced kindergartener produces as many words per sentence as a verbally slow sixth grader. This finding is all the more significant since the measure of words per communication unit advances in close step with the other measures of language development, such as the ability to control complex sentence forms of various types. Loban's measure of these other factors show that, on the average, the verbally advanced children in any grade will be using sentence structures the verbally slower children will not use until as much as three years later.

It is well to keep these points in mind as we consider techniques for teaching our students to write more elaborate sentences. We turn to these techniques now.

Teaching Grammar

If teaching grammar to children is to be of any real use, the methods we use must cause children to produce sentences with new forms and not just analyze someone else's sentences. We want them to use more versatile, more elaborate patterns of language, and not simply to know the names of grammatical items. *We* should have an explicit understanding of grammatical structures and terms in order to understand what the children are doing and help them grow. But the children's time should be spent reading, discussing, observing, and writing — not studying grammar as an end in itself.

Since approaches to grammar must differ considerably from early to later grades and with individual children who are more or less developed in language ability, we have divided the grammar activities that follow into three levels. Bear in mind that a normal classroom full of youngsters will vary as much as three years in language development, and thus some of the activities we designate for younger students will be useful for older students whose language is less developed and vice versa.

Activities for Primary Grades

Younger children cannot easily study language head-on, because the ability to consider language as a thing in itself and not just for the message it brings seems to be tied to children's cognitive development. First and second graders can begin to make progress in becoming better language users, however, with carefully planned teaching.

BOX 8.6
Sentence Patterns at Different Ages

Ages 5 and 6: Use all the basic sentence patterns; use pronouns; use present, past, and future verb tenses (Black English speakers omit some inflectional endings).

Average sentence length (speech): 6.8 words; most advanced children: 8 words; least advanced: 6 words.

Ages 6 and 7: Use more complex sentences, use more adjectives. Use *if . . . then* constructions or conditional dependent clauses: "If I have time then I will go."

Average sentence length (speech): 7.5; most advanced children: 8.1; least advanced: 6.6.

Ages 7 and 8: Use adjectival clauses with *which*: "I have a plant which I water every day." Use adverbial subordinate clauses with *when, if,* and *because*: "I like it when we go to movies." Use gerund phrases (verbs + *-ing*) as objects of other verbs: "I like going to movies."

Average sentence length (speech): 7.6; most advanced children: 8.3; least advanced: 7.

Ages 8, 9, and 10: Relate particular concepts to general ideas, using the connectors *meanwhile, unless, even if*: "She's a good dog, even if she snaps at people sometimes."

About 50 percent of this age group use the subordinating connector *although* correctly: "Although I was tired, I stayed to watch the movie." Participles, both past and present, appear: "Turning around, I saw the bear." "Having lost the key, she couldn't get inside."

Average sentence length (speech): 9; most advanced children: 9.3; least advanced: 7.5.

Average sentence length (writing): 8; most advanced children: 9; least advanced: 6.

Ages 10, 11, and 12: More complex thinking patterns are reflected in complex relations between sentences. These connectors appear: *provided that, nevertheless, in spite of,* and *unless*. Auxiliary verbs *might, could,* and *should* are more frequent.

Problems remain with some verb tenses, especially the different uses of past, past perfect, future perfect, and present perfect.

Nouns modified by participles and participial phrases appear: "His clothes, faded by the sun, were the color of straw."

Compounds and coordinate predicates also appear: "We tried out and bought the bicycle."

Average sentence length (speech): 9.5; most advanced children: 10.5; least advanced: 8.

Average sentence length (writing): 9; most advanced children 10.2; least advanced: 6.2.

SOURCE: From Walter Loban, *Language Development: Kindergarten Through Grade Twelve*. Urbana, Ill.: NCTE, 1976.

Talk as Grammar Practice. Most important at this level is real language practice. Above all else kindergarteners and first and second graders need plentiful opportunities to talk about things that matter to them with people they care about.

Of equal importance is hearing language used fluently to describe things they care about. As Jill Richards has pointed out, in the interest of getting children involved in activities that will make them curious and encourage them to talk, we must be careful not to separate them from fluent adult speakers who can supply words for the experiences they are engaged in (Richards, 1978).

If you want to expand the kinds of language practice they participate in, choose your topics systematically. Crowhurst (1979) found that the topics they discuss determine the kinds of grammatical structures they use in their writing. (The same is surely true of oral language.) If you want them to practice the future tense, set up questions for discussion like these:

— Where do you think you will be five years from now? What will you be doing?
— How many cnildren will you have when you grow up?
— (At the gerbil cage) What do you think will happen when Susan puts the lettuce in the corner of the cage?
— (At the science station) What do you think will happen when Richard puts the jar over the candle?

If you want children to practice clauses with *because,* ask questions with *why:*

— Why didn't the gerbil rush over to eat the lettuce?
— Why do you think the candle will go out?
— Why do you want to have fourteen children?

If you want them to practice sentences with conditional forms of verbs, share a filmstrip, story, or a skit that presents an unresolved problem, then ask questions like the following:

— What would you do if you were Henry?
— What do you think Henry's father would do if Henry did that?

Using Patterns from Literature. Although language arts and elementary English manuals contain many model sentence patterns for teaching grammar, children's literature is an even better source that can be shared, studied, and practiced. Good stories and poems have more finely crafted sentences in them than textbook exercises. Dorothy Grant Hennings (1978) suggests having the children listen to a poem such as Evelyn Beyer's *Jump or Jiggle*:

> Frogs jump.
> Caterpillars hump.
>
> Worms wiggle.
> Bugs jiggle.

Rabbits hop.
Horses clop.

Snakes slide.
Seagulls glide.

Mice creep.
Deer leap.

Puppies bounce.
Kittens pounce.

Lions stalk —
But —
I walk!

— Hennings, 1978, pp. 333–334

After listening to the poem, the children can read it chorally from a transparency or the board. Prereaders can recite it by echo reading, then choral reading, in the same way they would learn to recite a group dictated story (see Chapter Five). Next, the class or a group can develop a new version based on the same pattern, with individual children volunteering lines as you write them on the board or a story chart. (The volunteered lines need not rhyme as the model does, though you may want to press for a rhyme with the final pair of lines.)

With this procedure, the children are exposed to some colorful and interesting verbs, and the sentences also show them the inflectional pattern for plural subjects. When they make up new sentences following this pattern, they internalize and produce this inflectional pattern: "ants crawl," "bees buzz," and so forth. A natural variation on the pattern is to make the subjects all singular. Then they can practice inflecting verbs for singular subjects ("a frog jumps," "a caterpillar humps," and so on).

Such practice is especially helpful for exposing dialect speakers to the predictable patterns of standard English, but it is good for all children because it calls their attention on a conscious level to a pattern they already knew on a subconscious level and helps make them observers of language. There are books and poems that highlight just about every language pattern you might want to stress, from very easy levels to more difficult ones. *Brown Bear, Brown Bear, What Do You See?* by Bill Martin, Jr. (1970), for example, has an enjoyable pattern that is easily imitated and improvised on by young children. It gives them practice in the standard English word order for a wh-question, and it is rhythmical enough so that you can clap out the words with them if they cannot say the pattern unaided. This book also shows them the question mark in action (as well as commas between repetitions of the same word and after a noun in direct address, for those who are ready to attend to these matters). Some other books with a repetitive question format are Sesyle Joslin's *What Do You Say, Dear?* (1980) and *What Do You Do, Dear?* (1961); Mercer Mayer's *What Do You Do with a Kangaroo?* (1975); Robyn Supraner's *Would You Rather Be a Tiger?* (1973); and Walter Einsel's *Did You Ever See?* (1972).

Alphabet books belong in every primary classroom. They can be very useful in language study because many of them contain sentences or descriptive phrases about things in alphabetical order. The simplest alphabet books and picture dictionaries have only one word for each entry, such as *Brian Wildsmith's ABC* (1963) with one-word texts (for example, "cat CAT") and gorgeous illustrations. Some other very simple alphabet books present a list of common nouns associated with each letter, as in *Helen Oxenbury's ABC of Things* (1972) and *Bruno Munari's ABC* (1960). Books of this type are good for helping children name things and come up with many nouns.

Other alphabet books are more complex and are better suited for the later primary grades. *Hosie's Alphabet* (Baskin, 1972), for example, uses difficult words like "omnivorous swarming locust"; *City-Country ABC* (Walters, 1966) features alliterative descriptive sentences for each letter; *Apricot ABC* (Miles, 1969) and *Celestino Piatti's Animal ABC* (1966) have rhyming texts. Books such as these help children connect adjectives with nouns and adverbs with verbs, and they will enjoy making their own alphabet books and picture dictionaries and illustrating them with texts and a variety of pictures.

Like alphabet books, counting books are useful in language study, from the simplest "1–one bear, 2–two goats" type of text to more elaborate sentences and rhymes. Robert Allen's *Numbers: A First Counting Book* (1968) is an excellent simple book for early primary graders. It combines aspects of size and location with number concepts and shows various arrangements of the same number of things, such as apples in a row and apples in a circle or large tomatoes and small tomatoes. This type of book can prompt children to come up with varied sentences, such as "Eight apples are in a circle" or "Two baby goats are in the barn," putting an emphasis on nouns, modifiers, and prepositional phrases. Other counting books contain elaborated, sometimes rhyming, text like Brenda Seymour's (1969) *First Counting* ("1 red engine for my train, 2 new boots for snow and rain") and Harris Petie's (1975) *Billions of Bugs* ("1 praying mantis eating a grub; 10 walking sticks hide in a shrub"). Hoban and Selig's *Ten What?* (1974) is subtitled *A Mystery Counting Book*, and it is a mystery story in which the clues and story details all come in sets of particular numbers. Elaborate counting books like these offer many possibilities for language patterning and imitation.

Concept books are also extremely useful for primary graders. Comparisons and opposites are illustrated simply and effectively in Tana Hoban's *Push-Pull, Empty-Full* (1972) and *Over, Under and Through* (1973) and Peter Spier's *Fast-Slow, High-Low* (1972). Hoban's books feature sets of black and white photos for each pair of opposites; Spier's book uses intricate drawings that merit close examination and discussion. Locational concepts are featured in Betsy Maestro's *Where Is My Friend?* (1976) in which an elephant searches for her mouse friend under a rock, behind her, or through a gate. In Doris Lund's *I Wonder What's Under* (1970) a boy wonders if a monster is under his bed, then what's under the rug that's under the bed, then what's under the floor that's under the rug that's under the bed . . . and so on down to the earth under the cellar. Tana Hoban's *Shapes and Things* (1970) and *Look Again!* (1971) focus on identifying sets of objects and identifying a whole by looking at a part of it through a cut-out page. Tison and Taylor's *The Adventures of the Three Colors* (1971) uses colored transparent overlays to illustrate the effects of color mixing. These and other concept books elicit and model descriptive language.

As a general rule, a workable teaching pattern is: *listen, discuss, repeat, imitate and improvise,* and *illustrate.* First the children listen to the poem, story, or book as you read it. Then they discuss it, commenting on whatever strikes their fancy, while you call their attention to the pattern you want them to imitate and improvise on as well as other interesting features. Then they repeat the work, choral-reading the whole thing if they have access to copies or a transparency of it or speaking the repeated lines if not. Next they write their own versions, imitating the pattern in the version that was read to them but improvising with their own ideas. For young children or beginning writers, this stage can take the form of a line-a-child group approach, perhaps dictated to the teacher, who writes the lines on an experience chart. Finally they illustrate what they have produced: copying their own lines back onto a sheet of paper if they dictated them and drawing a picture to illustrate their work.

Since children will tire of this pattern if it is followed too rigidly, you should vary it in your teaching. Of course you'll want to make sure that they have the chance to hear and appreciate many stories and poems without having to imitate them and write their own.

After all, literature is more than a grammar lesson. The same point applies to the discussion stage, and sometimes it can be omitted. *Most* times it should bring out points about the work other than its pattern: the sounds of the words, how the children feel about certain images and characters, what the whole work reminds them of. The illustration can be omitted, or replaced by a skit or a group-illustrated mural drawn on a long piece of newsprint or other materials.

Using Dictated Stories for Language Elaboration. Some children in the primary grades may not yet have developed facility with elaborated, fully developed oral language. (You may recall that in Chapter Three some informal assessment devices were suggested to help you determine if they had mastered the basic grammatical forms in their speech and if their speech was elaborated or restricted.) Also, many primary graders are speakers of nonstandard English dialects. Many of them have elaborated, fully developed oral language within their own dialect but are not so fluent in using standard English, and they may have some difficulty reading standard forms. You can use dictated experience stories with both of these groups to help them speak more fluently and to become more familiar with standard English forms, while at the same time retaining the integrity of their spontaneous language.

As you may remember from Chapter Five, dictated experience stories are accounts dictated by one or more children and recorded on paper by the teacher. They are the foundation of the language experience approach to beginning reading, which has often been recommended as a useful and successful method for teaching young dialect speakers to read, since what they first read retains the familiar vocabulary and syntactic forms of their dialect (Cramer, 1971; Goodman, 1970; Hall, 1981).

Traditionally, dictated stories have been used without changing any aspects of what the children said. It was often thought that making any changes would imply that what the children had said was inferior in syntax or vocabulary and would demean the speakers (Cramer, 1971; Stauffer, 1980), but this is not necessarily so. If you proceed with sensitivity, you can modify their dictated accounts to draw their attention to particular areas of syntax and vocabulary and to expose them to standard English forms without doing violence to their language, ideas, or feelings about their language (Gillet and Gentry, 1982).

The traditional language experience lesson (described in Chapter Five) consists of discussing a stimulus object, event, or story; taking dictation; rereading chorally and individually until the rereading is fluent and confident; identifying words in context and then in isolation; integrating identified words into word banks; and beginning a new cycle with a new dictated story. This cycle can be modified in three steps.

In the first step the traditional sequence is followed, and the dictation is taken verbatim. At this stage you do not attempt to modify the children's utterances. This first version of the dictation keeps their utterances intact. What they said is what they read.

In the second step you write the dictated story over again in standard English, using many of the words from the original version. This step allows the children to practice recognizing the words they learned in the first step, but you also include in your new version patterns of organization, sentence structures, and new words you want them to become familiar with. You present and teach the new version in the same way you handle a dictated story: Read it aloud, then choral-read it repeatedly until they can reread it fluently and identify some single words and phrases in context and then in isolation.

Here, for example, is the first, verbatim version of a dictated story followed by a teacher-written standard English version:

The Firehouse

Arlen said, "We go to the firehouse."
Danny said, "One fireman he ride on the back
    of the truck."
Marcus said, "They blow the siren and we cover
    our ears real fast."
Bailey said, "Sometimes they be sleeping when the
    fire bell ring."

OUR TRIP TO THE FIRE STATION

Arlen, Marcus, Danny and Bailey went to
the firehouse. They saw where a fireman rides
on the back of the fire truck. They heard the
firemen use the siren. The siren made them
cover their ears! They saw where the firemen
sleep. Sometimes they are asleep when the fire
bell rings.

The rewritten version included the children's names and many of the terms
and ideas they used and also retained the same order of ideas. A few new (but
similar) terms like "fire station" were inserted and standard English sentence
structures and inflections were used. This story should be introduced as "another story about the firehouse trip." After the children have choral-read the
story and can reread it confidently, the two versions can be compared and
words that appear in both versions located. No attempt should be made to
compare the quality of the two versions or to imply that the second is an
improvement over the first.

In the third and final step, you have the children produce a revised version
of their original dictated story. You display the first version again and they
reread it. Then you encourage them to restate their original sentences, or make
up new ones, with the goal of making the sentences "longer and more colorful."
You suggest that they work together and offer comments about one another's
sentences. You conduct this oral revision activity in a lighthearted way, with
an emphasis on mutual support. Negative comments are strictly to be avoided
and strongly discouraged if the children begin to use them. You should be
careful to phrase directions and comments positively, saying, for example,
"How can you make your sentence longer?" or "Can you think of another way
to say . . ." rather than "How can you make this sentence better?" or "What
can we do to improve this part?"

You can also help, by judicious guidance, to direct their attention to
particular aspects of sentence or story structure or organization with questions
like "What was the *first* thing that happened . . .?" "Where can we add a
describing word that would tell us . . .?" or "How can we put these two short
sentences together to make one longer one?"

When they dictate their final version, they may spontaneously incorporate
some of the vocabulary and syntax that appeared in the second-step version,
but you should expect the third, revised, version to contain nonstandard usages.
These should be left intact. The emphasis in the third step is on *revision*, not
on perfection. A perfect version will never be produced! If the revised version
is somewhat more elaborate or descriptive or contains some standard element
that did not appear in the first version, then the goal of the whole process has
been achieved. Continued exposure to standard English and continuing oppor-

tunities to revise, rather than correct, their dictations will help move children toward familarity and facility with both elaborated sentences and standard syntax without forcing either one down their throats.

Activities for Middle Elementary Grades

By third grade, children are growing in their ability to think and talk about language and at that point it is possible to carry out activities that call their attention to language patterns in more detail. Just as important, they can appreciate differences in the way people say things and begin to consider matters of style. At this level, however, it is still necessary to stress meaningful language practice far more than the artificial manipulation of particular language forms. Keep this point in mind and try to imagine a balance that leans in favor of the listening, talking, reading, and writing activities we have discussed in previous chapters as you study the language activities presented in this chapter.

Using Patterns from Literature. Stories, poems, and other children's books continue to be a valuable source of language patterns for the middle elementary grades, and more complex sentence patterns can be introduced in these grades. Margaret Wise Brown's *The Important Book* (1949), for example, features evocative verses describing important features of common things: rain, snow, and the like. These verses have this predictable pattern:

The important thing about _____ is that it _____.
It's _____.
It's _____.
And it's _____.
But the important thing about _____
    is that it _____.

One or more verses can be sampled, then modified and improvised on, calling attention to the way descriptive phrases, pronouns, or other grammatical elements are constructed and sequenced.

Alphabet books are still useful in the middle grades, since many feature complex patterns and language. Maureen McGinn's *I Used to Be an Artichoke* (1973), for example, contains a fairly elaborate "I used to be . . . but then I . . . so I changed into . . ." pattern that models, among other things, the use of conjunctions to link simple sentences together. Dahlov Ipcar's *I Love My Anteater with an A* (1964) and Robert Tallon's *Zoophabets* (1971) feature a familiar alphabet game in which each letter is represented by a creature whose name begins with that letter, accompanied by what it eats, where it lives, and its good and bad characteristics, all beginning with the same letter. Similarly, Eric Carle's *All About Arthur (an absolutely absurd ape)* (1974) describes Arthur's many adventures in alliterative style — for example, Arthur left Atlanta because he felt all alone. Books like these are good because the text accompanying each letter or character is made up of interesting complex sentences with modifying phrases, adjectives, adverbs, and prepositional phrases, and these constructions are put together in a humorous, fanciful, and exaggerated context. They are much more fun to study and play with than grammar book exercises!

Another useful sentence pattern is the balanced sentence, with contrasting information divided into two sentences or into one longer sentence, as exemplified by Remy Charlip's *Fortunately* (1964). This amusing book invites children to come up with their own contrasting situations like: "Fortunately Ms. Willis got sick the day of the math test, but unfortunately the principal gave us the test anyway!" or similar patterns like "What good luck! I found a hundred dollar bill in the street. What bad luck! It was play money." Many areas of grammar could be studied in these humorous contexts: pronominalization, modifying words and phrases, conjunctions, and a variety of transformations, to name only a few.

Some books feature word play and parodies on familiar works, which middle-grade children will appreciate. George Mendoza's *A Wart Snake in a Fig Tree* (1968), for example, parodies the holiday carol "A Partridge in a Pear Tree." Frederick Winsor's *The Space Child's Mother Goose* (1958) parodies the old Mother Goose tales in a fashion children will find easy to improvise on. Word play on homonyms are featured in Fred Gwynne's *A Chocolate Moose for Dinner* (1973) and *The King Who Rained* (1970), Eth Clifford's *A Bear Before Breakfast* (1962) and Emily Hanlon's *How a Horse Grew Hoarse on the Site Where He Sighted a Bare Bear* (1976). Creating their own versions of these word plays is an entertaining way to help children focus on differences in word meanings. Similarly, Peggy Parish's *Amelia Bedelia* (1963) features amusing confusions of word meanings.

Cumulative tales are perenially interesting to middle-grade students and will be familiar to many. Cumulative tales are those like "The House that Jack Built" and "The Bremen-Town Musicians." Such tales can be found in any basic folk tale or children's literature anthology, and they contain ever-lengthening cumulative sentences, as in "The House that Jack Built" or repetitious sequential sentences, as in "Henny Penny," which can be fascinating for youngsters to study and experiment with. Some more modern examples of cumulative tales are Marjorie Flack's *Ask Mr. Bear* (1971), Maurice Sendak's *One Was Johnny* (1962), Barbara Emberley's *Drummer Hoff* (1967), and Harve Zemach's *Mommy, Buy Me a China Doll* (1975).

Yet another pattern you may want to use is that of adjectival forms including comparatives and superlatives like *big, bigger, biggest,* which is a classic pattern in folk tales, of course: The three bears, including their chairs, beds, and bowls of porridge; the three billy goats Gruff, and the three little pigs' various houses all exemplify this pattern, as well as many other classic tales. Most of the familiar tall tales of American heroes like Pecos Bill, Paul Bunyan, John Henry, and Mike Fink contain elements of exaggerated size, strength, or other characteristics. There are many volumes of tall tales, including Maria Leach's *The Rainbow Book of American Folk Tales and Legends* (1958), Walter

Blair's *Tall Tale America* (1944), Irwin Shapiro's *Heroes in American Folklore* (1962), and Alvin Schwartz's *Whoppers, Tall Tales and Other Lies* (1975).

Try to extend these language patterns into the children's own unstructured writings. After you have worked on a pattern one day in the usual listen, repeat, discuss, imitate and improvise, and illustrate format, remind them of that pattern when they are discussing their own papers with you. An excellent time to do this is during an editing conference that takes place between the teacher and a student after the student has written a first draft. Another appropriate time is during an editing workshop such as the kind developed by Cramer (1978). (The workshop and the conferences were discussed in Chapter Seven.) Although it bends the rules a little bit, if a paper has awkward or choppy sentences that could be improved by substituting a sentence form the children had studied, it is worthwhile to point this out, either directly, or by asking who can find a place where a sentence pattern the class had studied could be substituted for one or more sentences in the paper. The follow-up in the editing workshop would be to have the students search the papers they themselves had written for places where the studied form could be used.

Sentence Searches. Encourage students to look for interesting sentences in the independent reading they do, or even in their basals. When they bring you an interesting sentence pattern, one that seems applicable to the kinds of topics that other students might write about, ask the student who brought it to write it on the "interesting sentences" wall chart. Helpful practice can be gained by asking students either as a group or as a learning center activity to write their own sentences modeled after the one on the wall chart.

The opening sentence in Ruth Bornstein's *The Dancing Man* (1978) might catch some student's eye:

> Once, in a poor village by the Baltic Sea, there lived an orphan boy named Joseph.

The class might discuss what a good sentence this is to begin a story: It tells us *who, where,* and *when.* It includes the word *once,* which usually signals that what follows is a fanciful story. Ask the students if they can make up their own sentences about their own character in their own place, using this sentence as a model:

> Once, on a run-down farm by the Willis River,
> there lived a racked-up rooster named Crazy Bird.

> Once, in a BAD neighborhood by the East River,
> there lived a BAD DUDE named THE RIPPER.

> Once, in a cough drops box by the hot water
> bottle, there lived a little ant named Sue.

If the students are not bringing you interesting sentences or if you find that there are important sentence patterns that could aid their writing but have not been noticed by them in their searches for sentences, you may choose to select your own sentence patterns. In the discussion of sentence types in the first section of this chapter, several patterns were brought to light that are not used very readily by elementary age children. Among these are passive sentences:

Natasha was fooled by Boris's mustache.

sentences with noun clauses, which in children's language are especially rare in the subject position:

Harry's lying about his lunch money made the teacher mad.

appositives, or noun clauses that follow a noun and explain it:

Henrietta, the world's youngest magician, was very rich.

and many kinds of adverbial clauses:

Having found his lunch money, Robert was very happy.

When the rain stopped, we went outside.

The ambulance stopped where Mary lived.

Stand-Up Sentence Parts. To call attention to the grammatical classes of words (noun, verb, adjective, adverb, preposition, and so on), you can make up a sentence and write the words individually on pieces of tag board, have students stand with them in front of the class, and let other students think up other words that could be substituted for a given student's word.

Suppose these students stand up with the following sentence:

Ruth Tom Jeanne Ann   Ed   Tim Sally Pat
| The | | old | | man | | stood | | beside | | the | | big | | river |.

You might ask, "Who can think of a different word we could give to Ruth?" Sylvia thinks of *this,* so you write *this* on a piece of paper with a magic marker and hand it to Ruth, who holds the word on top of the word she is holding. You then ask for words that other children could hold, write these new words down, and hand them to the students who are standing. After several words have been suggested for each position, you ask one of the children to read all the words in his or her hand. You now name this class of words and ask the students if they can think of any others.

You can extend the activity by asking them to enter a heading in their notebooks for a particular word class they have talked about and also to write in at the top of the page the sample sentence with a circle around the member of the word class in question. You then have them list all the members of that word class they can think of, beginning with the ones the class came up with during the activity just described. If you stressed verbs, for example, a page of a student's notebook might look like this:

Verbs

The old man stood beside the big river.

 stays

 reads

 talked

 walked

Using Sentence Frames. A more systematic approach to identifying members of the form classes is to work with the test frames and other identifiers discussed earlier in this chapter. For nouns, for example, we suggested this test frame:

The _____ couldn't hide its _____.

Write this test frame on the board and ask the students to think of words that would fit in the blanks. Following a large group practice, they can write the heading "noun" in their notebooks, write in the test frame, and then list all the words they can think of that could fill the frame.

Those who catch on quickly to this activity might want to carry it further and try to construct test frames of their own. Many features of nouns wait to be discovered in this way: Your students may learn the difference between concrete and abstract nouns, "mass" and "count" nouns, animate and inanimate nouns, and other distinctive groups of nouns as they go about constructing and trying out test frames.

Form classes can also be identified by the affixes they will accept. For nouns, you can list the following affixes on the board (or in a learning center) and ask the students how many words they can think of that end with them: *-ment, -er, -ity, -ist,* and *-ness.* After they have thought of several words, they should then be asked to try them out in their test frame for nouns. Do they all fit? Are there any that will not fit?

Activities for identifying members of other form classes can be constructed along the same lines. Consult the earlier part of this chapter for test frames, lists of affixes, and so forth that can be used in designing such activities.

In all such activities, it is important to keep the goal of instruction in mind: Why do you want children to be able to identify members of form classes? Is it to make them observers of language and quick to notice and able to talk about effective ways to express thoughts? Is it to prepare them for further work in choosing interesting verbs, adjectives, adverbs, and nouns in their own speech and writing? These are defensible reasons.

Play on Form Classes. Some interesting poetic effects can be achieved by setting up activities that ask students to list words of a single form class. In playing on verbs, for example, the following can serve as a model:

Hilda could add, subtract, draw, multiply, divide, figure, calculate, analyze, investigate; but she couldn't chew gum.

The "punch line" makes the list more interesting.

Done with a large group, this exercise can ferret out quite a large variety of verbs. If there is doubt as to whether or not a word qualifies as a verb, ask the students to run it through the test for verbs.

Here is a sample from one child's work:

> She could walk, run, eat, hop, skip, jump, sing, write, chew gum, spell, read, climb, stomp, dance, ski, skate. But she couldn't do math.
>
> — Jessica, age 8

For adjectives, try a pattern like this:

> Chester is fat, gross, greedy, selfish, unfriendly, loud, rude, crude, and unattractive, but very smart.

Again, if there is doubt as to whether or not a word qualifies as an adjective, try it out in the test frame for adjectives:

> A _____ person is very _____.

Here is a child's sample:

> The tree was
> old,
> leaning over,
> ugly,
> bare,
> but lovely to climb.
>
> — Anna Brooke, age 9

With a bit more effort, the same activity can be extended to adverbs, using a pattern such as this:

> Our car runs poorly, slowly, roughly, badly, uneconomically, reluctantly, embarrassingly, but it gets us where we want to go.

Similarly, for prepositions, a pattern like the following can be used:

> We went over the rocks, through the bushes, around the guards, up the tree, down the ladder, across the creek, over the fence, by the machine gun nest, past the dogs, and out of the prison camp.

Note that in this pattern it is wise to retain the nouns that serve as objects of the prepositions. Otherwise, it will be difficult for the students to separate prepositions from adverbs of place.

The play on form class activities extends children's knowledge of the workings of grammar at the same time that it helps them gain power to use grammatical forms more expressively.

Moveability. Another interesting use of stand-up sentence parts is to demonstrate the important concept of the *moveability* of phrases within sentences. We can teach students the range of possible positions that different phrases and clauses can occupy, and thus enable them to write more varied and interesting sentences.

On pieces of tagboard, write phrases such as

| in the morning | | the lady | | felt much better |

Have three volunteers come to the front of the classroom and give a card to each. Then ask the other students to decide how many different ways the cards could be arranged and still sound like English. Once they get the idea with a limited set of phrases, try the activity with a longer set:

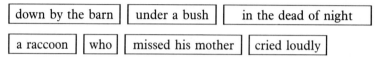

In the arrangements of the phrases there are a few best choices, a few unacceptable choices, and many in between. Your students will get more out of this exercise if you ask them to discuss each possibility that occurs to them and decide why it appeals or fails to appeal to them, not merely look for the best choices. Does the sentence arrangement flow? Does it make sense but sound stilted or awkward? Or is it nonsense? Does it leave the meaning in doubt? By discussing these issues you can help the students "tune" their ears for sound and sense in language.

Writing Patterned Observations and Poetry. Many of the poetry ideas developed by Kenneth Koch lead students to write complex sentence patterns. *I used to . . . / But now . . .* and *I seem to be . . . / But really I am* are good examples. You will find others in Chapter Seven of this book, or in Koch (1970).

The idea can be adapted to create many kinds of sentence patterns in which children can write real experiences and observations. Juanita Hazlegrove at Cumberland (Virginia) Elementary School had her fourth graders record their experiences of a particularly dramatic rain shower, using a series of sentences beginning, "When it rains . . . ," followed by another series beginning with "After it rains. . . ." Here is an example:

When it rains

When it rains it is cold.
When it rains the skys turn dark.
When it rains the sidewalks are slick.
When it rains it waters the plant.
When it rains it fills up streams, ponds,
lakes.

> After it rains
>
> After it rains the air smells clean.
> After it rains trees are heavy with water.
> After it rains there is mud everywhere.
> After it rains plants grow.
>
> — Matthew, grade 4

This idea could be extended to sentences beginning with "On my way to school I . . . ," "While eating lunch I . . . ," "When I get mad I. . . ."

Sentence Expansion. Sentence expansion is an activity that deals directly with an area in which virtually all elementary aged children need to grow. It provides practice in fleshing out "bare bones" sentences with colorful modifiers and descriptive phrases.

Beginning with a sentence such as

Elephants walked.

ask students one at a time to add words to the sentence that answer questions like:

What did the elephants look like?

How did they walk?

Where did they walk?

When did they walk?

These questions might lead them to build up this sentence:

The big gray elephants walked heavily down the trail yesterday.

If they have been led up to the sentence expansion activity by way of the earlier exercises in this section, you will be able to give them further guidance by telling them what kinds of elements to expand the sentence with. Once they know what P-groups (prepositional phrases) and adjectives are, for instance, you can give them more specific directions, as follows for the sentence *Elephants walked*:

— add an adjective that tells what the elephants *looked* like.
— add a P-group that tells *how* they walked.
— add a P-group that tells *where* they walked.
— add a P-group that tells *when* they walked.

These instructions will lead them to construct a sentence like:

The huge elephants walked with heavy steps along the trail on a summer day.

While you're introducing terms, you should tell them that in the shortened sentence *Elephants walked*, *Elephants* is called NP (for noun phrase) and *walked* is called VP (for verb phrase). The very simplest sentences consist of an NP and a VP (in traditional terms, a subject and a predicate). As you return to this exercise from time to time these terms will help you direct the students' attention to the parts of the sentence you want to expand.

You can derive the most benefit from the sentence expansion activity if you do it regularly and take the time to plan the elements of a sentence you want the children to work on. One sequence to follow starts with two-word sentences of the form NP + VP (*Elephants walked*; *Sheila fell*; *Henry runs*,) and works on the ways to expand the NP. NPs may take the form determiner + adjective + noun + P-group (*The ugly hyena in the park*) though all but the noun are optional. Later you can work on ways to expand the VP, stressing the addition of adverbs and P-groups and especially the different positions in which these can be added: adverb + NP + verb + adverb-of-place + P-group, and so on. (*Slowly, the sad boy walked home in the rain*).

For further development of skill in sentence expansion, have the students practice expanding the five basic sentence types (discussed in the earlier section of this chapter). To review them quickly, the five basic sentence types are:

1. Noun phrase/subject + intransitive verb + (adverb): *Rachel runs fast.*
2. Noun phrase/subject + transitive verb + noun phrase/direct object + (adverb): *Champions run laps willingly.*
3. Noun/phrase/subject + transitive verb + noun phrase/indirect object + noun phrase/direct object + (adverb): *Rachel gives everyone a good example.*
4. Noun phrase/subject + linking verb + noun phrase/predicate noun + (adverb): *Herbert is a stinker sometimes.*
5. Noun phrase/subject + linking verb + adjective/predicate adjective + (adverb): *Rupert was green with envy.*

We are certainly not suggesting that you try to get your students to learn all of the foregoing terminology but rather that you study and understand the patterns well enough yourself so that you can construct sentence expansion activities using sentences of each type as the basis for expansion.

The technique of sentence expansion has its limits. Beyond a certain point, sentences are not made better by having more modifiers added to them. It is tempting to create sentences like: *The old weary baggy-skinned elephants with the stubby tusks walked wearily with heavy footsteps down the narrow trail through the steaming jungle on a humid summer day in faraway Sumatra.* As Francis Christensen (1967) pointed out, however, a look at the work of professional writers shows that they do not elaborate their sentences in this way. The preferred method is to use adjectives, adverbs, and P-groups sparingly and achieve further elaboration by turning sentences into clauses and then subordinating them to other sentences like this: *As evening closed in, the elephants trudged on down the winding trail through the darkening jungle, foot following heavy foot, bodies obeying more reluctantly the prods of their unsmiling drivers.* A technique for teaching children to write sentences with more complex patterns, called *sentence combining,* is described later in this chapter.

Activities for Upper Elementary Grades

For children, the mechanical challenge of penmanship, the conceptual strain of spelling, and the discourse-related novelty of talking to an unknown and absent audience hamper the fluency of what they put down on paper. Through the third grade, the sentences they speak are more grammatically complex than the sentences they write. With older people, the situation is reversed, and the turning point comes, for most children, in about the fourth or fifth grade. It is then that the sentences they write catch and surpass in grammatical complexity the sentences they speak (Loban, 1976).

By fourth grade most of them seem to be sufficiently secure in the other basics of writing to pay more attention to differences in ways that sentences can be structured and thoughts expressed. Talking and listening, reading and writing in a wide variety of settings and for a range of real purposes should have center stage in the language program. Nevertheless, children can learn to write more effective sentences through certain kinds of directed practice, and this skill carries over to their everyday writing. Sentence expansion and writing pattern sentences may help, and they are recommended for younger students

in the fourth to eighth grade. Sentence combining, introduced in this section, can also help. This technique is especially suitable for students in the upper end of this age group, but we must repeat that all the techniques in this chapter, including sentence combining, are supplements to the basic activities of talking and listening, reading and writing.

Sentence Combining. Research has shown that children entering school have control over all of the basic sentence patterns. The ability to use transformed sentences, especially those derived from more than one simple sentence, evolves throughout the school years. A method that has been developed to help students in using transformed sentences is called *sentence combining* (Cooper, 1973; Mellon, 1969; O'Hare, 1973). It presents them with short simple sentences, shows them how they can be combined with a transformation, and then gives them practice combining other simple sentences using the same transformation.

> *Example:*
> I drank the milk.
> > Answer: The milk was in the refrigerator. (That)
> I drank the milk that was in the refrigerator.
>
> I want the bicycle.
> > Answer: The bicycle is in the garage. (That)

Like many of the other techniques discussed in this chapter, sentence combining directs children to manipulate sentences according to grammatical patterns but without requiring them to learn grammatical terminology. Here are some techniques for using sentence combining in the classroom.

Prepare duplicable worksheets. These worksheets should treat one combination at a time, first giving several examples of a completed combination, then providing up to a dozen sets of sentences for the students to combine using the same pattern. The exercises should have a consistent format and set of cues for the combinations required (see "An Outline of Sentence Combinations," in the appendix on page 348, for a suggested set of cues).

Keep the explanations of the grammatical operations to a minimum and avoid complicated terminology when you do talk about them. Matrix and imbedded sentences, two terms that you will have to use, might better be substituted by "receiver" and "giver" sentences, respectively.

Begin with the simplest combinations, then work up to the more difficult ones. Remember that the task of learning a new activity keeps students from working up to their capacity at first. Also, each time you introduce a new combination, practice it with them orally before they work the exercises on paper (it is helpful to have some additional exercises handy for this purpose).

It is best to assign the exercises frequently for short periods during the whole year. Mellon described a schedule of fifteen minutes a day, three days a week, throughout the school year. Better still, see that the exercises are continued from year to year throughout the elementary school curriculum.

Make sure the sentences used in the exercises are close to the language of the children. Where feasible, have the children themselves suggest the simple sentences after you demonstrate the pattern you are after. Try also for a carryover from sentence combining activities to their other writing. During editing sessions, point out opportunities to use sentence structures that have been practiced in sentence combining exercises. Take care to notice and praise them when they employ these structures in their everyday writing.

Finally, make sure that sentence combining exercises do not supercede their other writing opportunities. Sentence combining can improve their skill but only if they have the need and the opportunity to apply the skill in functional writing tasks.

The Appendix to Chapter Eight contains an outline of patterns of sentence combinations that can be imitated and extended in making up your own sentence combining exercises. These combinations, which are arranged in their approximate order of difficulty, are adapted from Cooper (1973) and Malmstrom (1968).

Teaching Standard English Usage. Usage is sometimes defined as the etiquette of language. Although expressions such as "I ain't got no money" or "She want two pencil" succeed in conveying their respective messages without confusion, in many social settings and in written form they are considered "bad grammar" or "uneducated speech." Such judgments are overly simplistic, of course, but they do reflect the widely shared view that schools should teach students to use standard English in circumstances where it is called for.

Pooley (1974) recommends that instruction in correct usage begin in the elementary grades, and he suggests several steps for the teacher. His suggestions include surveying the usage problems of the particular class of children, enlisting their interest in learning standard usage, striving for the "exact" word, recognizing the "social manners" of words, and using positive teaching techniques.

Surveying Usage Problems. It is impossible to compile one list of usage problems that is equally relevant to all elementary classrooms. Pooley tried (1974, p. 183) but the items on his list ("yourn," "hisn," "I knowed," and so on) are all typical of the usage problems teachers in the upper midwestern United States confronted in white children who had moved up from rural Appalachia in the 1950s and 1960s. Teachers today (as they presumably did then) work with children whose usage shows many different influences. Some youngsters from Brooklyn say "youse guys." Some blacks say "I be home directly" and "I have two pencil." Some Mexican-Americans say "I born in 1974" and "I am here since ten o'clock," both of which forms show interference from the Spanish versions of these English constructions. Children who come from Vietnamese, Haitian, Japanese, Chinese, Cambodian, or Arabic backgrounds may all have more or less prominent difficulties with some points of English usage, depending on factors such as the similarities and differences between their respective first languages and English.

The best solution is for teachers to compile their own lists of usage problems for each classroom. By monitoring the speech and writing of the students during the first few weeks of school, the teachers can compile lists of English constructions that are difficult for certain students. This need not be an arduous task, because the list does not have to be exhaustive, but it should have these features:

— *It should include those items that have high frequency:* It should be concerned with English constructions that are used most often in the students' speech and writing.
— *It should include those items that have the highest social penalty:* It should be aimed toward helping children to find substitutes for the constructions that are most likely to sound "uneducated" to society at large. By this criterion, "I ain't got no money" would make it onto the list of problem constructions but "Everyone has their own favorite" might or might not, depending on the importance of the other usage problems in a particular class of students.
— *It should be of limited length:* Within a given elementary school year, ten to fifteen items should be a suitable number for intensive attention. More than that may spread the students' attention too thin, especially those whose home language is such that they will have to work on a large number of items from the list.

Enlisting Students' Interest in Learning Standard English Usage. Pooley recommends that students be encouraged to keep their own lists of usage items that require attention and cross them off as they master each one. He also points out that they must see the value in learning standard forms and have reasons, embedded in real communication needs, to use them. "Only a priggish child," he writes, "can be interested in talking merely to 'improve' his usage or to show the teacher that he has improved" (1974, p. 176).

Recognizing the Social Propriety of Words. All children recognize that while some words and expressions can be used with their friends, they are not polite or appropriate to use in front of an adult (though teachers often have to reinforce this point). Some words are "rough" or crude; other words are "fancy." Actually, there is a considerable range between crude and fancy word choices. As Pooley suggests, we can ask what the difference is between "Beat it" and "Please leave" or between "Howdy" and "How do you do." Discussions of these differences can sensitize children to the suitability of certain word choices over others in speech and writing. Dorothy Grant Hennings (1978) suggests writing as many of these variations on the blackboard as the children can think of, then asking them to categorize the variations as "everyday language" or "written language." (Your class may think of different names for these categories). Once the categories have been well introduced, a wide range of usage differences can be discussed.

Role playing and writing exercises are good for expanding on a child's awareness of the "social manners" aspects of word choice. Consider these topics for role plays:

— a marriage ceremony (possibly one interrupted by a jealous suitor)
— a waiter or waitress taking orders in a restaurant
— a sales clerk waiting on an unusually large or small person in a clothing store
— a police detective interrogating a suspect about a crime (maybe a bum in one instance, the mayor of the city in another)
— a host or hostess introducing the President of the United States individually to members of the class
— the school principal interviewing a child who is coming to the school for the first time (or interviewing the parents of a child who is flunking out of school)

Role plays such as these can be played "straight" the first time and then modified with deliberately inappropriate language in subsequent versions. In the marriage ceremony, for instance, all participants would use formal language in one version, then everyday language or "street talk" in another. Scenarios such as these can be used as the basis for written exercises as well.

The realization that should emerge from these activities is, as Pooley puts it, ". . . that words are not 'right' or 'wrong' in themselves but rather in the setting in which they are used. This discovery is the foundation of a sound attitude toward usage" (1974, p. 178).

Choosing the Exact Word. "The difference between the right word and almost the right word is the difference between *lightning* and *lightning bug*." So wrote Mark Twain. The exact word is not just situationally appropriate; whether in slang or in formal English, the exact word is the one that sets off a flash of recognition, that evokes a clear image of what is being said.

An activity that teaches children to choose the exact word is to make up sentences that contain vague, overworked words and ask them to suggest synonyms. Taking "The man *walked* down the road," for example, you can ask them to think of other words for *walked*. They may suggest *sauntered*, *shuffled*, *strode*, *ambled*, or *stomped*. As each synonym is suggested, you can have the student get up and act out each version. To refine this activity further, you can suggest more precise variations of the subject, "the old man." Suppose it was "the crippled old man," or "the careworn old man," or "the proud young soldier," or "the deceitful thief." How would the verb *walked* be changed in each instance?

Another exercise is to take a poem or piece of literature where the words have already been well chosen and rewrite it in everyday language. What is the effect of the change?

Positive Usage Instruction. There are two extremes to be avoided in teaching usage. One is to make the instruction too abstract and isolated from the students' day-to-day communication needs. The other is to be too negative, too "picky," or too "snobbish." The first kind of error is typical of workbook or textbook approaches. Since they are written for all children everywhere, there is scant likelihood that the usage issues presented in these materials will exactly fit any one class. If usage instruction is abstract, if it focuses on problems that nobody has, or if it forces students to correct sentences they never would have said in the first place, it is not likely to make a significant impact on their language habits. On the other hand, if it is tailored to their actual needs and problems, we run the risk of constantly correcting them and calling them down. Any of us who has ever been in the situation of being constantly corrected when we were trying to get a point across knows how quickly we can become disenchanted with communicating at all in such a setting. The most important single requisite of a language arts classroom is that it be a place where all students feel free to communicate their ideas and feelings in an atmosphere of acceptance, mutual trust, and respect. And there is no doubt about it: If teachers insist that everything children say and write be first and foremost "grammatically correct," then the result will be correct but trivial and meaningless expression, or no expression at all.

The idea that there is some basic distinction between people who use textbook English and people who don't is simply untrue, and most students already realize this. If we teachers acknowledge it out loud, it enables us to start from the same side of the issue as the students, and we can look together at our English language as something that we all have in common but something that we each use in some unique ways. We can look squarely at the issue of social attitudes toward language and talk frankly about social prejudice and how shortsighted it is to judge people on the basis of their speech. We can also talk about what we are willing to do about it, individually and collectively, in our treatment of others and in our own preparation for life.

Summary

Grammar instruction used to stand at the center of the elementary language program. Now there are many educators who say it should not be taught. The critics point to the mindless way grammar got into the elementary school in the first place: from the Latin grammar of the Middle Ages to the "rules of etiquette" approach of the twentieth century. They also point to research evidence supporting the claim that traditional grammar instruction doesn't do any good.

Nevertheless, through modern linguistics, better, more accurate descriptions of grammar are available to us now than was the case in previous generations, and we can use these descriptions to understand what children know about grammar and what they have yet to learn. A brief sketch of the grammar of English sentences drawn from structuralist and generative-transformational linguistics occupied the first half of this chapter. This sketch showed new ways of identifying form classes (parts of speech), described the five basic sentence patterns, and showed the common grammatical transformations.

Most children know the basic sentence patterns by the time they reach school age. Learning to use the transformations is the real work of the elementary years (which was not accomplished by the traditional language program). Also to be learned are the social dimensions of the choice of styles, or registers, of speech. Speakers of nonstandard dialects as well as others must learn to use a range of speaking styles, from intimate to formal, and must learn to use them in appropriate situations.

Instruction in grammar should be differentiated for various age groups and for different levels of language development. In all cases, it should occupy only a fraction of the time devoted to reading, writing, dramatics, and discussion.

Primary grade children cannot productively study grammar. With the proper choice of topics to discuss and pattern books to read and imitate in writing, however, the teacher can systematically expose them to a range of grammatical patterns and encourage them to use those patterns. Dictated experience stories can be used for similar purposes, especially with speakers of variant dialects.

Middle elementary grade children also profit from exposure to well-written material and opportunities to imitate language patterns from literature. They can recognize and talk about some grammatical roles of words, which makes it easier for them to talk about the ways writing can be made more effective by using stronger and more vivid nouns, adjectives, verbs, and adverbs (the real reason for learning grammatical terminology). Thus stand-up sentence parts and the use of sentence test frames and other descriptions from structural linguistics were advocated here — but only to make the more expressive exercises such as sentence expansion or editing work more smoothly.

In the upper elementary grades, discussion and writing are both still recommended, as is imitating patterns for literature, but here we introduced the more advanced activity of sentence combining — the most widely acclaimed of the newer approaches to teaching grammar. Finally, we discussed approaches for dealing with usage problems. This aspect of grammar teaching worries us more than any other. It is true that language arts teachers have an obligation to the children not to let them go naively into the world using language patterns that may invoke prejudices against them. Yet the whole usage issue dates back to the time when unexamined social and racial biases pervaded our educational system. Children from groups who have often been alienated from schools are still at high risk of feeling rejected when the issue of usage comes to the fore. It is better that they feel welcome to express their vision of the world in their own voice than not to speak at all. Infinitely better.

APPENDIX TO CHAPTER EIGHT
An Outline of Sentence Combinations

Class I: Transformations That Create Compounds

Many different elements of a sentence — including noun phrases, verb phrases, adjectives, adverbs, and even prepositions — can be compounded.

A. *Compound noun phrase/subjects*

Henry likes football.
Herbert likes football.   (,)
Ron likes football.   (,)
Rachel likes football.   (, *and*)

• Henry, Herbert, Ron, and Rachel like football.

Sheila doesn't like snakes.
Pat doesn't like snakes.   (*neither . . . nor*)

• Neither Sheila nor Pat likes snakes.

Rupert likes string beans.   (*Both . . .*)
Doris likes string beans.   (*and . . .*)

• Both Rupert and Doris like string beans.

Cows chew their cud.   (*Not only . . .*)
Bulls chew their cud.   (*. . . but also . . .*)

• Not only cows but also bulls chew their cud.

B. *Compound noun phrase/objects*

Ruth wants *a baseball* for Christmas.
Ruth wants *a glove* for Christmas.   (,)
Ruth wants *a bat* for Christmas.   (, *and*)

• Ruth wants a baseball, a glove, and a bat for Christmas.

C. *Compound verbs*

The duck *quacked*.
The duck *swam*.   (,)
The duck *dived*.   (, *and*)

• The duck quacked, swam, and dived.

D. Adjectives in series

A Scout is *clean*.
A Scout is *brave*.   (,)
A Scout is *thrifty*.   (, *and*)

• A Scout is clean, brave, and thrifty.

The bicycle was *old*.
The bicycle was *rusty*.   (*and*)
The bicycle was *cheap*.   (, *but*)

• The bicycle was old and rusty, but cheap.

E. Adverbs in series

The band played *cheerfully*.
The band played *well*.   (*and*)

• The band played cheerfully and well.

Class II: Adjectives and Adjectivals

Most children's sentences could be improved by the addition of one or more well-chosen adjectives. Since combinations involving adjectives are relatively easy to demonstrate, they make a good starting point for sentence combining. Unless you have a reason to teach compounds first (previous section) start with adjectives. Then go on to nouns and adverbs and come back to compounds.

A. Simple adjectives

1. *Before the subject*

   The car ran poorly.
   The car was *big*.

   • The big car ran poorly.

2. *Before the direct object*

   She read us a story.
   The story was *silly*.

   • She read us a silly story.

3. *Before the predicate noun.*

   The play was a flop.
   The flop was *complete*.

   • The play was a complete flop.

4. *Before the object of a preposition*

They left in a wagon.
The wagon was *uncomfortable*.

• They left in an uncomfortable wagon.

B. Participles as adjectives

1. Forms with *-ing*.

We ran through the rain.
The rain was *pouring*.

• We ran through the pouring rain.

2. Forms with *-ed*★

The train rode on wheels.
The wheels were *rusted*.

• The train rode on rusted wheels.

Her foot caused her pain.
Her foot was *broken*.

• Her broken foot caused her pain.

As a more advanced exercise, the students can form their own participles from the verbs in the giver sentences:

The yard is full of dogs.
The dogs *bark*.   (*-ing*)

• The yard is full of barking dogs.

On the floor was a vase.
The vase had been *broken*.   (*-ed*)★

• On the floor was a broken vase.

C. Compound adjectives

The man made the *people* scream.
The man *ate fire*.   (_____ + *-ing*)

• The fire-eating man made the people scream.

The dog chased the wagon
The dog *loved fun*.   (_____ + *-ing*)

• The fun-loving dog chased the wagon.

★Note that although *-ed* signals that a past participle is needed, many verbs form their past participles with other endings: sweep-swept; break-broken; give-given, etc.

The car sped on.
The car was *splattered* with *mud*. (_____ + *-ed*)

• The mud-splattered car sped on.

The clown wept and wept.
His *heart* was *broken*.   (_____ + *-en*)

• The heart-broken clown wept and wept.

D. *Adjectival phrases*

More difficult than combinations that embed single words from the giver sentence to the receiver sentence are combinations that embed phrases. There are three common adjectival phrase embeddings. The second sentence, in which the students must create the prepositional phrase before embedding it in the receiver sentence, is more difficult than the first.

1. Prepositional phrases

   The air is dry.
   The air is in the *desert*.

   • The air in the desert is dry.

   We found the dog.
   The dog had *a broken leg*. (*with*)

   • We found the dog with a broken leg.

2. Appositive phrases

Appositive phrases are noun phrases that follow and qualify another noun. Appositives are usually set off with commas, though some forms like "my friend the butcher's child" are not. When in doubt, say the sentence aloud: If you detect pauses before and after the appositive, mark them with commas. If not, leave the commas out.

   My neighbor raises ducks.
   My neighbor is *Mrs. Crickett*. (, . . . ,)

   • My neighbor, Mrs. Crickett, raises ducks.

   My friend doesn't eat meat.
   My friend is *the butcher's child*.

   • My friend the butcher's child doesn't eat meat.

3. Participial phrases

   a. *Forms with -ing* (present participles)
      The police arrested the man.
      The man was *holding up traffic*. (*ing* + . . .)

      • The police arrested the man holding up traffic.

The girl stole across the goal line.
The girl was *carrying the ball.* (*-ing* + . . .)

• The girl carrying the ball stole across the goal line.

b. Forms with *-ed.*

We didn't like the play.
The play was *directed by Harold.* (*-ed* + . . .)

• We didn't like the play directed by Harold.

The car was the fastest.
The car was *driven by Annie.* (*-ed* + . . .)

• The car driven by Annie was the fastest.

Again, as a more difficult exercise, the students may convert the verbs in the following sentences to participles before embedding them.

The car was the fastest.
Sheila *drove* the *car.* (. . . *-ed by* . . .)

• The car driven by Sheila was the fastest.

The girl stole across the goal line.
The girl *carried* the *ball.* (. . . *-ing* . . .)

• The girl carrying the ball stole across the goal line.

4. Adjectival clauses with *that, whom, when, where*

The fish was a trout.
The fish *bit the hook.* (*that*)

• The fish that bit the hook was a trout.

The milk was sour.
Susan *bought the milk.* (*that*)

• The milk that Susan bought was sour.

Note that the word *that* can often be left out in sentences such as the one below:

The puppy was already sold.
Sherry wanted the *puppy.* (*that*)

• The puppy (that) Sherry wanted was already sold.

E. *Adjectival clause embeddings using* **who, whom, where,** **or that**

People get on my nerves.
People *talk like that.* (*who*)

• People who talk like that get on my nerves.

The person is Harold.
I want to nominate the person.   (*whom*)

- The person whom I want to nominate is Harold.

The store burned down.
I bought my bike at the store.   (*where*)

- The store where I bought my bike burned down.

The part was the end of the movie.
The part *annoyed Leslie*.   (*that*)

- The part that annoyed Leslie was the end of the movie.

F. Multiple combinations

After one or more combinations have been introduced and practiced singly, you can set up exercises that require students to repeat the same kind of transformation or combine different transformations in the same sentence. Here are some examples.

The neighborhood is full of dogs.
The dogs *bark*.   (*-ing*)
The dogs *yelp*.   (*-ing*)
The dogs *trouble mother's sleep*.   (*that*)

- The neighborhood is full of barking, yelping dogs that trouble mother's sleep.

A car was rattling down the street.
The car was *big*.   (*,*)
The car was *dirty*.   (*,*)
The car was *black*.
The car had *broken windows*.   (*with*)
The street was empty.

- A big, dirty, black car with broken windows was rattling down the empty street.

Class III: Transformations That Create Noun Clauses

A. Clauses with **that** and **the fact that**

These noun clauses can be used as either subjects or objects of verbs. As objects, they are very common and appear early in children's sentences, according to Loban (1976). As subjects, however, they are rarer and appear much later. A dummy word (something) is used in the receiver sentence to hold the place that the embedded noun clause will fill.

1. As objects of the verb

Paul knows (something).
Stealing is wrong. (*that*)

• Paul knows that stealing is wrong.

Sherry said (something).
She was cold. (*that*)

• Sherry said that she was cold.

2. As subjects of the verb

(Something) caused great excitement.
School let out early. (*The fact that*)

• The fact that school let out early caused great excitement.

(Something) was plain for all to see.
Hilda was guilty. (*that*)

• That Hilda was guilty was plain for all to see.

B. Infinitive clauses with to and for . . . to . . .

Like *that* clauses, noun clauses with infinitives are more common in the direct object slot, although they may appear in the subject slot as well.

1. As objects of the verb

Mrs. Thatcher doesn't like (something).
The boys act silly. (*for . . . to . . .*)

• Mrs. Thatcher doesn't like for the boys to act silly.

The dog wants (something).
The dog goes for a walk. (*to . . .*)

• The dog wants to go for a walk.

The dog wants (something).
You take him for a walk. (*. . . to . . .*)

• The dog wants you to take him for a walk.

2. As subjects of the verb
These forms are rare and may be too advanced for many children.

(Something) is dangerous.

(Someone) rides a bike with no hands. (*to*)

• To ride a bike with no hands is dangerous.

(Something) makes me sad.
You tell me this. (*For . . . to . . .*)

• For you to tell me this makes me sad.

C. *Gerund phrases*

(Something) was her favorite sport.
(Someone) played tennis.   (*-ing*)

• Playing tennis was her favorite sport.

He hated (something).
(Someone) did mathematics.   (*-ing*)

• He hated doing mathematics.

The coach couldn't understand (something).
Jim dropped the ball.   (*-'s* + *-ing*)

• The coach couldn't understand Jim's dropping the ball.

(Something) kept the baby awake.
The wind was howling.   (*-'s* + *-ing*)

• The wind's howling kept the baby awake.

D. *Question clauses*

Roscoe never understood (something).
His car would not run (for some reason).   (*why*)

• Roscoe never understood why his car would not run.

(Something) made him sick.
He ate (something) for supper.   (*what*)

• What he ate for supper made him sick.

Sheila wonders (something).
The snake was going (somewhere).   (*where*)

• Sheila wonders where the snake was going.

Randy wondered (something).
He would do the job (somehow).   (*how*)

• Randy wondered how he would do the job.

The ticket seller knew (something).
The movie would last so long.   (*how long*)

• The ticket seller knew how long the movie would last.

The people wondered (something).
The pitcher could throw so well.   (*how well*)

• The people wondered how well the pitcher could throw.

Rachel knew (something).
(Someone) puts in so many eggs.   (*how many*)

• Rachel knows how many eggs to put in.

The science teacher did not say (something).
Someone waters the plants so often.   (*how often*)

• The science teacher did not say how often to water the plants.

Class IV: Transformations That Create Adverbs

Adverbial clauses are produced in two ways: *subordinate clauses* ("When she had finished, the girl rested"), and *absolutes* ("Having finished the job, the girl rested"). Subordinate clauses, being more common, are more accessible to elementary aged children. Subordinate clauses and absolutes can appear in three positions in a sentence:

$$\left.\begin{matrix}\text{Adverb}\\\text{Clause}\end{matrix}\right\} + \text{Subject} + \left\{\begin{matrix}\text{Adverb}\\\text{Clause}\end{matrix}\right\} + \text{Verb} + \left\{\begin{matrix}\text{Adverb}\\\text{Clause}\end{matrix}\right.$$

Loban found that children spontaneously insert subordinate clauses only in the last position. Hence, exercises that require them to put them elsewhere will be more difficult but still possible.

Absolutes are rarer and more difficult and best suited for advanced or older upper elementary students.

A. Subordinate clauses

Subordinate clauses are formed by placing a *subordinator* before a sentence. Subordinators are:

after	for	unless
although	if	when
because	since	while
before	though	as

The children went to the ball game.
They washed the dishes.   (*after*)

• After they washed the dishes the children went to the ball game.

I will go.
You will go.   (*if*)

• I will go if you will go.

The house burned.
The family looked on.   (*as*)

• As the family looked on, the house burned.

Chester said goodbye to his friends.
He left town.   (*before*)

• Chester, before he left town, said goodbye to his friends.

B. *Absolutes*

Absolutes are formed with participles (*-ing* and *-ed* forms of verbs).

1. with *-ing* forms

    The cowboy raced on.
    His horse was galloping madly.   (absolute)

    • His horse galloping madly, the cowboy raced on.

    The cowboy rode hard.
    His hands gripped the reins.   (absolute: *-ing*)

    • The cowboy rode hard, his hands gripping the reins.

2. with *-ed* forms

    The runner neared the finish line.
    Her face was streaked with sweat.   (absolute: *-ed*)

    • Her face streaked with sweat, the runner neared the finish line.

    The car sped on.
    Its windshield was spattered with mud.   (absolute: *-ed*)

    • The car sped on, its windshield spattered with mud.

After the students can make combinations using subordinate clauses and absolutes, they could try designing exercises that call for more than one of each in the same sentence.

    The car rattled ahead.
    It hit the lamp post.   (*after*)
    Its headlight was dangling uselessly.   (absolute: *-ing*)

    • After it hit the lamp post, the car rattled ahead, its headlight dangling uselessly.

Note: The sources for much of this material are Cooper (1973) and Weaver (1979).

CHAPTER NINE

*Understanding
and Teaching
Handwriting and Spelling*

CHAPTER OUTLINE

This chapter discusses two major aspects of writing mechanics: handwriting and spelling. The first half of the chapter deals with handwriting and is divided into two sections: understanding handwriting, in which the process of learning handwriting is linked to theories of perception and learning, and teaching handwriting, in which methods of handwriting instruction are described. The second half of this chapter is devoted to spelling and it too is divided into two sections: understanding spelling, which details the theoretical and empirical bases for the study of spelling as a developmental process, and teaching spelling, which demonstrates methods for analyzing and teaching spelling across the grades.

Understanding Handwriting

Handwriting instruction has undergone a quiet revolution in the past decade, a revolution caused largely by basic changes in our understanding of the nature of handwriting skill and how it is developed. Handwriting instruction has often been overlooked in favor of more newsworthy topics in language arts such as composition, creative dramatics, or the grammar controversies, but it is an important skill. Like spelling and usage, one's handwriting is sometimes used by others as an indicator of one's level of education or culture, however unfounded and unfair such judgments may prove to be. Since legible, facile handwriting makes a child's written work easier and more successful, understanding how it develops and how to teach it effectively are important for teachers of all grades.

Psychology and Handwriting Instruction

The current changes going on in handwriting instruction can be traced to shifts in psychology away from behaviorist theories toward developmental and cognitive theories of knowledge and learning.

Behaviorists advocate breaking complex behaviors down into small, discrete skills that are actively taught by the teacher. Parts are to be mastered before wholes.

In contrast, cognitivists believe that where a symbol system such as writing is concerned, children should be exposed to the system as a whole and as it is actually used. They believe that children have built-in sense-making mechanisms that enable them to actively explore and form concepts about their environment as a whole, including the writing system. Since concept formation always works from whole to part, from big picture to small detail, children should explore writing as a whole before they are taught individual letters.

Differences between these two views lead to differences in teaching. Besides the whole/part controversy, there are disagreements over the amount of initiative to leave to the students. Behaviorists tend to give teachers responsibility for teaching everything directly, while cognitivists suggest that teachers guide them to learn concepts through their own explorations — that is, teachers should follow the lead set by children's own sense-making operations.

Neither of these views has been shown to be dramatically superior to the other in guiding educational practice. Cognitive-based teaching styles are clearly on the rise, while behaviorist approaches, which dominated education in the sixties and early seventies, appear to have waning influence. Because educational practice always lags behind changes in theory, most commercial approaches to handwriting instruction in use today are derived from behavioral theory. Hence, they put little emphasis on a child's discovery powers as a source of learning, they exhort teachers to guard against letting children practice bad habits and handwriting, and they generally assume that everything must be taught directly, without analyzing what the task of learning handwriting is like from a child's point of view. On the other hand, they are systematic and tailored very closely to what children are able to do. If they sometimes bore average and above-average students by failing to acknowledge what they already know about writing, they help slow learners by giving them work in small increments and following up with frequent assessments of progress and lots of feedback.

In the next section, "Teaching Handwriting," we will include some of the best aspects of the behaviorist theories, especially the systematic approach to instruction. In the meantime, however, we will explore an important contribution that perceptual psychology has made to the teaching of handwriting: a detailed description of how the task of learning to write presents itself to children, what concepts of written language are formed in the process of learning about print, and how and in what order they are formed.

Children's Perception and Writing

In Chapter Two we described the way youngsters go about naming things. We noted there that words are labels for concepts and that concepts are really the same thing as *categories* of objects or events that act or appear or can be treated the same way and hence qualify for the same name. Children's earliest categories for things are very general, and they typically lump things together that adults would call by many other names. A two-year-old's "dog" may, for example, refer to dogs, sheep, wolves, opossums, raccoons, and even ponies. With experience, of course, each of these animals will be given its own name, and "dog" will be reserved for true canines. The reason a particular animal is assigned to a category in the first place is presumably because it shares the *features* that the child has implicitly decided make up that category. The early concept of "dog" probably had features such as *animal, four-legged, furry, protruding muzzle*, and so on. Characteristics that are used to define membership in a category are called *distinctive features*.

Children's early concepts are differentiated by distinctive features that are *global* — that is, they tend to focus on the most obvious features and ignore subtle differences. As they mature and have more experience with objects and events, their concepts change; they begin to notice, and to consider important, more features as well as features that are less immediately apparent. Mental categories become more finely differentiated, and additional categories are developed to account for new experiences.

Writing and alphabet letters are part of the world of things young children encounter. They learn to differentiate between writing and pictures, between writing in different alphabetic systems, and between or among different letters in the same way they learn to differentiate between dogs and cows or collies and spaniels: by perceiving features, first globally and then in finer discriminations, until they can recognize even subtle differences between highly similar letters or recognize similarities in the same letter produced in different type faces or handwriting styles.

Let's try an informal experiment in perception and concept formation. Look at Figure 9.1 while you count quickly to five. Then close the book and try to write exactly what you saw. Do this now before you read on.

Compare your figures to Figure 9.1. How close an approximation could you make? In contrast, repeat the procedure with the array in Figure 9.2. Do this before you read on.

Now compare your results again. You probably reproduced the Roman letters in Figure 9.2 much more accurately, and with much greater ease, than

Figure 9.1   Characters

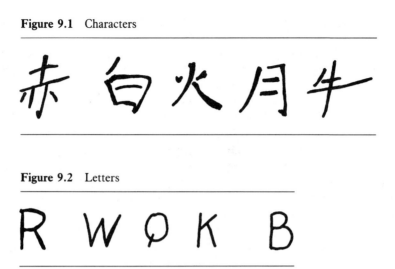

Figure 9.2   Letters

R W Q K B

the Chinese characters in Figure 9.1. Why? Because you already have stable concepts for the Roman letters: You know what parts make them up and how they differ from each other. Unless you can write Chinese, you probably don't know what is distinctive about each character. You probably left out parts, perhaps whole characters, and even put in marks that weren't in the originals. Without a concept for the whole, the parts don't fit together.

Children appear to develop concepts about writing and written letters before they can produce letters. Several studies show that their concepts about writing develop from general to specific and that their awareness of distinctive features sharpens as they grow older and have more experience with print.

Features of Writing in Children's Early Graphics

In one study (Lavine, 1972) three-, four-, and five-year-olds looked at cards with various visual arrays on them, such as those in Figure 9.3, and indicated which arrays were *writing*. The youngest subjects chose as "writing" arrays that were arranged in horizontal lines (linearity), those that had more than one character (multiplicity), and those in which characters differed from each other (variety). Figure 9.4a shows some arrays the younger subjects selected as writing. Included were arrays of geometric shapes and writing systems other than English; excluded were some arrays of Roman letters. The older subjects did not use the global features of linearity, multiplicity, or variety; instead they used individual letters as features. Regardless of how the arrays were arranged, they were selected as writing if they contained letters or letter-like characters, as in Figure 9.4b.

Marie Clay's work (1975, 1977) directly reveals what features children perceive about print before they can read or write. Clay observed five-year-olds

Figure 9.3   Cards from Lavine's experiment

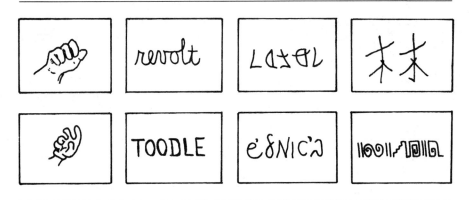

SOURCE: From L. Levine, "The Development of Perception of Writing in Pre-Reading Children: A Cross-Cultural Study," Unpublished Ph.D. thesis, Cornell University. Used by permission.

Figure 9.4   Linearity and variety were distinctive to younger children, and Roman letters were distinctive to older children

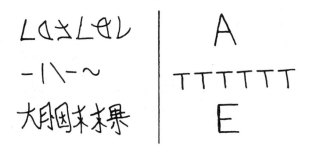

SOURCE: From L. Levine, "The Development of Perception of Writing in Pre-Reading Children: A Cross-Cultural Study," Unpublished Ph.D. thesis, Cornell University. Used by permission.

captions for them but were not given any formal reading or writing instruction. In the course of a year, the youngsters enthusiastically produced a large volume of writing-like figures, which Clay analyzed for similarities across children. Clay found that elements of adult writing were present in virtually all of their early attempts at writing. It seemed to her that these prereaders were, by their active experimentation with print, discovering principles of written language that literate people use to produce real writing.

The ways these principles of writing appear in a young child's attempts to write are very important. First, they show once again that children attend first to global features, then to particular features of individual letters, evidence in

BOX 9.1
Clay's Principles of Writing

Recurring Principle: The same marks are made repeatedly in writing.

Generative Principle: A small number of different marks are used repeatedly but in various orders.

Linear Principle: Figures are arranged in horizontal lines across the page.

Flexibility Principle: Adding marks to some letters merely embellishes them, but adding other marks, or marks to other letters, changes the letters' identity. Some embellishments are "allowable" and others are not.

Sign Principle: The writing is intended to be read by others, not just the writers, and they can ask others to read back what they have written.

favor of a cognitive theoretical position on teaching handwriting. Second, they show the informed teacher how ready a particular child may be to profit from handwriting instruction.

The principles of writing Clay explained are summarized in Box 9.1 and detailed in the next section.

The Recurring Principle. Clay observed that very young children tended to produce the same mark over and over again, as in Figure 9.5. The recurring principle is similar to the *multiplicity* feature Lavine's youngest subjects used. This strategy does not produce writing that looks very adultlike, and it is soon replaced by more elaborate strategies, which are discussed below.

The Generative Principle. Children soon sense that the same mark made over and over is not much like the writing they see in books or newspapers. "Real"

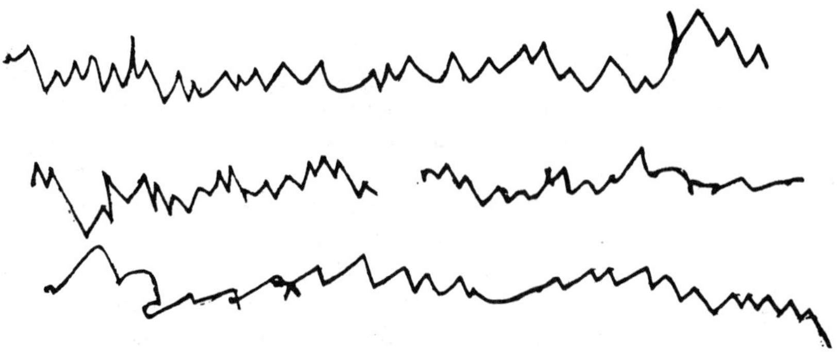

Figure 9.5 A four-year-old's writing, showing the recurring principle

writing is not made up of only one mark repeated but of various marks. When they discover this principle they begin to vary their marks, using several in different orders to create a large amount of writing, writing that looks more interesting. The generative principle, which is similar to Lavine's *variety* feature, is demonstrated in Figure 9.6.

The Linear Principle. As children look at the writing of adults, they begin to perceive that the figures themselves are arranged in a particular way: in hori-

Figure 9.6   A kindergartener's writing, showing the generative principle

zontal rows or lines. But where do the children begin? They have to be shown that we start at the left, move to the right, then return to the left to begin again. We are so used to this feature that we may forget it is arbitrary; other writing systems may move vertically and right-to-left, as Chinese does, horizontally right-to-left, as Hebrew does, or even horizontally left-to-right, then right-to-left, then left-to-right again, as in an ancient Greek writing style called *boustrophedon*, meaning "as the ox plows the field."

In Figure 9.7, Helen handled the left-to-right arrangement of her first line correctly but placed the remaining letters in a line above instead of below. In Figure 9.8 Anna Brook arranged her line linearly but right-to-left; in Figure 9.9 Walt "hedged his bet" by writing his name in *both* directions!

The direction in which writing is arranged and in which individual letters must face is often a fluid concept for children in kindergarten, first grade, and even higher grades. This fact is not so surprising when we stop to think that

Figure 9.7   The linear principle

Helen, grade 2

Figure 9.8   The linear principle

Anna Brook, age 5

Figure 9.9 The linear principle

Walt, age 4

letters are virtually the only thing in a child's environment whose identity changes with direction. Daddy turned around is still Daddy; a chair knocked over is still a chair; but *b* turned around is *d*, a different letter. Upside down, it could be *p* if arranged one way or *q* if arranged another. The linear principle requires quite a different sort of perception from the task of recognizing people, animals, or other objects, and this difficulty is not always recognized by educators. Note in Figure 9.10 that the ditto sheet given to Shelley, a kindergartener, required her to fill in the letters between *a* and *z*, but because of the orientation of the snake she wrote the letters *k* through *r* in a row arranged from right to left. As can be seen by her corrections, Shelley first wrote *k* correctly but then decided that she should take her cue from the reversed line, so she reversed all the letters in the backward-moving line until she reached the part that moved from left to right again. It is clear that the ditto sheet threw unnecessary hurdles in the way of a child who was just coming to grips with the linear principle. Neither the person who designed the worksheet nor Shelley's teacher was apparently aware of this difference in perception between children and adults.

The Flexibility Principle. Children do not learn the letters of the alphabet all at once. They learn a few at a time, beginning at the age of three or four. They usually learn the letters in their own first names first, perhaps along with *a*, *b*, *c*, and a few others. Most children go through a fairly lengthy period — several

Figure 9.10 Shelley, kindergarten. The *A* and *Z* were already printed

years, in many cases — during which they know some letters but not others, and that is when some interesting problems arise. Each time they see print, whether it is on a book cover, a magazine, a cereal box, or the signboard of a favorite restaurant, the print they see is likely to vary from the print they are most familiar with in two ways: (a) It will contain some unfamiliar letters, and (b) it will contain familiar letters written in unfamiliar styles. (Think, for example, of all the different ways you may see the letter *a* written on a given day.)

Marie Clay has observed that this dual variety in letters makes it hard for children to tell what keeps one letter from turning into another (1975). If, for example, t and t are variations of the same letter, then are T and J variations of the same letter also? In the same vein, if $\mathsf{|}$ and I are seen interchangeably, then is there any important difference between $\mathsf{|}$ and T ? Or F and E and L ? These questions do not exist for those of us who know how to read, but children must find answers to them before they can learn to recognize or reproduce all the letters of the alphabet. Clay terms this a question of *flexibility*, since what is at issue is how much a single letter can change stylistically and still remain the same letter. There is more involved in the flexibility principle than recognition of letters, however. Psychologists note that the ability to recognize forms develops before the ability to produce the same forms. In speech, this means children can understand a word spoken by someone else before they can say it themselves. In writing, it means they can recognize letters before they can write them themselves. Here another aspect of the flexibility principle comes in: if they already know how to produce a certain letter — say, F — then by embellishing it slightly they can produce another letter that previously they could recognize but not produce, such as E. Many preschool, kindergarten, and early first-grade children can be seen producing variations of letters they know, presumably in an attempt to discover ways to produce letters they did not have under control. Those who do not yet know all of the letters, however, often do not know if their new creations are real letters or not. Note in Figure 9.11 for example, the way Carla experimented with *e* and *m* to create some unallowable variations.

The Sign Principle. This term refers to the growing awareness that writing is not simply a personal activity, but a social one, that writing is intended to be read and understood by others. As children discover this principle they often expect to find a pictorial relationship between symbols and meaning, and they sometimes intermix pictorial symbols with letters and letterlike figures. When children discover the sign principle, they may begin to show their writing to someone and demand that it be read to them, or they may ask "What did I write?" By doing this they show that they understand that writing is to be read, but they reason that because they cannot yet read, *they* are unable to read their writing. Only others, especially adults, will be able to do so.

Both Clay's and Lavine's work shows us that children perceive global features of writing before they can turn out recognizable writing, features that contribute to their concepts of what writing is and how it is produced. At first

Figure 9.11 The flexibility principle

Carla, age 4

the features they perceive and try to write in their own graphic productions are global, but they become more finely differentiated as they experiment with writing and compare their productions to standard writing. Clay (1977) advises teachers to allow them to explore writing and experiment with it *before* formal handwriting instruction begins; we concur with Clay that this experimentation is necessary for children to acquire the global writing concepts they will need to make sense of handwriting instruction.

Teaching Handwriting

Any teacher who has ever compared the graceful penmanship modeled in the current handwriting textbooks to the infinitely varied — and sometimes illegible — handwriting of his or her students has had to wonder, Is is possible to teach children to write like this? Is that what these materials are for? The answer is, of course, no. Handwriting is individual and unique, and the materials we use to teach it are intended as illustrative models, not as *the* way everyone should write. The goal of teaching handwriting is to help children write *legibly* and *comfortably*. Effective writing must be readable in order to convey a message to anyone other than the writer, but it must be done without frustrating or fatiguing the writer. To achieve these goals, handwriting instruction should not be discouraging or frustrating to children, fraught with overcorrection. However, it should be deliberate, systematic, and well organized as well as humane. Box 9.2 lists some general guidelines for teaching handwriting.

Readiness for Handwriting Instruction

Handwriting instruction usually begins during the first semester of first grade. By then, most children are ready to profit from instruction, although some can be successfully taught in the second half of kindergarten (Enstrom and En-

---

BOX 9.2
Guidelines for Teaching Handwriting

Follow one method consistently. This procedure helps children learn how to form letters and minimizes confusion and forgetting.

Make your handwriting a good model. When you write on the board or on students' papers, use the style you are teaching.

Display the handwriting models prominently. Post the letters, upper and lower case, so the class can refer to them. Primary grad-ers should have model letters written on narrow strips taped permanently to their desks.

Use real writing tasks for handwriting practice. Deemphasizing artificial drills and emphasizing real tasks like writing captions, recipes, game rules, and ads makes handwriting practice more interesting and natural.

Keep direct instruction periods short. Small muscles tire quickly; fifteen minutes a day of direct instruction, with practice throughout the day in real writing tasks, is most effective.

strom, 1971), while still others would best be delayed until second grade. Whether or not a child can profit from instruction at a given time is a matter of *readiness*, which can be thought of in two ways. First is the question of maturation, especially in motor coordination. The second is the matter of the prerequisite concepts about written language, concepts that enable children to make sense of handwriting instruction. Here are some psychomotor signs of readiness (based on Gessell and Ames, 1947; Gillet and Temple, 1982; Petty and Jensen, 1980, p. 478; Van Der Zanden, 1981):

1. *Facility in Using Crayons, Scissors, Brushes, and Pencils in a Variety of Activities*. Children should be reasonably adept at making these implements do what they want them to. Otherwise, instruction in how to form particular letters will be frustrating and unproductive if they can't get their pencils to follow orders! The remedy for manual clumsiness is plenty of *unforced* opportunities to use watercolor paints, markers, crayons, chalk, and pencils, beginning at home or preschool when possible and certainly in kindergarten and first grade.

2. *Ability to Copy Simple Shapes*. This skill is partly a matter of manual coordination and partly an ability to scan a shape for its features and their relationships and to reproduce those features and relationships on a piece of paper. It is an important skill, yet most young children seem to generate figures of their own more ably than they can copy figures done by someone else. If students cannot copy very well, assigning them some copying tasks could help, but such assignments should represent only a small percentage of the child-directed painting, drawing, and play-writing activities. Copying is terribly tedious and frustrating for the child who cannot do it well.

3. *Established Hand Dominance*. Hand dominance refers to a preference for using one hand more readily than the other for tasks requiring higher degrees of coordination, such as holding a spoon, throwing a ball, or using a pencil. Hand dominance usually begins by the age of two, is well under way by age four, and is normally stable by age six. Roughly nine out of ten children are right-hand dominant, the other left-handed, with an exceptional few being ambidextrous. Those who are left-handed often show a less resolute preference than right-handers and they may vary from one hand to another. Not having a dominant hand is likely to make such children less skillful with pencils and crayons. Provide them with plentiful opportunities to practice challenging motor activity and then encourage them to use more exclusively whichever hand appears dominant. If they are equal in first grade, it is probably advisable to encourage the child to use the right hand, since the world heavily favors right-handers. Trying to get left-handers to write with their right hands is likely to be more harmful than helpful, and may result in nervousness, impaired confidence, and delayed manual skill.

4. *Well-developed Pseudowriting*. When children are encouraged to play at writing, to write play shopping lists for the kindergarten grocery store center,

to write letters to friends, or to write captions to pictures they have drawn, we see their play writing develop from being little more than scribbles to becoming forms that look very much like real writing. In fact, these later productions often have recognizable letters in them, even though the children have had no formal teaching in handwriting.

Play writing is the most powerful of all the indicators of handwriting readiness. When children have developed to the point where they use discrete letters or letterlike symbols arranged in varied sequence in horizontal lines across the page, then it is clear that their perception of print has moved from the global features up to the specifics, and they are now ready to study the production of individual letters.

In kindergartens and first grades where children are encouraged to "play at writing," you can monitor their progress and spot evidence of readiness for instruction by using Clay's writing principles as criteria (refer back to Box 9.1).

If evidence of these principles appears consistently in play writing, instruction in letter formation can begin. If not, further exposure to print and play writing is needed. In the latter case, children should be read to frequently and shown the print the reader is looking at, they should have objects around them named and labeled, they should see adults write down what they say, as in dictated experience stories (see Chapter Five), and they should be encouraged to play at writing and experiment with it without criticism of what they produce.

Manuscript and Cursive Writing

In most schools in North America, children are taught two forms of handwriting: *manuscript* (or "printing") and *cursive* (fluid, connected writing). Manuscript is introduced first and mastered before the children are led to make the transition into cursive writing. There are sound reasons for introducing manuscript writing first, according to Herrick (1955): (a) Because it consists of straight lines and curves, it comes more easily to young hands whose fine muscles are still maturing (large muscles become coordinated before fine ones), and (b) it closely resembles the print that children are learning to read in books. By learning manuscript first, they avoid the task of learning two symbol systems at the very beginning of their schooling. Also, it is more easily read by both child and teacher.

The transition from manuscript to cursive is approached differently from one school to another. Some schools change over as early as the end of first grade, but the usual time is in grade three. Studies have shown that eventual legibility or rate of children's writing are not significantly affected by early versus late transition, although Herrick (1955) observed that the later the move is introduced, the more rapidly they are able to achieve the transition to cursive.

Some commercial methods teach cursive writing with little reference to manuscript writing, but most teach children to add transitional strokes to change letters from manuscript to cursive (see Figure 9.12). One such program

Figure 9.12 Connective approach for transition from print script to cursive

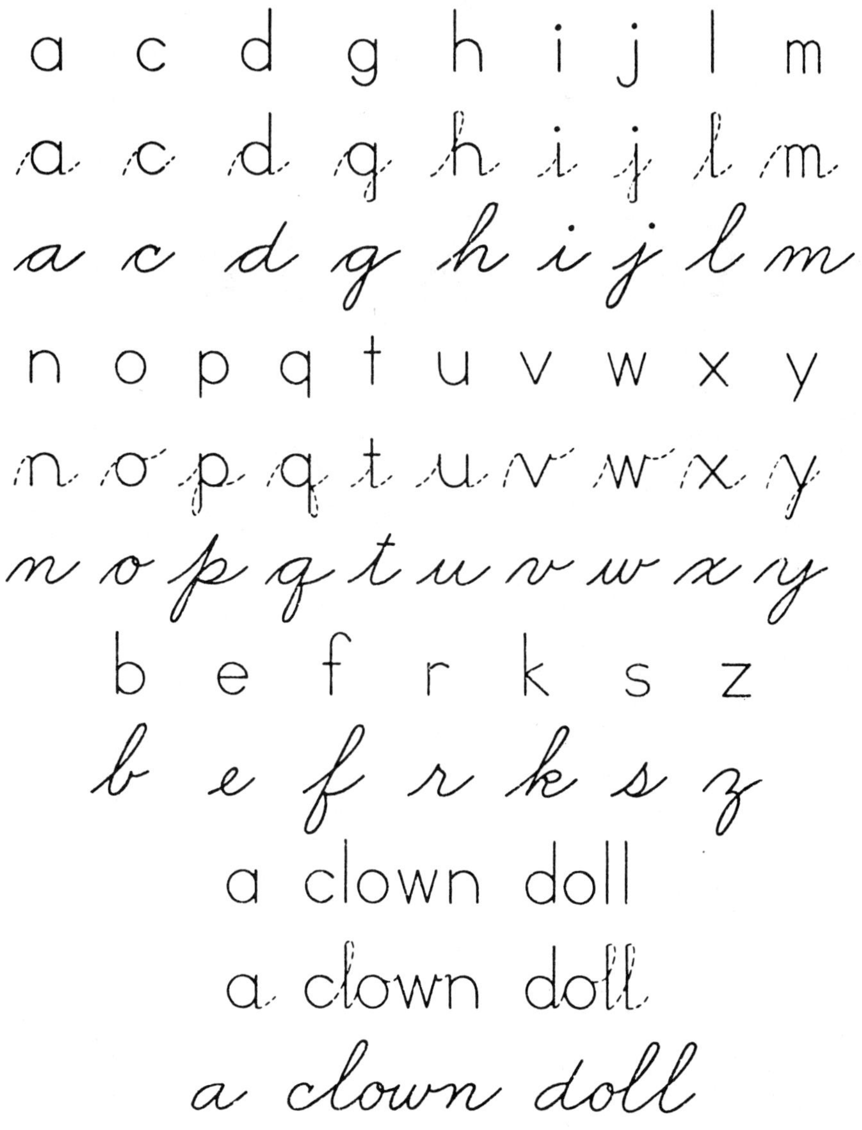

a c d g h i j l m

a c d g h i j l m

a c d g h i j l m

n o p q t u v w x y

n o p q t u v w x y

n o p q t u v w x y

b e f r k s z

b e f r k s z

a clown doll

a clown doll

a clown doll

is the D'Nealian system published by Scott, Foresman (Thurber, 1978) in which the manuscript letters are made somewhat more rounded than conventional manuscript. Thus the transition to cursive, when it comes, is made easier because there is less difference between the two forms. Most letters written by the D'Nealian method can be converted from manuscript to cursive by adding only a single stroke.

A final note on manuscript versus cursive: A study by Otto and Anderson (1969) found that in terms of legibility, rate, and ease of writing, children would be as well or better off if they stayed with manuscript and never made the transition to cursive writing. They advocated the development of a single style of handwriting that could be taught once and for all, but this proposal seems a long way from general acceptance.

Tools and Surfaces for Writing

In the past it has sometimes been a popular practice to have children "write in the air," making large-motor gestures in space before they tried their hand at pencil and paper. Current views, however, recognize that they learn to write best by writing letters rather than spending a great deal of time writing circles or other letter parts. Similarly, letters should be practiced in the context of real words and done at the board or on paper.

Five- to seven-year-olds have yet to develop finger strength and coordination, and many teachers advocate practicing with chalk at the board or with paints or large felt pens at an easel. At their desks, beginners may be most comfortable using chalk, crayons, felt pens, or thick primary pencils. If regular pencils are used they should have soft leads and not be sharpened to a fine point.

Holding a regular pencil is different from using a crayon, chalk, or felt pen; children holding a pencil too close to the point or too tightly find writing fatiguing. Pencils should be held comfortably (not gripped) at the bottom of the painted portion. A bit of tape on the pencil will help a beginner remember where to hold it.

Primary writing paper is usually large (12″ x 18″) and unlined. Unlined paper can be folded horizontally and the crease used as a guide when making the transition to lined paper. As their ability to control the size of their letters grows, children can begin to use smaller sheets with narrower lines. They should be offered 8½″ x 11″ paper as soon as they want it; many children identify standard-size lined paper with being a "big kid" and they should have plenty of practice using it.

Teaching Letter Formation:
The Perceptual-Motor Approach

An approach to teaching letter formation based on principles of perceptual-motor learning (Furner, 1969) can be applied to any particular handwriting style or method. Furner believes that children must begin with a clear, accurate concept of how each letter appears, then develop ways of producing each letter. Observing how letters are formed, verbalizing how they are shaped and formed, and practicing letter formation contribute to visual, auditory, and kinesthetic learning. The sequential steps in teaching letter formation by this approach are detailed below and summarized in Box 9.3.

BOX 9.3
Perceptual-Motor Approach to Letter Formation

Modeling: Write the letter on the board, modeling shape and component strokes.

Guided Observation: Call attention to the component features while writing the letter — how many strokes, the size of circles or lines, where to start and stop.

Verbalizing Description: Have children say aloud how to make component strokes and features. Help them describe each step explicitly.

Writing While Verbalizing: Have them say aloud how to make each letter while they carry out the steps on their own paper.

Comparing Productions with a Standard: Have them compare letters made in previous step to model letters on desk-top letter strips or transparent overlays. They should describe similarities and differences aloud and make necessary corrections. They should also select examples of their best work.

Modeling. Mark lines on the board corresponding to lines on the children's writing paper. Write the letter being introduced on the board within the lines, thus modeling the letter's shape and its component strokes.

Guided Observation. Describe the letter's individual features, one at a time, as you write it. Ask volunteers to tell you how many strokes there are, how many straight lines, how large circles should be, and so on. Repeat this procedure until all features have been pointed out and described.

Verbalizing Description. Here children describe aloud how each letter part is formed, giving each step explicitly and in sequence. Precise terms like *baseline*, *stroke*, and *clockwise* should be modeled and defined by the teacher, then properly used by the students. You can write out and post their descriptions of letter formations for their reference later.

Writing While Verbalizing. In this step they practice saying aloud the steps they formulated in the previous step, while acting out the steps at their desks with paper and pencil. This routine helps them associate the steps with the physical action. Small groups or pairs can practice with one, then another pupil reading (or reciting) the steps while the others follow the directions.

Comparing Productions with a Standard. After they have practiced verbalizing the letter formation steps while writing the letter, they should compare what they produced to a standard model, which is easily done if you pass out transparencies with the letter written on it in wax pencil or transparency marker. They can place these overlays over their papers and describe how they are similar and different from the standard. Then they should remove the overlay and make any corrections on their papers. (Transparencies can be collected, wiped off, and reused many times.) After they have mastered a letter they can select an example of their best work for display or sharing with parents.

Furner (1969) advocated introducing letters not in alphabetical order but in groups of letters shaped similarly: the lower case *circle letters* (such as *o*, *a*, and *e*), *straight line letters* (such as *l* and *i*), *point letters* (such as *v* and *w*), *tail letters* (like *y* and *g*), and *hump letters* (like *m*, *n*, and *u*). Children should be encouraged to note and describe how members of a group resemble one another and how they differ.

Helping Left-Handed Children

About one child in ten is left-handed, so a typical classroom will have two or three "lefties" in it. These students face problems not encountered by other children. School desks may be easy for right-handers to get in and out of but awkward for left-handers. Pencil sharpeners favor right-handers, causing lefties to break more points. Worst of all, since we write from left to right, left-handed children's left hands obscure and smear what they have just written.

There are several things you can do to make life easier for lefties in your class:

1. Identify your left-handed students and plan to provide special support for them. Do *not* try to make them write with their right hands!
2. Have a left-handed teacher or older pupil with good handwriting model letter formation for them. Left-handers have difficulty following a right-handed model.
3. Show them how to turn their writing paper so that it is opposite to the way right-handers have it (see Figure 9.13).
4. Have their desk tops lowered. Left-handers can better see what they have written if it is situated farther below their eyes. Most desks have tops that

Figure 9.13 (*a*) Position of paper in cursive writing for the right-handed; (*b*) position of paper in cursive writing for the left-handed; (*c*) a recommended position for manuscript writing for the right- and left-handed pupil

SOURCE: From Dallmann, *Teaching the Language Arts in the Elementary School*, 3rd Edition. © 1966, 1971, 1976 Wm. C. Brown Publishers, Dubuque, Iowa. All rights reserved. Reprinted by permission.

can be raised or lowered with an adjustable wrench; ask your maintenance staff.

5. Help them find the most legible form of each letter that they can produce with reasonable ease and encourage them to use that style, no matter how it may differ from the standard the right-handers are following.

Maintaining Legible Handwriting

We can help children develop the habit of legible handwriting by systematically integrating handwriting practice into everyday writing activities, encouraging them to write their final-draft compositions in careful handwriting, and consistently modeling good handwriting ourselves. As they move up in the grades, however, direct handwriting instruction is deemphasized because the other school subjects demand more, and faster, writing. Consequently handwriting tends to drift farther away from the style taught and may become less legible.

Although developing an individual written "hand" is natural, legible handwriting should become a lifetime habit. The major emphasis in composition must be on content, but maintaining legibility can be achieved by following the guidelines discussed below and summarized in Box 9.4.

1. *Separate working drafts from finished drafts.* When writers are actively creating, appearance necessarily suffers. Getting thoughts on paper is hampered by overconcern with spelling, punctuation, and letter formation. As discussed in Chapter Seven, early drafts should be focused on content; final drafts should be edited, proofread, and copied over in neat handwriting. A messy final draft shows a lack of respect for one's readers. Motivation to produce neat final drafts is increased if work is shared with others, not just turned in to the teacher, so final products should be displayed, illustrated and bound, mailed, or whatever is appropriate. There should be a *real* outcome for the writing.

2. *Encourage awareness of the impact of legibility.* Children often don't realize that others may have trouble reading what they write. Burns and Broman

---

BOX 9.4
Guidelines for Maintaining Legible Handwriting

Separate working drafts from finished drafts. Neat, legible writing is important in final drafts only.

Encourage awareness of the impact of legibility. Discuss how illegible writing creates negative impressions of the writer.

Make handwriting interesting. Introduce and explore topics like calligraphy, handwriting analysis, hieroglyphics and picture writing, and the history of alphabet systems.

Make sure children write every day. Illegible handwriting is often caused by a sheer lack of practice.

(1979) suggest making transparencies of legible and illegible handwriting samples and discussing what makes the latter hard to read. (Examples should be from students the same age as your pupils but *not* from your class.) The children can discuss the impression that poor handwriting may convey. Older students might prepare a survey in which adults look at samples of handwriting and judge the writers' responsibility, academic potential, employability, and the like. The results may be surprising and persuasive!

3. *Make handwriting interesting.* There are many areas related to handwriting that students may enjoy exploring. Because writing is one of the most important inventions of humanity, much has been written about topics like picture writing, smoke signals and other visual codes, hieroglyphics, and the evolution of various alphabet systems. Burns and Broman (1979, pp. 350–351) suggest the following books of interest to elementary children:

Cahn, William, and Rhoda Cohn. *The Story of Writing.* Irvington-on-Hudson, New York: Harvery House, 1963.

Dugan, William. *How Our Alphabet Grew.* New York: Golden, 1972.

Gourdie, Tom. *The Puffin Book of Lettering.* Baltimore, Md.: Penguin Books, 1961.

Hofsinde, Robert (Gray-Wolf). *Indian Picture Writing.* New York: Morrow, 1959.

Irwin, Keith Gordon. *The Romance of Writing.* New York: Viking Press, 1957.

McCain, Murray. *Writing.* New York: Farrar, Straus & Giroux, 1964.

Ogg, Oscar. *The Twenty-Six Letters,* rev. ed. New York: Crowell, 1971.

Russell, Solveig. *A Is for Apple and Why: The Story of Our Alphabet.* New York: Abingdon Press, 1959.

Scott, Joseph and Lenore Scott. *Hieroglyphs for Fun.* New York: Van Nostrand Reinhold, 1974.

Other topics of interest may be *calligraphy*, the ancient art of decorative lettering, and *graphology*, the analysis of handwriting. Calligraphy is enjoying a renaissance of popularity, and you may be able to draft an older student or adult to teach it to your class. Graphology is a controversial topic: Like astrology, some believe strongly in its powers to reveal hidden personality traits through handwriting while others scoff at what they believe is "pseudoscience." When explored in a lighthearted, positive way, however, the topic can be fun for older students. Some books on calligraphy and graphology you might find useful are:

FURTHER READINGS ON CALLIGRAPHY

Angel, Marie. *The Art of Calligraphy: A Practical Guide.* New York: Charles Scribner's, 1978.

Baker, Arthur. *Arthur Baker's Historic Calligraphic Alphabets.* New York: Dover, 1980.

Baron, Nancy. *Getting Started in Calligraphy*. New York: Sterling, 1979.

Butterworth, Emma M. *The Complete Book of Calligraphy*. New York: Harper & Row, 1980.

Fairbank, Alfred. *A Book of Scripts*, 2d ed. Winchester, Mass.: Faber & Faber, 1977.

Gillon, Edmund V. *Pictorial Calligraphy and Ornamentation*. New York: Dover, 1972.

Gourdie, Tom. *Calligraphy for the Beginner*. New York: Taplinger, 1981.

Gray, Nicolete. *Lettering as Drawing*. New York: Taplinger, 1982.

Jarman, Christopher. *Fun with Pens*. New York: Taplinger, 1979.

Jessen, Peter. *Masterpieces of Calligraphy: Two Hundred and Sixty-One Examples, 1500–1800*. New York: Dover, 1981.

Korn, Ellen, ed. *Teach Yourself Calligraphy: For Beginners from Eight to Eighty*. New York: Morrow, n.d.

Lehman, Charles. *Italic Handwriting and Calligraphy for the Beginner: A Craft Manual*. New York: Taplinger, 1982.

Parkhurst, Christine and Marian Fellows. *Script Ease: A Step-by-Step Guide from Manuscript to Calligraphy*. Tucson, Ariz.: Kino Publishing, 1982. (Grades 1–12)

Reynolds, Lloyd J. *My Dear Runemeister: A Voyage Through the Alphabet*. New York: Taplinger, 1982.

Shepherd, Margaret. *Learning Calligraphy: A Book of Lettering, Design and History*. New York: Macmillan, 1978.

Studley, Vance. *Left Handed Calligraphy*. New York: Van Nostrand Reinhold, 1979.

FURTHER READINGS ON GRAPHOLOGY

Engel, Joel. *Handwriting Analysis Self-Taught*. New York: Elsevier-Nelson Books, 1980.

Falcon, Hal. *How to Analyze Handwriting*. New York: Trident (div. of Simon & Schuster), 1971.

Hartford, Huntington. *You Are What You Write*. New York: Macmillan, 1976.

Hughes, Albert E. *What Your Handwriting Reveals*. North Hollywood, Calif.: Wilshire, 1978.

Mann, Peggy. *The Tell-Tale Line: The Secrets of Handwriting Analysis*. New York: Macmillan, 1976.

Meyer, Jerome S. *The Handwriting Analyzer*. New York: Simon & Schuster, 1974.

Robie, Joan. *What Your Handwriting Tells About You*. Nashville, Tenn.: Broadman Press, 1978.

Ruiz, Mary and Karen K. Amend. *The Complete Book of Handwriting Analysis*. North Hollywood, Calif.: Newcastle, 1980.

Figure 9.14 Unpracticed handwriting, twelve-year old

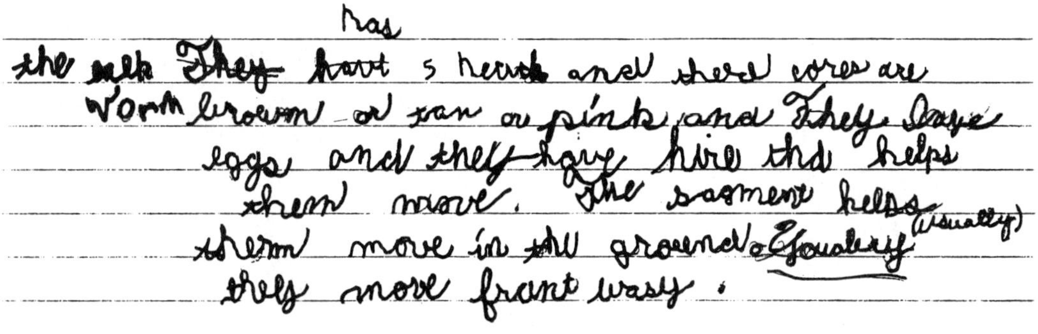

Ruiz, Mary and Karen K. Amend. *The Complete Book of Handwriting Analysis.* North Hollywood, Calif.: Newcastle, 1980.

Solomon, Shirl. *Knowing Your Child Through His Handwriting and Drawing.* New York: Crown, 1978.

Wyland, Johanna L. *Your Paths in Ink: Graphoanalysis and the Personality.* Smithtown, New York: Exposition Press, 1980.

4. *Make sure children write every day.* Lack of practice may be the biggest single reason for illegible penmanship. Handwriting is a motor act; it improves with practice and grows rusty with disuse. Children at every grade should be doing extended writing every single day — not ditto sheets or workbooks but paragraphs and pages of connected text. Figure 9.14 shows the handwriting of a student who wrote almost nothing on a daily basis. Frequently the poorest writers are the ones who do the least writing, so they have the least opportunity to improve. Mina Shaughnessy, a teacher of academically disadvantaged college students (basic writing students in the quotation below), had this to say about high schoolers' writing experience; her words bear on students of all ages:

> Compared with the 1000 words a week that a British student is likely to have written in the equivalent of an American high school or even the 350 words a week that an American student in a middle-class high school is likely to have written, the basic writing student is more likely to have written 350 words a semester. It would not be unusual for him to have written nothing at all. He is often therefore still struggling with basic motor-mental coordinations that have long ago become unconscious for more practiced students. And as long as the so-called mechanical processes involved in writing are themselves highly conscious or even labored, the writer is not likely to have easy access to his thoughts. Thus matters like handwriting and punctuation and spelling become important, if only because without some measure of ease, without being able to assign some operations to habit, or even to indifference, the novice writer is cut off from thinking.

> . . . the answer to this is practice — writing and more writing, preferably in modes that encourage a flow of words (journals, free writing, notations or observations), until the pen seems a natural extension of the hand, and the hand of the mind itself.
>
> — (Shaughnessy, 1977, pp. 14, 16)

When students at any grade level begin to do extended writing, for handwriting practice or any other purposes, another aspect of writing mechanics — spelling — becomes important. The subsequent sections of this chapter take up this important topic.

Summary

Theories of handwriting instruction today reflect a general trend in psychology away from behaviorist learning theories, advocating part-to-whole sequences and breaking up tasks into small increments, toward a cognitive learning position, which advocates whole-to-part sequences and discovery learning. Commercial handwriting materials, however, tend to reflect the behaviorist position of teaching parts of letters before whole letters in lock-step sequences of skills. Recent work in the field of perceptual learning and by observers of young children reveals that they tend to perceive global features of writing such as its horizontal line arrangement, variety in written characters, and general features of characters before they perceive or produce specific characteristics of letter formation. Observers of young children advocate allowing them to "play at writing" and "explore with a pencil" before attempting to teach handwriting formally.

"Play writing" can be examined for features such as repetition of the same marks, horizontal lines, generation of new marks, and evidence of communicative intent on the part of the writer to determine if children are approaching readiness for handwriting instruction.

When they are ready for it, systematic handwriting instruction helps them develop habits of legibility and comfort while writing. Teachers should use one method or style consistently, provide a good model in their own handwriting, keep handwriting models prominently displayed for the children's reference, use real writing tasks for handwriting practice, and keep direct instruction periods short. Psychomotor signs of readiness include facility with using crayons, scissors, and brushes, ability to copy simple shapes, established preference for the left or right hand, and well-developed "play writing."

Manuscript writing, or printing, is introduced first in most schools. Transition to cursive, or connected, handwriting generally takes place at about third grade. With either system, children should have plenty of practice in real writing tasks, at the board and on paper. The size of the paper and writing instruments is important; larger tools and paper are appropriate for younger children. Letter formation in either system can be facilitated by using a perceptual-motor teaching method with sequential steps of modeling, guided observation, verbalizing description, writing while verbalizing, and comparing productions with a standard.

About one in ten children is left-handed, and left-handers need special help to make their writing comfortable. Turning the paper at a different angle from right-handers, lowered desk tops, and some leeway in letter formation are helpful.

Older students can be helped to maintain legible handwriting habits by encouraging them to attend to neatness only in final drafts, encouraging their awareness of the impression legible handwriting conveys, introducing interesting topics such as calligraphy (decorative lettering), history of writing systems, and handwriting analysis, and providing daily extended writing practice.

Understanding Spelling

Spelling is an area of the language arts curriculum that is poorly understood by many teachers. We have been teaching spelling in schools for centuries, and in many ways spelling instruction has not changed much. Many people are confused by how children learn to spell correctly and how good spellers and poor spellers differ in what they know or do. In this section we will attempt to help you understand how different aspects of our language are represented in the ways we spell words, how children demonstrate their growing knowledge of language by their spellings, and how these concepts can be related to the teaching of spelling.

The Nature of Our Spelling System

A time-honored belief about spelling is that the letters we use to spell words represent the speech sounds we use to pronounce those words. Evidence for this belief can be found in the many words that can be "sounded out" and read or spelled accurately by assigning a particular speech sound to each of the letters, such as *c-a-t*.

It does not require a very great leap in logic, then, to arrive at the conclusion that written letters, and the ways they are combined in spelling, exist *only* in order to represent speech sounds. This too has been a popular idea for many decades. The fact that there are twenty-six letters, called *graphemes*, in our alphabet and forty-four different speech sounds, called *phonemes*, requires that some letters or letter combinations must represent more than one sound in speech. (An example of this is the fact that we use the *th* letter combination to stand for two different phonemes: the sound you hear at the beginning of *thin*, and the somewhat different sound you hear at the beginning of *there*.)

According to this position, the ways that our twenty-six letters represent our forty-four speech sounds are not very efficient. An obvious solution to the problem is to "reform" our alphabet and our ways of spelling words so that each of the forty-four phonemes can be represented by a grapheme that is used only for that sound. In this way, a one-to-one correspondence between graphemes and phonemes would be created, and spelling would become a simple matter of remembering the grapheme for each sound. Over the years many attempts have been made to reform spelling by introducing either a new, forty-four-grapheme alphabet, such as the Initial Teaching Alphabet, or ITA (Mazurkiewicz and Tanzer, 1963), or by retaining the twenty-six-grapheme alphabet while simplifying spelling rules to conform with common pronunciations, such as changing *dripped* to *dript* and *thorough* to *thoro* (Venezky, 1980).

Spelling reform has been proposed repeatedly for generations. It appears to have hit its zenith in the first decade of the twentieth century under the enthusiastic patronage of President Theodore Roosevelt, who in 1906 ordered the Public Printer to begin producing all government documents in simplified spelling. (Public and Congressional outrage soon convinced him of the foolhardiness of his action, and he quickly rescinded his order.) Spelling reform movements and groups persist to this day but, according to Venezky (1980), ". . . it is undeniable that in terms of its own goals, the reform movement has failed" (p. 29).

Why has spelling reform failed in its many attempts to make spelling and pronunciation coincide? Because the basic premise of spelling reform, that orthography reflects *only* speech sounds, is too simple. Spelling patterns preserve features of *meaning* and common origin in writing as well as features of pronunciation. Meaning features are contained in *morphemes*, the smallest units of meaning in language.

Since morphemes are units of meaning, they can be represented in speech or in writing as whole words, parts of words, syllables, or single letters or sounds. For example, *cat* is a word made up of one morpheme; *cats* is a word made up of two morphemes, the base *cat* and the ending *-s*, which indicates the plural concept. Likewise, *roll* is a single-morpheme word, and *unroll* is made up of two morphemes; the base *roll* and the prefix *un-*, which contributes a particular meaning to the word *unroll* as a whole.

When the morphemes *un-* and *-s* are added to *roll* and *cat*, the base words don't change in their pronunciation. Many words *do* change, however, in their pronunciation when their morphemic components change, such as *Canada–Canadian* and *critic–criticize* (Henderson, 1981). Venezky (1980) offers the example of *cone* and *conic*. He wrote,

> If CONE and CONIC, for example, were spelled KON and KANIC, their shared semantic base would not be so immediately obvious. (p. 29)

In these examples as in many, many others, the shared meaning relationship between base words and their derived forms is not immediately apparent in our pronunciation but *is* obvious in, and is preserved by, our spelling system.

Here is another example. *Sign* is a fairly common word, which to a spelling reformer appears to have a totally useless silent letter (*g*) in it. SIN (or even SINE) would conform much more closely to our pronunciation of this word. However, the *g* in the spelling exists because the word is semantically and etymologically, or historically, related to words like *signal*, *signature*, and *signet*, all of which retain the pronunciation of the *g*. And all of these words derive from the same Latin base word, *signum*, as do *resign* and *resignation*, *design* and *designate*, *malign* and *malignant*. By changing the spelling of *sign*, *resign*, and the like to conform to their pronunciation, the meaning relationships encoded in their spelling would be lost. Our written language would lose more than it would gain by such "simplification."

The position that spelling reformers have long held, that English spelling is impossibly irregular and capricious, has been refuted many times. Perhaps most influential was the elegant explanation by linguists Noam Chomsky and Morris Halle (1968) that because writing reflects both semantic, or lexical, information and phonological, or pronunciation, rules, our English orthography is nearly optimal for its purposes.

Chomsky and Halle were not the first, however, to propose that spelling reflects meaning relationships as well as speech sounds in written words. In 1913, Henry Bradley presented a paper to the British Academy that is little known today but which predated Chomsky and Halle's insights by fifty-odd years. In this paper, he wrote that advocates of spelling reform were mistaken in believing that writing should represent speech sounds precisely. Bradley insightfully made the point that if this were to come to pass, one could then compare written English to written musical notation, with each mark accurately representing a particular sound to anyone who has mastered the system. Then he brilliantly refuted this point, writing,

> The truth is that between written music and written language there is one all-important difference. In written music the representation of sounds is the absolutely ultimate end. In written language it is only a means. We use visible symbols for the sounds of speech because spoken sounds are symbols of meaning. The ultimate end, and for most purposes, though not for all, the only important end of written language is to convey meaning.
>
> — (Bradley, 1913, p. 2)

So we can see that although English spelling does not always precisely conform to our pronunciation of words, it does encode in visual symbols important cues to the meaning of words and the meaning-based relationships among them, cues that would be lost if spelling were made to conform strictly and only to pronunciation. Since spelling patterns encode word meaning cues, then *thinking* and *understanding* must be involved in mastering correct spelling. In other words, there must be more to correct spelling than rote memorization or "sounding out." With this conclusion we return to the idea introduced previously, that although spelling instruction has been solidly founded on both memorizing and sounding out, teachers have long realized that neither memorizing nor sounding seem to make their pupils spell correctly. We must turn, then, to *cognition* (thinking and understanding) in order to discover what it is children do when they spell, both correctly and incorrectly. And it is here that a rich and informative body of research has been focused for roughly the last fifteen years, research that shows quite clearly how children use logic and knowledge about spoken and written words as they learn to spell.

Cognition and Invented Spelling

In recent years much attention has been directed toward the study of children's attempts to spell words they have not been taught. In particular, the writing and spelling of preschoolers and primary grade children who may be prereaders or very beginning readers, have been examined closely (Beers and Henderson, 1977; Bissex, 1980; Chomsky, 1971a and b, 1979; Gentry, 1978, 1981; Liberman et al., 1980; Read, 1971, 1975, 1980; Zutell, 1979; and others). A number of important insights have come from this work. Perhaps the most important generalization is that children develop *strategies*, which they use systematically and predictably to help them spell (Marsh et al., 1980; Read and Hodges, 1982). These strategies frequently result in misspellings, but these misspellings can be extremely informative. By examining them we can see how children use what they have learned and invent strategies for what they don't yet know in spelling. Their *invented spellings* progress through about five rough but recognizable stages, which occur in a predictable order, as they grow toward correct spelling.

Long before they enter school most children begin to write. At the earliest stages their "writing" is actually more like scribbling and is unintelligible to others and, frequently, to the writer as well. If they are given any encouragement at all, children of three and four will produce a prodigious amount of such "pseudowriting," which they often embellish with drawings and enjoy "reading" to others, blithely making up stories and dialogues that the marks might represent. Because their scribbles may bear little, if any, visual resemblance to actual print and because they take part in this behavior playfully and with gusto, many adults underestimate its importance in the child's journey toward literacy. Look back at Figures 9.5 and 9.11 in the section "Handwriting," for some examples of pseudowriting.

Prephonemic Spelling. By about age four or five, much of their writing begins to approximate adult standards more closely. If they have been read to and have had experience with words and letters in the environment, they begin to use letters and letterlike forms and their writing begins to look a lot more like "real" writing to adults, although it is still unreadable. Many preschoolers and most kindergarteners are able to recognize and produce some, or even all, of the letters of the alphabet, as well as some numerals. Look back at Figure 9.6, a good example of an unreadable array of letters. When writing is made up entirely of letters and letterlike forms (which include numerals and letters formed incorrectly or backward), then we say that the writing represents the first stage of spelling — the *prephonemic* stage.

At the beginning of the prephonemic stage, which often coincides with children's entrance to school and the kindergarten year, they "throw letters at the page." They produce arrays of letters, usually arranged in horizontal lines, but they may use a small number of letters over and over, and the letters may be reversed or upside down.

Figure 9.15   Jessie, four-year-old preschooler

Figures 9.15 and 9.16 are examples of prephonemic spelling. In Figure 9.15 Jessie, at age four, has arranged "words" in separate lines; in Figure 9.16 Phillip, a kindergartener, has written an account to accompany his picture; Phillip's writing is entirely prephonemic, but he was able to "read" it to his teacher, who wrote down what he said on the back of his paper.

The primary similarity in these examples, and the characteristic that makes them typical, is that although the writing is made up entirely of recognizable

Figure 9.16 Phillip, kindergartener

BOX 9.5
Characteristics of Prephonemic Spelling

Prephonemic spelling:

Is made up of letters and letterlike forms, such as numerals and incorrectly formed or made-up letters.

Is unreadable; letters and forms are used randomly, not to represent sounds.

Is usually arranged in horizontal lines.

May be made up of unbroken lines of letters or arranged in wordlike configurations with spaces between.

Shows that the child is aware that words are made up of letters and that print is arranged horizontally.

Is typical of older preschoolers, kindergarteners, and many first graders.

---

letters, the letters used bear no relationship to the sounds in these words. Since there is no way these spellings could be sounded out to determine what words they represent, they are called *prephonemic*, because these children, who are prereaders, have not yet discovered that letters in writing represent sounds in spoken words. They have discovered that words are made up of letters, and not numerals, scribbles, or other marks, but they have yet to discover the relationship between letters and sounds. Box 9.5 summarizes the characteristics of prephonemic spelling.

Early Phonemic Spelling. As youngsters are exposed to beginning reading instruction and have further experience with print in books and other materials, they discover that letters in print "have sounds," or represent sounds in spoken words. This concept is called the *alphabetic principle,* and it is a critically important one. When children realize that letters stand for sounds, they can begin to write words that are at least partly readable by others, and they can begin to use letter-sound correspondences, or phonics, to figure out the identity of words others have written.

When they first begin to spell phonemically, they use letters to represent sounds in words, but the spellings they produce still don't look much like adult spellings. Look at Figures 9.17 and 9.18, which represent early phonemic spellings by primary graders. In Figure 9.17, Nina spelled some words correctly, which she memorized and can recognize when she sees them in print, as well as some words that are unfamiliar. She spelled several words entirely correctly. (She also spelled *dog* correctly aloud but reversed her written *d.* When she tried to spell *dip,* she also called the first letter she wrote a *d* but reversed it. Since she was confident she'd written a *d,* we'll consider it as such.) Her spellings of BA for *baby,* MAY for *mother,* KGI for *car,* BNA for *dip,* and YWI for *wall* are invented spellings.

In these inventions Nina has represented the initial sound in each word, then added other letters randomly except in BA, where she has represented both

Figure 9.17   Nina, first grade

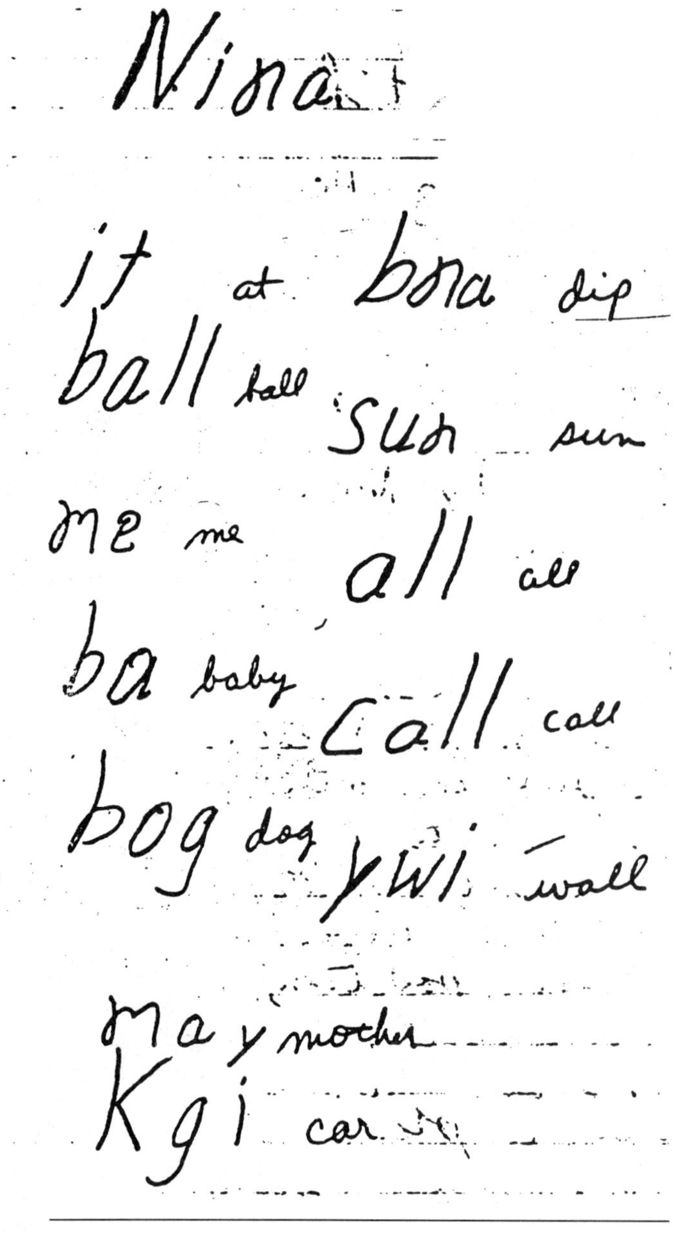

Nina

it   at   bona dip

ball ball sun sun

me me all all

ba baby call call

bog dog ywi wall

may mother

Kgi car

Figure 9.18 Brian, first grade (Sept.)

I love my mother. Me and my mother. Me and my dog.

I LNMNA MNG MAMDG

I like my mother. Me and my mother. Me and my dog.

the initial and medial vowel sound. Remember, Nina thought she'd written a *d* as the first letter of her invention of *dip*. (YWI for *wall* may confuse you, but we'll explain her strategy here shortly.)

In Figure 9.18, Brian drew a picture of his mother and then wrote something about his drawing. His teacher transcribed what he read back over his own writing: "I love my mother. Me and Mother. Me and my dog." Brian spelled only one word, *dog*, correctly; for the rest, he used only one letter for each one-syllable word and two letters for the two-syllable word *mother*. The letters used represent all the initial sounds, and the final sound in *mother*. Unlike Nina, Brian did not use any other letters to make his spelling look more wordlike — he's content with one-letter words.

In Figures 9.19 and 9.20 Kerrie and Scott have consistently represented initial and final consonant sounds and long vowel sounds but no other sounds: WD and YD (*would*), HM (*him*), KP (*keep*), F (*for*), YE (*we*), NAM (*name*), FED (*feed*). If you are curious about why Scott used Y in spelling *we* and *would*, we'll explain the strategy he used, along with Nina's YWI (*wall*) shortly.

Nina, Brian, Kerrie, and Scott have all included at least one phonemic feature in each invented spelling, but their inventions are quite incomplete, one of the characteristics of early phonemic spellings summarized in Box 9.6. Why do early phonemic spellers attempt only one or two sounds in their invented spellings? Many adults say it is because they "don't hear the other sounds." However, since they not only could pronounce these words correctly, including all their sounds, but also characteristically go through a great deal of oral sounding out as they try to spell (Graves, 1982; Temple, Nathan, and Burris, 1982), we can assume that "not hearing" all the sounds is not what causes these primitive spellings.

A more accurate explanation has to do with the process of *phonemic segmentation*, or the ability to break apart sounds in spoken words (Liberman et

---

BOX 9.6
Characteristics of Early Phonemic Spelling

Early phonemic spelling:

Is made up entirely of letters, usually in short strings of 1–4 letters; single letters are often used to represent whole words.

Represents the discovery of the alphabetic principle: Letters are used to represent *some* of the sounds in words.

Commonly features the use of consonants to represent initial sounds; sometimes final sounds and/or other important, clearly discernible sounds are represented too, but the spellings are very incomplete.

Shows the child's discovery that letters in print represent sounds in spoken words and indicates the beginning of the ability to segment phonemes.

Is typical of very beginning readers, some kindergarteners, most first graders, and some older children just beginning to read.

Figure 9.19 Kerrie, kindergartener

If I had a dinosaur I WDNAmHm
DINe IWDKPHm kerrie

If I had a dinosaur I would name
him Dine. I would keep him.

Figure 9.20 Scott, kindergartener

al., 1980; Liberman, Shankweiler, Fischer, and Carter, 1974; Morris, 1980).
If we try to spell an unfamiliar word by using the sounds we hear, we have to
go through a multistep process like this:

1. Determine what word will be written: "I want to spell *twins*."
2. Separate (or *segment*) the first sound from the rest of the word: "Twins
   . . . /t/ . . . /t/ . . . "
3. Determine what letter represents that first sound: ". . . /t/ . . . /t/ . . . *t*!"
4. Recall how letter is formed: "How do you make a *t*? Oh, two lines . . . "
5. Determine where to write the letter: "Where do you start writing? Over
   here? . . . "
6. Proceed with the motor act of forming the letter: "A line like this, and
   then a line like this . . . "
7. Recall the word being spelled: "What was it I was writing? Oh yeah, *twins*
   . . . where was I?"
8. Segment the second sound heard: "Twins . . . /t/ . . . /w/ . . . /w/ . . . "
9. Repeat steps 3 through 7: "What letter says /w/? How do you make a *w*?
   Where does it go, on the right or left of the *t*? . . . "
10. Repeat steps 2 through 7 for each succeeding sound.

Adult writers, of course, don't go through each of these steps discretely,
but young writers or very uncertain spellers do, and you can see how easy it
would be for them to lose track of the process. Indeed, young spellers like
Nina, Brian, Kerrie, and Scott get through the first few steps, complete the
process of putting down the first (or most important) sound they hear, and
then simply go on to the next word. This is understandable, because young
writers who are trying to create some kind of message, as Brian was, are
naturally concerned with getting whole thoughts and images down on paper as
well as whole words and could easily forget what they were trying to say at any
point in that laborious process. Liberman et al. (1974, 1980), Morris (1980),
and others have shown that young children who are not yet fluent readers have
great difficulty segmenting sounds within words and following the sequential
process of representing each sound.

As they become more fluent readers and acquire greater facility with phonemic segmentation, after they have mastered beginning reading and decoding
skills, they get better at representing in words more of the sounds, more
accurately. This marks their transition into the next spelling stage.

Letter-Name Spelling. Letter-name spellings take on many more recognizable
features and reflect a burgeoning awareness of letter-sound relationships in
words. Although the sound features are represented in each word, the words
themselves still may look quite strange to adult readers, but it is the concepts
about spelling their spellings reflect, and not their correctness or lack of it,
that is interesting and informative here. Let's look at some typical letter-name
spellings in Figures 9.21, 9.22, and 9.23.

These spellings are like those of early phonemic spellers except that they are more filled out. Virtually every sound we hear in these words as we speak them has been given its own letter, and the strategies used to spell the sounds in the words are very interesting. First, let's look at the words with long vowel sounds. Since long vowels "say their names," it is easy to use these letter names, or consonant letter names, to spell long vowel sounds, as Billy, Frank, and Jesse did in these words:

HATS	hates	FID	find
LIKS	likes	MI	my
PLAG	playing	LIF	life
NIT	night	CRI	cry
LUSTUTH	loose tooth	B	be
WOK	woke	LONLE	lonely

Figure 9.21 Billy's spelling: letter-name

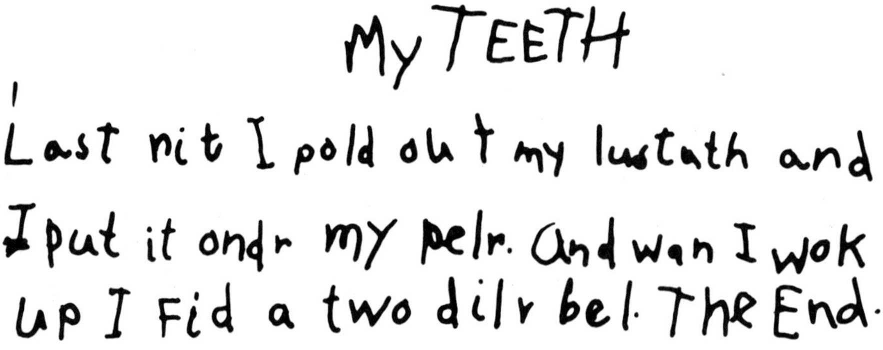

My TEETH

Last nit I pold out my lustath and I put it ondr my pelr. And wen I wok up I Fid a two dilr bel. The End.

SOURCE: From Jean Wallace Gillet and Charles Temple, *Understanding Reading Problems: Assessment and Instruction.* Copyright © 1982 by Jean Wallace Gillet and Charles Temple. Reprinted by permission of Little, Brown and Company.

Figure 9.22 Frank's spelling: letter-name

DONALD HATS ME DONALD LIKS PLAG SOKR DONALD OLWES bREGS A SNAK

SOURCE: From Jean Wallace Gillet and Charles Temple, *Understanding Reading Problems: Assessment and Instruction.* Copyright © 1982 by Jean Wallace Gillet and Charles Temple. Reprinted by permission of Little, Brown and Company.

Figure 9.23 Jesse, a letter-name speller in kindergarten

If I had a dinosaur I WOODROW WUD CRI BCS HE run would cry because he

FUR MI LIFE HE WUD BLOW LE JESSE
For my Life, He would would be lonely.

In adult spelling, we usually "mark" these long vowels by using some other letters as signals, letters that are not sounded themselves but which are called "vowel markers": the final *e* in *hates, likes, loose, life, lonely,* and *woke*; the *-gh* in *night* and the *y* in *cry*. Young spellers using phonemic and letter-name strategies, however, rarely use letters that do not stand directly for a sound. Because they are concentrating on the alphabetic principle that letters stand for sounds, they are as yet unaware that letters also are included for other reasons beyond sound. This awareness comes later as they learn more about words and the vagaries of letters and sounds.

Two other characteristics of letter-name spelling are evident in Figures 9.21, 9.22, and 9.23. One is the omission of certain letters and the use of single letters to represent entire syllables, as in PLAG (*playing*), SOKR (*soccer*), BREGS (*brings*), ONDR (*under*), PELR (*pillow*), and DILR (*dollar*). In SOKR, ONDR, PELR, and DILR these children have used the single letter *r* to stand for the syllables that adults would spell with a vowel and *r*. (Billy pronounced *pillow* like "piller," hence his use of *r*.) In adult spelling we would use *-er* as in *soccer*, *-ar* as in *dollar*, and *-or* as in *sailor* in these unstressed syllables, although all we hear is the sound of the *r* because the vowel sound is reduced almost completely. Similarly, we use a vowel in unstressed final syllables like *-om* in *bottom*, *-le* in *little*, *-on* in *wagon*, and *-en* in *kitten*; young spellers characteristically omit the vowel in these syllables and represent only the consonant sound. In these spellings we can also see other letters omitted, such as the *n* before *g* in *playing* and *brings*. Letter-name spellers characteristically omit the letters *m* and *n* when they occur in *-ing* endings or before consonants, as in *monster* or *bumpy*. In the case of *m*'s and *n*'s before consonants, the sounds of these two letters simply seem to disappear when the words are pronounced. Why does this happen?

To see how this works, say aloud *cat* and *can't* several times in succession while you hold your nose. Concentrate not on the sound but on the *feel* of the words and the position of your tongue, palate, and jaws. The position of these parts of the mouth doesn't change at all when you pronounce these two different words; the only difference is that when you say *can't* you direct a small amount of air through your nose. Because of that, linguists call these sounds "nasals," and they are the ones that you can't pronounce clearly if your nasal passages are blocked, as when you have "a bad code id your dose." When young spellers try to spell these sounds, they concentrate more on the position of the parts of their mouth than on the minor variations in the sounds they produce, and in spelling they generally omit the nasals before other consonants completely.

Another very interesting characteristic of letter-name spelling can be seen in Billy's and Frank's (Figures 9.21 and 9.22) representation of short vowel sounds using a letter-name strategy.

Using the *names* of letters, it is fairly easy to figure out what letter to use for the vowel sound in words like *play* (PLA), *fly* (FLI), *likes* (LIKS or LICS), *night* (NIT), *woke* (WOK), or *loose* (LUS). If, however, you had not yet been taught what letters represent the vowel sounds in words like *brings, found, dollar, bill, under, pulled,* and *snack,* how would you know what letter to use? The letter-name strategy causes children to make some very logical, albeit incorrect, guesses about how short vowel sounds are spelled. It is not until they become fairly facile at early reading, and have had a good deal of direct instruction in spelling and decoding short vowel words, that they begin to represent short vowels correctly.

To explain short vowel strategies we must return to the idea of the position of the mouth, tongue, teeth, and palate when pronouncing words. Each of the short vowel sounds is "made" in a particular position in the mouth, a position that is the same, or very nearly the same, as a long vowel sound. The trouble is, the two sounds don't go with the same written letter!

Let's say that, like Billy, you wanted to write *when* but didn't know the letter that went with the short vowel. Like Billy, you'd first write a *w,* then try for the vowel. Say *when* aloud, and concentrate on the *e* sound and on the parts of your mouth when you say it. Now try saying a vowel-letter name for that sound and choose one that has the same position. An adult would spell that *ĕ* sound with a letter *e,* but if you say "ehh . . . eeey . . . ehh . . . eeey" aloud you'll feel your jaw close and your tongue change position when you say "eeey," so it's unlikely that you, or Billy, or any other letter-name speller would guess that *e* goes in *when.*

How about *a?* Try it: "ehh . . . ay . . . ehh . . . ay. . . ." Your mouth moves very little, if at all! Since they're formed in the same place, *a* must stand for "ehh" or the short *e* sound in *when.* So, you'd likely choose WAN as Billy did for *when.*

Let's try the sound of *ĭ,* as in *brings.* Adults would spell it with an *i,* but say "ih . . . ah-ee . . . ih . . . ah-ee", gliding the "ah-ee" as you do when you say the letter-name *i.* Are they made in the same position? No, *i* is more open, whereas *ĭ* is rather closed and made at the front of your mouth. Likewise, "ih . . . ay . . . ih . . . ay" isn't a very good match, so it's unlikely you'd choose the letter *a* either. How about "ih . . . eee . . . ih . . . eee"? There's a match! Frank, and other letter-name spellers, would choose the letter *e* to represent the vowel sound of short *i* as in Frank's BREGS for *brings* and Billy's PELR (*pillow*) and BEL (*bill*).

The other short vowel positions and long vowel names match up in similar fashion: The short *u* sound in *pulled, put,* and *under* is made in the same position as the name of the letter *o,* so we have spellings like Billy's ONDR, POT, and POLD, as well as Jesse's WOD for *would* and RON for *run.* The vowel sound in *found,* which is glided, sounds like "ah" at the beginning, as does the sound of *o* in *dollar;* "ah" and "aw," variant pronunciations of *o* as in *dollar* and *dog,* are made in the same position as the name of the letter *i,* so we get DILR for *dollar* and FID for *found.*

What about short *a,* as in *snack?* Both *ă* and *ĕ* are made in nearly the same position, as you can feel if you say "man-men" in succession; both are very close to the letter-name *a,* and so letter-name spellers often choose *a* for *ă* as well as for ĕ, as in SNAK (*snack*) and WAN (*when*). The *a* in SNAK turns out to be a correct usage by adult standards, but it is the only case in which the letter-name substitution for a short vowel sound is correct!

The short vowel sounds are frequently substituted in these ways:

a for ă: BAT for *bat*, HAV for *have*

a for ĕ: BAT for *bet*, WAN for *when*

e for ĭ: BET for *bit*, BEL for *bill*

i for ŏ: HIT for *hot*, DILR for *dollar*

o for ŭ: BOT for *but*, POT for *put*

The vowel *u* can be used for the *oo* sound as in LUSTUTH or in PUL (*pool*), or it can be used as Jesse did in WUD (*would*).

The letter-name strategy takes its name from this characteristic use of vowel-letter names to represent short vowel sounds, but there are a few consonant letters that letter-name spellers also trip up on: *h*, *w*, and *y*. None of these letter names contains the sound the letter usually has, as *b* ("bee") or *d* ("dee") or *f* ("eff") do.

Look back now to Figure 9.17 and Nina's YWI for *wall*. Nina used the letter name *y* ("wy") for the sound adults would represent with a *w*. Likewise, look back at Figure 9.20, where Scott used YE for *we* and YD for *would*. Scott also used the name of the letter *y* for the sound we spell with *w*. Nina and Scott are primarily early phonemic spellers, but they both used one letter-name strategy in these samples. They will soon move more fully into the letter-name stage.

We recall a first grader who had carefully drawn an elephant and wanted to label it "Dumbo." "How do you spell Dumbo?" he demanded, and we encouraged him to give it a try: What did you hear at the beginning? Brow furrowed, he muttered "DUM-bo . . . DUM-bo. . . ." Then a triumphant grin lit his face as he cried "*Double*-you!" and proceeded to proudly label his elephant WBO, an example of the stunning logic behind letter-name spellings.

In summary, letter-name spelling (summarized in Box 9.7) shows us how active a role children's inventive processes play in their learning to spell. All children will show a tendency to use letter-name spelling when they get to that point of development — if they can be persuaded to write down words they don't know how to spell. Thus it appears that for them to learn to spell correctly is not just a matter of learning new words from scratch but to test the words against the intuitive concepts of spelling structure they have already devised and gradually amend these concepts to bring them into line with the spelling structures of the words they see around them. The changes their spelling strategies go through as they revise their concepts to incorporate more and more features are the bases for the next two spelling stages, transitional and derivational (see Box 9.7).

BOX 9.7
Characteristics of Letter-Name Spelling

Letter-name spelling:

Shows children's firm awareness that letters represent sounds, so the letters they use stand for sounds with no silent letters included.

Is still incomplete: Some sounds clearly evident in words are systematically omitted, such as *m*'s and *n*'s before consonants, vowels in unstressed syllables, and many short vowels until late in this stage; however, more sound features are represented than in earlier spelling stages.

Uses the *names* of letters to represent sounds in words as well as the *sounds* of letters.

Is often characterized by: long vowels used appropriately, but unmarked (as with a silent *e*); short vowels predictably substituted by using vowel-letter names or omitted altogether; verb tense and plural endings spelled as they sound: *t, d,* and *id*; *s, z,* and *iz*; use of *jr, gr,* and *chr* for sounds adults spell with *er-* and *dr-*.

Is typical of beginning readers, who can read a little but are not yet fluent. Most first and many second graders fall into this group.

Transitional Spelling. Transitional spellings represent a turning away from invention strategies and incorporating more features of standard spelling. As children become more fluent readers, the decoding and spelling rules they have been taught begin to make sense and are used more reliably. Hence, transitional spellings look more complete and often more adultlike than those of previous stages.

The transitional stage coincides with the advancement from beginning reader to independent reader and depends in large part on continued contact with print. Many children move into transitional spelling, and its reflection of advancing word knowledge, in late first or second grade, with less able readers moving into it later in the elementary grades. This stage is a persistent one because it involves testing hypotheses and rules, experimenting and learning rule exceptions, and figuring out spelling regularities. Transitional strategies may persist for several grades and are not unusual in poor readers in middle school or above.

Figures 9.24 through 9.27 are examples of transitional spelling, all produced by first graders. The three children who wrote these four compositions all differ in their spelling skills and word knowledge, but all show a degree of orthographic awareness that letter-name spellers lack.

One characteristic of transitional spellers is that they mark patterns for vowel sounds, especially the common final *e* marker. Letter-name spellers, you may recall, are most apt to use an unmarked vowel letter to represent its long (or tense) sound and to represent short (or lax) vowel sounds by using the vowel-letter name that is closest in point of articulation to the desired vowel

Figure 9.24 Mosby, first grade, transitional speller

eohs Thsr was d mrshin and a man
(came) (space)
Jdm to spdse and the mrshin dad a spdes
(star)
gun and blew-up a stare. and the man blew-
up the mrshin that was the ond
of the mrshin.

"Once there was a Martian and a man came to space and the Martian had a space gun and blew up a star and the man blew up the Martian that was the end of the Martian."

Figure 9.25   Mosby, first grade, transitional speller

"Once there was a little train. It was going to Minnesota with lots of toys for girls and boys. One day they ran out of coal so they had to get out. Another train was coming. They said can we borrow the coal. Yes! said the other train. And the trains went down the track."

sound. Transitional spellers, moving toward mastery of the range of vowel sounds, are aware of such rules for marking vowels as the "silent final *e* rule." They begin using markers in their spellings, although often inappropriately.

In Figures 9.24 and 9.25, Mosby experimented with marking with a final *e*. He omitted the marker in some long vowel words like CAM (*came*) and TRAN (*train*) but showed his growing awareness of marking in SPASE and SPAES (*space*), STARE (*star*), and BRWROE (*borrow*). Likewise, Amy (Figure 9.26) applied a final

Figure 9.26 Amy, first grade, transitional speller

AmyM.

Amy McDowell

One day I had some floere frends
and some sum frend. and I likd
them and thay likd me too.

Make a vest.
If you want to make a vest, you hare
to get some meatium-size
buttens and then some neadles
a id threds and then some
light Mateerial for the back
Make sure it is white mateea
and Make sure that the ves
is brown or tan then start
Soing. Make sure it has
no arms eather. Moke sure it
has three buttens then you hare
a rest to wear.
You will Know how to make a vest

Josiah

e to FLOERE (*flower*), and Josiah (Figure 9.27) used a vowel pair to mark long vowel sounds in MEATIUM (*medium*), NEADLES (*needles*), EATHER (*either*), and MATEERIAL (*material*).

Transitional spellers generally represent short vowel sounds fairly accurately, since they have largely abandoned the letter-name strategy that results in short vowel substitutions. They concentrate on the sounds rather than the names of letters, which results in some readable, albeit incorrect, spellings for words with short vowel sounds, such as THER (*there*), UTHR (*other*), SED (*said*), CUMING (*coming*), HAED (*had*), BUTTENS (*buttons*), and THREDS (*threads*). Mosby's MINTUSOUDU (*Minnesota*) is an interesting example of a transitional speller's attempt to sound out an unfamiliar word with short vowel sounds.

Transitional spellers may also render plural and past tense endings phonetically. In English, there are three different pronunciations for the -*ed* ending:

/t/ as in *picked* and *shopped*

/d/ as in *planned* and *sewed*

/əd/ as in *traded* and *painted*

Adults, who know that these three pronunciations are all spelled the same way, would use -*ed* in each case. Letter-name and transitional spellers, however, depend heavily on how words are pronounced, so they would likely use a *t* at the end of *picked* (PIKT), a *d* at the end of *planned* (PLAND), and *d* with a vowel at the end of *traded* (TRADID).

Likewise, adults use -*s* and -*es* on present tense verbs (*runs, washes*) and plural nouns (*birds, glasses*) although there are several pronunciations for these endings:

/z/ as in *birds* and *runs*

/s/ as in *cats* and *likes*

/əz/ as in *glasses* and *washes*

Letter-name and some transitional spellers are apt to spell these just as they sound: BERDZ or BERZ, LIKS or LICS, GLASEZ or GLASIZ.

Mosby, Amy, and Josiah negotiated these patterns fairly successfully. Amy is still in the process of mastering these regularities: Note her use of the -*ed* ending in HAED (*had*) and her omission of the *e* in LIKD (*liked*). Mosby and Amy appropriately used an *s* in forming plurals, but their spellings of TOWEE'S (*toys*), GRAL'S (*girls*), BOY'S (*boys*; note Mosby's reversed *b*), TRAN'S (*trains*), and FREND'S (*friends*) reveal their beginning awareness of apostrophes. Mosby and Amy need continued exposure to print before they can sort out the differences between plurals and possessives.

Transitional spellers, especially those in primary grades, may temporarily trip up over sounds that are spelled in different ways, like the sound at the beginning of *coal* and the end of *track*. Mosby spelled that sound correctly in *track*, but using the same letters created an error in CKOLL (*coal*). This is a good example of how it happens that transitional spellers, who may know quite a bit about spelling patterns, can make errors *because* of their knowledge. It is important for them to experiment and try out their spelling hunches without penalty, even though their hunches may turn out to be wrong.

Another feature, which adults often find very confusing, is the way letter-name and transitional spellers may represent the sounds we would spell with *tr-* and *dr-*. In reading instruction, we usually don't introduce these and similar letter pairs, which we call *blends* (*tr*, *dr*, and other consonant groups that are pronounced in rapid succession), until well after single letter sounds have been taught, often late in first grade or in second. But long before this instruction occurs, children find they need to write words with these sounds. A letter-name or transitional speller can solve this problem in some fascinating ways.

The sounds we spell with *tr* and *dr* actually sound quite a bit like the sounds we also represent with *j*, *g* (as in *gerbil*), and *ch*. Say these word pairs aloud and see if you can actually hear much difference in the beginning sounds: *drain–jrain, train–chrain*. There are subtle but unimportant *sound* differences; as adults we know, however, that English words don't begin with letter combinations like *jr*, *chr*, or *gr* when the *g* is pronounced like *j*. Letter-name or transitional spellers often don't know these conventions yet, so they may use GR, JR, and CHR to spell these sounds.

When they attempt to spell two-syllable words, the problem of marking pronunciation arises all over again. When, for example, we add *-ing* to *sit*, the *i* in *-ing* acts as a silent marker letter that makes the *i* in *sit* long: *siting*. We don't intend for this lengthening of the first *i* to occur, so in order to prevent it we must "insulate" the first *i* from the lengthening effect of the second. We do this by doubling the final consonant: *sitting*. Children who have learned the rules for spelling single-syllable words must revise those rules when it comes to spelling words of more than one syllable. Such revision extends the transitional stage somewhat, as children who have mastered spelling one-syllable words may go through a period of confusion and relearning when they attempt polysyllabic words. The characteristics of transitional spelling are summarized in Box 9.8.

Derivational Spelling. This stage represents the last developmental plateau before the achievement of largely correct, fluent spelling. Spellers in the derivational stage (Henderson, 1984) have mastered the sometimes confusing phonemic system of English spelling; they have learned and can use spelling rules involving marking of vowels, consonant doubling, and adding of inflections and affixes to many words.

What is still lacking is a working knowledge of how spelling may reflect historical and meaning relations among words that are derived from the same base words, which is an advanced form of word knowledge: Words are viewed not as individual entities but as members of related families and networks. At the derivational stage words cannot be spelled by using phonemic or sound-

BOX 9.8
Characteristics of Transitional Spelling

Transitional spelling:

Is nearly complete; all phonemes are represented, long and short vowel sounds are generally spelled correctly or typically: HED (head).

Shows an awareness of marking systems such as silent letters and consonant doubling but uses markers inappropriately: RUNING (*running*), MAKKING (*making*), DUCKE (*duck*).

Is largely readable by others.

May show several different attempts at the same word, sometimes abandoning a correct for an incorrect spelling.

Shows an awareness of inflectional endings, but words are often spelled phonemically: PICKT (*picked*), WANTID (*wanted*).

Is typical of young pupils beyond the beginning reading stage and older ones who are still unfluent readers.

based spelling patterns; the speller must also consider what the word means, how it relates to other words in the same family, even from what language it was derived. It is a stage of mastering spelling intricacies, one many older students and adults never fully complete.

To successfully negotiate the derivational stage, students need wide, rich exposure to written language that is complex, precise, and challenging in vocabulary and usage. In addition, they have to actively and directly explore how different forms of words relate to each other, they have to know how words enter our language from other languages and how history changes them, and they have to compose frequently and critically.

Derivational spellers typically have difficulty recognizing that spelling patterns persist across different forms of the same word, regardless of changes in pronunciation from one form to another. Some examples are SAIL–SALER or SALOR, BOMB–BOMMER, SINE–SIGNAL. In many words, vowel sounds that are clearly heard in one form may reduce to schwas in related forms, yet the spelling of the vowels remains the same in both forms, as in *final* and *finality*, *legal* and *legality*, *define* and *definition*, *desperate* and *desperation*. Derivational spellers, largely unaware of how these relationships are preserved by spelling, may produce errors like FINLE–FINALITY, LEGLE–LIGALITY, DEFINE–DEFENITION, or DESPERITE–DESPERATION.

In addition, they may confuse the spellings of affixes or morphemes that remain constant in different words, like *bio-, -graph, -phone* and *circum-*. Thus they may use the form correctly in one word and incorrectly in another, as in BIOLOGY–BIAPSY, TELEPHONE–SYMFONY, or PHOTOGRAPHY–BIBLIOGRAFY. The characteristics of the derivational stage are summarized in Box 9.9, and Figure 9.28 shows a spelling test of a ninth grader in this stage. Paul is a good speller; he has successfully negotiated transitional spelling and can correctly spell adult words. His difficulty with *wreckage, patient,* and *prosperity* are attributed to treating these words as unrelated to derived forms like *wreck* and *prosper*.

BOX 9.9
Characteristics of Derivational Spelling

Derivational spelling:

Shows mastery of most of the phonemic and rule-governed spelling patterns, such as vowel marking and consonant doubling, that trip up transitional spellers.

Shows lack of awareness of relational patterns among words derived from the same source.

Is typical of older students and adults who have not read widely, written copiously, and studied word derivations directly.

Figure 9.28 Paul, ninth grade, derivational spelling

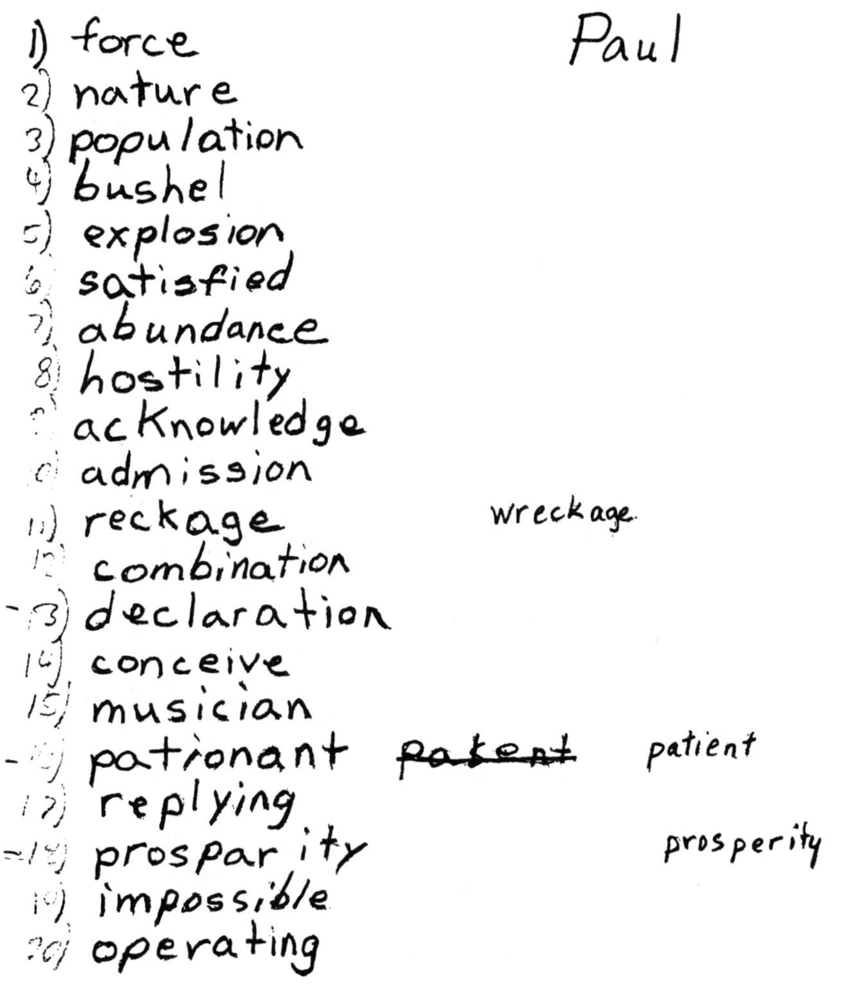

Paul

1) force
2) nature
3) population
4) bushel
5) explosion
6) satisfied
7) abundance
8) hostility
9) acKnowledge
10) admission
11) reckage   wreckage
12) combination
13) declaration
14) conceive
15) musician
16) pationant   ~~patent~~   patient
17) replying
18) prosparity   prosperity
19) impossible
20) operating

Implications for Teaching Spelling

The research cited in the foregoing discussions has overturned some of our long-held, cherished beliefs about how children learn to spell. From this body of work we can draw these conclusions:

1. Learning to spell is a developmental and conceptual process.
2. Children's strategies for spelling unfamiliar words change as their knowledge base and experience with print grows.
3. Their spelling errors reflect the attainment of successive developmental stages.
4. Such stages, as well as the development of word knowledge, can be determined by studying their spelling errors.
5. The development of spelling strategies is characterized by extensive exploration, invention, and trying out hypotheses.

From these conclusions we can see that learning to spell correctly is a process that is integrally linked with experience and experimentation and that it requires a good deal of time, learning, and maturation to become a competent, confident speller.

Development in any area takes time — to learn to talk, to read, to perform complex motor acts, and to master correct orthography. Development also means that there will be many attempts, and many failures, before mastery is achieved and that failures and errors are a necessary part of learning. How can we support and encourage our students as they make the journey toward correct spelling?

One of the best ways is to *allow children at all levels to do a great deal of writing, while accepting their "best guesses" for words they don't know how to spell.* The combination of a wealth of writing experience and acceptance of invented spellings has been recommended widely (Beers, Beers, and Grant, 1977; Bissex, 1980; Chomsky, 1971a and b,; 1979; Cramer, 1976; Forester, 1980; Gentry and Henderson, 1978; Lancaster, Nelson, and Morris, 1982; Temple, Nathan, and Burris, 1982; and others). Developing spellers need to be immersed in a learning environment in which they are constantly exposed to print through books, labels, experience charts, and other written language while simultaneously producing their own approximations of standard spellings. In this way they can continually compare their own inventions to standard adult spellings, which helps them grow toward correct spelling by successive approximations.

Young spellers' attempts at unfamiliar words deserve *reinforcement and reward,* with correct or logical aspects of their invented spellings pointed out directly (Gentry and Henderson, 1978; Lancaster, Nelson, and Morris, 1982; and others). For example, Elaine, a first-grade transitional speller, wrote about her pet: I CAN DRCK WOTTRE. ("It can drink water.") Elaine's teacher reinforced and rewarded her attempts by saying:

"You did a good job of trying to spell *drink* and *water*. In *drink* you've put in both the beginning and ending sounds, and in lots of words the /k/ sound is spelled with *ck*. *Drink* has an *i* and an *n* in it; see, D-R-I-N-K. You've made an especially good try on *water*; you've put in letters for all the sounds, and your spelling is very close. Here's how *water* is written: W-A-T-E-R."

Elaine's teacher sincerely praised her attempts, modeled correct spelling, and allowed her to contrast her inventions with a standard, without negative comments.

Encouraging children to create a "best-guess" invented spelling when they are stuck is also a helpful procedure. When children ask, "How do you spell _____?" don't be too quick to spell the word for them, and try to avoid the temptation of giving a quickie spelling lesson at every such request. Sometimes it's best to give the spelling — when they are deeply involved in composing and you don't want to sidetrack that self-expression or when they are checking rough drafts for revision — but if you provide spellings routinely, they will begin to depend on you, instead of on themselves, for correct spellings, and they will begin to infer that they are incapable of making a good try.

Encourage youngsters to attempt spellings by saying the word over to themselves, trying to segment the phonemes and put down a letter for the first sound, then the next, and so on. Very young or very unfluent spellers may be able to represent only the first sound; remember, this is a characteristic of early spelling development. Encourage them to put down a letter for that sound and draw a line for the rest of the word: *d* _____ (*dog*). This will reinforce the idea that there is more to the word than one letter. Praise attempts rather than shortcomings.

Sometimes teachers are uncomfortable with the proposition that they should accept spelling errors or say something positive to a child about what is so obviously an error. A teacher once told us, "My job is to *prevent* children from being wrong, not to *encourage* it." These feelings are understandable, but is the teacher's role really to "prevent errors"? Can learning take place without mistakes? Do children ever learn to do anything without first trying and failing? The answer is, of course not. Children themselves don't expect to be able to do things perfectly the first time; they spend their whole childhood practicing and working toward mastery of everything they do. Only adults seem to believe that doing something imperfectly the first time is a bad thing! It is only when we place a high premium on correctness, and treat the imperfect attempt as something to be avoided at all costs, that children lose their willingness to take the risk of being wrong. In spelling, this attitude has a number of very unfortunate results. They can be seen in fearful students who can write only if the teacher tells them how to spell every word and in the constricted, unexpressive writing of students who use only words they are sure of. Gentry and Henderson (1978) put it well:

1. Encourage creative writing.
2. De-emphasize standard spelling.
3. Learn to respond appropriately to nonstandard spelling. (p. 637)

In the next section we will explore various methods of teaching spelling.

Teaching Spelling

As we have seen from the foregoing discussions, learning to spell is built on a process of discovery and experimentation with print. Discovery and experimentation do not exist in a vacuum, however; it is often systematic teaching that plants the seed of inquiry, and only an active classroom environment can nurture it. Effective spelling instruction has two fundamental goals: (a) to teach children a body of words they can spell correctly without hesitation and (b) to encourage exploration of and reflection on patterns in spelling at all levels with systematic word study and plentiful writing.

Effective spelling instruction begins with matching what the students know to what is to be presented, which entails assessing what they know.

Assessing Grade Level Placement: The Informal Spelling Inventory

Commercial spelling series are designed to teach children up to several hundred words a year. Words are selected for various levels in order of difficulty, with the lower levels focusing on words that are common and have predictable spelling patterns. The upper levels contain less common words and more variant or unpredictable patterns. Implicit in the series concept is the assumption that all children in one grade will be appropriately challenged by learning the selected words. This concept, however, is as false as the expectation that all children in one grade could comfortably read from the same basal reader. They must be placed in appropriate spelling materials, regardless of their age or grade.

You can determine what level of spelling book any student should work in by using a simple, teacher-made test called an *informal spelling inventory*. (The procedures for teaching children who are placed in different spelling levels are given later in this chapter.) Here are the steps in compiling and using an informal spelling inventory:

1. Get a copy of the spelling book for your grade and also those for the preceding two grades and succeeding two grades (up to five levels).
2. Construct a list for each level of randomly selected words; twenty words is fine for first and second grades, twenty-five words each for levels above second.
3. Begin administration with the lowest level list you have. Spread out administration over several days, giving only one list at a time. All students should be tested on the lowest list.
4. When giving the test read each word once, clearly but without exaggerated pronunciation. Allow sufficient time for the pupils to write the word or attempt it. They should make a guess if they are unsure and draw a line if they have no idea.

5. Pass out a duplicated list so they can check their own work; spot-check their accuracy.
6. All pupils scoring better than 70 percent should be given the next list.

The instructional level for spelling is a score between 55 and 70 percent correct (Stauffer, 1975). At that level a child has many words to learn but will encounter a reassuring number of already mastered words. Continue testing upward until each youngster's instructional level has been determined. Those scoring below 55 percent on the lowest list can be given lists from still lower levels, if available, or simply begin the first-grade book. First graders scoring below 55 percent on the first-grade level should probably not begin formal spelling instruction for a few months but work instead on developing a basic sight vocabulary, learning to spell some of their sight words, and playing at writing.

The informal spelling inventory yields *quantitative* information about what level of commercial spelling book would be appropriate for instruction. It does not tell you what stage of spelling development a child has reached. Let's say, for example, that on one level the target word was *nature,* and five pupils spelled it incorrectly in the following ways:

Betty	*Arnold*	*Kim*	*Lauren*	*Doug*
BZRLD	NR	NAHR	NACHER	NATIOR

Quantitatively, all five pupils got one word wrong, but *qualitatively,* each used a different strategy and is in a different developmental stage. Betty's spelling is prephonemic, with no sound relation between *nature* and the letters she used. Arnold, representing two sounds, is an early phonemic speller. Kim represented all the salient sounds and used a letter name, "aitch," for the medial sound. Lauren used conventional spelling patterns such as *ch* and *er*; she is a transitional speller. Doug's spelling is derivational, showing an awareness of derivational patterns such as the pattern and sound in *nation.*

We can use *spelling features lists* to determine any child's developmental spelling stage, which will help us design appropriate activities to use once a child is instructionally placed in a spelling level.

Assessing Stages of Spelling Development: The Spelling Features Lists

Spelling features lists are collections of words that we expect children will *not* be able to spell correctly. To assess development we look at errors, not correct spellings, to see what strategies they use when they generate spellings on their own. We can analyze errors that occur in free composition, but this has two drawbacks. One is that many children try to avoid using words in compositions if they are unsure of the spellings. The other is that if they have been taught to write freely without overattending to spelling in first drafts, they may misspell words they really know. Administering a list of unfamiliar words, with proper encouragement, gets us around both of these problems. Tables 9.1 and 9.2 contain suggested lists; the first is for students aged five, six, or seven, and the second for pupils over seven. Lists can be administered to whole classes or smaller groups, with younger children attempting the words in two sittings. All students should be told beforehand that these are *new* words not studied before, that not knowing some (or even all the words) is expected, and that it is their *attempts* you are interested in. Papers are not scored; instead you should analyze each pupil's attempts for strategies that represent an overall developmental level.

Table 9.1 Beginners' features list (five-, six-, and seven-year-olds)

Part I: One session[a]

Fish	I caught a fish.
Bend	Can you bend your arm?
Jumped	I jumped over a log.
Yell	We can yell all we want outside.
Learned	I learned to count in school.
Shove	Don't shove your neighbor in the lunch line.
Witch	Hansel and Gretel met a witch.
Piece	I want a piece of cake.

Part II: Another session

Late	I stayed up late.
Bench	We sat down on a bench.
Drive	I'm too young to drive a car.
Wet	Your hair is all wet.
Chirped	The cricket chirped in the yard last night.
Neck	She wore a gold chain around her neck.
Trained	I trained my dog to shake hands.
Tick	There was a tick on my dog.

May be given at one sitting if the children don't tire too quickly.

NOTE: Repeat each word two to three times, but don't exaggerate its pronunciation.

Table 9.2 Advanced features list (seven- to eleven-year-olds)

Setter	My dog is an Irish setter.
Shove	Don't shove your neighbor in the lunch line.
Grocery	I'm going to the grocery store.
Button	A button popped off his jacket.
Sailor	My cousin is a sailor.
Prison	If you break the law, you may go to prison.
Nature	We went for a hike on the nature trail.
Peeked	The spy peeked out from his hiding place.
Special	Birthdays are special days.
Preacher	The preacher talked for an hour.
Slowed	The truck slowed down for the curve.
Sail	The boat had a torn sail.
Feature	We went to see a double feature.
Batter	The first batter struck out.

Classifying the Errors. Do not analyze correct spellings. If a child gets more than half of the beginners' list correct, administer the advanced list. Use these guidelines for assigning each misspelling to a category:

1. *Prephonemic.* Consider a spelling prephonemic if there is no evidence that any of the letters in the spelling stand for any of the phonemes in the test word. Assign each prephonemic spelling a 1.

Examples: DLD for *once,* RZF for *witch*

2. *Early Phonemic.* Consider a spelling early phonemic if salient phonemes in the test word are omitted (but not *n*'s or *m*'s before consonants, nor vowels before *m, n, r,* or *l* in unstressed syllables; these are omissions associated with the following letter-name stage of spelling). Assign each early phonemic spelling a 2.

Examples: ND for *wind,* JD for *jumped,* HD for *shed*

3. *Letter Name.* Consider a spelling letter-name if most of the phonemes in the test word are represented on the basis of a similarity between the phonemes and the sound of the letter name. Silent letters are omitted, as are *n* and *m* before consonants and vowels in unstressed syllables ending in *n, m, l,* or *r.* Short vowels are often spelled by the closest long vowel-letter name: *i* for *ŏ, e* for *ĭ, a* for *ĕ.* Long vowels will be spelled without markers. Assign each letter-name spelling a 3.

Examples: HEK for *chick,* LRND for *learned,* PECT for *picked*

4. *Transitional.* Consider a spelling transitional if short vowels and digraphs (*ch, sh, th*) are spelled correctly and if the letters *y, w, c* ("soft sound"), and *g* ("soft sound") have their conventional spellings. Silent letters can be present but incorrectly used. Consonant blends such as *tr* and *dr* can be spelled CHR and JR, respectively. The /sh/ or /ch/ sounds in *nature, grocery,* and *special* can be spelled CH, SH, and SH, respectively. Past tense endings will be spelled incorrectly, just as they sound. Consonant doubling may be omitted in two-syllable words. Assign each transitional spelling a 4.

Examples: LURND for *learned,* GROSHRY for *grocery,* CHRAEND for *trained,* BUTUN for *button*

5. *Derivational.* Consider spellings deviational if the /ch/ or /sh/ sounds in *grocery, special, preacher,* or *feature* are spelled with *ti, si, ci, sy,* or *ty* but not with *ch* or *sh.* Consider spellings derivational if the stems in *sail* and *sailor* are spelled the same way. *Prison* may be spelled PRISION. Assign each derivational spelling a 5.

Examples: SAILER for *sailor,* NATIUR for *nature,* SPETIAL for *special.*

After some practice with these guidelines, you will have little difficulty assigning each misspelling to a category. If you get completely stuck on a word, discount it and concentrate on the others.

For each child, determine which category has the most examples. If there are large accumulations of errors in other categories, these too can be revealing. Spelling development is unidirectional. It moves from prephonemic to early phonemic to letter name, and so on, not the other way around. Thus if students have 50 percent of their errors in the transitional category and 30 percent in the letter-name category, it is an indication that they have recently moved into the transitional stage, with vestiges of the earlier letter-name strategies remaining. If they have 60 percent in the transitional and 30 percent in the derivational stage, this suggests that they are moving beyond transitional spelling and into the derivational stage.

If a youngster gets more than half of the advanced list correct, or has more unclassifiable errors than classifiable ones on either list, the *error log* will be more useful than the features list analysis.

The Spelling Error Log. An error log is a collection of spelling errors maintained over an extended period of time. Errors can be collected from many sources, not just spelling work: tests, worksheets and workbook pages, creative writing (later, not early, drafts), journals, and other assignments.

Collect spelling errors for a two- or three-week period, until you have ten to twenty-five errors. Then analyze them as in the foregoing procedure, assigning each misspelling to a category and determining what stage is most representative of the errors overall.

Teaching Spelling Word Lists

Research conducted by Thomas Horn (1969) has suggested that the most successful method of teaching spelling is the test-retest method. Traditionally, the method consists of a pretest on Monday, after which the students check their own papers. The words they missed are written on a list for special study and studied on Tuesday. Wednesday they are tested again on all the words. Those who get all the words right on the Wednesday test are exempted from further testing. The others restudy the words they missed and on Friday have a posttest covering all the words.

This method is useful because it focuses children's attention on the words they need to study rather than on those they already know, and it leads to concentrated effort through repeated testing. Its drawback is that it places an uneven burden on the class. If the same list is administered to all the students, then some will know almost none of the words the first time around and some will already know most of them. Therefore, an individualized approach is better. Stauffer (1975) adapted the test-retest model to cover children with any number of different spelling levels simultaneously. You first ascertain the spelling instructional level of each child by means of the informal spelling inventory. Stauffer suggested that formal teaching of spelling lists be held off until October of the second grade because (a) it gives the children the first-grade year in which to explore the relationship between language and print without pressure for achievement or correctness and (b) allows time at the beginning of the second grade year for the teacher to determine the instructional spelling level for each child.

Once the spelling level has been determined (see procedures in the previous section), you should obtain a year's list of spelling words for each spelling level. If you are using a commercial spelling series, then simply procure books that correspond to the instructional level indicated in the informal spelling inventory. If you constructed the inventory yourself, the matching of spelling level with textbook will be automatic.

After you have determined the range of spelling instructional levels in your class, create spelling instructional groups by grouping together children whose levels are the same or very close (much as you do in forming reading groups). Three or four groups in a classroom is typical. With the children assigned to spelling level groups, and an entire year's list of words available for each group, you are ready to begin individualized instruction.

The teaching plan is based on a weekly schedule. On Monday, read the word lists and have the children write the words; on Wednesday, read the list again, and on Friday, read it a final time. At each administration, however, you should read as many lists as there are spelling levels in the class. This works as follows: Each spelling level group is numbered one, two, three — as many numbers as there are groups. Let's say you have three groups. The first word you read is for the first group to spell, the second word for the second group, the third word for the third group, the fourth word for the first group again, the fifth word for the second group, and so on. Thus you read twenty words for each group, and since the children from one group are writing their word while the ones from the next group hear theirs, three or four lists can be read in only a little more time than it takes you to read a single list and pause for the children to write.

After you have called all the words, have the children correct their own papers against a duplicated list of correct words and tell them to place a check mark by each incorrectly spelled word they find. As in the informal spelling inventory, you should move among the children to check the accuracy of their correcting. If you find that one has missed an error, say so, but don't identify the missed word. Thus the child must compare his or her paper against the correct list, only this time more carefully. Write the number of misspelled words at the top of the page.

Immediately following the spelling test, have all the children study the words they misspelled. Stauffer recommended this technique for aiding memorization:

1. Study the correct order of the letters in the word, repeating the spelling to yourself over and over.
2. Close your eyes and picture the word in your mind as you repeat the spelling to yourself.
3. Open your eyes and look at the word again, repeating the order of the letters to yourself.

4. Cover up both the misspelled word and the correction and write the word from memory beside the two.

5. Finally, check to see if you have spelled the word correctly in step 4. If so, proceed to the next misspelled word on the list and study its correct form the same way. If not, restudy the word by repeating these five steps.

As Stauffer notes, "In the beginning, this is time-consuming, but it is worth every second of it. In a month or so the children will have caught on so well that everything will proceed easily and efficiently" (1975, p. 214).

The entire batch of lists is read again on Wednesday, and each group spells all the words on that group's list. The children who misspell any words on this second testing study those words as before. They will be tested again on their entire list on Friday. Those who got all the words right on Wednesday are exempted from Friday's test.

Being allowed to skip the test on Friday and read or draw instead is looked at as a special privilege, and it is a motivation for children to study especially hard at the beginning of the week. One advantage of Stauffer's multiple list method is that all the children are working on a spelling list that pretesting has shown to be on their level, and so they all have a roughly equal chance to master the entire list by Wednesday.

Stauffer suggested further steps to challenge abler spellers and keep from frustrating less able ones. For the more able spellers, longer lists can be administered — twenty-five to thirty words. Also, they can be given a new list of words on Friday if they consistently score 100 percent on Wednesday's test. Either way they move through more than a year's spelling level in the course of the school year.

For less able spellers, the number of words on the test can be reduced so that no child has more than three misspelled words to study at one time. Reducing the number to only ten or fifteen per week may help to keep the children succeeding and moving ahead rather than failing, becoming frustrated, and making little forward progress at all.

Teaching Spelling Concepts

When children are placed at their appropriate level, their spelling ability will be enhanced by integrating *spelling concepts* into the teaching of spelling lists. At their different developmental spelling stages they need instruction based on concepts they already have and those they need to acquire. In a typical first grade they will likely be functioning from prephonemic through transitional strategies; a typical fourth grade will probably have one or two early phonemic spellers, some letter-name spellers, and a large number of transitional and derivational spellers. Each group needs to acquire different concepts and take part in different activities to maximize their spelling potential.

Prephonemic Spellers. Look back at Figures 9.15 and 9.16. These spellings are prephonemic because the letters used do not represent the sounds in the words. These spellings show us that although these youngsters have not yet discovered the alphabetic principle, they do know a good deal about print: They use only letters, arrange them in wordlike configurations, and demonstrate both generativity (the use of different marks) and linearity (horizontal lines).

Their writing is typical of many preschoolers and those in early primary grades, although youngsters who have had extensive experience with print and play writing may be over this stage by school entry. Kindergarteners and first graders who write like this need to explore print and note certain features of it that they can produce in their play writing. These features include these concepts:

1. Words are made up of letters, are bounded by spaces on either side, and are read left to right.
2. Similar-sounding words often contain the same letters.
3. Letters stand for sounds in words.

Activities that will help prephonemic spellers establish these concepts are:

1. Frequent reading to children, positioning the book so they can see the print, running a hand under the words being read. This should be done daily both at home and in school.
2. Labeling objects at home and in the classroom, naming the objects and pointing to the labels, and drawing attention to the initial sound and initial letter in words.
3. Creating displays of words and corresponding pictures from magazines, catalogues, and grocery labels. Also, encourage students to use these words in play writing and drawing.
4. Creating individual or group "word books" of words and pictures as above, reviewing the words and noting initial letter-sound correspondences as with labels.
5. Using dictated experience stories and voice pointing while reciting memorized text (see Chapter Five).

Early Phonemic Spellers. Look back at Figure 9-19, written by Kerrie, an early phonemic speller in kindergarten. Kerrie has discovered the alphabetic principle, and she uses letters to represent important sounds in words. As yet, her spellings are abbreviated, since she is still developing the *ability to segment phonemes* within words and the *concept of word*, the ability to separate spoken words in the stream of speech and keep them separate mentally while they are being spelled.

Early phonemic spellers need encouragement and support as they fully develop the following concepts:

1. Spoken and written words are separate units.
2. The spellings of some words can be memorized, such as one's own name.
3. Writing is communicative; both writer and reader can learn to read it.

The activities listed in the previous section for prephonemic spellers are still beneficial for early phonemic spellers, and the following activities are also helpful:

1. Play word games aloud, such as rhyming games, making up or orally completing simple rhymes and verses, and word games like "Pig Latin" — remember "ig-pay atin-Lay"? Such activities help children manipulate individual words mentally.

2. Continue daily reading, pointing now to individual words as you read them at a natural speaking rate.

3. Continue using dictated stories and choral reading of simple verses, primer stories, and the like but have the students practice voice pointing as they recite the memorized text. Here we are trying to reinforce the concept of the match between spoken and printed words.

4. Encourage them to memorize spellings of a few common, high-frequency words such as their own and friends' names, words they are especially interested in learning, and words they are learning to read as sight words. Recognizing a few words at sight and being confident of their spellings helps them master voice pointing and provides an important feeling of mastery at this early spelling stage.

5. Encourage them to develop a collection of "favorite words," and those they want to learn to read and spell, printing the words they ask for on small cards (Ashton-Warner, 1963). These words can be used in writing, sentence building, word games, and for making picture dictionaries.

6. Do word matching (Clay, 1981) by making a duplicate of dictated stories or single sentences, cutting one copy apart into lines, phrases, and single words and have the children reconstruct the whole by putting the parts in order. As this is mastered the original can be removed and only the parts used to re-create the whole.

7. Let them practice segmenting familiar printed words by cutting apart lines of words that are repeated without spaces:

JIMMYJIMMYJIMMYJIMMYJIMMYJIMMYJIMMYANNANNANNANNANNANN
ANNANN

Words used for this activity should be highly familiar, such as each other's names. They may need a model, so write the separated words on the board (Temple, Nathan, and Burris, 1982).

8. Encourage a great deal of writing; ask them to "read" what is written and transcribe what was read, as Brian's teacher did in Figure 9.18.

9. Be sure the classroom is rich in print; not just books but posted dictations, instructions, descriptions of class events, poems, and other materials that are periodically read to the children, referred to, and changed. Such displays reinforce the communicative importance of print.

Letter-Name Spellers. Look back at Figures 9.21, 9.22, and· 9.23. Letter-name spellers differ from early phonemic spellers only in that they have the ability to represent almost all of the sounds in words with letters. This new ability comes not from any great advancement in auditory discrimination but rather in the ability to make words hold still mentally while they analyze their sounds and find letter-name matches for them.

For letter-name spellers, we have four main goals toward which their spelling instruction should be directed:

1. They should learn to examine the spellings of words and derive concepts about their structure.
2. They should acquire specific concepts about the structure:
   a. common spellings for short vowels
   b. the highest frequency spellings for long vowels
   c. the spellings for high-frequency beginning consonant sounds
   d. the common structures of one-syllable words
3. They should continue to experience reading and writing as valuable means of receiving and expressing stories and ideas.
4. Their willingness to experiment with spellings should not be dampened by overemphasis on correctness.

Activities for spelling instruction should focus their attention on common, predictable patterns in written words and on nurturing their curiosity about words. Suggested activities include the following:

1. Help each child make a *word bank,* a collection of words recognized at sight, gathered from experience stories, trade books, labels and signs, easy basal readers, and similar sources (see Chapter Five). If one can read but not spell some of these words, they can be used as spelling words.

2. Word bank words can be used for *word sorts* in which children find and group together words with shared features, such as the same initial consonant sound, vowel pattern, or final sound. Provide two or three example words, pointing out the features in common, and refer to the examples as they search their word banks, locate words fitting the patterns, and place the word cards in a group (Gillet and Kita, 1979; Morris, 1982).

3. After words that fit the pattern have been selected, encourage them to describe orally how the words are similar: "They all start with the /b/ sound and the letter *b,*" for example. This procedure helps them to focus on the shared feature and learn to describe it accurately.

4. Words that go together should be listed together in an individual "key word book" or spelling dictionary, and new word groups should be added regularly.

5. During writing, use key word books or spelling dictionaries as sources of words or for looking up words the children want to use, thus giving them an introduction to looking up words in a standard dictionary.

6. They can take part in *word hunts* in which they search magazine and newspaper pages, trade books, and other materials for word bank words or for new words that fit a specified pattern. Word hunts help them learn to perceive patterns in new words and hold a pattern mentally while considering different words.

7. They should use one-syllable words from word banks and other sources to practice creating *word families* by segmenting the initial sound from the rest of the word, as in *s*-ail or *b*-ake, then substituting other initial sounds to create new words, like *sail–bail–fail–mail–nail* or *bake–cake–make–rake–sake–take*. This activity helps to improve their phonemic segmentation and ability to mentally manipulate words.

8. Letter-name spellers' invention of short vowel sounds should be accepted, but common short vowel (and long vowel) words of one syllable should be taught directly so that they will begin to contrast standard spellings with their intuitive hunches about these sounds.

9. When presenting patterns for direct teaching, as in 8 above, work first on regular patterns that occur most often in print: CVC (consonant–vowel–consonant) patterns with short vowels, like *hat–bed–sit–hot–mud*; CVCe (consonant–vowel–consonant–silent *e*) patterns with long vowels, like *make–hide–rope–rule*; CVVC (consonant–vowel–vowel–consonant) patterns with long vowels, like *sail–feet–boat–pool*. Patterns that occur less often, such as CVCe patterns of short vowels (*come, give, love, have*) and CVVC patterns with variant sounds (*veil, ruin*) should be introduced *after* common, predictable patterns have been well established.

10. Continue to emphasize daily writing activities. Encourage the students to use their word banks, key word books, bulletin board displays of words, picture dictionaries, and similar sources to find correct spellings of words they want to use. Also encourage them to use standard spellings for words directly taught and memorized, while at the same not deterring them from judiciously guessing the spellings for other words they want to write.

11. Begin to emphasize the creation of rough and final drafts in composition (see Chapter Seven), in which words are checked and standard spellings used whenever possible. Absolute correctness in final drafts is unreasonable to expect, but it is not too early for children to develop the habit of objectively examining their own work, choosing words they are uncertain of, and comparing their attempts to standard spellings.

Transitional Spellers. Bill, who produced the writing in Figure 9.29, is a transitional speller. He represented all the phonemes in the words he misspelled (GIT–*get*, WEN–*when*, SUM–*some*, DIGING–*digging*, PAD–*paid*, WORKT–*worked*, PROBBALY–*probably*, DUS–*does*, RAN–*rain*) with the exception of one misspelling: SIP–*skip*. He represented both long and short vowel sounds, used common short vowel patterns (SUM, DUS), represented inflectional endings (DIGING, WORKT), and had typical difficulty with consonant doubling rules (DIGING, PROBBALY).

Figure 9.29 Bill, transitional spelling

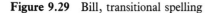

> Dere Bill
>
> Today is a sip day as we git out at 1:10 today.
> Wen I git home I am going to do sum work for a man
> down the street. I am diging trenches for him I git
> pad 3.50 an hour and I have workt for him for
> 10:00 hour and today I will probbaly work for about 3.00
> more today. If it dus not ran.

He is just entering the transitional stage and retains some letter-name spellings of long vowel sounds that he has not attempted to mark in any way (PAD, RAN). Bill is beyond the beginning reading stage, and the reading and spelling instruction he experienced has helped him figure out how to accurately represent consonant sounds, how short vowel patterns are most often spelled, and the correct spellings of many words. Now he is struggling to master more advanced spelling concepts like long vowel marking patterns, short vowel spellings that are irregular (as in *some* and *does*), consonant doubling rules, and inflectional endings.

Most children progress through transitional spelling by about the end of third grade, although many will continue to make transitional errors for some years. Some, however, become stalled at this point of development. Adolescent and adult poor spellers who still spell primarily by sounds in words generally are both poor readers and reluctant writers. Figure 9.29 is a good example of this, because Bill is a high school student.

Commercial spelling programs, with their systematic introduction of spelling patterns, selection of words fitting particular patterns, and review activities, do quite a good job of helping transitional spellers learn patterns. By the time they enter the transitional stage, students can read well enough and know enough about words to benefit from such systematic instruction.

Activities for transitional spellers should include the following (Henderson, 1984):

With early transitional spellers

1. Review initial consonant substitution in one-syllable words, dividing such words after the initial sound.

2. Review common initial consonant spellings, short vowel patterns, and most common long vowel patterns (CVCe and CVVC).
3. Introduce initial consonant blends and digraphs (*br, pl, st,* and so on and *th, ch, sh*).
4. Introduce words with *m* or *n* before other consonants, which letter-name spellers usually omit, such as *lamp, find,* and *stand.*
5. Introduce words ending in *-ve* (*move, have, shove, love*) and short vowel patterns with doubled final consonants (*fell, miss, well, pass, toss,* and so on).
6. Introduce standard spelling of the past tense (*-ed*) ending and contrast it with its pronunciation in different words (such as in *showed, hiked,* and *wanted*).

With later transitional spellers

1. Review the concepts listed above (3–6).
2. Introduce variant vowel patterns like *-ight, -aight,* and *-eigh.*
3. Introduce vowel dipthong (glided) patterns, as in *foil, trial,* and *south.*
4. Introduce *r*-controlled vowel patterns, as in *far, herd, forest, sir,* and *fur.*
5. Introduce rules for adding *-ing* and *-ed* to one-syllable words with long and short medial vowels, as in *get–getting, ride–riding, hop–hopping, hope–hoping* and *pad–padded, trade–traded.*
6. Introduce rules for adding *-er* and *-est,* as above: *late–later–latest, fat–fatter–fattest.*
7. Introduce compound words and how they are divided: *houseboat, baseball, rainbow.*
8. Introduce homonyms, words that sound alike but are different in meaning and spelling: *wait–weight, sale–sail, meet–meat.*
9. Introduce the meaning and spelling of common prefixes like *un-, sub-, pro-,* and *re-.*
10. Introduce patterns of plural endings and adjective and verb forms in one- and two-syllable words, including words requiring that letters be changed or added, as in *try–tried–tries* and *happy–happier.*

Most spelling series introduce, explain, and model patterns like these beginning at about the end of second grade or early in third, so the task of teaching such patterns is made easier by referring to appropriate lessons. What is taught in a spelling lesson, however, should also be consciously referred to in the reading and handwriting lessons. Transitional spellers can usually read fairly well and are able to recognize many words at sight, so they may not look carefully at the structure of words they are reading unless their attention is drawn to these patterns. Word sorts, word hunts, and discussions of the history of particular words will help foster their continued interest in and curiosity about word structures.

Derivational Spellers. Negotiating the derivational spelling stage requires that instruction focus on how groups of words are related to each other and how they derive from the same bases. At this point spelling instruction and vocabulary development must come together, as students learn to use word meanings to relate spellings, particularly with words in which pronunciation changes across forms, as in *prosper–prosperity* and *alternate–alternative*. Activities should include the following:

1. Explore the concept of *morphemes,* units of meaning that can stand alone or must be attached to other morphemes. *Free morphemes* can stand as single words: *cat, want, silly. Bound morphemes* must be attached to other morphemes, to which they contribute meaning: cat*s,* want*ed,* silli*ness.* Some free morphemes can be joined to others to form compound words: *campground, airport, baseball.* Some bound morphemes have clear historical roots, like the Latin forms *-graph, -phone, auto-* and *circum-.* Awareness of their meaning in words like *autograph, graphology, telephone, phonetics, automobile, autonomy,* and *circumnavigate* is a great aid to both spelling and vocabulary development.

2. Examine words for historical bases and word parts that occur in other words and work at relating meanings. Examples might include *si*gnature, *si*gnet and re*si*gnation, *demo*cracy and *demo*graphics, or photo*graph,* *graph*eme, and *graph*ic.

3. Examine words with common prefixes such as *re-, in-,* and so on, which are assimilated into the spellings of the morphemes they are attached to. *In-,* meaning "not," retains its spelling in words like *inoperable* and *insincere,* but before *b* or *p,* the *n* changes to *m*: *impossible, impatient, imbalance.* Before *r,* the *n* becomes another *r*: *irrelevant, irreverent, irrespective.* Similarly, *ad-,* "to or toward," is assimilated in words like *acclimate, affirm,* and *apprehend.*

4. Explore derived forms of nouns, adjectives, and verbs with the same base words and show how morphemes are added to indicate the word's grammatical function. Rules for using *-tion* or *-sion* and *-able* or *-ible* can be explored in words like *hesitate–hesitation, divide–division, break–breakable,* and *reverse–reversible.*

5. Explore the spelling of reduced vowels in derived forms by referring to different forms of the same word. Reduced vowels, which occur in unstressed syllables, cannot be spelled by simply listening to the word, since reduced vowels sound like schwas, but remembering how the vowel is spelled in a related form helps: irrit*a*te–irrit*a*ble, prosp*e*r–prosp*e*rity, inv*i*te–inv*i*tation, and so on.

As with spellers in previous stages, extended reading, word sorting, word hunts, and systematic discussion of word patterns and histories are most helpful to derivational spellers. Word sorting should focus on grouping together words with shared morphemes or base words. Derivational spellers should routinely use dictionaries, and a class set of a modern, readable, well-illustrated student dictionary is a must.

There are many good books available that will help your students to learn about the *etymology*, or historical sources, of words in interesting ways. You might find the following books useful:

Bickerton, Derek. *Roots of Language.* Ann Arbor, Mich: Karoma, 1981.

Bodmer, Frederick. *The Loom of Language.* New York: Norton, 1982.

Cohane, John P. *The Key.* New York: Crown, 1969.

Diamond, Arthur S. *History and Origin of Language.* Secaucus, N.J.: Citadel Press, 1965.

DiBlasi, Augustine. *Did You Know? Word Derivation Made Simple.* New York: William-Frederick Press, 1980.

Funk, Charles E. *Thereby Hangs a Tale: Hundreds of Stories of Curious Word Origins.* New York: Warner Paperback Library, 1972.

Gallant, Roy A. *Man Must Speak: The Story of Language.* New York: Random House, 1969.

Hogben, Lancelot. *The Mother Tongue.* New York: Norton, 1964.

Kelling, George W. *Language: Mirror, Tool and Weapon.* Chicago: Nelson-Hall, 1974.

Mitchell, Richard. *Less Than Words Can Say.* Boston: Little, Brown, 1979.

Pei, Mario. *The Families of Words.* New York: St. Martin's Press, 1962.

Revesz, Geza. *The Origins and Prehistory of Language.* Westport, Conn.: Greenwood Press, reprint of 1956 ed.

Train, John. *Remarkable Words: With Astonishing Origins.* New York: Crown, 1980.

Weekly, Ernest. *An Etymological Dictionary of Modern English.* New York: Dover, 1967.

———. *Something About Words.* Darby, Pa.: Arden Library, 1977.

Word Origins. Secaucus, N.J.: Lyle, Stuart, 1980.

Summary

A common belief about English spelling is that letters are used only to spell sounds in spoken words, but the twenty-six letters are used in a variety of ways to spell the forty-four phonemes in English. Some people believe spelling would be easier to learn if there were forty-four different letters, one for each sound, or if spelling were changed so that silent letters and the like were not used. These attempts to reform spelling have not been successful, because spelling reflects meaning relations among words as well as sounds in speech. Spelling patterns can be visual cues to word meanings and word relationships, and spelling reforms would remove these cues from print.

When children begin to write, before they know how to read or spell many words, they use letters to represent sounds in words. A large body of research shows that they systematically use strategies to invent spellings and that their inventions reveal what concepts they have about print, sounds, and letters. They seem to move through sequential stages of spelling development, stages represented by the typical strategies they use and the errors resulting from such strategies. Development from the earliest to the latest stage usually covers several years, from preschool or early primary grades to later elementary grades or beyond. The stages of spelling development are:

— *prephonemic:* Letters are used to create wordlike configurations, but there is no evidence of relationship between letters and sounds.
— *early phonemic:* The alphabetic principle of letter-sound correspondence is discovered and one or two letters are used to represent whole words, such as M or MR for *mother.*
— *letter name:* More, but not all, sounds in words are represented either by a letter's most common sound or by the letter's name, such as *h* for the beginning sound in *church.* Typically, many sounds are omitted and invented spellings are difficult to read.
— *transitional:* Typical spellings of most sounds are correctly represented and common spelling patterns begin to appear, but they are used incorrectly, as in DUCKE for *duck* and NACHER for *nature.* Conventional rules for marking vowels, doubling consonants, and so on are confused at this stage.
— *derivational:* Common patterns and conventions confused in transitional spelling are mastered, but words are considered separate entities rather than members of families. Thus knowing how to spell one form of a word, like *prosper,* does not help in spelling a derivation of the same word, like *prosperity,* which might be spelled PROSPARITY.

General guidelines for teaching spelling include encouraging a great deal of writing, reacting appropriately to invented spellings, reinforcing and rewarding correct or logical aspects of invented spellings, and inducing children to try to spell words themselves. Teachers should help them learn to correctly spell a body of words as well as fostering their curiosity and awareness of patterns and their willingness to experiment.

An informal spelling inventory of graded words can be made up to determine at what level a child should be placed in a commercial spelling series. A features list of unfamiliar words can be administered to help determine what developmental stage a youngster is presently in. An error log can be used instead of a features list.

Individualized instruction from spelling books can be accomplished by placing children in appropriate spelling levels based on difficulty and by using spelling groups like reading groups. A test-retest method can be employed even when all children are not working in the same level.

Concepts can be taught in conjunction with a commercial program by being aware of what stage each speller is currently in and what concepts are typical of that stage. Instruction should focus on introducing concepts required for progress to the next developmental stage.

CHAPTER TEN

The Language Arts Program

CHAPTER OUTLINE

Having discussed the "why" and the "how" of teaching talking and listening, reading and writing, grammar, handwriting, and spelling, it is now time to turn to a set of issues that is common to all of them.

In the present chapter we will make a case for integrating the language arts as you teach them. Though we have presented them separately for the sake of clarity in the preceding pages, experience and research suggest that children learn the language arts best when they are taught in combination with each other. We will make a case for combining the language arts first and then suggest ways they can efficiently be taught in combination.

This leads to the planning of lessons, which in turn raises the issue of involving students in the planning of their own activities. Evaluating the students' work as well as the on-going language arts program come next. Because the goal of language arts teaching is to help students to make more productive use of language, in this section we present a number of active alternatives to paper and pencil tests, which tell us much more about the students.

Language is used for communication, and communication requires both communicators and audience. Unless we take charge of the grouping of students in the classroom, the teacher is the only one who gets adequate practice using language! Ways of grouping students and managing the activities of groups is the next topic.

A language arts classroom needs more than teachers and students, so the next topic is the list of tape recorders, books, chart stands, games, costumes, and other devices that a language arts teacher should plan to have on hand. One resource that is finding its way into more and more classrooms is the microcomputer. This device offers so many challenges and possibilities that we discuss it in its own section. Many classes have additional human resources available, in the form of aides and parent volunteers. How to make the most of their help is the next topic.

Finally, how do you get better as a teacher year after year? Ways to grow as a teacher, to stay intellectually alive and to keep being nourished by work with the children, comprise the last topic in the book.

Integrating the Language Arts

The organization of the language arts curriculum often suggests that reading, composition, spelling, handwriting, grammar, listening, and speaking are separate subjects. When schools purchase a different set of materials for each subject and when "methods" courses emphasize conducting discrete lessons for each subject, the language arts become fragmented. It will be up to you to find ways to tie together the reading, speaking, listening, and writing your students do every day.

Throughout the preceding nine chapters we have shown again and again how the language arts support one another. The oral language development children experience before school entry and in the early primary grades forms the foundation for their use of language as readers and writers. The concepts about stories and the experience with book language they gain when they listen to you read to them help them remember and understand stories they read and enable them to write stories themselves. The writing they do in every grade helps them learn to organize their information and ideas and convey them precisely in oral and written form. Early attempts to spell unfamiliar words allow them to test their hypotheses about how letters and sounds work in words, which contributes to their word recognition abilities. Both reading and writing contribute in important ways to their vocabulary and grammatical development. Laboring over a composition to clarify meaning and choose just the right word, phrase, or image helps them to appreciate the beauty and power of good quality literature, as does wide exposure to prose and poetry through reading and listening. Each topic in language arts contributes to the others, for all are interrelated, and, to be most effective, instruction must preserve and foster this interrelatedness.

In addition, language arts and the other content subjects of the curriculum should be integrated. Language arts are communicative media. They are used to study and convey some other content; they have no real content of their own. Thus when you are planning for instruction in one of the elementary grades, think of opportunities for using language arts when you are formulating lessons in health, in science, or in social studies.

A useful way of conceptualizing the relationship between language arts and other subjects is to think in terms of *content* and *process goals*. Content goals refer to the matter, the facts, concepts, and principles the children should learn. Process goals refer to skills that they gain in the course of recording, investigating, summarizing, and communicating the matter they have studied.

Both content and process goals are important. While we want students to carry away the main concepts, generalizations, and pertinent facts of a social studies lesson, for example, we also want their experience in that lesson to teach them something about learning: about observing, recording, analyzing, reaching conclusions, and communicating them. In other words, we want them not just to learn the material but to become better learners and communicators.

Most of the process goals we are referring to are language arts concerns. Observing a spider spinning a web and finding words to describe its actions is a language activity. Recording observations of the spider and its web in a notebook over a period of days is a language activity. Comparing observations made by other students of other spiders in order to arrive at a general description of spider behavior is a language activity. Making an oral presentation to the class, making a poster, and writing a book on spider behavior are language activities. More than language arts is involved here. The students are learning to operate from the perspective of a scientist; they are using a certain kind of language that is factual rather than fanciful, objective rather than personal. The study of spiders would go nowhere, however, without language to communicate the findings, and the study of language arts would not be all it could be if children did not have interesting topics such as those provided by science and social studies and other day-to-day issues that stimulate them to use their language skills.

In the preceding nine chapters we have described general and specific activities for various aspects of language arts. Most of them are just as useful for content subjects. When you are teaching science, math, social studies, or other content subjects, you can integrate the language arts by including activities such as these in your content lessons:

Speaking

— listing ideas (brainstorming)
— classifying examples of a certain category
— comparing and contrasting ideas
— rank-ordering several ideas
— thinking of concrete examples of a generality
— innovating or improvising on a model
— planning a solution to a problem
— role-playing a situation
— finding a principle or generality in a body of data
— interviewing a resource person
— taking part in a panel discussion
— presenting findings of a study to a group or to the whole class

Listening

— listening to stories, poems, and songs about other places, cultures, and times
— listening for ways a classmate can improve a paper he or she has written
— listening to a guest speaker, demonstration, film, skit, or oral report
— listening to a debate or to divergent points of view
— interviewing others

Reading

— reading for information in a book, magazine, newspaper, reference book, or other writing
— reading correspondence from people to whom letters have been written
— reading what you yourself and other students have written
— reading summaries, reviews, synopses, or abstracts to get an overview of longer pieces
— reading stories, poems, plays, biographies, and nonfiction works about a topic, person, or event

Writing

— recording observations
— taking notes from a discussion, demonstration, or other activities
— transcribing an interview
— writing questions for an interview or questionnaire
— writing invitations, letters, and requests for information
— writing scripts for a drama presentation
— writing summaries, synopses, and steps in a procedure
— writing newspaper articles

Planning Lessons

It is impossible for us to teach you specifically how to plan your lessons in language arts, because there are just too many variables involved: the grade you teach, the materials your school requires you to use, how closely you have to follow those materials, the range of abilities in your class in reading and writing, your students' interests and prior experiences, your own interests, strengths, and attitudes, and your personal teaching philosophies. There is no ideal lesson, nor is there any particular "right" way to plan. Some lessons can be used, with modifications, from the materials you have, some can best be planned jointly with students; some, like the cultural journalism projects described in Chapter Seven, evolve as the children become caught up in them; some may take only part of a period to complete, while others may extend over several weeks.

We can, however, suggest some overarching guidelines and strategies to include in every phase of your lesson planning, and we have summarized these in Box 10.1.

The first thing to consider in lesson planning is the *goal*: What do you want your students to learn, to appreciate, or to be able to do? These goals are often referred to as *objectives*, a term that has come to mean the superspecific, molecular skills statements often seen in basal reading programs. Lesson goals or objectives need not, and probably should not, be so very specific; overly-

BOX 10.1
Guidelines for Planning Lessons

Decide what you want students to learn from any lesson (the *why*) before you plan.

Take their own interests, goals, and motivations into consideration when you plan.

Involve them in planning and give them choices and alternatives.

Involve them actively so they are moving about, manipulating things, and learning by direct and concrete experience. Deemphasize passive activities whenever possible.

Consider the full range of their abilities and interests, not just that of the "typical" students.

Include evaluation *before* and *during* lessons, not just *after*.

---

precise objectives make it too easy for us to lose sight of the forest for the trees. Keep your goals fairly general, reasonably open, and explainable.

The last point is an important one. Lesson goals establish the *why* of a lesson, and children have as much right to know why as anyone. It is fair and reasonable for them to want to know how a lesson will contribute to their progress, and when you can explain that you show them that you are directing them with judgment and confidence. When they can understand why you want them to do something, they are much more likely to give it an enthusiastic effort.

Consider also what the students themselves want to learn about or learn to do. Interest and motivation come from within each learner; they are not applied from the outside, even when we use "motivators" like praise, criticism, approval, grades, privileges, and smiley face stamps. A basic tenet of learning is that we learn faster and better when we are interested in the topic or the vehicle for learning.

Students become involved in learning when they share in the planning of what they will do. Why? Because when they have a hand in the planning, they are much more likely to understand what a lesson is for, what its aims are. When they understand what the aims of a lesson are and what they should get out of it, they apply themselves more willingly and more diligently to the learning tasks than they would otherwise. Many teachers have noted that students will subject themselves to much harder tasks through self-initiated activity than to teacher-assigned activities.

Another reason for involving them in planning is that it gives them an opportunity to learn to be responsible and to make decisions, which are important learnings in themselves. Still another reason is that it makes the school day far more interesting. Children enjoy going to school more when they are actively involved and when they feel that they have a stake in what goes on there.

There are many possible levels of student participation in planning. Howes (1974) has described several such levels in Table 10.1.

Student participation can be approached at any point in a lesson plan: the goal, the activities and means by which the goal is to be achieved, and the means of evaluation. Involving students in planning need not mean asking, figuratively or literally, "What should we do?" although it might. It may be just as effective to offer them a restricted choice. You might suggest two or three activities for practicing a new skill, for example, and let groups or individuals select which to do, or describe several activities you have selected and allow them to determine the order in which they will be accomplished. Even very young children can participate in these structured choices, and they will feel more involved and more autonomous because of that participation.

What your students will do to achieve an objective is critical. Too often we rely on passive activities that fail to let children move about, talk, or examine, feel, hear, and taste things. This may be because passive activities are generally quieter, neater, and more orderly than those that actively involve the children; but too much quiet, neatness, and order are stultifying. Children are concrete thinkers, and they must be involved physically in their learning. An old proverb says: "I watch and I forget; I listen and I remember; I do and I understand." As a general rule, children in all elementary grades should be *doing*: creating, illustrating, acting out, building, talking, writing.

Table 10.1   Teacher and student: How much does each plan?

LEVELS OF DECISION MAKING "WHO MAKES THE DECISION?"	DECISION-MAKING PHASES "WHAT DECISIONS CAN BE MADE?"			
	GOAL "WHAT"	PLAN "HOW"	ACTION "DOING"	EVALUATION "RESULTS"
Level 4 Pupil — develops options, teacher is resource. Pupil — decides, using teacher as needed.				
Level 3 Teacher and pupil — develop alternatives. Pupil — decides in concert with teacher.				
Level 2 Teacher — states choices. Pupil — selects.				
Level 1 Teacher — suggests and decides. Pupil — "cops out."				

SOURCE: Reprinted with permission of Macmillan Publishing Company from *Informal Teaching in the Open Classroom,* by Virgil M. Howes. Copyright © 1974 by Virgil M. Howes.

Teaching should begin with concrete experiences and move gradually to the abstract. The list in Table 10.2 includes a number of activity types arranged from more concrete to more abstract. Note that nearly all of the language arts are on the abstract end! Reading, listening, talking, and writing are all at least a step removed from direct, concrete experience. To be most effective, language arts teaching, especially with younger elementary grade students, should come in as an extension, as an elaboration, a recording, a reflection, an analysis, and an evaluation of concrete experience.

Building on concrete experiences means taking advantage of what is going on around you, using the flow of daily activities in and around school to suggest topics and activities. Let's say, for example, that the street outside your classroom window is being torn up and repaved and your students' interest is drawn toward the scene. You could of course, close the windows to shut out the noise, punish those who dawdle near the construction site, and doggedly pursue your preplanned lessons. Or you could seize the moment and use the scene outside as a vehicle for study in a variety of areas. What could be learned from the street repair? Look at how many topics in math, social studies, science, reading, and writing one class came up with after a brainstorming session (see Figure 10.1).

Table 10.2   Concrete to abstract: The range of activities

MOST CONCRETE	Hold an out-of-class, concept-related activity.
↑	Do something
	Construct artifacts, models, dioramas, etc.
	Stage a simulation.
	Do an experiment, investigation, or demonstration.
	Do a role play or dramatization.
	Take a field trip.
	Participate in a debate.
	Complete independent readings.
	Illustrate a concept with pictures and examples.
	Read for information in a textbook.
	Participate in a discussion.
	Write a report of readings.
	Complete a categorization exercise.
	Watch a demonstration.
	Listen to a guest speaker.
	View still pictures.
	Listen to a record or tape.
	Listen to an oral reading or lecture.
↓	Have a question-and-answer session.
	Read and answer questions.
MOST ABSTRACT	Look up vocabulary words.

SOURCE: From Thomas H. Estes and Joseph Vaughan, *Reading and Learning in the Content Classroom*, pp. 212–213. Copyright © 1978 by Allyn and Bacon, Inc. Reprinted by permission.

Another point to consider in selecting activities is to make sure they really provide practice in the competency you want to develop. If your goal is for students to learn to read and apply information, then they should read and apply information — real information, in real applications. If the goal is to learn to write, have them write — write a lot, about real subjects of real interest that other real people will read. Somehow the idea has crept into American education that learning activities don't matter very much. As long as they can be said to be addressing some specific objective, then worksheet exercises can be substituted for more direct experience. As a result, we sometimes might see a teacher teaching about the parts of a book using only ditto sheets: During the course of the lesson, the children never pick up a book! This sort of lesson is objectionable on at least two grounds. First, it does not usually teach what it purports to teach. Second, and perhaps a more serious objection, is that it promotes a sort of tour-bus approach to reality. Children do not experience things directly; the lessons have been predigested and neatly sliced by the textbook publishers.

So, if the goal is to read, read. If the goal is to talk and listen, talk and listen. If it is to write, write. When you find it necessary to break these things apart and talk about the pieces, so be it, but be sure to put them back together again, and be doubly sure that the children spend more time experiencing the real thing than studying the parts. Where elementary language arts are concerned, we are trying to produce good drivers, not good mechanics.

If students are to talk, read, or write, it is more motivating for them to have something to talk, read, or write *about*, and some clear purpose for doing so. Sometimes this motivation can come from an event that you decide to harness as a learning experience, such as the street repair unit. At other times it may be something that you bring in deliberately to start things off. A film about space exploration could be such a device. Is there life on other planets? Which planets are most likely to support life? What would life be like on another planet? What is the world's scientific community doing to investigate this question? What have they found out?

A story that you or the students read or a skit they act out can pose a moral dilemma. Is it *ever* right to steal, for example? This question can lead to a small group discussion, the writing of more stories, or the creation of a new play (see Reimer, Paolitto, and Hersh, 1983).

With older students, you can ask *focusing questions*, especially if the lesson is not too long. What do they already know or believe about the topic at hand? Such a discussion should press for specific answers, and you should write them on the board for all to consider. After the discussion you should highlight areas that the students need to know more about and then let them go about their listening, reading, and discussion with set purposes in mind (see the DRTA discussion in Chapter Five).

Every classroom has children representing a wide range of abilities, from

Figure 10.1 The web: The flow of interests and questions from a child's observation

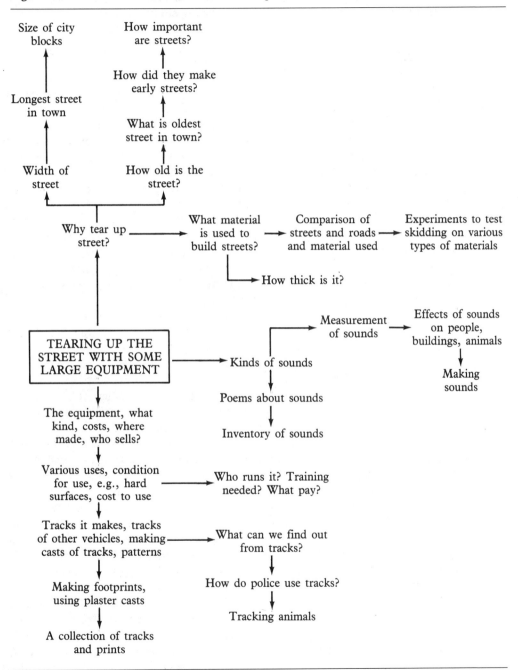

SOURCE: Reprinted with permission of Macmillan Publishing Company from *Informal Teaching in the Open Classroom* by Virgil M. Howes. Copyright © 1974 by Virgil M. Howes.

low to high, in reading, writing, spelling, and other areas. A typical fourth grade, for example, will have a range of reading abilities from beginning readers to those reading at sixth- or seventh-grade levels or above (Estes and Vaughan, 1978).

The range of abilities means that the lessons must be appropriate for every learner, which means, of course, that each student will not be required to do the same things. It means selecting activities that are within the capabilities of each student and which challenge each student in some way. Many learning activities should be *collaborative*; that is, the children should cooperate in pairs, small groups, or teams to complete an assignment. With a cooperative effort to lean on, they will have support, help, and the benefits derived from the diverse interests and experiences of other students.

A systematic way to incorporate children with different abilities into the same lesson is to use *learning contracts*. Contracts begin with the goals or objectives for the lesson. Once these are determined, the teacher and the student discuss how to go about the lesson. A student could be asked to choose activities from a range of activities of different types, choosing, for example, to participate in a small group discussion, to help make a poster with one other student, to read certain material, or to write a report. The teacher negotiates with the students the type or amount of work they will do. For those with different reading abilities, it is better to give an option in the kinds of reading and writing to be done rather than in the amount. If books are available on different difficulty levels, let the slower student read two easy ones to another student's hard one. Or give the slower student the option of listening to one or more books on tape. For the sake of fairness, it is not advisable to let a slower student contract to do less of the same work than another; it is better to differentiate the work, finding work that makes both students work hard and productively, but in different material, for the same outcome.

Evaluation should take place before, during, and after a lesson. "Before" means determining what children already know. It is important to achieve a balance in this sort of evaluation. If it is approached too formally, it can be time-consuming. Some commercial programs require so much testing that they inundate teacher and students with paper — before any actual instruction takes place. One commercial reading program, for instance, devotes 30 to 35 percent of the instructional time to testing (Kita, 1981). Surely the children would learn more if they spent this extra time simply reading. On the other hand, their time can be wasted if they are routinely made to work "the next chapter in the book" without regard to the question of whether they already know it or not. Those who consistently get "hundreds" on spelling tests without making much effort, for example, would be better served if they were placed in more difficult lessons. The happy medium is to be alert to the question of placement: Be prepared to ask the question, "Which of my students really needs to learn this?" as you plan a lesson. Do some checking in cases of reasonable doubt and place students accordingly.

The "during" evaluation is the checking done to see if the lesson is going well. If the lesson is a longer-term unit stretching over days or weeks, it is especially important to understand what the students are doing, to check whether their motivation is still keen, and to see to it that they have the resources to do what is expected of them. Are they finding the materials they need? Do they know how to work in the learning center? Are they able to read and learn from the textbook? Do they have a clear idea of how to do the writing involved? Since we don't know how they are able to perform as learners until we watch them trying to learn, this kind of evaluation is extremely important not only to the lesson at hand but also their education in general.

If we're going to do just one kind of evaluation, the "after" evaluation is normally the one we think of doing. In the next section we will discuss means of evaluation in greater detail, so for now we will simply say that the evaluation at this stage should meet these criteria:

1. It should accurately reflect what the children were attempting to learn and do so as globally as possible: testing real reading, real writing, real understanding.
2. It should also be clear to the students themselves as to how they did and why it was important.
3. It should include some evaluation of the learning activity itself in addition to the student's progress.

Maintaining Ongoing Evaluation

Evaluation is an integral part of planning and conducting lessons and not reserved for the time following a lesson. As a plan, keep in mind these questions:

— What do good readers do? How much of this do my students do? How accurately is my instruction aimed at getting them to do what good readers do?
— What do good writers do? How much of this do my students do? Is my instruction making them better writers, in the full sense that I first described?
— What do effective talkers and listeners do? How do my students stack up? How likely is my instruction to make them more expressive and articulate talkers and more active and discerning listeners?

These are the "big questions" in language arts, the ones that will help you keep your program aimed toward real language growth. Take the time to examine carefully each aspect of your program against the questions listed above. Don't be taken in by what the teacher's guide says the books are supposed to teach, and don't assume that the diagnostic tests fully measure significant ability and growth in the language arts. We have never seen a program, be it commercially published or produced by a school system, that could not be greatly enriched by the teacher's own ideas or, in many cases, substantially modified by the teacher.

Observation

"Observational skills," as David Elkind writes, "are among the most important tools a teacher can acquire" (1973, p. 171). Observation means finding out what a student can and can't yet do by observing the student in typical, real, and natural situations rather than by testing. During your teaching day you will be constantly in touch with your students and will probably be observing them more than you realize. You may happen to observe a child going about studying a list of spelling words, or writing a paper; or you may observe a small group of students having a discussion and see who talks, who doesn't, and how they go about taking turns in the discussion. You may observe them outside of instructional tasks, playing games, having arguments, or just getting along. Such observations can help you decide who may be having difficulty, who appears to need intervention, and who is succeeding in a given situation.

To become the best teacher you can to the most students, you will have to

do more than this happenstance observation; you will have to go at it systematically. You can do so by taking a few minutes every few weeks to read down the names on your class list, and for each child's name ask yourself: "What's going on in this student's life? Do I know as much as I should about this child's progress and learning experience in my class?" There will be youngsters for whom your answer to the last question is no. Note the names and set up a schedule for yourself, giving yourself two or three days to observe each one as carefully as your time permits.

Observation will reveal things tests don't. Here are some aspects you can observe:

Speaking and Listening

— How much, and how successfully, do the students converse with other students?
— How well do they listen to others?
— How well do they follow oral directions?
— How well do they understand standard English?
— How attentively do they listen to stories?
— How do they use the various language functions (see Chapter Two)?

Reading

— How much do they read in a typical day?
— Do they read for pleasure?
— Are they able to comfortably read assigned textbooks and related materials?
— Are they able to read silently?
— Are they able to read while others move, talk, or do other things nearby?
— What do they like to read?

Writing

— Do they write enthusiastically or reluctantly?
— Do they write first drafts, or do they try to get everything right the first time?
— How do they handle the spelling of unfamiliar words?
— Where do they get ideas for writing?
— Do they have problems with letter formation? Is their handwriting legible?

This list is by no means complete, since its contents will vary depending on the age and grade of your students and what you need to find out about an individual.

Note, however, that observation has limitations; it can sometimes intimidate the children and they may not show off the full range of language competencies. It should be supplemented by work sampling and informal testing.

Work Sampling

Each student should keep a year-long work folder in which dated samples of work in various areas are filed weekly. Particularly in the areas of composition, spelling, and handwriting, comparing work over time will help you determine where the children are making rapid progress and where problems persist.

What tendencies are showing up in their handwriting? Are they having trouble with the same things in current papers as in earlier ones? Is the handwriting getting neater and more controlled? Is the composition showing growth? Is more attention paid to beginnings and endings, to main points? Is the vocabulary growing? Are the compositional forms of story, explanation, description, persuasion, and so on getting more distinct and better controlled? Are the same words misspelled?

A long-term study of work samples can reveal answers to many of these questions. What is more, showing children their earlier papers and pointing out to them the ways they have grown can be tremendously encouraging to those who feel that their writing, spelling, or handwriting "isn't any good." All children need to see concrete evidence of their own progress in order to believe in themselves. Work samples are also a very effective means of informing parents about a student's progress. Often they are more meaningful than test scores, grades, and other data we routinely share with parents.

Informal Testing

The last topic we will discuss in this section is informal testing. There are some aspects of reading, writing, spelling, and even oral language that are not made completely clear by observation, at least not during the limited amount of time we have to observe individual students in our classrooms. They may not demonstrate some particularly fascinating or problematical behavior they have during the time that we are nearby. In work samples, they may "play it safe" and not show us the outer reaches of what they can do.

Informal testing is a deliberate sampling of a certain kind of behavior (unlike observation, which is a general, unspecified sampling of behavior). It is intended to resemble as closely as possible the real activity that we are sampling, which does not mean multiple choice questions or filling in the blanks. It means real reading, real composing, and real talking. What we want is qualitative rather than quantitative information. We're not looking for percentile scores or who's best and who's worst. We seek rather to know what children do when they read, write, spell, or speak. Let's consider some examples.

In reading, one example of informal testing is the informal reading inventory, the procedure that is used to find out on what level a child is reading (see Chapter Five). It can also be used to determine if a child is having problems with word recognition, comprehension, or reading rate. Other informal testing procedures also described in Chapter Five are the cloze and the maze procedures. These informal reading tests can sometimes show us more than observation because they show a student's performance in a range of reading material, from very easy to very hard, something we are not likely to see in an observation. What they don't show us, however, is the way children read in material they have selected themselves out of interest. Since interest is a key factor in comprehension, this is an important limitation on informal tests of reading and suggests that these tests should be supplemented by observation of a child's day-to-day reading behavior.

In spelling, the informal spelling inventory and the spelling features list are both informal testing devices that show how particular children spell (see Chapter Nine). The informal spelling inventory tells us in what level of spelling book they should be placed. The spelling features list shows the stage of conceptual spelling development they are operating in. Both instruments may be more efficient than analyzing their writing samples, simply because both give us uncorrected examples of their spellings for words they might not ordinarily choose to spell.

In connection with oral language, we mentioned several informal testing procedures in Chapter Three, including the mean length of utterance measure and sentence modeling, but these measures deal with a fairly narrow range of language behavior. For one thing, they study language behavior outside of a normal communicative context — a necessary condition for efficient testing, perhaps, but a seriously limiting one insofar as the more recent definitions of language competencies are concerned. These informal testing procedures can, however, give us an indication of how limiting or facilitating the child's syntactic competence may be, which is a central aspect of most definitions of language ability. Nevertheless, these measures too should be supplemented by observation.

In composition, no really good informal writing test exists. It is better to have children write and analyze the results, as we discussed in Chapter Seven. All that we might add to the evaluation procedures we laid out in that chapter is that you should deliberately assign topics that address different subjects for different purposes and for different audiences to get a broadly based sample for analysis. As we have seen, writing stories is different from writing expressive pieces, which is different from writing papers that have some transactional purpose such as explaining, describing, or persuading.

Grouping Students

There are fourteen, or eighteen, or twenty-five, or thirty of them, and one of you. If you work with one, all the others are out of contact with you, and if you work with them all simultaneously, your contact with each child is greatly diluted. Every day you will probably spend some time working with individuals and some time with the whole class, but much of your time and theirs will be spent in group work. This is a necessary and, in most cases, a positive thing. How, then, can you make the best of learning groups?

The most important single rule is to *group flexibly*, which means varying activities so that each day they do some work individually, some in small groups, some in larger groups, and some as a whole class. It also means forming groups in changing patterns so that they don't always work with the same set of peers.

In order to make groups work successfully in your classroom, consider what kinds of activities groups of different sizes are best suited for, and find ways to get them going.

It is useful to think in terms of four different sizes of groups: large groups, small groups, pairs, and individuals.

1. *Large Groups.* Any group with more than a dozen members is large. Large groups are best suited for listening and observing, when little two-way interaction is required, and for films, field trips, lectures, sing-alongs, or creative dramatics, either participating or as an audience for others. A large group can listen to a story, though it is best if younger children can sit close in a circle around the reader or storyteller so that there is eye contact and physical proximity with the children. If the group is too large for this, then subdividing the group is advisable. Also, some kinds of testing can be done in a large group with students beyond primary grades.

The large group is *not* well suited for discussions, demonstrations where the students must observe details, or for taking turns reading.

2. *Small Groups.* Small groups range from three to about eight members, with five being close to ideal. In a small group, two-way sharing of ideas is possible. The group is small enough to be cordial and relaxed but large enough to provide a sounding board for an individual's ideas and to be a source of varied experiences and opinions. Small groups are good for discussing many topics, planning and problem solving, group collaboration on a story or a poem, listening and responding to a member's composition, and peer editing. They are good for putting on puppet shows and skits, even when no audience is present, and they are ideal for group reading-and-discussing activities.

3. *Pairs.* Each member of a pair has more time to talk and listen, so pairs are good for tutoring (one student helping another), interviewing to get a composition started, and proofreading compositions. With fewer people to address an issue, pairs can work faster than small groups, which makes them worthwhile if you want to get students to talk about or react to something quickly. They lack the diversity of opinion that small groups have, however, so there may be little constructive divergence in discussions. Pairs are ideal for activities where "two heads are better than one," as in interviewing a resource person, checking writing for mechanical problems, learning spelling words, writing a script or doing other collaborative writing, sharing books, "buddy reading," reviewing word banks, and library research.

4. *Individuals.* Individual work can be restful and satisfying for limited periods of time. It offers a quieter respite from group activity and an opportunity to explore one's individual interests and work at one's own pace, but too much of it can make children feel cut off from their friends or even neglected by the teacher. The younger the child, the shorter such periods should be.

Appropriate activities for individual work are reading, journal writing, free writing, word searches, listening to tapes at a listening center, some learning center or learning packet activities, and handwriting practice.

Often, though by no means always, you will assign students to groups. For direct instruction, as in reading and spelling, such groups are often formed by calling together pupils of approximately the same ability level, and because grouping this way is so ubiquitous, we sometimes forget that groups can be formed on any other basis. Then the "ability group" becomes a fixed entity, and the same children always work together. This should be avoided, because it has a way of socially and intellectually isolating classmates from one another.

For some activities, groups should be formed on the basis of interest, particular skills needs, and to encourage diversity. Interest groups can conduct discussions or debates, listen to stories together, and do collaborative writing and drama activities on a specific topic they are all interested in. Needs groups can be brought together for direct instruction and practice in a particular area in which they need help, such as word analysis skills, handwriting practice, oral language activities, editing, and proofreading. Divergence groups, in which children work together who might ordinarily never work together because of widely different interests, needs, or backgrounds, are good for certain kinds of ungraded collaborative writing, brainstorming and consensus discussions, debates, listening activities, and dramatics.

Without consistent efforts to form groups on bases other than general reading or other abilities, groups can become a social and academic ghetto. Don't let your students stagnate in the same groups all year: seek out topics and activities they can work on together but in new combinations. Members of a group learn as much from one another as from their teacher, so let each student have plenty of opportunities to work with all the other students.

Gathering Resources

Creating a physical environment that nourishes and promotes the language arts doesn't require heaps of money, but it does require thought and creativity. Since most communities cannot provide all the funds that schools need and deserve, teachers quickly become skilled at making a little money go a long way. In previous chapters we have suggested what a well-stocked language arts classroom should have, including numerous lists of books and related source materials for various subject areas. In this section we will suggest other kinds of resources for your classroom.

1. *Books and more books* are essential for every grade. Establish a collection that has a wide range of difficulty levels, with plenty of very easy books. Be sure nonfiction, poetry, biographies, how-to books, and humor are well rep-

resented as well as fiction. Arrange with the librarian to keep a good selection of titles in your room for, say, a month at a time.

2. *Non–book materials* like magazines, newspapers, catalogues, and brochures are a must for every grade. Some should be for reading, others for cutting up for projects.

3. *Reference materials* like dictionaries, encyclopedias, atlases, a thesaurus, and books of records should always be on hand. Be sure these are fairly easy: picture and junior dictionaries and encyclopedias for children.

4. *A comfortable place for reading* with books displayed on low shelves or a table and a rug or floor pillows to curl up on, away from high-traffic areas, is essential for all grades. Optional, but great, are beanbag chairs, a reading carrel, and a rack for displaying books and magazines.

5. *Costume items, props, and floor space for dramatics* should be available in all grades. (See Chapter Three for specific suggestions.) A trunk, footlocker, or packing case doubles as storage and as a prop when needed.

6. *Puppetry materials* are essential for primary grades and great for all. Include materials for making puppets and a simple stage (see Chapter Three).

7. *Games,* homemade and commercial, like Spill-'n'Spell, Scrabble, Perquackey, Boggle, card and board games, Link Letters, and magnetic letters should always be standard equipment.

8. *Basic A-V equipment* such as a record player, overhead projector and transparency film, and cassette tape recorder is very useful if you can get it. The students can use these for listening to records and tapes, recording scripts and sound effects for drama, editing in group workshops, transcribing interviews, and many other language activities. Nearby keep spare projector bulbs, transparency markers and tissue for cleaning transparencies, blank and recorded tapes, records, and extension cords or batteries.

9. *Musical instruments* for singing, rhythm, and movement are essential for primary grades. A piano, autoharp, guitar, or dulcimer is wonderful; if unavailable, the children can make rhythm band instruments like castanets, bells, drums, and tambourines with clean cans and other containers, dried beans, and the like. These make good art projects.

10. *Writing materials* of all kinds are essential for all grades. These include: *paper of all kinds* (computer printout sheets, large newsprint, rolls of adding machine tape or shelf paper, and lined paper); *tools for writing* (large and fine pencils, chalk, paints and brushes, felt pens, and transparency markers); *tools for revising* (scissors, tape, colored markers); *materials for illustrating and publishing* (wallpaper and fabric scraps, cardboard, sewing supplies, rulers, glue, scissors, crayons, paints, felt pens, calligraphy pens and ink, and a portable typewriter).

11. *Display space* for writing, pictures, dictated stories, word collections, bulletin boards and so on is also a must. Use doors, backs of bookcases, an easel or chart stand, any wall space, windows, bulletin boards, and walls outside your classroom. For primary graders, display work at *their* eye level, not yours!

In addition, there are a host of optional items you *could* get along without but which would add greatly to your students' experience: simple cameras and film, especially instant cameras, a movie camera or videotaping equipment, a personal computer and word processing software, a simple printing set, a telephone, a hand-held two-way radio set, an aquarium and live animals, a microscope, and many other items.

Beyond a core of things that most language arts programs demand, the list of resources is as variable as the interests and talents of the teachers and students in the classroom. We think of Alex Garcia in Victoria, Texas, a teacher and TV newscaster, whose fourth-grade language arts program revolved around a radio station his students operated in the classroom; of Paul Brown in Geneva, New York, whose middle-school language arts classes became the nucleus of a community theater that staged three ambitious musicals each year: of Marsha Jones in Cumberland, Virginia, whose interest in sculpture could be seen in the ceramics and wood scrap sculpture her first graders made. All of us have strong interests and special talents that are infectious to children. They, after all, want to get good at things that matter to adults. As we expand on our interests and deepen our talents we become more interesting people and more influential teachers. The last section in this chapter addresses this issue and describes some things you might want to learn to do better. First, however, we must describe three other critical classroom resources: computers and volunteers and aides.

Using Classroom Computers

In 1983 *Time* magazine broke with a half-century-old tradition and named a machine the "Man of the Year." The machine was, of course, a microcomputer, the suitcase-sized descendant of those enormous electronic brains that fill whole floors and cost millions. These smaller, cheaper computers have developed from nowhere to tens of thousands of sales almost overnight. Each new model seems more advanced and yet lower priced than the last, and it won't be long before schools, even elementary schools, will be buying microcomputers to go into each classroom. Even now, quite a few schools have at least one microcomputer in the library or media center. It seems fair to say that if you teach presently or plan to begin teaching next fall, your job will require that you know something about the application of microcomputers to classroom instruction. In this section we discuss this topic.

We will begin by describing microcomputers, their accessories, and what they do. Then we will discuss their most popular classroom applications, including computer-assisted instruction, word processing, programming, and taking dictation in language experience programs. Finally, we will discuss means of evaluating computer software and give sources of current information on computing and the available materials that go into or that describe the use of computers.

Description of the Microcomputer

A microcomputer is a typewriter keyboard with an electronic memory storage in it. The memory does two things: First it stores information, either letters, numbers, or other kinds of commands such as those that will enable it to produce drawings, tunes, or even speech sounds. Second, it stores and lets the user insert new commands for manipulating the information in memory or manipulating new information the user types in. A set of commands that tells a computer how to manipulate information is called a *program*, and the act of feeding such commands into a computer is called *programming*. Programming is done by typing letters and numbers on the keyboard. Unfortunately, you cannot freely use plain English to program a computer, because English, like other natural languages, is fraught with ambiguities that require listeners to use their imaginations in order to understand. Computers do not have imaginations, so we must communicate with them through an unambiguous *programming language* such as BASIC. If a computer has been *preprogrammed* to do so, however, it can accept and act on information written in plain English. A computer that accepts plain English is said to be "user-friendly."

Computers can be programmed to carry out their many functions in two ways: (a) you can type commands into the machine using BASIC or some other programming language or (b) you can use a program of commands that some other programmer has prepared. Such programs, called *software*, are available on pieces of celluloid called *floppy discs* or on cassette tapes. Later in this section when we describe the programs that are available as instructional aids for spelling, grammar, and other functions, you should bear in mind that these programs come in the form of discs or tapes that cost from about fifteen dollars up to several hundred dollars.

Besides the computer itself, other machines, or *hardware*, are needed for successful computing. One necessary machine is a television screen, sometimes referred to as a *cathode ray tube* or *CRT*. Just as you communicate with a computer by typing print into the keyboard, the computer communicates with you by displaying print or other graphics on a television screen.

Another machine that is important to have for language arts applications of computers is a *printer* — an electronic typewriter that is linked to the computer and that allows anything that can be shown on the television screen to be printed out on business-size sheets of paper. The printer can type out several copies of the same page very rapidly. When a computer is used to teach writing, or in a language experience program, or to edit and print out children's work into books, having access to a printer is essential.

A *speech synthesizer* is another piece of hardware that greatly expands the contribution computers can make to language arts teaching. As the name implies, this is a device that under the direction of the computer makes humanlike speech sounds. It can be programmed through the keyboard to pronounce any words you desire, including (on some models) both the phonemes as well as variations in pitch. The speech synthesizer can also work in conjunction with preprogrammed software that uses spoken words. Spelling programs, for instance, make good use of speech synthesizers by pronouncing a word and asking the student to spell it on the keyboard.

Usually, computers are purchased for school use with more than language arts concerns in mind. If you as a language arts teacher are in a position to influence the decision as to what kinds of computer equipment are purchased, you would do well to ask for a printer and, if possible, a speech synthesizer. You should also make sure that provision is made to purchase *word processing software* as well as other software with specific applications to language arts. We describe such software below.

Word Processing

In Chapter Seven of this book we described the use of computers to teach children the writing process. Word processing capabilities require that a computer have both a CRT screen as well as a printer. The word processing software itself usually comes in the form of a floppy disc, which is inserted into the computer, and it enables you to type a page and have it displayed on the CRT screen before it is printed out. With the page on the screen you can manipulate the writing a variety of ways simply by typing in words and commands. You can add, erase, or change the order of words, lines, or whole paragraphs of print. You can have the computer call attention to repetitions of the same word (some programs will even suggest synonyms!) and point out words that are misspelled. Since it is possible to store a piece of writing indefinitely in the computer or on a floppy disc without printing it out, you can work on the same piece of writing for short periods of time stretched out over a number of days or weeks. When you are satisfied with the text as it appears on the screen, you can have it printed out on paper. Many word processors will go so far as to arrange straight margins on both sides of the page, something that once only professional typesetters could do.

Word processing makes a delight out of the task of trying out a piece of writing many ways to see which way looks best. The possibilities for rearranging text and the challenge of typing the correct commands into the computer add a dose of motivation to what to less prolific students may seem an onerous task. According the Eileen Gress, an educational computing expert from the Fairport (New York) school district, the potential of word processors to encourage writing, reviewing, and revising — in short, to foster professional writing habits — may be their biggest contribution to language arts instruction (Gress, 1983). It is also one of the most time-consuming uses of the computer, however, and may be necessary to have two computers in each classroom to afford each student an adequate opportunity to write on one. In any event, you certainly should not limit the students' writing time to the amount of time they are able to find a word processor available. Writing needs daily practice and, fortunately, pencils and paper are still a bargain!

Computer-aided Instruction

Personal computers are widely used in language arts to provide drill and practice, mostly in the areas of spelling, grammar, some reading skills, and some aspects of prereading. Since the computer can provide students with feedback on their responses as they work, these activities are commonly used as independent work while the teacher works with other individuals or a group.

Generally speaking, these drill activities are very similar to workbook activities; the major differences are not in the tasks the children perform but in the immediate feedback they receive from the computer. According to *Swift's 1982 Educational Software Directory*, representative activities include:

Prereading

— alphabet letter matching
— alphabet letter ordering
— shape, color, and numeral matching

— learning letter names
— upper- and lower-case letter matching

Reading

— completing cloze exercises
— following directions
— identifying main ideas
— sequencing story events
— phonics and structural analysis skills
— reading rate drill
— literal comprehension of paragraphs
— dividing words into syllables

Spelling

— unscrambling anagrams
— identifying misspellings in text
— producing correct spellings from words flashed visually or by voice simulation
— replicating correct spellings

Grammar

— identifying word classes: nouns, verbs, adjectives, and so forth
— subject-verb agreement
— capitalizing
— punctuating sentences
— identifying sentence types
— matching synonyms and antonyms
— matching words and definitions
— identifying sentence fragments

Most of these activities closely resemble the drill-and-practice tasks provided by workbooks, skill building kits, and duplicator worksheets. The familiar, convergent response formats of matching, multiple choice, and fill-in-the-blanks are most common. The major difference between workbooks and computer tasks is that workbooks and duplicator sheets have to be corrected and returned while the computer provides immediate feedback. Software programs "respond" in different ways to students, most often with printed messages like "Good work" or "Try again," smiley faces or bursts of music. However cute or polite such responses may be, they are not human responses. It is important to remember that in the long run, children need responses from peers and teachers more than from machines.

There are relatively few software programs for writing instruction other than word processing software. Bolt Beranek and Newman, Inc. (50 Moulton Street, Cambridge, Mass. 02138) produces Story Maker, which allows children to produce stories with alternative events and endings, sometimes called "branching stories." Other than for word processing, most software programs advertised for writing instruction are really traditional grammar and mechanics exercises like capitalizing, punctuating, and locating spelling errors in preprogrammed, not student-produced, text.

Programming

In many schools teachers are using computers to familiarize students with computer functions, improve computer literacy, and teach basic programming. The rationale for such instruction is that, because computers are so widely used in everyday life, "computer literacy is important to effective participation in today's society" (D'Angelo, 1983). Also, teachers like the fact that learning programming puts children in charge of the operations of the computer rather than merely responding to the computer's initiatives, as they do in computer-assisted instruction.

Wholesale computer programming is probably out of reach of all but the exceptional pre–high school student, according to Meredith Richards (1983), a cognitive psychologist and computer expert. Such programming requires that the student have reached an abstract level of thinking that most elementary students do not attain. Nevertheless, some greatly simplified programming languages exist that allow children to take the initiative and do creative things on computers. One such language, called LOGO, is available for the Apple computer. More programs that include the creation of graphic designs and interactive games are becoming available for Apple and for other computers. These will expand the range of operations young children can carry out.

As with the word processor, teaching children to program on the classroom computer is likely to limit the use of the machine to one or two students for large blocks of time. In order to allow more students to use it you may have to limit its use during class. Nevertheless, when you see how fascinating programming can be to students and the interesting things they can do with computers, and consider that otherwise they may be pumping quarters into the video games at the corner deli, you may well decide to schedule extra time for those who want to use the classroom or library computer.

Language Experience Uses for Computers

An innovative and productive use of word processing software in primary grades is in conjunction with the language experience approach to beginning reading, as described in Chapter Five. In this approach children dictate experience stories that are written down and reread chorally and silently to teach sight word recognition and help forge a link between speech and print. Word processing software allows a teacher or aide to print neat, attractive copies of dictated stories for the children to take home or keep at school, print compilations of stories for groups, and help in changing and extending original stories. It also stores their work for later production and revision. This use of computers takes much of the tedious work out of copying and duplicating dictated stories and makes it easier for teachers to use language experience methods in the classroom (Barber, 1982; Hennings, 1981).

Other Uses of Computers

Aside from word processing, computer-assisted instruction, programming, and taking dictation, there are many other areas where computers are useful. Whether they are of real help to you will depend on what your teaching requires. Software is available that does many things you may not need to have done! If you are managing the instruction of thirty children by keeping track of their progress through many individually measured specific objectives, you could productively use a microcomputer to organize and keep your records. However, unless this kind of management is specifically mandated by your school system, you may find it more helpful to maintain a folder of writing samples and observations for each student instead. There is certainly no reason to use a computer to do things that would not otherwise be justified on educational grounds.

Several writers have recently advocated using microcomputers to perform readability estimates on reading materials that are being considered for adoption or in which you might wish to place children with limited reading abilities (Judd, 1981; Keller, 1982; and Schuyler, 1982). If you do this, however, you will have to *type* samples of at least three hundred words each into the computer for each book you survey, vis-à-vis *counting* sentences and polysyllabic words in the same-sized samples if you used readability formulas without the help of a computer. It is difficult to see how using the computer in this instance could actually save effort, and, besides, readability estimates are very inexact measures (see Gillet and Temple, 1982, for discussion). Simply having a computer calculate an estimate based on a questionable formula does not improve the accuracy of the readability measurement.

Evaluating Computer Software Packages

As a teacher you will have to decide whether or not to use available computer materials and to recommend whether or not some software packages you might use should be purchased. The following guidelines will be helpful to you:

1. Seek out some of the numerous journals and newsletters that evaluate commercial software and read the reviews critically
2. Look beyond the surface features of programs and determine what the instructional goal of the activity really is, as well as what children do while completing it.

Although the educational computer market is growing so rapidly that you cannot keep current without spending time on such an effort, there are a number of journals and sources of information about computer software that will help you evaluate what is available. One of the best sources is the International Council for Computers in Education (ICCE, 135 Education, University of Oregon, Eugene, Oregon 97403). ICCE publishes *The Computing Teacher*, a journal devoted to information on computers, using computers, teacher education, and the impact of computers on the school curricula. ICCE also publishes numerous booklets such as:

Introduction to Computers in Education for Elementary and Middle School Teachers
Parents' Guide to Computers in Education
Learning Disabled Students and Computers: a Teacher's Guide Book
Evaluator's Guide for Microcomputer-Based Instructional Packages
Teacher's Guide to Computers in the Elementary School
School Administrator's Introduction to Instructional Use of Computers

Another valuable source of information is the Minnesota Educational Computing Consortium (MECC, 2520 North Broadway Drive, St. Paul, Minnesota 55113). MECC is presently one of the largest developers of software and a national leader in applying computers to education. MECC sponsors conferences for teachers and publishes an informative newsletter, *User's*.

Other sources of evaluative information on software are:

Computer Using Educators Newsletter
1776 Educational Park Drive
San Jose, Calif. 95101

Curriculum Product Review
520 University Avenue
Palo Alto, Calif. 94301

Educational Computer
P.O. Box 535
Cupertino, Calif. 95015

Educational Technology
140 Sylvan Avenue
Englewood Cliffs, N.J. 07632

Info World
530 Lytton Avenue
Palo Alto, Calif. 94301

The Journal of Courseware Review
20863 Stevens Creek Boulevard
Building B-2, Suite A-1
Cupertino, Calif. 95014

Microcomputers in Education
Queue, Inc.
5 Chapel Hill Drive
Fairfield, Conn. 06432

MicroScope and Jem Reference Manual
Jem Research
Discovery Park, University of Victoria

P.O. Box 1700
Victoria, British Columbia
V8W 2Y2 Canada

North Carolina Dept. of Public Instruction
Materials Review and Evaluation Services
Division of Educational Media
Raleigh, N.C.

Peelings II
P.O. Box 188
Las Cruces, N.M. 88004

Purser's Magazine
P.O. Box 466
El Dorado, Calif. 95623

Softalk Magazine
11021 Magnolia Boulevard
North Hollywood, Calif. 91601

School Courseware Journal
1341 Bulldog Lane, Suite C4
Fresno, Calif. 93710

If your school has microcomputers, your library or staff development office should be receiving *The Computing Teacher* and as many other journals and newsletters as possible. (If they are not available, talk to your media specialist or staff development official.)

Sometimes you will not have expert reviews available, or programs may be already purchased and you must decide whether or not to use them. To make this decision, you should look beyond the seller's claims and beyond the surface features of the program. Most are made to be visually appealing by using bright colors, spaceships, monsters, and other features of computer and video games, but are the activities really worthwhile? Do they:

— enhance children's natural use of language?
— encourage them to do divergent thinking?
— help them learn to solve real problems?
— encourage them to read and write real text?
— use their mistakes as a sign of real learning?
— help them to integrate skills into productive reading and writing?

Or, do they:

— engage them in fragmented or artificial activities?
— focus on convergent thinking only?
— rely on blank-filling and multiple choice selection?
— reinforce the notion that errors are negative and always to be avoided?
— take time away from real reading, writing, and speaking activities?

These are critical questions to ask and to answer. Since computerized learning is a new field, many computer programs used in schools are written by computer programmers, not teachers. Their fundamental criterion is not necessarily what a real and valuable learning activity is but rather what a computer can be made to do. As a result, quite a few programs are interesting but of little real learning value. They may be nothing more than the same old tired workbook drills dressed up in a computer format.

If your review of the program indicates that it is worthwhile, there are still some practical questions to be asked.

— Is the program flexible enough to accommodate students who are working at the range of proficiency you find in your classroom?
— Are the instructions clear enough for them to work independently at it?
— Are the activity sequences planned so that they can have a satisfying instructional episode within a reasonable amount of time, so that several students can use it during one class period?

If the answers to these questions are negative, then you will often find yourself leaving your other teaching activities in order to help children who should have been functioning independently with the computer.

Working with Aides and Volunteers

No matter what the organizational scheme or class size, every classroom is limited by the ratio of one teacher per X students, and you simply will not be able to give all the students as much of your time and attention as they need. A workable solution is to involve other adults and older students in your classroom. Volunteers can add to the number of hours available to children for doing meaningful activities in the language arts classroom. These hours, more than any accumulation of skills on a checklist, are what add up to language growth.

There are a few important guidelines to success in working with aides and volunteers. They are:

1. Plan and demonstrate precisely what the aide or volunteer is to do and *not* do and why.
2. Find out what the aide or volunteer wants to do, likes to do, and feels confident doing and build on those.
3. Let the students know positively and firmly that they must extend to the aide the same courtesies, attention, and respect they would show to a teacher or parent.

Aides and volunteers can perform a wide variety of support functions for you and your students. Some of these involve direct contact with the children and others are behind-the-scenes activities. Both are important, and the volunteers themselves should decide which they would rather do, or both. What, specifically, can aides and volunteers do?

With Children

— Read aloud and tell them stories.
— Listen to them read and tell stories.
— Take dictation.
— Choral-read dictated stories and pattern books.
— Help them review word bank words and do word sorting and word searches.
— Help them find books for pleasure reading.
— Help them locate materials in the library and references for reports.
— Help them with spelling and handwriting practice.
— Supervise their seatwork and practice activities.
— Play games with them.
— Supervise book binding.
— Talk to and listen to them.
— Sing songs and read poetry to them.
— Cut apart dictated stories and help them match sentence and word strips with the original.
— Share hobbies and interests with them.

Behind the Scenes

— Make games and puppets.
— Sew pages together for book binding.
— Make read-along tapes.
— Type and duplicate group dictated stories, newspaper articles, and the like.
— Collect books for the classroom library.
— Collect materials for rhythm band instruments, art projects, and drama activities.
— Help make or put up bulletin boards and displays.
— Copy poems onto posters for display.
— Type final draft writing onto pages for bound books.
— Collect illustrations and make a picture file for writing assignments.
— Make labels for objects in the primary classrooms.

These lists are only the beginning. Your particular teaching situation and the skills and interests of your aides and volunteers will shape the role they play in your classroom.

Growing as a Teacher

Elementary age children, especially those in middle childhood, have a consuming interest in learning how to do things. Psychologists refer to this as the *sense of industry* (Erikson, 1963), which shows itself in their interest in sports and games, collecting, making things, fantasy and role playing, arts and crafts, playing musical instruments and dancing, taking care of animals, and helping adults at work. Before the onset of adolescence, children are still greatly influenced by the adults around them. As elementary teachers, one of the most powerful influences we can have is to nurture their industry by sharing with them our own personal skills and interests.

Many of us can still clearly remember elementary teachers who profoundly influenced us in positive ways. Often they were the ones who taught us new skills and introduced us to new interests by sharing what they themselves enjoyed doing. What we probably never realized was that by doing so they made their work more interesting for themselves and fostered their own continuing growth as teachers.

There are two ways you can grow as a teacher. One is by working at improving and building on those basic skills you want your students to practice: reading, writing, speaking, and listening. The second is by sharing your hobbies and interests with your students and seeking out new things you would like to learn to do yourself (Kohl, 1976).

To be most effective as a teacher of reading, writing, and oral language, you must be a good model. Do you read for pleasure? Do you talk about books with your friends? Do you go to the library or buy books for yourself? If you don't read outside the classroom, it is hard to be genuinely enthusiastic about reading in school. If you are a reader, share it with your students: Talk about books you like, bring a book to school to read with your lunch, and let your students know you read. If you're not a reader, make a start. Buy or borrow a best seller, a book from which a current movie was made, or a friend's favorite; then set aside some time every day to read. If you don't like the book, try another, but don't give up. If you think you read too slowly, you'll find that practice helps enormously.

The same is true of writing; if you don't like to write, you'll have more difficulty getting your students fired up about it. Few of us write much for pleasure, so few of us feel really comfortable with it. You need to write a lot to get very good at it. Buy a notebook or an attractively bound blank book (available at most bookstores and large stationery stores) and start keeping a private journal. Write a little every day, just for self-expression. Then look at your daily activities and see how you can put more writing into them. Next time you head for the phone for a long-distance chat, write a letter instead. Letters "reach out and touch someone" too, and they do it much less expensively! If you are already an enthusiastic pleasure writer, look into taking a creative writing course in your spare time.

Think about what you like to do in you leisure time. Do you like to sew? Paint? Refinish furniture? Repair toys? Garden? Watch birds? Sing or play an instrument? Make pottery? Weave? Play computer games? Take photographs? Cook? Dance? Participate in sports? Play the stock market? Travel? Share what you like to do with your students. Teach them part or all of what you know. Your enthusiasm for your hobby or skill will shine through and may infect a child who has never experienced what you enjoy.

Then think about things you don't presently do but would like to learn. Grab an opportunity to learn a new skill or hobby. Look into local clubs and classes and learn from friends. Explore something you've never done before: pottery, tennis, a foreign language, computers, identifying edible wild plants, cookery, dramatics, playing a musical instrument, gardening, auto repair, hiking, toymaking, dance, archeology, writing poetry. When you do so, you do more than just learn a new skill: You put yourself back in the role of the learner. And to stay in touch with children, we must continue to be learners ourselves. The best teachers are those who never stop learning.

Summary

The organization of most language arts programs suggests that reading, writing, speaking, listening, spelling, and the other components are separate subjects. In reality each supports and reinforces the others, and language arts must be taught as a complex of interrelated language processes. In addition, the language arts are integral parts of the study of all other subjects and should be integrated into the entire curriculum.

Planning effective lessons begins with determining the goal or objective of any instruction, planning the means by which the goal can be achieved, and then evaluating the lesson and the students' performance before, during, and after the lesson. Lesson planning should include the students' own interests and motivations, should involve them in making choices and selecting alternatives, and should engage them actively, not passively, in activities. Learning activities should move from concrete to abstract, with plenty of experience at the concrete end of the continuum.

Evaluation must be an ongoing process, and it should be built into lessons as you consider how the things you teach promote real reading, writing, and language growth. Observation of students at work helps you determine general areas in which they may have particular ease or difficulty, as well as how much reading, writing, and oral language they typically engage in. Work sampling helps you see growth in particular areas across time and is an effective way of demonstrating their progress to them and to their parents. Informal testing can help you gather qualitative diagnostic information about a youngster's strengths and needs in a specific or general area.

Grouping students in the classroom is most effective if grouping is done flexibly, ensuring that everyone works in groups of different sizes, including working with a partner and alone, for different tasks. Groups should be formed on the basis of shared interests and the specific instructional needs the students share as well as on the more common basis of general ability in reading or overall achievement.

A well-equipped language arts classroom for any grade must have plenty of books, magazines, newspapers, and reference sources for pleasure and informational reading, a comfortable and attractive place for reading and book displays, drama and puppetry materials, learning games, audiovisual equipment, music supplies, a variety of writing and publishing materials, and space for displaying student work. A most valuable resource for any classroom is the human one: aides and volunteers who perform a wide variety of services and who give pupils additional individual time and attention. The keys to success in working with these paraprofessionals include building on their individual skills and interests, agreeing on responsibilities clearly beforehand, and properly preparing students to work with paraprofessionals.

Growing as a teacher means extending our personal and professional horizons by polishing our own language skills, sharing our own skills and interests with students, and actively seeking out new skills to learn. By doing so we continue to grow and learn, and we can better stay in touch with the learners with whom we work.

Bibliography

Adams, Marilyn J. and Allen Collins. "A Schema-Theoretical View of Reading," in *New Directions in Discourse Processing*, Roy O. Freedle, ed. Norwood, N.J.: Ablex, 1979.

Adler, Mortimer J. and Charles Van Doren. *How to Read a Book*. New York: Simon & Schuster, 1972.

Albert, Burt. "Burt Albert's Complete Guide to Writing," *Instructor* (Sept. 1981):93–103 (Part 1); (Feb. 1982):72–79 (Part 2).

Allen, Roach Van. *Language Experiences in Communication*. Boston: Houghton Mifflin, 1976.

Allen, Robert. *Numbers: A First Counting Book*. Bronx, N.Y.: Platt & Monk, 1968.

Anderson, Paul S. and Diane Lapp. *Language Skills in Elementary Education*, 3rd ed. New York: Macmillan, 1979.

Anderson, Richard C. "The Notion of Schemata and the Educational Enterprise," in *Schooling and the Acquisition of Knowledge*, Richard C. Anderson, Rand J. Spiro, and William Montague, eds. Hillsdale, N.J.: Lawrence Erlbaum, 1977.

Applebee, Arthur N. *The Child's Concept of Story*. Chicago: University of Chicago Press, 1978.

Arbuthnot, May Hill. *The Arbuthnot Anthology of Children's Literature*, 4th ed. Glenview, Ill.: Scott, Foresman, 1976.

Ashton-Warner, Sylvia. *Teacher*. New York: Knopf, 1963.

Bank Street Writer. New York: Bank Street College of Education and Intentional Publications, Inc., 1982.

Barber, Bill. "Creating BYTES of Language," *Language Arts* 59, no. 5 (May 1982):472–475.

Barron, Richard F. "The Use of Vocabulary as an Advance Organizer," in *Research in Reading in the Content Areas: First Year Report*, Harold Herber and Peter Sanders, eds. New York: Reading and Language Arts Center, Syracuse University, 1969, pp. 29–39.

Bartlett, Frederick C. *Remembering*. Cambridge, Mass.: Cambridge University Press, 1932.

Baskin, Leonard. *Hosie's Alphabet*. New York: Viking Press, 1972.

Beers, James W., Carol S. Beers, and Karen Grant. "The Logic Behind Children's Spelling," *Elementary School Journal* 77, no. 3 (Jan. 1977):238–242.

Beers, James W. and Edmund H. Henderson. "A Study of Developing Orthographic Concepts Among First Graders," *Research in the Teaching of English* 11 (Fall 1977):133–148.

Bellugi, Ursula. "Some Language Comprehension Tests," in *Language Training in Early Childhood Education*, Celia S. Lavatelli, ed. Urbana, Ill.: University of Illinois Press, 1971.

Bernstein, Basil. "Elaborated and Restricted Codes: Their Social Origins and Some Consequences," in *Communication and Culture*, George Smith, ed. New York: Holt, Rinehart & Winston, 1966, pp. 427–441.

Betts, Emmett A. *Foundations of Reading Instruction*. New York: American Book Co., 1946.

Bissex, Glenda. *GNYS at WRK: A Child Learns to Write and Read*. Cambridge, Mass.: Harvard University Press, 1980.

Blair, Walter. *Tall Tale America*. New York: Coward-McCann, 1944.

Bloomfield, Leonard. *Language*. New York: Holt, Rinehart & Winston, 1933.

Bolinger, Dwight. *Aspects of Language*. New York: Harcourt Brace Jovanovich, 1975.

Bormuth, John R. "Cloze Test Reliability: Criterion Reference Scores," *Journal of Educational Measurement* 5 (Fall 1968b):189–196.

———. "Readability: A New Approach," *Reading Research Quarterly* 1, no. 3 (Fall 1966):79–132.

———. "The Cloze Readability Procedure," *Elementary English* 55 (Apr. 1968a):429–436.

Bornstein, Ruth. *The Dancing Man*. New York: Seabury Press, 1978.

Bostain, James C. "The Dream World of English Grammar," *NEA Journal* 55, no. 6 (Sept. 1966):20–22.

Braddock, Richard, Richard Lloyd-Jones, and Lowell Shoer. *Research in Written Composition*. Urbana, Ill.: NCTE, 1963.

Bradley, Henry. *On the Relations Between Spoken and Written Language with Special Reference to English*, proceedings of the British Academy, vol. VI. London: Oxford University Press, 1913.

Britton, James. *Language and Learning*. Harmondsworth, England: Penguin, 1970.

Brown, Margaret Wise. *The Important Book*. New York: Harper & Row, 1949.

Brown, Roger. *A First Language*. Cambridge, Mass.: Harvard University Press, 1973.

Brown, Roger and Ursula Bellugi. "Three Processes in the Child's Acquisition of Syntax," in *New Directions in the Study of Language*, Eric H. Lenneberg, ed. Cambridge, Mass.: MIT Press, 1964.

Burns, Paul C. and Betty L. Broman. *The Language Arts in Childhood Education*, 4th ed. Chicago: Rand McNally, 1979.

Calkins, Lucy McCormick. "Make It Messy to Make It Clear," unpublished manuscript, University of New Hampshire, n.d.

———. "Notes and Comments: Children's Rewriting Strategies," *Research in the Teaching of English* 14, no. 4 (Dec. 1980b):331–341.

———. "The Craft of Writing," *Teacher* (Nov.–Dec. 1980a):41–44.

———. "Work in Progress: One School's Writing Program," *The National Elementary Principal* 59, no. 4 (June 1980):34–38.

Carle, Eric. *All About Arthur (An Absolutely Absurd Ape)*. New York: Franklin Watts, 1974.

Carlson, Ruth Kearney. *Enrichment Ideas*, 2nd ed. Dubuque, Iowa: Wm. C. Brown, 1976.

Chall, Jeanne. "The Great Debate: Ten Years Later, with a Modest Proposal for Reading Stages," in *Theory and Practice of Early Reading*, vol. I, Lauren Resnick and Phyllis Weaver, eds. Hillsdale, N.J.: Lawrence Erlbaum, 1979.

Charlip, Remy. *Fortunately*. New York: Parents Magazine Press, 1964.

Chomsky, Carol. "Approaching Reading Through Invented Spelling," in *Theory and Practice of Early Reading*, vol. 2, Lauren Resnick and Phyllis Weaver, eds. Hillsdale, N.J.: Lawrence Erlbaum, 1979.

———. "Invented Spelling in the Open Classroom," *Word* 27, nos. 1–3 (Apr.–Dec. 1971b):499–518.

———. *The Acquisition of Syntax in Children from Five to Ten*. Cambridge, Mass.: MIT Press, 1969.

———. "Write First, Read Later," *Childhood Education* 47 (Mar. 1971a):296–299.

Chomsky, Noam. *Aspects of the Theory of Syntax*. Cambridge, Mass.: MIT Press, 1965.

———. *Language and Mind*, enlarged ed. New York: Harcourt Brace Jovanovich, 1975.

Chomsky, Noam and Morris Halle. *The Sound Pattern of English*. New York: Harper & Row, 1968.

Christensen, Francis H. *Notes Toward a New Rhetoric*. New York: Harper & Row, 1967.

Chwast, Seymour. *The House that Jack Built*. New York: Random House, n.d.

Clay, Marie M. *Concepts About Print Test*. Exeter, N.H.: Heinemann Education Books, 1972.

———. *What Did I Write?* Exeter, N.H.: Heinemann Educational Books, 1975.

Clifford, Eth. *A Bear Before Breakfast*. New York: Putnam, 1962.

Coger, Leslie Irene and Melvin R. White. *Readers Theatre Handbook: A Dramatic Approach to Literature*, rev. ed. Glenview, Ill.: Scott, Foresman, 1973.

Cohen, Sandra and Stephen Plaskon. *Language Arts for the Mildly Handicapped*. Columbus, Ohio: Charles Merrill, 1980.

Cooper, Charles R. "An Outline for Writing Sentence-Combining Problems," *English Journal* 62, no. 1 (Jan. 1973):96–108.

Cottrell, June. *Teaching with Creative Dramatics*. Skokie, Ill.: National Textbook Co., 1975.

Craft, Ruth. *Play School Play Ideas*. London: British Broadcasting Corp., 1971.

Cramer, Ronald L. "The *Write* Way to Teach Spelling," *Elementary School Journal* 76, no. 8 (May 1976):464–467.

———. *Children's Writing and Language Growth*. Columbus, Ohio: Charles Merrill, 1978.

———. "Dialectology: A Case for Language Experience," *The Reading Teacher* 15, no. 1 (Oct. 1971):33–39.

Crowhurst, Marion. "Developing Syntactic Skill: Doing What Comes Naturally," *Language Arts* 56, no. 5 (May 1979):522–525.

Dale, Philip S. *Language Development: Structure and Function*, 2nd ed. New York: Holt, Rinehart & Winston, 1976.

Dallmann, Martha. *Teaching the Language Arts in the Elementary School*, 3rd ed. Dubuque, Iowa: Wm. C. Brown, 1976.

D'Angelo, Karen. "Computer Books for Young Students: Diverse and Difficult," *The Reading Teacher* 36 (Mar. 1983):626–633.

Danner, F. W. "Children's Understanding of Intersentence Organization in the Recall of Short Expository Passages," *Journal of Educational Psychology* 68 (1975):174–183.

Deighton, Lee C. *Vocabulary Development in the Classroom*. New York: Teachers College, Columbia University Press, 1959.

DeVilliers, Jill and Peter DeVilliers. *Language Acquisition*. Cambridge, Mass.: Harvard University Press, 1978.

Downing, John and Derek Thackray. *Reading Readiness*, 2nd ed. London: Hodder & Stoughton, 1975.

Eimas, P. D. "Linguistic Processing of Speech by Young Infants," in *Language Perspectives: Acquisition, Retardation and Intervention*, R. L. Schiefelbusch and L. L. Lloyd, eds. Baltimore, Md.: University Park Press, 1974.

Einsel, Walter. *Did You Ever See?* New York: Scholastic Books, 1972.

Ekwall, Eldon. *Diagnosis and Remediation of the Disabled Reader*. Boston: Allyn & Bacon, 1976.

Elbow, Peter. *Writing With Power*. New York: Oxford University Press, 1981.

———. *Writing Without Teachers*. New York: Oxford University Press, 1976.

Elkind, David. *Child Development and Education*. New York: Oxford University Press, 1973.

Emberley, Barbara. *Drummer Hoff*. Engelwood Cliffs, N.J.: Prentice-Hall, 1967.

Enstrom, E. A. and Doris Enstrom. "Signs of Readiness," *Elementary English* 48, no. 2 (Feb. 1971):215–220.

Erikson, Erik H. *Childhood and Society*, 2nd ed. New York: Norton, 1963.

Estes, Thomas H. and Joseph L. Vaughan. *Reading and Learning in the Content Classroom*. Boston: Allyn & Bacon, 1978.

Evans, Bergen and Cornelia Evans. *A Dictionary of Contemporary English Usage*. New York: Random House, 1957.

Fader, Daniel. *The New Hooked on Books*. New York: Berkley, 1976.

Flack, Marjorie. *Ask Mr. Bear*. New York: Macmillan, 1971.

Flavell, John. *Cognitive Development*. Englewood Cliffs, N.J.: Prentice-Hall, 1977.

Forester, Anne D. "Learning to Spell by Spelling," *Theory into Practice* 19, no. 3 (Summer 1980):186–193.

Friedman, Paul. *Listening Processes: Attention, Understanding and Evaluation*. Washington, D.C.: National Education Association, 1978.

Fries, Charles. *American English Grammar*. New York: D. Appleton-Century, 1940.

———. *The Structure of English: An Introduction to the Construction of English Sentences*. New York: Harcourt Brace, 1952.

Frye, Northrup. *Anatomy of Criticism: Four Essays*. Princeton, N.J.: Princeton University Press, 1957.

———. *On Teaching Literature*. New York: Harcourt Brace Jovanovich, 1972.

———. *The Educated Imagination*. Bloomington, Ind.: Indiana University Press, 1964.

Furner, Beatrice. "Recommended Instructional Procedures in a Method Emphasizing the Perceptual-Motor Nature of Learning in Handwriting," *Elementary English* 46, no. 8 (Dec. 1969):1021–1030.

Gág, Wanda. *Millions of Cats*. New York: Coward-McCann, 1928.

Gardner, Richard and Beatrice Gardner. "Teaching Sign Language to a Chimpanzee," *Science* 165:664–672.

Gentry, J. Richard. "Early Spelling Strategies," *Elementary School Journal* 79, no. 2 (Nov. 1978):88–92.

———. "Learning to Spell Developmentally," *The Reading Teacher* 34, no. 4 (Jan. 1981):378–381.

Gentry, J. Richard and Edmund H. Henderson. "Three Steps to Teaching Beginning Readers to Spell," *The Reading Teacher* 31, no. 6 (Mar. 1978):632–637.

Gerbrandt, Gary L. *An Idea Book for Acting Out and Writing Language, K–8*. Urbana, Ill.: NCTE, 1974.

Gessel, Arnold and Barbara Ames. "The Development of Handedness," *Journal of Genetic Psychology* 70 (1947):155–175.

Gibson, Eleanor J. *Principles of Perceptual Learning and Development*. New York: Appleton-Century-Crofts, 1969.

Gillet, Jean Wallace and Charles Temple. *Understanding Reading Problems: Assessment and Instruction*. Boston: Little, Brown, 1982.

Gillet, Jean Wallace and J. Richard Gentry. "Bridges Between Standard and Nonstandard English with Extensions of Dictated Stories," *The Reading Teacher*, 36, no. 4 (Jan. 1983): 360–364.

Gillet, Jean Wallace and Mary Jane Kita. "Words, Kids and Categories," *The Reading Teacher* 32, no. 5 (Feb. 1979):538–542.

Gleason, H. A., Jr. *Linguistics and English Grammar*. New York: Holt, Rinehart & Winston, 1965.

Goodman, Kenneth S. "Dialect Rejection and Reading: A Response," *Reading Research Quarterly* 4 (Summer 1970):600–603.

Graves, Donald H. "Research Update: Andrea Learns to Make Writing Hard," *Language Arts* 56, no. 5 (May 1979):569–576.

―――. *Writing: Teachers and Children at Work.* Exeter, N.H.: Heinemann Educational Books, 1983.

Gress, Eileen. Personal communication, Mar. 20, 1983.

Guthrie, John T., Mary Siefert, Nancy A. Burnham, and Ronald I. Caplan. "The Maze Technique to Assess Monitor Reading Comprehension," *The Reading Teacher* 28, no. 2 (Nov. 1974):161–168.

Gwynne, Fred. *A Chocolate Moose for Dinner.* New York: Dutton, 1973.

―――. *The King Who Rained.* New York: Windmill, 1970.

Hall, MaryAnne. *Teaching Reading as a Language Experience*, 3rd ed. Columbus, Ohio: Charles Merrill, 1981.

Hall, MaryAnne, Jerilyn K. Ribovich, and Christopher Ramig. *Reading and the Elementary School Child*, 2nd ed. New York: Van Nostrand, 1979.

Halliday, Michael. *Explorations in the Functions of Language.* London: Edward Arnold, 1975.

―――. "Learning How to Mean," in *Foundations of Language Development: A Multidisciplinary Approach*, vol. I, Eric Lenneberg and Elizabeth Lenneberg, eds. New York: Academic Press, 1975.

Hammond, W. Dorsey. "The Effects of Reader Predictions on the Recall of Relevant and Incidental Information Found in Expository Material," paper presented at the annual meeting of the International Reading Association, Atlanta, Ga., April 1979.

Hanlon, Emily. *How a Horse Grew Hoarse on the Site Where He Sighted a Bare Bear.* New York: Delacorte Press, 1976.

Henderson, Edmund H. *Learning to Read and Spell: The Child's Knowledge of Words.* Dekalb, Ill.: Northern Illinois University Press, 1981.

―――. *Teaching Children to Spell English.* Boston: Houghton Mifflin, 1984.

Henderson, Edmund, Thomas Estes and Susan Stonecash. "An Exploratory Study of Word Acquisition Among First Graders at Mid-Year in a Language Experience Approach," *Journal of Reading Behavior* 4, no. 3 (Summer 1972):21–31.

Hennings, Dorothy Grant. *Communication in Action.* New York: Rand McNally, 1978.

―――. "Input: Enter the Word-Processing Computer," *Language Arts* 58, no. 1 (Jan. 1981):18–22.

Herrick, Virgil E. "Children's Experiences in Writing," in *Children and the Language Arts*, Virgil E. Herrick and Leland B. Jacobs, eds. Englewood Cliffs, N.J.: Prentice-Hall, 1955.

Hetherington, Mavis and Ross Parke. *Contemporary Readings in Child Psychology.* New York: McGraw-Hill, 1977.

Hittleman, Daniel R. *Developmental Reading: A Psycholinguistic Perspective.* Chicago: Rand McNally, 1978.

Hoban, Russell and Sylvie Selig. *Ten What? A Mystery Counting Book.* New York: Charles Scribner's Sons, 1974.

Hoban, Tana. *Look Again!* New York: Macmillan, 1971.

―――. *Over, Under and Through.* New York: Macmillan, 1973.

―――. *Push-Pull, Empty-Full.* New York: Macmillan, 1972.

―――. *Shapes and Things.* New York: Macmillan, 1970.

Horn, Thomas. "Spelling," in *Encyclopedia of Educational Research*, 4th ed. New York: Macmillan, 1969, pp. 1282–1289.

Howes, Virgil N. *Informal Teaching in the Open Classroom.* New York: Macmillan, 1974.

Huey, Edmund B. *The Psychology and Pedagogy of Reading.* Cambridge, Mass.: MIT Press, 1968 (originally published 1908).

Hunt, Kellogg W. *Grammatical Structures Written at Three Grade Levels: NCTE Research Report #3.* Urbana, Ill.: NCTE, 1965.

Ipcar, Dahlov. *I Love My Anteater with an A.* New York: Knopf, 1964.

Jacobson, Ira D. "Comments on the Use of Computers in Public Schools," paper presented to the Advisory Committee of St. Anne's-Belfield School, Charlottesville, Va., October 1982.

Jenkins, Peggy Davidson. *The Magic of Puppetry: A Guide for Those Working with Young Children.* Englewood Cliffs, N.J.: Prentice-Hall, 1980.

Jones, Margaret and Edna Pikulski. "Cloze for the Classroom," *The Reading Teacher* 17, no. 6 (Mar. 1974):432–438.

Joslin, Sesyle. *What Do You Do, Dear?* Reading, Mass.: Addison-Wesley, 1961.

———. *What Do You Say, Dear?* New York: Scholastic Books, 1980.

Judd, Dorothy H. "Avoid Readability Formula Drudgery: Use Your School's Microcomputer," *The Reading Teacher* 35, no. 1 (Oct. 1981):7–8.

Keller, Paul F. G. "Maryland Micro: A Prototype Readability Formula for Small Computers," *The Reading Teacher* 35, no. 7 (Apr. 1982):778–782.

Kita, Mary Jane. Personal communication, 1981.

Klein, Marvin L. *Talk in the Language Arts Classroom.* Urbana, Ill.: NCTE, 1977.

Koch, Kenneth. *Rose, Where Did You Get That Red?* New York: Random House, 1973.

———. *Wishes, Lies and Dreams.* New York: Random House, 1970.

Kohl, Herbert. *On Teaching.* New York: Schocken Books, 1976.

Labov, William. *The Study of Nonstandard English.* Urbana, Ill.: NCTE, 1970.

Lancaster, Willie, Laurie Nelson, and Darrell Morris. "Invented Spellings in Room 112: A Writing Program for Low-Reading Second Graders," *The Reading Teacher* 35, no. 8 (May 1982):906–911.

Larrick, Nancy, ed. *Somebody Turned on a Tap in These Kids: Poetry and Young People Today.* New York: Dell, 1973.

Lavine, Linda O. *The Development of Perception in Writing in Pre-Reading Children: A Cross-Cultural Study*, Ph.D. dissertation, Cornell University, 1972. University Microfilms International, Ann Arbor, Mich. 73-6657.

Leach, Maria. *The Rainbow Book of American Folk Tales and Legends.* Cleveland, Ohio: World, 1958.

Liberman, Isabel, Alvin Liberman, Ignatius Mattingly, and Donald Shankweiler. "Orthography and the Beginning Reader," in *Orthography, Reading and Dyslexia*, James Kavanaugh and Richard Venezky, eds. Baltimore, Md.: University Park Press, 1980.

Liberman, Isabel, Donald Shankweiler, F. W. Fischer, and B. Carter. "Explicit Syllable and Phoneme Segmentation in the Young Child," *Journal of Experimental Psychology* 18 (1974):201–212.

Livingston, Myra Cohn. *When You Are Alone It Keeps You Capone: An Approach to Creative Writing with Children.* New York: Atheneum, 1973.

Loban, Walter. *Language Development: Kindergarten Through Grade Twelve.* Urbana, Ill.: NCTE, 1976.

Lund, Doris. *I Wonder What's Under.* New York: Parents Magazine Press, 1970.

Lundsteen, Sara. *Children Learn to Communicate.* New York: Holt, Rinehart & Winston, 1978.

McConaughy, Stephanie. "Using Story Structure in the Classroom," *Language Arts* 57, no. 2 (Feb. 1980):157–165.

McGinn, Maureen. *I Used to Be an Artichoke.* St. Louis, Mo.: Concordia, 1973.

Macrorie, Ken. *Writing to be Read*, rev. 2nd ed. Rochelle Park, N.J.: Hayden Books, 1976.

Maestro, Betsy. *Where Is My Friend?* New York: Crown, 1976.

Malmstrom, Jean. *Introduction to Modern English Grammar.* Rochelle Park, N.J.: Hayden Press, 1968.

Mandler, Jean M. and Nancy S. Johnson. "Remembrance of Things Parsed: Story Structure and Recall," *Cognitive Psychology* 9 (1977):111–151.

Manning-Sanders, Ruth. *Robin Hood and Little John.* London: Methuen, 1977.

Manzo, Anthony V. "Guided Reading Procedure," *Journal of Reading* 18, no. 4 (Jan. 1975):287–291.

Marsh, George, Morton Friedman, Veronica Welch, and Peter Desberg. "The Development of Strategies in Spelling," in *Cognitive Processes in Spelling*, Uta Frith, ed. New York: Academic Press, 1980.

Marshall, Nancy and Marvin D. Glock. "Comprehension and Connected Discourse: A Study into the Relationships Between the Structure of Text and the Information Recalled," *Reading Research Quarterly* 14, no. 1 (1978–1979):10–56.

Martin, Bill, Jr. *Brown Bear, Brown Bear, What Do You See?* New York: Holt, Rinehart & Winston, 1970.

Martin, Bill, Jr. and Peggy Brogan. *Bill Martin's Instant Readers.* New York: Holt, Rinehart & Winston, 1971.

————. *Sounds of Language.* New York: Holt, Rinehart & Winston, 1974.

Mayer, Mercer. *What Do You Do with a Kangaroo?* New York: Scholastic Books, 1975.

Mazurkiewicz, Albert J. and Harold J. Tanzer. *Early to Read: ITA Program.* New York: Initial Teaching Alphabet Publications, 1963.

Mellon, John C. *Transformational Sentence Combining.* Urbana, Ill.: NCTE, 1969.

Mencken, H. L. *The American Language*, one-vol. abridged ed. New York: Knopf, 1977.

Mendoza, George. *A Wart Snake in a Fig Tree.* New York: Dial Press, 1968.

Merritt, John. *Reading, Writing and Relevance.* London: Open University Press, 1978.

Meyer, Bonnie J. *Organization of Prose and Its Effects on Recall.* Amsterdam: North Holland, 1975.

Miles, Miska. *Apricot ABC.* Boston: Little, Brown, 1969.

Miller, Robert H. "Discovering the Christensen Rhetoric," in *Teaching Writing K–8*, Jack Hailey ed. Berkeley, Cal.: Instructional Laboratory, University of California, 1978.

Minsky, Marvin. "A Framework for Representing Knowledge," in *The Theory of Computer Vision*, P. H. Winston, ed. New York: McGraw-Hill, 1975.

Moffett, James and Betty Jane Wagner. *Student-Centered Language Arts and Reading, K–13.* Boston: Houghton Mifflin, 1976.

Moray, Neville. *Listening and Attention.* Baltimore, Md.: Penguin Books, 1969.

Morris, R. Darrell. "Beginning Readers' Concept of Word," in *Cognitive and Developmental Aspects of Learning to Spell*, E. H. Henderson and J. W. Beers, eds. Newark, N.J.: International Reading Association, 1980.

————. "'Word Sort': A Categorization Strategy for Improving Word Recognition Ability," *Reading Psychology* 3, no. 1 (Sept. 1982):247–259.

Munari, Bruno. *Bruno Munari's ABC.* Cleveland: World, 1960.

Murray, Donald. "How Writing Finds Its Own Meaning," in *Eight Approaches to Teaching Composition*, Timothy R. Donovan and Ben W. McClelland, eds. Urbana, Ill.: NCTE, 1980.

Nelson, Katherine. "Structure and Strategy in Learning to Talk," *Monographs of the Society for Research in Child Development* 38, nos. 1, 2 (1973).

Norton, Donna E. *The Effective Teaching of Language Arts.* Columbus, Ohio: Charles Merrill, 1980.

Office of Bilingual Education. *Manual for Bilingual Education Institute*. Austin, Tex.: Texas Education Agency, 1978.

Ogilvy, David. *Confessions of an Advertising Man*. New York: Atheneum, 1980.

O'Hare, Frank C. *Sentence Combining*. Urbana, Ill.: NCTE, 1973.

O'Neill, Mary. *Hailstones and Halibut Bones*. New York: Doubleday, 1961.

Otto, Wayne and Dan W. Anderson. "Handwriting," in *Encyclopedia of Educational Research*, 4th ed. New York: Macmillan, 1969.

Oxenbury, Helen. *Helen Oxenbury's ABC of Things*. New York: Watts, 1972.

Parish, Peggy. *Amelia Bedelia*. New York: Harper & Row, 1963.

Petie, Harris. *Billions of Bugs*. Englewood Cliffs, N.J.: Prentice-Hall, 1975.

Petty, Walter and Julie Jensen. *Developing Children's Language*. Boston: Allyn & Bacon, 1980.

Pflaum, Susanna. *The Development of Language and Reading in Young Children*, 2nd ed. Columbus, Ohio: Charles Merrill, 1978.

Piaget, Jean. *The Construction of Reality in the Child*. New York: Basic Books, 1954.

———. *The Language and Thought of the Child*, 3rd ed. London: Routledge & Kegan Paul, 1959.

Piatti, Celestino. *Celestino Piatti's Animal ABC*. New York: Atheneum, 1966.

Pilon, A. Barbara. *Teaching Language Arts Creatively in the Elementary Grades*. New York: Wiley, 1978.

Pooley, Robert C. *The Teaching of English Usage*. Urbana, Ill.: NCTE, 1974.

Premack, David. *Intelligence in Ape and Man*. Hillsdale, N.J.: Lawrence Erlbaum, 1976.

Rankin, Earl F. and Joseph W. Culhane. "Comparable Cloze and Multiple-Choice Comprehension Test Scores," *Journal of Reading* 13, no. 3 (Dec. 1969):193–198.

Read, Charles. *Children's Categorization of Speech Sounds in English*. National Council of Teachers of English Research Report #17. Urbana, Ill.: NCTE, 1975.

———. "Creative Spelling by Young Children," in *Standards and Dialects in English*, T. Shopen and J. M. Williams, eds. Cambridge, Mass.: Winthrop, 1980.

———. "Preschool Children's Knowledge of English Phonology," *Harvard Educational Review* 41 (1971):1–34.

Read, Charles and Richard E. Hodges. "Spelling," in *Encyclopedia of Educational Research*, 5th ed. New York: Macmillan, 1982.

Reimer, Joseph, Diana Prichart Paolitto, and Richard H. Hersch. *Promoting Moral Growth*, 2nd ed. New York: Longman, 1983.

Rice, Mabel. *Cognition to Language: Categories, Word Meanings, and Training*. Baltimore, Md.: University Park Press, 1980.

Richards, Jill. *Classroom Language; What Sorts?* London: George Allen and Unwin, 1978.

Richards, Meredith Martin. Personal communication, March 1983.

———. *Word Processing Activities for Children*. Reston, Va.: Reston, 1984.

Rimanelli, Geose and Paul Pinsleur. *Poems Make Pictures, Pictures Make Poems*. New York: Pantheon, 1972.

Rumelhart, David. "Notes on a Schema for Stories," in *Representation and Understanding: Studies in Cognitive Science*, D. Bowbrow and Allen Collins, eds. Academic Press, 1975.

Saltz, Eli, Elaine Soller and Irving E. Sigel. "The Development of Natural Language Concepts," *Child Development* 43, no. 4 (Dec. 1972):1191–1202.

Samuels, S. Jay. "The Method of Repeated Reading," *The Reading Teacher* 32, no. 4 (Jan. 1979):403–408.

Sapir, Edward. *Language: An Introduction to the Study of Speech*. New York: Harcourt, 1921.

Schuyler, Michael. "A Readability Formula for Use on Microcomputers," *Journal of Reading*, 25 no. 6 (Mar. 1982):560–591.

Schwartz, Alvin. *Whoppers, Tall Tales and Other Lies*. Philadelphia: Lippincott, 1975.

Sendak, Maurice. *One Was Johnny*. New York: Harper & Row, 1962.

Seuss, Dr. *Hop on Pop*. New York: Beginner Books, 1963.

Seymour, Brenda. *First Counting*. New York: Walck, 1969.

Shapiro, Irwin. *Heroes in American Folklore*. New York: Messner (div. of Simon & Schuster), 1962.

Shaughnessy, Mina P. *Errors and Expectations: A Guide for the Teacher of Basic Writing*. New York: Oxford University Press, 1977.

Silverstein, Shel. *Where the Sidewalk Ends*. New York: Harper & Row, 1974.

Sloan, Glenna Davis. *The Child as Critic: Teaching Literature in the Elementary School*. New York: Teachers College Press, 1975.

Smart, Mollie S. and Russell E. Smart. *School-Age Children: Developmental Relationships*. New York: Macmillan, 1973.

Smith, Frank. *Understanding Reading*, rev. ed. New York: Holt, Rinehart & Winston, 1978.

Sowers, Susan. "Young Writers' Preference for Non-Narrative Modes of Composition," paper presented at the Fourth Annual Boston University Conference on Language Development, Boston, Mass.: 1979.

Spier, Peter. *Fast-Slow, High-Low*. New York: Doubleday, 1972.

Stauffer, Russell G. *Directing the Reading-Thinking Process*. New York: Harper & Row, 1975.

———. *The Language-Experience Approach to the Teaching of Reading*, rev. ed. New York: Harper & Row, 1980.

Stein, Nancy. *How Children Understand Stories*. Urbana: University of Illinois Center for the Study of Reading, Technical Report #69, March 1978 (ERIC:ED, 153–205).

Strunk, William and E. B. White. *The Elements of Style*, 3rd ed. New York: Macmillan, 1979.

Sullivan, Joan. "Round Is a Pancake," in *Sounds Around the Clock*, by Bill Martin, Jr. New York: Holt, Rinehart & Winston, 1972, pp. 26–32.

Supraner, Robyn. *Would You Rather Be a Tiger?* Boston: Houghton Mifflin, 1973.

Swenson, May. "Southbound on the Freeway," *To Mix with Time*. New York: Charles Scribner's Sons, 1963, p. 59.

Swift's 1982 Educational Software Directory. Austin, Tex.: Sterling Swift Publishing, 1982.

Tallon, Robert. *Zoophabets*. New York: Bobbs-Merrill, 1971.

Taylor, Barbara M. "Children's Memory for Expository Text After Reading," *Reading Research Quarterly* 15, no. 3 (Spring 1980):399–411.

Taylor, Wilson. "Cloze Procedure: A New Tool for Measuring Readability," *Journalism Quarterly* 30 (Fall 1953):415–433.

Temple, Charles, Ruth Nathan and Nancy Burris. *The Beginnings of Writing*. Boston: Allyn & Bacon, 1982.

Thoreau, Henry D. *Walden*. New York: Time Inc., 1962 (originally published in 1854).

Thorndike, Edward L. *Educational Psychology, Volume II: The Psychology of Learning*. New York: Teachers College Press, Columbia University, 1913.

Thorndyke, Perry. "Cognitive Structures in Comprehension and Memory of Narrative Discourse," *Cognitive Psychology* 9 (Jan. 1977):77–110.

Thurber, Donald N. *D'Nealian Handwriting*. Glenview, Ill.: Scott, Foresman, 1978.

Tierney, Robert J., John E. Readence, and Ernest K. Dishner. *Reading Strategies and Practices: A Guide for Improving Instruction*. Boston: Allyn & Bacon, 1980.

Tison, Annette and Talus Taylor. *The Adventures of the Three Colors*. Cleveland, Ohio: World, 1971.

Tough, Joan. *Focus on Meaning: Talking to Some Purpose with Young Children*. London: George Allen and Unwin, 1973.

Vacca, Richard T. *Content Area Reading*. Boston: Little, Brown, 1981.

Van Der Zanden, James W. *Human Development,* 2d ed. New York: Knopf, 1981.

Venezky, Richard L. "From Webster to Rice to Roosevelt," in *Cognitive Processes in Spelling*, Uta Frith, ed. New York: Academic Press, 1980.

Vonnegut, Kurt, Jr. *Breakfast of Champions*. New York: Dell, 1974.

Vygotsky, Lev. *Thought and Language*. Cambridge, Mass.: MIT Press, 1962.

Walters, Marguerite. *The City-Country ABC*. Garden City, N.Y.: Doubleday, 1966.

Weaver, Constance. *Grammar for Teachers*. Urbana, Ill.: NCTE, 1979.

White, T. H. *The Once and Future King*. New York: Berkeley Medallion Books, 1966.

Wildsmith, Brian. *Brian Wildsmith's ABC*. Lexington, Mass.: D.C. Heath, 1963.

Winsor, Frederick. *The Space Child's Mother Goose*. New York: Simon & Schuster, 1958.

Young, Richard, Alton Becker, and Kenneth Pike. *Rhetoric: Discovery and Change*. New York: Harcourt Brace Jovanovich, 1970.

Zavatsky, Bill and Ron Padgett. *The Whole Word Catalogue 2*. New York: McGraw-Hill, 1977.

Zemach, Harve. *Mommy, Buy Me a China Doll*. New York: Farrar, Straus & Giroux, 1975.

Zutell, Jerry. "Spelling Strategies of Primary School Children and Their Relationship to Piaget's Concept of Decentration," *Research in the Teaching of English* 13, no. 1 (Feb. 1979):69–80.

Acknowledgments *(continued from page iv)*
tin, *Brown Bear, Brown Bear,* pp. 1–5. Copyright ©
1970 by Holt, Rinehart and Winston, Inc. Reprinted
by permission. *Page 165*: "Dark Girl" reprinted by
permission of Harold Ober Associates Incorporated.
© 1963 by Arna Bontemps. "Heaven" copyright 1947
by Langston Hughes. Reprinted from *Selected Poems
of Langston Hughes,* by Langston Hughes, by per-
missin of Alfred A. Knopf, Inc. "Chester" from
*Where the Sidewalk Ends: The Poems and Drawings of
Shel Silverstein.* Copyright © 1974 by Shel Silverstein. Reprinted by permission of Harper & Row,
Publishers, Inc. *Pages 166–168*: Deborah Tall poems
used by permission of Deborah Tall.

Chapter 7 *Pages 240–241*: From Donald H.
Graves, "Research Update: Andrea Learns to Make
Reading Hard," *Language Arts,* Vol. 56, no. 5 (May
1979). Reprinted by permission of the National
Council of Teachers of English. *Pages 240–246*: From
Donald H. Graves, *Writing: Teachers and Children at
Work* (Exeter, N.H.: Heinemann Educational Books,
1983). Reprinted by permission. *Pages 272–275*:

Poems from Ronald L. Cramer, *Children's Writing
and Language Growth* (Columbus, Ohio: Charles E.
Merril, 1979). Reprinted by permission. *Page 281:
From New & Selected Things Taking Place* by May
Swenson. Copyright © 1963 by May Swenson. First
appeared in *The New Yorker.* By permission of Little,
Brown and Company in association with the Atlantic
Monthly Press. *Page 288*: From Jean Wallace Gillet
and Charles Temple, *Understanding Reading Prob-
lems: Assessment and Instruction.* Copyright © 1982 by
Jean Wallace Gillet and Charles Temple. Reprinted
by permission of Little, Brown and Company.

Chapter 8 *Pages 326–327*: Evelyn Beyer's
poem from *Another Here and Now Story Book* by Lucy
Sprague Mitchell. Copyright © 1937 by E. P. Dutton. Copyright renewal 1965 by Lucy Sprague Mitchell. Reprinted by permission of the publisher, E. P.
Dutton, Inc.

Chapter 9 *Pages 381–382*: From Mina P.
Shaughnessy, *Errors, and Expectations: A Guide for
the Teacher of Basic Writing* (N.Y.: Oxford University
Press, 1977). Reprinted by permission.

Index